FRAMING THE PAST

The Historiography
of German Cinema
and Television

Edited by

**Bruce A. Murray and
Christopher J. Wickham**

Southern Illinois University Press
Carbondale and Edwardsville

Library of Congress Cataloging-in-Publication Data

Framing the past : the historiography of German cinema and television
  / edited by Bruce A. Murray and Christopher J. Wickham
        p.   cm.
    Includes bibiographical references and index.
    1. Motion pictures—Germany—History.   2. Historical films—
Germany—History and criticism.   3. Motion pictures in
historiography.   4. Television broadcasting—Germany—History.
5. Television and history.   I. Murray, Bruce Arthur.   II. Wickham,
Christopher J.
PN1993.5.G3F67   1992
791.43′75′0943—dc20   91-39848
ISBN 0-8093-1756-7   CIP

Contents

Contents

Acknowledgments

As with all collections of essays, the contributions to this volume provide, to some extent, their own reception context. Their sequential organization between the covers of this book and the order in which they are read affect their individual and collective signification and, perhaps, significance. They by no means represent a unified critical voice, indeed their strength as a collection rests not least in their diversity of method, theoretical premise, scholarly goals, and style. Despite their heterogeneity, they remain at all events in dialogue with each other.

When considering the contextuality and intertextuality of these essays, it should not be forgotten that their theses first came together at the conference "Concepts of History in German Cinema," held in October 1988. It was here, in the auditorium of the music department of the University of Illinois at Chicago, that resonances and dissonances initially played themselves through; the articles have in most cases been fine tuned as a result of that event. The editors would like to thank the authors for their thoughtful responses to suggestions for revision.

Thanks are due also to all those who attended the conference and contributed, both formally and informally. The editors acknowledge their debt to the National Endowment for the Humanities, the Max Kade Foundation, the Goethe Institute Chicago, the German Department, the College of Liberal Arts and Sciences, and the Student Activities Funding Committee at the University of Illinois at Chicago, the Film Center of the School of the Art Institute of Chicago, Lufthansa German Airlines, the Chicago International Film Festival, and the Robert Bosch Corporation for their contribution to the success of the conference. Thanks are also due to the Institute for the Humanities of the University of Illinois at Chicago, Richard Martin, Kris Szremski, David Orsay, and anonymous readers for assistance with preparation of the manuscript, and to Southern Illinois University Press for outstanding cooperation.

Certain chapters herein were previously published elsewhere in altered form. We acknowledge the following publishers for permission to reprint:

Oxford University Press for "Leni Riefenstahl's Feature Films and the Question of a Fascist Aesthetic," by Linda Schulte-Sasse.

Indiana University Press for "On the Difficulty of Saying 'We': The Historians' Debate and Edgar Reitz's *Heimat*," by Eric L. Santner, and "History and Film: Public Memory in the Age of Electronic Dissemination," by Anton Kaes.

Framing the Past

Introduction

Bruce A. Murray

History . . . is neither the past as such, nor yet a discourse in which the past is revealed, but rather a set of discourses in which the past is constructed.[1]

Fixing, securing, or pinning down of the past as coherent is not attempted for the past's sake but for the sake of the present—such a representation appears to ward off the threatening anxiety of having to recognize the inability of an individual to control and master the self-as-subject.[2]

Controlling change is necessary because the logic of late capitalism requires change to be equated with progress and civilization itself, as only a philosophy of the "good life" based on change will lead to further and further consumption.[3]

Contemporary Trends in the Historiography of Cinema[4]

Issues of historiography have attracted much attention during the past two decades in what many now seem comfortable characterizing as the era of the postmodern. Responding to the insights of poststructuralist thought (Derridean deconstruction, Lacanian psychoanalysis, Althusserian Marxism, Foucauldian historiography, etc.) and to a multitude of unacceptable social experiences (environmental pollution, dysfunctional interpersonal relationships, the arms race) that now more than ever have become associated with a problematic commitment to instrumental reason, scholars from a wide variety of disciplines have taken significant steps in reassessing the modalities of historical representation.[5] The result has been a dramatic shift in three interrelated perceptions. First, instead of assuming the ability of language systems to mediate between an archeologically accessible past and the present in ways that enable verifiable cognition of the past, "history" now appears as little more than a system of discourses we use to fabricate a coherent past from whatever traces of it we might locate in the present. Second, instead of assuming larger social goals as the motivating force for generating historical discourse, we now seem more willing to acknowledge that our overwhelming concern may very well be to use history as we do myth to cope with a personal sense of powerlessness in a world of symbolic multivalence and indecidability. And finally, instead of perceiving a clear separation between supposedly value-neutral historical discourse and value-laden ideology, we now contemplate the ways in which psychologically motivated representations of the past intersect with the discourse of politics and economics to influence the ideological organization of social life in specific temporal and spatial contexts. As Fredric Jameson suggested in his seminal essay on postmodernism, one might even claim that the "weakened historicity" of much contemporary scholarly discourse about the past is intimately linked to the cultural logic of late capitalism.[6]

Among the early expressions of these perceptual shifts in film scholarship was the critical interpretation of essays from journals such as *Cahiers du Cinéma* and *Cinéthique* in the British film periodical *Screen* during the first half of the 1970s.[7] Here contributors such as Colin MacCabe and Stephen Heath analyzed popular culture, above all cinema, in an attempt "to understand cultural processes as systems of signification," "to link questions of signification to questions of subjectivity," and "to explain the way in which capitalist relations reproduce themselves in non-coercive ways."[8] The inquiry led in many directions, including the focus on "Film: History/Production/Memory" at the Edinburgh Film Festival in 1977.[9] Within that context Mark Nash and Steve Neale, the authors of my first introductory citation, emphasized the necessity for reassessing the relationship between cinema and history in each of its three major articulations: "the history of cinema, history in cinema, and cinema in history."[10]

In all three cases Nash and Neale stressed the need to perceive cinema as a social institution and history as a set of discursive practices. For them the term institution meant not only a location of social practice but a system of standards for production, distribution, and reception that

2

produces and reproduces ideology, hence defining subjective as well as intersubjective positions. Consequently, history was to be studied as a particular mode of discourse within the institution of cinema with the capacity to influence the organization of individual experience into ideological perspectives in the present. From this vantage point, a number of questions became relevant. For example, what factors influence the narration of film history and with what effects? How can histories of cinema specify the "differentiations and articulations, the struggles and contradictions, crossing and constituting the cinematic institution?" To what extent have the narrative strategies of historical films encouraged an identity between the past, the text, and spectating subjects? How and under what circumstances have they participated in securing imaginary perceptions of the subject in time, and how might they draw attention and facilitate the transition to symbolic forms of subjectivity and social interaction? And how do cinematic forms of discourse influence the developing ideology of history? What images of historical agency does cinema foster and in what social context does this occur?

Over the past decade or so, film scholars have engaged in a variety of projects that address such questions. Representative of these projects were the annual events sponsored by the Center for Twentieth Century Studies at the University of Wisconsin-Milwaukee. Coinciding with and influenced by the work of *Screen* at the end of the 1970s and into the 1980s, the meetings provided an exemplary forum for discussing semiotic revisions of all aspects of the "cinematic apparatus."[11] Within that framework, international groupings of film scholars worked to explode conventional histories of cinema as well as explore the influence of cinematic narration in constituting images of historical agency. The published documents of the "Cinema Histories, Cinema Practices" conference of 1981, for example, included important essays on the relationship between the crisis in the historiographic imaginary at the turn of the century and the development of a narrative imaginary in classical cinema, as well as on the potential for writing the history of cinema as a history of visual pleasure.[12] The 1981 event also led to the publication of a collection of essays in feminist film criticism that challenged all manifestations of the relationship between film and history by considering their foundation in patriarchal modes of discourse.[13] They drew attention to the relationship between gender and film in ways that questioned affirmative associations between historical agency and male protagonists, narrative strategies of (often gendered) binary opposition, and logocentric film scholarship.

As the revision of cinematic historiography (understood in the terms Nash and Neale suggested) continues into the present, so, too, does the focus on its foundation in and influence on the process of human identity formation and its relationship to other forms of ideological discourse in specific social settings.[14] It should come as no surprise then that my second and third introductory citations are from very recent work on this project. The second originates in Janet Staiger's analysis of what she perceives as discursive forms of a repetition compulsion that constitutes the intertextuality of "historical" films. As the citation indicates, Staiger links the tendency of publicity articles, talk-show interviews, and reviews to strengthen the suggestion of "historical" reality in films like *The Return of Martin Guerre* (1982) with the human desire for the omnipotence and corresponding security associated with the pre-oedipal imaginary. In other words, our experience of weakness and fallibility in what appears to be a disorderly (if not chaotic) everyday world feeds our childlike compulsion to (re)assert the existence of an orderly historical development and our ability to understand and represent it. The author of the third citation, Mas'ud Zavarzadeh, criticizes the psychoanalytically informed work of scholars like Staiger, noting its lack of attention to the specific political and economic contexts within which the narrative strategies of cinema develop. But he also demonstrates a reliance on contemporary psychoanalytic models to assert the conservative function of nostalgia in mainstream films of late capitalism like *Lost in America* (1985). While scholars like these narrow their focus on history in cinema, others continue work on histories of cinema and on the function of cinema in history. Here, one might mention the studies of early and classical Hollywood cinema by Miriam Hansen and David Bordwell et al. or the contributions to the feminist "re-vision" of film history by Annette Kuhn, Mary Ann Doane, E. Ann Kaplan, and Tania Modleski, among many others.[15] Their work includes increased attention to female filmmaking, spectatorship, and criticism, raising new questions about the ways in which cinema has influenced perceptions of agency and, at least tangentially, historical development.

The Historiography of German Cinema and Television

The first substantial histories of cinema in Germany appeared at least as early as the 1920s. They included annual reports on the industry, popular illustrated accounts by major journals, and critical analyses of the developing relationship between cinema and other art forms.[16] Research into the relationship between cinema and social behavior and thus on cinema in history began even earlier.[17] But before either of these activities attracted widespread attention, Germans began to employ the medium of film to represent the past. Among the first efforts were films about the Prussian heritage. They began attracting audiences before the turn of the century.

Since then, German films ranging from *Der alte Fritz* (*Old Fritz*, 1896, remake in two parts, Gerhard Lamprecht, 1927) to *Kolberg* (Veit Harlan, 1945), *Die Mörder sind unter uns* (*The Murderers Are among Us*, Wolfgang Staudte, 1946), *Heimat* (Edgar Reitz, FRG, 1984), and *Das schreckliche Mädchen* (*The Nasty Girl*, Michael Verhoeven, FRG, 1990), but also others, including *Battleship Potemkin* (Sergei Eisenstein, 1925), *Gone with the Wind* (Victor Fleming, 1939), and *Holocaust* (Marvin Chomsky, 1978) have fascinated and entertained audiences. They have promoted history as a component of personal/cultural/national identity. They have offered perceptions of historical change to individuals, interest groups, and national communities engaged in debates about the meaning of the past for social development in the present and future. They also have served as one important object of study for those who have investigated the interweaving relationships between history, narration, and subjectivity in a social environment that has become permeated by filmic images of the past.

German cinema and television consistently have focused attention on the past, but the selection and treatment of specific subjects has changed. While commercial cinema slowly established its institutional

5

foundation during the initial decade of this century, religious, political, and even military organizations recognized film's mass appeal and began using it to influence public opinion.[18] The more or less blatant use of film for political purposes continued with the programs of the Universum Film AG (Ufa) during and after World War I, the activity of various politically oriented companies, including the Social Democratic Film und Lichtbilddienst and the Communist Prometheus in the Weimar era, and the propagandistic films of various producers throughout the Third Reich.[19] In each case films with historical subjects figured prominently in the struggle to influence public opinion and thus social development.[20]

Of course, entertainment films with far less obvious ideological agendas have dominated mainstream German cinema and television from their beginnings. Between 1895 and 1945, heroic figures such as Frederick the Great, Queen Luise, Otto von Bismarck, as well as figures from other European countries and from world history appeared frequently. It also was during this epoch that Ernst Lubitsch set standards for the historical pageant, combat films about World War I emerged, and light-hearted film operettas portrayed eighteenth-century Prussian and Austrian society as the site of romance.[21]

Following World War II, commercial competition between what were perceived as distinct national cinemas, ideological competition between the cinemas of the two German states, and the emerging competition between cinema and television influenced the production of German films in which Hitler and other National Socialist leaders replaced the prominent figures of the more distant past. Such films employed the Third Reich as a setting for comedy, love stories, even soft pornography. Others attempted honestly to "come to terms" with the National Socialist past as the two Germanies formulated and reformulated their identities.[22] Of at least equal significance, both typical and unique figures from everyday life received greater attention in the post-1945 German cinemas and in the newer medium of television. Moreover, while German films with historical subjects prior to 1945 often employed a variety of narrative techniques to convince spectators of their authenticity, cinema and television in the postwar Germanies (especially since the emergence of New German Film) more frequently drew attention to the constructedness of their portrayals and have challenged spectators to ascribe meaning to images of the past in playful/critical dialogue with them.[23] It also must be emphasized that, while German texts were offering their portrayals of the past to consumers of film and television, so, too, were those of the other cultures, foremost among them texts produced in the United States, the Soviet Union, Great Britain, and France.[24]

Although it is relatively easy to document changes in the selection and treatment of historical subjects in German cinema and television, it is much more difficult to determine precisely which factors have motivated those changes. What has been the role of the institutions with their developing systems of production, distribution, and exhibition? What has been the role of subsidy, contingency, and censorship laws? How have political, economic, and aesthetic factors influenced the narrating of the past in these media? What has been the impact of specific events, such as World War I, the world economic crisis of 1929, World War II, or the cold war and its apparent conclusion?

It also is difficult to answer questions about the relationship between the production of films about the past and their reception. Why, for example, was the figure of Frederick the Great so popular among film audiences in the Weimar era? How do marketing and journalistic criticism affect the reception of films about the past? What effect does the reception of such films have on the production of subsequent films with historical subjects? What potential/actual effect do films about the past have on our perceptions of social development? How do they affect our evaluation of contemporary issues? The urge to articulate and consider questions like these has motivated much of the research on the relationship between film and history throughout this century. Difficult though these questions might be, they have been posited as central to the useful study of cinema, television, and their relationship to society—even for those who discount the possibility and doubt the value of formulating conclusive answers to such queries.

The historians, film scholars, and German studies specialists who have contributed to this volume address these and other questions from a variety of perspectives. While their interests and methods differ, each is keenly aware of the complex network of developing social institutions and discourses that have influenced the historiography of German cinema and television. As has been the case with the study of cinematic historiography in general, one can find in this anthology increasing attention to questions often associated with poststructuralist perspectives—questions applying to all articulations of the relationship between film and history.[25] The work gathered here offers a wealth of insights into the constructedness of film history, history in film, and film in history. While some explore psychoepistemological motivations for narration in greater detail and others pay more attention to sociopolitical factors, a sense of the dynamic link between psychology and social history informs the analyses of most. Their perceptions also lead some contributors to apply the same critical scrutiny they bring to bear on the narration of history to their own accounts. In these and other ways the essays gathered here contribute significantly to the discussions about the historiography of German cinema and television that are in the foreground of media studies today.

The most lively discussions about the link between cinema, television, and history in Germany have developed around three interrelated issues during the last two decades. The first is the reception of Weimar cinema, which for most film scholars continues to be mediated to one extent or another by Siegfried Kracauer's work. The second is the inscribing of fascism in cinema and television, understood as establishing and practicing institutional guidelines for the making and consuming of texts in each medium but also as "coming to terms" with this as part of the cultural heritage—a process that has included the production and reception of films about fascism in postwar Germany. The third is the nature of and potential for alternatives to mainstream cinema and television, perceived as significant components of the dominant public sphere for the organization of past and present experience into ideological perspectives for the present and future.

The Reception of Weimar Cinema

Kracauer's *From Caligari to Hitler* has attracted the attention of almost every postwar film scholar with an interest in Weimar cinema.[26] From the very beginning, reviews of the work foregrounded its "framing" of film history. While earlier critics were satisfied with exposing how Kracauer's inductive method encouraged him either to disregard or recast aspects of Weimar cinema that failed to confirm his thesis about the tendency of films to reflect a "national character," more recent studies have sought to explain the motivations for his leveling of difference and to confront it with accounts capable of reasserting the richness of cinema in Germany during the 1920s. Among the many examples one might cite, those of Thomas Elsaesser and Patrice Petro have received the most critical attention during the past decade.

In his frequently cited essay on film history and visual pleasure, Elsaesser challenges us to consider how not one but a variety of imaginaries constituted the developing institution of cinema in the Weimar Republic. According to him, virtually all who were attracted to the medium of film in the 1920s affirmed those forms of production and reception that might help them to regain a sense of plenitude, wholeness, unity, and omnipotence in a culture of scarcity, fragmentation, opposition, and helplessness. While Kracauer focuses above all on the ways in which cinema responded to the petit-bourgeois spectator's desire for the imaginary specular relations of Wilhelminian culture, Elsaesser suggests the need to pay more attention to the filmmaker's "Edisonian" imaginary and the scholar's desire to create a "master narrative" of Weimar film history. In the first case, all those associated with the apparatus of cinematic representation become fascinated with their ability to create and thus be the masters of their own worlds. In the second, the scholar, like the film historian Kracauer, combats the indecidability of the text (Weimar cinema) by forcing it to conform with a model of teleological causality that implies verifiable knowledge and restores historiographic certainty. It is worth noting how Elsaesser not only calls into question Kracauer's effort to create an accurate history of German film in the 1920s. While encouraging more differentiated investigations of the developing institution of cinema, he also resists the urge to formulate some final, authoritative account. Elsaesser seems far more interested in raising questions and stimulating dialogue than in finding answers and coming to conclusions about Weimar film. He thus invites his readers to abandon the desire for closed master narratives in favor of the pleasure associated with intellectually creative process.

According to Petro, despite the apparent difference between Kracauer's and Elsaesser's accounts of cinema in 1920s Germany, they can be perceived as similar insofar as both perpetuate a conflation of "narrative with national identity, national identity with subject, and all three terms with male subjectivity and male identity in crisis" (xiii). She alleges that the image of male identity in crisis elides the existence of female spectatorship and the distinct address to female spectators in Weimar cinema. In addition, Petro asserts, by identifying the crisis of male subjectivity as the driving force behind the production of what are characterized as protofascistic texts, the conventional approach to this period in German film implicitly advocates restoring patriarchal models of mastery and control.[27] If the historiography of German film in the 1920s is ever to transcend the limitations of such thinking, she argues, it must open itself to the manifestations of female spectatorship.

Petro's study not only continues the work of those feminist film scholars who challenge conventional histories of cinema and history in cinema by emphasizing their rootedness in patriarchal forms of cognition.[28] In her search for signs of an address to female spectators and the contours of female spectatorship, Petro moves beyond the conventional focus on film production and reception to investigate the intertextuality of cinema and photojournalism in Weimar culture. To this extent she practices the kind of "thick reading" many associate with New Historicism.[29] She and to some extent Elsaesser, while employing psychoanalytic and feminist models to review Weimar cinema, remain committed to investigating the relationship between cinema and the other forms of discourse Germans employed to negotiate the meaning of their everyday experience in the 1920s. In contrast to Elsaesser, Petro also seems confident that, although standard accounts of Weimar cinema are flawed, it is possible to ascertain and present accurate knowledge about specific periods in the development of film in Germany.

In the opening essay in this volume, Thomas Saunders offers his own revision of the discursive framing of Weimar cinema. He asks us to consider how imagining German cinema as a national phenomenon in the 1920s has influenced the narration of Weimar film history ever since. Saunders investigates the rhetoric of cultural competition that predated the Weimar Republic, characterized most perceptions of World War I, and contributed to the focus on rivalry in Weimar cinema. He outlines in detail the developing sense of competition as the prestige and commercial power of producers in other countries, especially the United States and Soviet Union, increased. According to Saunders, the rivalry assumed national and then nationalistic contours when producers in Germany failed to compete successfully in foreign markets and struggled to succeed at home. Within this framework, political, intellectual, journalistic, and other discourse about cinema gradually promoted a concept of culture and cultural development based on the conflation of particular interests with those of the German nation in opposition to those of other nations.

In light of Elsaesser's insights about the variety of imaginaries at work in the historiography of Weimar cinema, it seems appropriate to investigate the trend Saunders highlights more specifically as the product of similar phenomena. One could ask, for example, whether discursive efforts to posit a national cinema (and to assert the threat of opposing national cinemas) indicate psychological distress in German society. They might be seen as responses to a social environment that required but also inhibited the transition from perceptions of cultural homogeneity and omnipotence to the acceptance of new forms of cultural and intercultural pluralism. They do seem to suggest the inability and/or unwillingness of Germans to formulate new concepts of self and culture in a framework of interpretive negotiation on national and international levels. They also could be perceived as examples of a broader trend in Western culture, according to which allegiance to nation appeared more as the expression of a psychological response to the process of modernization in a variety of social settings.

Within the current context, it also seems worthwhile to ask whether ongoing efforts to portray Weimar and other periods of German cinema as developments in a unified national cinema reproduce a discourse of conflation and demonstrate persisting difficulties in negotiating cultural pluralism. Is it more accurate to claim that such efforts, precisely because of their interest in difference, are dedicated to maintaining a plurality of cultures? Is it only possible to sustain one at the cost of the other? And what is the value of questions about the verifiability of historical accounts for such considerations?

The next two essays encourage further attention to such questions. Like Saunders, Sabine Hake and Marc Silberman seem less interested in discovering how Weimar cinema might reveal something about the process leading to the Third Reich and more in the degree to which it was a reaction to social conditions in the aftermath of World War I. However, while Saunders pays greatest attention to the descriptive and normative discourse about making and going to films, Hake and even more so Silberman focus more narrowly on the analysis of particular cinematic texts. Both have selected films in which geographical and temporal displacement serve as tactics for grappling with a sense of insecurity in the present, and both analyze the ways in which such tactics created broad semiotic parameters for Germans to reconstitute cultural hegemony.

As the title of her essay indicates, Hake sees the historical pageants that Ernst Lubitsch produced for Ufa as texts with which film-makers, journalists, and spectators could express their attitudes about post–World War I Germany. From her perspective, the postwar transition from monarchy to parliamentary democracy, from bourgeois to mass culture, and from sexual conservatism to sexual liberalism was perceived as a threat to the German social imaginary. The production and reception of films such as *Madame Dubarry* (*Passion*, 1919) and *Anna Boleyn* (*Deception*, 1920), she asserts, can be understood as efforts to reaffirm it. Thus, Lubitsch's films offered spectators displaced images of monarchical rule, affording reassuring visual pleasure of it as spectacle without requiring the destabilizing experience of its negative aspects. Their international commercial success allowed Ufa producers and journalists to portray such films as avenging the loss of World War I and empowering the German nation in cultural competition with other nations. They also provided Lubitsch the opportunity to establish a reputation as master of *mise en scène*, allowing him to challenge modernist fragmentation with visions of historical plenitude and unity created in part with reference to male desire and female victimization.

Marc Silberman's essay complements Hake's work with a focus on cinematic portrayals of the French Revolution. He argues that the dramatic presentation of aggravated conflict, rupture, and irreversible change in Lubitsch's *Passion*, Dimitri Buchovetzki's *Danton* (*All for a Woman*, 1921), and Hans Behrendt's remake of *Danton* (1931) referred less directly to revolutionary France than to the experience of crisis in the Weimar era. Reinforcing Janet Staiger's claim about narrating history,

12

Silberman bases his analysis on the perceived relationship between cinematic interpretations of the past and conflicts of the present. His essay demonstrates clearly how the highlighted films offered possible responses to questions raised in the broader discussion about Germany's transition from monarchy to republic. Each film implicitly criticized the long overdue bourgeois revolution in Weimar Germany. At the same time, they raised suspicion about the adequacy of any historical subject to bring about revolutionary change, a suspicion implying a preference for imagined prewar German cultural strength and harmony. Like Hake, Silberman, too, emphasizes the tendency of such films to articulate attitudes about change by associating its negative aspects with uncontrolled male desire and female sexuality.

While investigating Weimar cinema, Silberman acknowledges the tendency of his analysis to establish a historical narrative in his present. That narrative emphasizes the degree to which films about the past express the desire to transform one's own relation to reality. Without expressly stating his desire, Silberman encourages all producers of historical narratives to scrutinize their own interest in the past. The essays of Saunders, Hake, and Silberman together encourage further discussion about the ways in which the developing institution of cinema in the Weimar Republic did inhibit the transition to forms of cultural and intercultural pluralism. Their authors, like Petro, contribute to a "thick reading" of Weimar culture, suggesting that German films about the past and the discourse surrounding such narratives participated foremost in reestablishing the specular relations of pre–World War Germany. Their attention to cinematic, journalistic, and other discursive forms also indicates the absence of a unilateral political, economic, aesthetic, or even cultural program for the development. Advocates of apparently differing ideological orientations from various social institutions in German, French, U.S., and other cultures, they suggest, voiced skepticism and reluctance about dramatic changes in German society. If this was the case, perhaps there is some more basic motivation for narrative expressions of fear about transition in German/Western society and the corresponding recourse to concepts of cultural integrity and hegemony. In other words, it may be necessary to consider in greater detail how the process of individual and cultural identity formation, which is implied by terms such as the *imaginary* and *social imaginary*, influences the relationship between film and history.

The attention Hake and Silberman pay to cinematic gender coding also encourages us to consider further the possible link between the desire to sustain patriarchal relations of power and the intersecting images of male desire, female sexuality, and threatening change in the production and reception of German films about the past. Such a focus might help to qualify Petro's perception of an address to female audiences and female spectatorship in Weimar cinema. If one adopts Petro's approach, it becomes necessary to ask whether the highlighted films and the discourse surrounding them must be seen as addresses to and expressions of a specific gender. Certainly, their alleged emphasis on recouping a sense of mastery and control recalls what Petro criticizes as the conflating discourse of male identity in crisis. It also might be possible to interpret the production/reception of the featured films as occurring in a society where male and female experiences of crisis at least partially overlapped. If this is the case, perhaps the narrative address in some films about the past, as well as in discourse about such films and about German cinema generally can be perceived as less gender specific than Petro suggests. Of course, there likely were attempts to address women specifically with portrayals of the past in Weimar cinema, and, insofar as the experience of crisis did differ for men and women, their responses to films with historical subjects probably differed, too.

The essays by Saunders, Hake, and Silberman also invite continued attention to the process whereby the historiography of film in the Weimar Republic becomes the problematic story of a homogeneous nation and national cinema, focusing attention too narrowly on the texts of a few mainstream German filmmakers and their work. One might ask how the story would change if, for example, it accounted for leftist discourse about cinema and leftist feature as well as documentary filmmaking. And what would be the effect of considering the German reception of films from other cultures, such as *The Gold Rush* (Charlie Chaplin, 1925) or *Mother* (Vsevolod Pudovkin, 1927)?

Inscriptions of Fascism in Film and Television

In his essay on teaching and writing about German feature films from 1933 to 1945, Eric Rentschler calls for a revision of cinema in

14

the Third Reich with attention to similar questions.[30] He notes how conventional studies of Nazi film concentrate on the activity of the state-run industry and its leading figures or on major directors, genres, and individual films. They do so, he asserts, either to condemn the cinema of this period as a propaganda machine for National Socialist ideology or to vindicate it by identifying pockets of resistance and highlighting the production values of its many entertainment films. Rentschler bemoans such accounts for leveling the cinema of the Third Reich in ways similar to standard accounts of Weimar film. At the same time, he praises the recent work of Gertrud Koch, Karsten Witte, and others, calling for additional, more differentiated investigations with contemporary semiotic, feminist, and New Historical trajectories that consider cinematic texts as aesthetic constructs. He advocates greater attention to psychoanalytical motivations for specific narrative techniques, including gender coding. He also promotes more detailed analysis of the abundant theoretical and technical discourse about media in the Third Reich, the relationship between National Socialist cinema and those of the Weimar Republic and the Adenauer era, and the relationship between Nazi and other state-run and commercial cinemas, such as those of Spain, Japan, the Soviet Union, and classical Hollywood. In addition, he encourages more analysis of the controversy about the cinema of the Third Reich in postwar East and West Germany.

Rentschler seems primarily interested in revising the history of film in the Third Reich, but his suggestions also apply to analysis of the other intersections between film, television, and history. The essays in this volume by Jan-Christopher Horak, Linda Schulte-Sasse, and William Uricchio contribute significantly to the project Rentschler has outlined. Horak and Schulte-Sasse continue the focus on the possible link between gender coding in films about the past, patriarchy, and attitudes about modernization, but they broaden their scope to offer insights about the relationship between cinema in the Weimar Republic, those of other periods in German history, and other discourses in other cultures. While they concentrate foremost on the analysis of individual films, Uricchio returns our attention to discourse about a specific medium of textual production. In this case, the medium is television, and the discourse is that surrounding its development in the Third Reich but also historiographical accounts of the phenomenon in the postwar context. Together these essays not only raise questions about narrating the past of National Socialist cinema and television. They also focus critical attention on fascist representations of the past and their influence on concepts of historical agency.

Horak subjects cinematic narratives of the Prussian past to sociopsychological scrutiny, drawing a connection between the males who considered such portrayals to be appealing and German fascism. He focuses on texts about love, sexuality, duty, and death in late nineteenth- and early twentieth-century Prussian culture, indicating that the mythically portrayed willingness of Prussian males to abandon women and serve their country encouraged German men to accept a patriarchal, fascist authority. Referring to Freudian concepts of love, Horak asserts that films about the Prussian heritage demonstrate how German fascist ideology nurtured obsessional male types who were fanatically dedicated to duty and willing to sublimate their erotic libidinal economies in favor of an aggressive thanatos drive. According to his study, the corresponding valorization of Germany and German men as the primary agents in world historical development helped lay the groundwork for total war. The essay also provides evidence for claims about the continuity between the pre-Nazi past, the Third Reich, and the postwar era, suggesting that texts with similar narrative strategies were constitutive elements of Wilhelminian culture and continued to appear after 1945.

Schulte-Sasse extends the volume's attention to gender roles and their inscription in German films about the past by analyzing Leni Riefenstahl's *Das blaue Licht* (*The Blue Light*, 1932) and *Tiefland* (1954). It is Schulte-Sasse's contention that these films, too, establish a tension between a modern present and a premodern past. In each film a naïve, mysterious female figure, played by Riefenstahl, embodies a more positive natural world of former times, while most male figures represent an evil modern world of instrumental reason. But Schulte-Sasse is cautious about defining the aesthetic quality of such films as fascist. In contrast to Horak's emphasis on the link between National Socialism and the content-based glorification of the military and death, she focuses on the structural tendency of fascist ideology to respond to dissatisfaction with modernity by dissolving the boundaries between an aestheticized past and real life in the present. From Schulte-Sasse's perspective, Riefens-

16

tahl's films, like countless modern narratives, ranging from sociopsychological dramas in the second half of eighteenth-century Germany to the
political discourse of the late twentieth century in the United States,
foreground the tension between a contemporary reality dominated by
instrumental reason and something other (nature, woman, or art) as well
as a nostalgic longing for the other as a space of reconciliation.

At the same time, Schulte-Sasse considers the distinction between modern and fascist aesthetic models tenuous enough to warrant
suspicion about the capability of most "modern" texts to function similarly
to fascist texts in contemporary Western societies. In this way she, like
Horak, encourages more critical attention to continuities in aesthetic
movements. However, while Horak limits his discussion to German
culture, Schulte-Sasse joins Saunders in raising questions about histories
of German film based narrowly on the perception of national distinctions.
Her essay also challenges narratives of film history, like Petro's for
example, that seem to conflate patriarchal with male-produced gender
codes. Referring to John Berger's concept of the split self engendered in
women by Western culture and focusing on Riefenstahl's status as direc-
tor/actress, Schulte-Sasse indicates the possible narcissistic motivations
for females to contribute to the generation of patriarchal images of
gender.

Each of the contributions discussed to this point indicates the
possibility of analyzing efforts to negotiate change in German society
during the first decades of the twentieth century as dramatic examples
of the strained process of individual and cultural identity formation in
modernity. They find expressions of such tension manifested in cinematic
narratives and in the various texts surrounding them—ones filled with
nostalgia for a perceived past of cultural wholeness, stability, and strength
but also expressing hope for a future with similar qualities. While some
of the essays investigate the relationship between such longing in the
filmmaker's, spectator's, or critic's present and the cinematic portrayal
of the past, others consider how such inscriptions of desire also influence
the historiography of earlier developments in German cinema and television in our present.

William Uricchio contributes to both endeavors with his analysis
of discourse about the emergence of television in Germany. He analyzes

numerous sources of archival information and considers their intersections as sites where valuable insights about the connection between concepts of technology, progress, nation, and television in the Third Reich become apparent. At the same time, he considers how accessible documents from the National Socialist past have influenced efforts to narrate the past of German television in the postwar era.

The essay's focus on political, economic, and technological discourse in government and industrial circles, the trade press, and popular journals suggests a contradiction between public and private accounts of television's development. Uricchio notes the tendency of more widely publicized documents to emphasize the prospect of unbounded technological progress, the national origins of technological innovation, and the general benefit of such innovation. Less publicized and private records reveal a deep-seated contradiction between such perceptions of national strength and unity and the reality of a culture in which the desire for progress exceeded capabilities, multinational cooperation facilitated the introduction of television, and only a minority of German households received the medium—one which also could assist a powerful minority in controlling the development of public opinion if available to most. Invoking Enlightenment notions of universal historical progress and recasting them in a national context—so the study implies—created a legitimizing mask for the political and economic self-interest of the National Socialist leadership, the directors of competing ministries, and multinational corporations.

Uricchio also discovers such masking in the postwar period as first Allied and then German scholars privileged self-legitimizing histories of television in the Third Reich. He describes how Allied accounts, often formulated by corporate employees with government assignments, paid little attention to multinational cooperation, focusing more on German innovations and military applications. Some West German accounts relied on easy access to Propaganda Ministry documents that emphasized using the medium to dictate public opinion, and East German accounts frequently referred to available Postal Ministry records of cooperation between government and industry. The resulting portrayals were of a National Socialist culture as negative other in opposition to positive postwar (East or West) German and Allied Western culture. Relying on documents from one ministry more than another also enabled the two German states to reinforce perceptions of similar opposition between them in the present. As Uricchio outlines, the evidence in Postal Ministry archives supported the East German concept of a link between fascism and capitalism, thus strengthening the corresponding view of West Germany as quasi-fascist in contrast to a supposedly socialist East Germany. The evidence in Propaganda Ministry archives supported the West German image of a connection between fascism and totalitarianism, reinforcing the image of the GDR as quasi-fascist in opposition to an allegedly democratic FRG.

The essays by Horak, Schulte-Sasse, and Uricchio indicate that the historiography of cinema and television as it manifested itself during the Third Reich both predated 1933 and remained operative after 1945. These contributions expose a persistent and widespread reluctance to abandon perceptions of cultural strength and wholeness. When faced with the cultural and intercultural complexity of modernity, they assert, German, but also other Western filmmakers, spectators, and critics often have reverted to conventional narrative strategies to recoup positive images of individual and cultural integrity.

Uricchio's essay is especially thought-provoking for two additional reasons. When considered in connection with those by Saunders, Hake, and Silberman, it raises questions about the extent to which German and other Western politicians, corporate leaders, and journalists intentionally encouraged perceptions of national strength and unity as a mask for serving their own interests before 1933. As we have seen, such images found expression in all articulations of the relationship between film and history in the Weimar era. This suggests the generation of a sociopsychological anachronism consisting of the private acceptance and public rejection of cultural and intercultural complexity. Does the anachronism persist in more recent efforts to narrate the past of German cinema and television as that of a unified nation? What are the costs and benefits of such schizophrenic behavior and what would be necessary to overcome it? Uricchio offers one possible answer by emphasizing how increasing numbers of German scholars have developed more differentiating approaches to the study of television in the Third Reich. In the process he draws attention to the postwar trend toward experimenting with alternatives to the mainstream histories of German cinema and television. Such efforts hold the potential for replacing anachronistic portrayals, stressing cultural harmony/hegemony and intercultural competition, with others emphasizing cultural fragmentation/fallibility and intercultural cooperation. Once again, such endeavors become visible at every possible intersection between cinema, television, and history in German culture and with increasing frequency and intensity in the postwar era, especially during the past two decades. Such projects are the focus of the final group of essays in this volume.

Alternatives to Mainstream Cinema and Television

Discussions about the nature of and potential for alternatives to mainstream cinema and television often have accompanied efforts to revise German film history. Roughly coinciding with the German student movement and motivated by the desire to learn from the past what might be of use in establishing a counterpublic sphere in the present, various film scholars published studies of the German left's critique of commercial cinema and efforts to produce alternative films in the 1920s.[31] These accounts, like those of Elsaesser, Petro, and others, shared an interest in exposing weaknesses in conventional histories of Weimar cinema. However, instead of acknowledging the semiotic impediments to creating any ultimately accurate account, most claimed that their efforts would help to correct and/or fill the gaps of standard histories. With the proper (dialectical-materialist) method, they asserted, it would be possible to acquire verifiable knowledge about the developing process of German cultural production in the 1920s and to use such knowledge in modifying the process in accordance with the needs of contemporary society.[32]

Of course, those who did investigate leftist film activity in the Weimar Republic found filmmakers and critics who promoted divergent alternatives to mainstream portrayals of the past in cinema.[33] The result was growing attention to the issue of cinematic agency in general and to corresponding specific questions about the influence of history in cinema on the function of cinema in history. If the goal of leftist alternatives was to empower German citizens to participate in the organization of social life, what role should narrative play? During the 1920s, Proletkult advocates and other leftist radicals considered it impossible to democratize

German society from above without encouraging spectators to construct their own narrative histories cooperatively and critically from below. Was it necessary to experiment with techniques capable of undermining the filmmaker's authority to narrate the past in the postwar present? Perhaps it was possible to develop models of production and reception that would collapse the conventional separation between the notions of producer/ideology/above and recipient/material existence/below. Such experiments might more effectively contribute to a public sphere in which all Germans might participate creatively in the intertextuality of historical and political discourse.

While historians of leftist film activity documented these theoretical insights, analyzed their impact on filmmaking in the past, and suggested their potential influence on cinema and television in the present, a new generation of filmmakers began considering similar questions in attempting to establish their alternatives to mainstream cinema, beginning in the 1960s.[34] During the past three decades, West German filmmakers ranging from Helma Sanders-Brahms, to Alexander Kluge, Edgar Reitz, and Margarethe von Trotta, but also East Germans such as Frank Beyer, Heiner Carow, Rainer Simon, and Konrad Wolf have done so by referring to the cinema of the Weimar Republic, the cultural heritage of National Socialism, and to the insights of orthodox Marxism, Critical Theory, and feminist theory. However, above all they have done so in critical dialogue with the existing public spheres of East and West German society and their methods for organizing everyday experience in the past and present into ideological discourse. They have defined the public sphere as governed either by the principles of consumer capitalism or orthodox Marxism but also by overarching patriarchal defense mechanisms that have inhibited the productive negotiation of the National Socialist past. In other words, the questions about cinematic agency so prevalent in film theory debates in the Weimar Republic often have found expression in discussions about the ways in which the postwar institutions of cinema and television in Germany have blocked the process of healthy individual and cultural identity formation and the ways in which alternatives might facilitate the project.

It is important to note here that many German filmmakers and a significant number of the film scholars who have studied their work have demonstrated a greater interest in drawing critical attention to the constructedness of cinematic and television narration. To cite just one of many possible examples, by the beginning of the 1980s Timothy Corrigan had found material adequate for a booklength study of the self-reflexive narrative techniques employed by New German filmmakers as a challenge to classical Hollywood techniques of self-effacing narration.[35] In addition, filmmakers and scholars have stressed more the relationship between conventional narrative strategies and the desire for mastery and control as a product of sociopsychological developments, focusing foremost on the relationship between historically specific forms of social interaction such as consumer capitalism, Stalinism, or patriarchy and the process of individual/cultural identity formation. Although there are notable exceptions, most contemporary German filmmakers and scholars of German cinema and television have appeared less interested in investigating the ways in which psychological phenomena, independent of a specific social setting, drive the process of signification.

Most (New) German filmmakers and their critics also have been more willing to perceive signification as a process with a degree of openness sufficient to engage larger numbers of participants in negotiating meaning, but not so undecidable that at least temporary consensus is precluded. They have been unwilling to abandon the attempt to perceive cinema and television as modes of discourse for the social organization of everyday experience into ideological perspectives. In other words, although intersecting concerns and approaches render clear distinctions inappropriate, the Frankfurt School, Habermasian concepts of public sphere, and the Brechtian aesthetics of alienation and learning seem to have exerted a greater influence than French poststructuralism and Derridean strategies of deconstruction. If the historiography of German cinema and television has become more interested in facilitating something like the Lacanian transition from imaginary to symbolic forms of social interaction, then it more often than not has done so by encouraging spectators and readers to nurture and acclimate themselves to a social environment in which both the text and its interpreters enact the tension between the multivalence of the signifier and the desire to fix its meaning as a precondition for communicating the terms of cooperative cultural production. Perhaps nowhere has this been clearer than in the produc-

tion and critical reception of films about German fascism, and some of
the work in this volume comes from authors who have contributed
significantly to the trend.[36]

In his contribution, Barton Byg analyzes the consistent generational quality of debates about the narrating of German history in the
GDR and discusses the influence of those debates on *Berlin um die Ecke*
(*Berlin Around the Corner*, Gerhard Klein, 1965/1987), *Die Russen
kommen* (*The Russians Are Coming*, Heiner Carow, 1967/1988), and
Jadup und Boel (Rainer Simon, 1980/1988). Each of these Deutsche
Film-AG (DEFA) narratives is set in the Third Reich or in a postwar
present concerned with that past. Each also was originally forbidden but
rediscovered and presented to East and West German audiences with a
great deal of publicity in the second half of the 1980s. Similar to Uricchio,
but referring only to the GDR, Byg notes how political and cultural
political leaders who experienced the Third Reich as adults and helped
to establish the GDR favored narratives about the National Socialist past
that legitimized their actions by identifying East Germany positively as
antifascist. His analysis of the highlighted films characterizes them as the
products of younger filmmakers and spectators who embrace cinema as
a medium for formulating individual and cultural identity in opposition
to this older generation and its authority to narrate the past. According to
Byg, the struggle to influence the process of identity formation expressed
itself in the alternative thematic orientations (above all the focus on
generational conflict) and narrative strategies of the three films, in the
initial decisions to censor them, and in their reappearance in the 1980s.

The development of this particular struggle over more than two
decades also raises questions about the dynamic relationship between
history in film and film in the history of German socialism. While Byg
convincingly illustrates the desire of an older generation to sustain
skewed images of personal and cultural integrity and the eventually
successful efforts of younger Germans to challenge those images, it is
less clear whether the challenge indicates another step in the cultural
transition from imaginary to symbolic relations. Perhaps the production
and reception of more recent DEFA films about the Third Reich and the
GDR, including the screening of forbidden films and accompanying
publicity, do suggest a greater willingness to affirm subjective/cultural

ambivalence, fallibility, and interdependence. This is especially likely if such projects nurture cooperation between people of different generations (and among various cultures) in narrating the National Socialist past in ways that encourage the perception of common interests and shared responsibility. However, it also is possible for such discourse to function as a means for yet another generation of Germans (and for other cultures) to narrate a kind of self-legitimizing distance between themselves and perceived negative others, in this case an older generation of Germans who appear as guilty of mistakes in the National Socialist and postwar past.

With this in mind, it will be fascinating to monitor future German and other efforts to narrate the past of GDR cinema. What will their more detailed analysis reveal about forbidden and other DEFA films about German fascism? Will they also consider the discourse surrounding such films? What narrative strategies will such projects employ and how will they influence the process of individual and cultural identity formation in the united Germany and elsewhere? Perhaps they will define East German cinema narrowly with reference to DEFA, but they may also consider the significance of the institutions of cinema in West Germany, the United States, the Soviet Union, and other cultures. Will they identify similarities between cinema in the GDR and other cinemas or concentrate on drawing distinctions? And what will be the portrayal of the specific relationship between cinema in East and West Germany, as well as between those cinemas and that of the Third Reich?

As the remaining essays in this volume suggest, especially since the 1960s, at least some similarities in the treatment of the National Socialist past have appeared in the cinemas of the two Germanies. Like their counterparts in the East, younger West German filmmakers often have raised questions about historical continuity, challenging the older generation's denial of responsibility for the National Socialist past. They, too, have formulated their challenges cinematically with alternative thematic orientations and narrative styles. The contributions here also suggest an intensifying effort among filmmakers in the FRG to abandon one-dimensional images of individual/cultural integrity and infallibility—efforts that influence all intersections of the relationship between cinema, television, and history.

Michael Geisler's essay contributes to the process by returning our attention to the medium of television and its treatment of Jewish persecution in the Third Reich. Popular claims about the impact of the NBC docudrama *Holocaust* in the FRG provide the point of departure for his critique of West German television films about the National Socialist past. Geisler asks why West German films from the 1950s to 1970s have attracted less attention than *Holocaust,* whether or not the docudrama really was a watershed event in the media development of the Federal Republic, and if it succeeded in changing discourse on the Holocaust. By focusing on *Holocaust* in this way, Geisler participates in the narrative reframing of West German television's treatment of Nazi atrocities. Instead of portraying television as a distinctly national institution, he, like Uricchio, acknowledges the influence of programming from other cultures. His survey of West German films also challenges traditional claims about television's lack of attention to the Third Reich and about the medium's inability to facilitate a productive "coming to terms" with the National Socialist past.

Similar to other contributors, Geisler notes the tendency among (West) German filmmakers to narrate the past as a method for recouping images of individual/cultural innocence, capability, and progress. However, in the postwar context the National Socialist past appears less as a compensatory realm in which such images take root and flourish than one from which Germans seek refuge in the present. Geisler explains how narratives, ranging from Claus Hubalek's *Die Festung (The Fortress,* 1957) to Egon Monk's *Die Anfrage (The Inquiry,* 1962) and Rolf Hädrich's *Mord in Frankfurt (Murder in Frankfurt,* 1968) encouraged spectators to identify with the opponents and victims of German fascism, to condemn atrocities as the crimes of parents who burdened their children with inherited guilt, and generally to assume the position of detached observers of something portrayed as distant. He also perceives these displacing gestures in West German efforts to block the domestic broadcast of *Holocaust* (or alternately to build a network of mediating public programs to accompany it) and in other phenomena of the 1980s, ranging from the Bitburg event to the Historians' Debate.

Geisler criticizes such distancing techniques, whether their initiators claim the need and ability to document the past objectively or attempt to legitimize their efforts by disparaging as melodramatic the "culture industry's" portrayals while valorizing more critical, intellectual approaches. Noting how such projects remove German fascism from the realm of everyday personal experience, he locates the attraction and value of *Holocaust* precisely in its capacity to personalize Nazi terror and embed it in the everyday life of the German people. This, he argues, enables the kind of aesthetic experience capable of modifying grandiose concepts of self and society, engendering more complex perceptions of ambiguity and fallibility in the past, as well as continuity between the past and the present. Geisler links the experience encouraged by *Holocaust* to the kind of "mourning" Alexander and Margarete Mitscherlich pre-scribed in their seminal work on postwar German culture. However, he also identifies a number of fascinating West German television projects with similar agendas, including Eberhard Fechner's *Klassenphoto (Class Photograph,* 1971), Paul Karalus's *Endlösung (Final Solution,* 1979), and Pavel Schnabel's *(Rhina) "Jetzt - nach so viel Jahren" ([Rhina] "Now After All These Years,"* 1981). It is in their collecting personal oral histories of everyday life in the Third Reich, their dialogic and visual collapsing of the distance between the perpetrators and victims of Na-tional Socialism, and their experimenting with other forms of interactive and cooperative narration that Geisler perceives the greatest promise for a positive working through of the past as images of the Nazi era move progressively from the realm of personal memory to that of public mem-ory, from the domain of contemporary history to that of general history.

Attention to the relationship between postwar German identity formation, the labor of mourning, and film continues in the next essay. Like Geisler, Eric Santner invokes the insights of the Mitscherlichs, but he recasts them explicitly within the framework of post-Freudian psychology and the postmodern to articulate the failure of Germans to complete the task of creating more complex images of themselves and their culture. Santner identifies a double bind associated with the labor of mourning, indicating that Germans first must work through the primitive narcissistic injury represented by the shattering of specular relations that provided the psychological foundations of National Socialism. Only when they no longer mourn the loss of perceived unity associated with National Socialist ideology, Santner claims, can Germans exit the realm of imaginary continuity, enter the world of postmodern contiguities between self and other, and begin to acknowledge shared responsibility for and sympathize with the victims of National Socialism as distinct others who are worthy of respect.

According to his reading of recent events in West German culture, a compulsion to repeat self-legitimizing strategies in narrating the past continued to figure strongly in the 1980s. If National Socialism projected the threat to perceived national unity and strength onto Jews (and others) in the destabilizing modern culture during the first half of the twentieth century, then, Santner asserts, West Germans often repeat this strategy when faced with postmodern challenges to traditional concepts of everything from subjectivity to national culture. His essay reviews the major contributions to the Historians' Debate, illustrating how this compulsion finds expression in narrating the past with a desire to recoup conventional notions of the (German) subject's centrality and homogeneous national identity in virtually all of them. Thus, Ernst Nolte appears to discredit the victors' accounts of the Holocaust and valorize German interpretations. Michael Stürmer also seems confident in the ability of Germans to ascribe meaning collectively to the National Socialist past in ways capable of nurturing healthy individual/cultural identity in the present. At the same time, Santner notes, one of the most prominent scholarly narrators of the past, Andreas Hillgruber, promotes a myopic vision of events on the Eastern front, fostering images of German soldiers as tragic figures who attempted to salvage what they could for the German nation in the face of the approaching Red Army.

Like other contributions to this volume, Santner's offers examples of such narrative defense strategies in various forms of discourse. In his "thick reading" of contemporary West German culture, Edgar Reitz's alternative to mainstream inscriptions of German fascism like *Holocaust* also appears complicit in the trend toward psychological regression. Seen from this perspective, *Heimat*, similar to the Riefenstahl films as described by Schulte-Sasse, encourages nostalgia for an imagined past that appears lost to modernity. It chastises those who abandon their homes (*Weggeher*) for disrupting communal integrity, focusing on the consumer capitalism of the United States (and the Jews who found refuge there) as primary initiators of social fragmentation and erosion in Western culture today. In its larger critique of modernity, guilt for the National Socialist past once again is displaced in ways capable of restoring an image of individual German innocence and the longing for a region in which Germans might cohabit harmoniously, free of (post)industrial threats.

Santner's provocative rethinking of German mourning is compelling, but it also raises a number of questions. Although he outlines Jürgen Habermas's challenges to neoconservative positions in the Historians' Debate and affirms the corresponding work on a "postconventional" identity in contemporary West German culture, his narrative focuses narrowly enough on expressions of psychological regression to evoke a perhaps overly pessimistic image of cultural homogeneity. Does the Habermasian strategy of a postmodern identity formation that is less tied to conventional concepts of distinct individual/cultural boundaries and binary opposition figure prominently enough in German culture now to warrant cautious optimism? If this is the case, Santner's effort to convince his readers of persistent impediments in the German labor of mourning might be perceived as perpetuating the kind of self-legitimizing discourse that, while criticizing the narrated other, implies one-dimensionally positive images of the narrator.[37] In addition, Santner's analysis of *Heimat* may appear unduly harsh to some. While others, too, have discussed the cited shortcomings in the miniseries, most affirm its attempt to expose the negative effects of modernity, including mass media, on individual and cultural identity formation. Some also perceive in Hermann's recording session at the conclusion of *Heimat* an effort to interweave the past and present, personal experience and mass media, producer and recipient into a highly ambiguous text—one suitable as a potential model for individual/cultural identity formation in the postmodern present. Is it possible to see Reitz's and other New German alternatives to mainstream cinema and television, especially those Geisler highlights in his essay, as nurturing the transition to a greater acceptance of individual/cultural ambiguity in a postmodern world of instability? Under what circumstances would Santner affirm cultural development in contemporary Germany?[38]

With what many now recognize as a characteristically enigmatic, but consistently thought-provoking presentation of insights, Thomas Elsaesser expresses a similar degree of skepticism about the labor of mourning in West German culture, focusing specifically on New German Cinema. Like Byg and Geisler, Elsaesser cites generational conflict as a significant factor in filmic portrayals of German fascism during the past two decades. The experience of the past as mediated by life under the patriarchal authority of the family (and other social institutions) in the present, he asserts, established the context for a younger generation to emerge from a political amnesia in the late 1960s and 1970s and "oedipalize" their narration of the past. According to this notion of the historical imaginary, many New German filmmakers appear to narrate identification with and rejection of selected aspects of the past simultaneously, breaking radically with what is perceived to be negative and embracing nostalgically allegedly positive elements that seem to be lost. Referring specifically to *Heimat* and intending an allusion to the use of media in the Third Reich, Elsaesser indicates how this selective process becomes a kind of elegiac editing, constructing images of continuity and discontinuity narcissistically and, consequently, transforming history into what he describes as an "old movie." Or as Schulte-Sasse might formulate it, New German Cinema's labor of mourning begins to resemble the fascist tendency to dissolve the boundaries between an aestheticized past and real life in the present, reinforcing positive images of self as innocent, whole, and capable.

At the same time, Elsaesser sees another, overlapping paradigm at work in New German Cinema's efforts to problematize the representation of the past. Recalling the perceived link between warfare, capitalism, and electronic media in the work of Weimar intellectuals such as Ernst Jünger, Walter Benjamin, and Siegfried Kracauer, his essay reinforces my introductory remarks on alternatives to mainstream cinema and television by constructing a narrative of continuity between the Weimar past and West German culture of the late 1960s and 1970s. According to this narrative, New German filmmakers, including Kluge (*Die Patriotin* [*The Patriot*, 1979]), Hans-Jürgen Syberberg (*Hitler, ein Film aus Deutschland* [*Our Hitler*, 1977]), and Rainer Werner Fassbinder (*Lili Marleen*, 1980) continue earlier media-critical investigations into the status of cinema as historical agent. They emphasize how commercial cinema often mobilizes public opinion about the past just as much as it might nurture the private process of remembering. Elsaesser seems to applaud New German films that expose the extent to which the mobilizing spectacle of cinema and television has permeated all realms of everyday life, rendering distinctions between private and public sphere—even cinema and history—increasingly tenuous. But, he also questions the power of such films to nurture a sphere in which individuals can have personal experiences and organize them with any degree of autonomy. Unlike Geisler, Elsaesser perceives the personal labor of mourning as becoming more and more esoteric as the "industrialization of consciousness" progresses, especially through the medium of television.

The essays by Byg, Geisler, Santner, and Elsaesser indicate no strong consensus about the potential for alternatives to mainstream narratives about the past to positively influence the process of individual/cultural identity formation in contemporary German culture. Each of them criticizes the conventional narrative tendency to rejuvenate notions of integrity and capability based on the Enlightenment teleology of progress. However, while some sustain hope for developing a sphere in which personal experience might serve as the catalyst for work on identities of complexity, ambiguity, and fallibility, others seem to doubt the possibility and even the efficacy of such projects. If, as Elsaesser implies, we now live in a (postmodern) culture of pastiche that has substantially undermined all notions of the subject's ability to shape its own identity, then what is the value of projects dedicated to autonomous identity formation? If the goal is to abandon the desire for mastery and control in relationships between self and other, might it not be more effective to embrace the postmodern as that which shows us the way? As one might expect, Elsaesser's relatively open narrative provides no clear answers. Instead, it stimulates dialogue and, especially when combined with Byg's, Geisler's, and Santner's perspectives, invites readers to contemplate whether a conclusive assessment is possible and even desirable.

In the volume's final essay, Anton Kaes contributes further to this process by positing New German Cinema as a postmodern alternative to the "culture industry." Building on Critical Theory's (foremost that of the Frankfurt School) and Jean Baudrillard's assessment of modern mass media, Kaes refers specifically to miniseries representations of history, observing how they have begun to replace all other images, thus reducing the experience of historical events to the act of receiving narrativized media events. Like Geisler and Elsaesser, he questions the future of a public memory created by humans who are capable of organizing their own experience of history unfettered by the constraints of technological memory. However, Kaes reinforces Geisler's notion of productive experimentation more than Elsaesser's view of an overwhelmingly powerful and stifling media system. While he also shares with Elsaesser and Santner the image of a West Germany in transition from modernity to postmodernity, he consequently assesses the production of images about the National Socialist past within this context of transition more positively than either of them.

Refocusing our attention on media events such as the *Holocaust* broadcast, the Bitburg visit, and the controversy over building new museums of German history in Bonn and Berlin, Kaes identifies in the accompanying debates a tendency to reinvigorate the capacity for public remembering. His own exemplifying readings of *Our Hitler, The Patriot*, and Claude Lanzmann's *Shoah* (1987) illustrate a contemporary desire to engage the imaginations of individuals, encouraging them to cooperate creatively in narrating the past. According to Kaes, such (postmodern) projects deconstruct the power of technological images and their producers to commercialize and homogenize the past, abstracting it ever further from the realm of personal experience and memory. In the place of such self-effacing commodification, he argues, Syberberg, Kluge, and Lanzmann offer texts committed to foregrounding the act of construction. They challenge mainstream stories of continuity and closure with open-ended narratives, consisting of innumerable shorter, contiguous stories.

While Kaes might agree with Elsaesser about the extent to which mainstream cinema and television have colonized the human conscious, he thus shares with Geisler the hope for alternative narrative constructions of the past emanating from the margins. In contrast to both Santner and Elsaesser, he expresses little apparent concern for the possibility that such alternatives might be part of a new generation's attempt to assert individual/cultural innocence and autonomy at the expense of others. Kaes perceives postmodern German culture as one in which the narrative hegemony of commercial cinema and television can be challenged effectively by experimental, destabilizing, heterogeneous, and self-reflexive constructions of the past. In other words, he suggests, the history in New German Cinema and television can merge productively with cinema and television in the developing story of German culture.

The Historiography of Cinema and Television in Postmodernity

Of course, my essay, too, is a narrative construction of history. It organizes the contributions to this volume sequentially by following the chronology of textual production to which they refer: the essays on Weimar cinema appear first, those on film and television in the Third Reich next, and the others on film and television in the postwar era last. One potential consequence of such an organizing principle is the suggestion of a teleological development in which specific political, economic, technological, and/or aesthetic events influence others in a process of progressive linear change. While it may be impossible to ignore the developing nature of the historiography of cinema and television in Germany, the essays gathered here demonstrate clearly the complex and dynamic nature of such development and the variety of mediating factors in any attempt to formulate a verifiable account. In addition, as scholars such as Elsaesser assert, the longing for unimpeachable accounts might be stimulated by the desire for mastery and control that has attracted so much critical attention during the recent past.

Given the substantial problems with a teleological approach, I would like to offer a variety of other possible strategies for organizing the essays gathered here and encourage readers to experiment with grouping them in a process of creative interaction, perceiving each to exist in critical dialogue with every other. One could, for example, connect and contrast the contributions by those authors who focus narrowly on cinematic or television texts, those who concentrate more on analyzing the discourse surrounding the production of such texts, or others who are more concerned with the discourse about the developing medium of production. Following this strategy, one might further consider the nature and significance of insights derived from each focus and the extent to which each might complement the others. A further possibility is to link and consider the relative value of those essays with a greater interest in specific articulations of the relationship between cinema, television, and history, as well as those that consider the extent to which they influence each other. What gaps, blind spots, and other limitations emerge from narrative constructions based, for example, only on the analysis of history in individual films?

As indicated by their sequential organization, the essays also invite readers to perceive continuities in narrating the past in/of German cinema and television. Thus it is tempting to consider groups of essays with a focus on gender coding (Hake, Silberman, Horak, Schulte-Sasse) and generational conflict (Byg, Geisler, Elsaesser) or even larger groups focusing on inscriptions of nationalism/fascism or on efforts to overcome such orientations and the intersections between such groups. One might also ask what other continuities exist and what kind of insight can be gained from exploring them.

Despite the heterogeneity of the essays in this volume, it is also impossible to overlook the extent to which most of them emphasize the relationship between narrating the past and the (German) subject's effort to formulate individual and cultural identities in the present. This is the most striking continuity in the authors' analysis of the historiography of film and television in Germany. Whether their topic is the narration of film or television history, the narrating of history in cinema and television, or the influence of cinema and television in history, they appear to reinforce consistently the claim formulated in the second introductory citation from Janet Staiger. Beginning at the turn of the century and continuing to the present, historians, filmmakers, critics, and spectators all seem to have participated to some extent in the discursive practice of "fixing, securing, or pinning down the past" in correspondence with "the threatening anxiety of having to recognize the inability of an individual to control and master the self-as-subject."

According to Saunders, Hake, and Silberman this strategy found expression in cinematic discourse about the past and in discourse about German cinema during the Weimar Republic but also in subsequent accounts of that period in German film history. Combining their contributions with those of Horak and Schulte-Sasse reinforces the perception of continuity in this practice from literature to film, journalism, and historical discourse; from Germany to other European nations and the United States and at least from the time of the Weimar Republic through the Third Reich and into the postwar era. The essays of Uricchio and Geisler illustrate the extent to which the developing medium of television provided an additional context within which Germans and others have perpetuated strategies for formulating conventional images of self and society in the process of narrating the past. And while Byg, Santner, Elsaesser, and Kaes all perceive the desire of younger generations of German filmmakers to nurture new models of identity formation and to accomplish this in part through critical dialogue with their cultural heritage, they reach no clear consensus about the potential for or actual success of such projects. Is it possible that even the most energetic attempts to develop alternatives to the mainstream historiography of German cinema and television remain to a large extent bound by an unshakable allegiance to imaginary specular relations? If it is possible to abandon such an allegiance, what is the hope of doing so effectively in a culture many have described as offering fewer and fewer opportunities for individuals to formulate identities independent of the constraint associated with terms like the culture industry, the industrialized conscious, and technological memory? What are the prospects for the historiography of cinema and television in post–cold war, postmodern Germany?

In their own attempts to challenge the conventional historiography of German cinema and television and to encourage new trends, many of the contributors to this collection offer a variety of potentially valuable responses. If there will be meaningful change, then it will involve continued attention to the issues of nationality and national cinema that have been treated in the contributions of Saunders, Uricchio, Byg, Santner, and others. The ongoing discussion about Weimar film history, for example, could profit substantially from continued evaluations of the extent to which notions of national cinema nurtured and/or inhibited cultural pluralism in the 1920s. The same applies to current efforts to narrate the past of German cinema and television, including those with a focus on the two Germanies during the postwar era. It also seems important to encourage greater attention to the issues of patriarchy, gender coding, and gendered spectatorship as discussed by Hake, Silberman, Horak, and Schulte-Sasse. Here it will be important to refine further existing models for analyzing how patriarchal notions of gender have influenced cinematic and television discourse about the past. Perhaps the most difficult challenge of this project will be to document responsibility for such discourse and distinctions between the male and female experience of it in ways that avoid recourse to self-legitimizing strategies of binary opposition along gender lines.

The greatest challenge of all will be to narrate the past of divided Germany in cinema and television. Will the German labor of mourning progress in the electronic media of the united Germany and to what extent will it construct continuities and discontinuities between the various phases in the development of twentieth-century German culture? Will the National Socialist past fade into what Geisler calls general history, and how will film and television mediate the personal experience of life in divided Germany? Will political, economic, technological, and aesthetic trends, including movement toward a United States of Europe, global economics, cable networking, and interactive modes of communication foster more flexible notions of individual and cultural identity? Will the "industrialization of the conscious," as Elsaesser describes it, render it impossible for individuals to shape identities with any degree of autonomy? And if this is the case, will the result be negative? Although the answers to these questions are unclear, it seems certain that they will stimulate the discussion about the relationships between cinema, television, and history in Germany for the foreseeable future.

Notes

1. Mark Nash and Steve Neale, "Film: 'History/Production/Memory,'" *Screen* 18 (Winter 1977/78): 77.
2. Janet Staiger, "Securing the Fictional Narrative as a Tale of the Historical Real," *South Atlantic Quarterly* 88 (1989): 399.
3. Mas'ud Zavarzadeh, "Change, History, Nostalgia," *Seeing Films Politically* (Albany: State U of New York P, 1991) 153.
4. In this essay I assume multiple connotations of the term historiography. As the reference to the work of Mark Nash and Steve Neale below indicates, historiography articulates a variety of possible intersections between cinema,

television, and history. These include narrating histories of cinema and television, cinema and television's narration of history, and cinema and television's participation in historical development.

5. See, among many other examples, F. R. Ankersmit, "Historiography and Postmodernism," *History and Theory* 28.2 (1989): 137–53; Linda Hutcheon, *A Poetics of Postmodernism: History, Theory, Fiction* (New York and London; Routledge, 1988), esp. "Historiographic Metafiction: 'The Pastime of Past Time,'" 105–23; and Hayden White, *The Content of the Form: The Narrative Discourse and Historical Representation* (Baltimore: Johns Hopkins UP, 1987). Much of what has been referred to recently as New Historicist scholarship also participates in this reassessment. See, for example, *The New Historicism*, ed. H. Aram Veeser (New York and London: Routledge, 1989).

6. Fredric Jameson, "Postmodernism, or the Cultural Logic of Late Capitalism," *New Left Review* 146 (July/August 1984): 53–92. See also his book *Postmodernism, or the Cultural Logic of Late Capitalism* (Durham: Duke UP, 1991).

7. For an introductory account of this process, see Colin MacCabe, "Class of '68: Elements of an Intellectual Autobiography," in his *Tracking the Signifier. Theoretical Essays: Film, Linguistics, Literature* (Minneapolis: U of Minnesota P, 1985) 1–32.

8. MacCabe 6–7.

9. The winter 1977/78 issue of *Screen* includes articles on the festival topic. See, Nash and Neale 77–91; and Keith Tribe, "History and the Production of Memories" 9–22.

10. Nash and Neale 77.

11. See Teresa de Lauretis and Stephen Heath, eds., *The Cinematic Apparatus* (London: MacMillan, 1980), esp. Stephen Heath, "Technology as Historical and Cultural Form," 1–13; Peter Wollen, "Cinema and Technology: A Historical Overview," 14–22; and Douglas Gomery, "Towards an Economic History of the Cinema: The Coming of Sound to Hollywood," 38–46.

12. See Patricia Mellenkamp and Philip Rosen, eds., *Cinema Histories, Cinema Practices*, American Film Institute Monograph Series (Frederick, MD: University Publications of America, 1984), here Philip Rosen, "Securing the Historical: Historiography and the Classical Cinema," 17–34; and Thomas Elsaesser, "Film History as Visual Pleasure: Weimar Cinema," 47–86.

13. See Mary Ann Doane et al., eds., *Re-vision: Essays in Feminist Film Criticism*, American Film Institute Monograph Series (Frederick, MD: University Publications of America, 1984).

14. Of the many examples that would document ongoing trends I mention three representative groups here: revisions of early and classical cinema that create histories of narrative strategy, feminist critiques of reified patriarchal film history that deploy current psychoanalytic theory, and the critique of ideology studies that link film history and historical films with affirmative as well as subversive political practice. See among many, many others, Miriam Hansen, *Babel and Babylon: Spectatorship in American Silent Film* (Cambridge: Harvard UP, 1991); David Bordwell et al., *The Classical Hollywood Cinema* (New York: Columbia UP, 1985); Mary Ann Doane, *The Desire to Desire: The Woman's Film of the 1940s* (Bloomington: Indiana UP, 1987); and Mas'ud Zavarzadeh. It is worth noting here that, while each of the

suggested groups in some way links cinematic historiography with issues of ideology, almost all studies resist any notion of verifiable class-specific intentionality that could drive production and lock criticism into the search for corresponding inscriptions. Zavarzadeh's study is a thought-provoking exception to this rule.

15. Constance Penley, ed., *Feminism and Film Theory* (New York: Routledge, 1988); Tania Modleski, *The Women Who Knew Too Much* (New York: Routledge, 1988); E. Ann Kaplan, *Women and Film: Both Sides of the Camera* (New York: Methuen, 1983); Annette Kuhn, *Women's Pictures: Feminism and Cinema* (London: Routledge, 1982).

16. Of course, as soon as critics began to consider the development of cinema, they engaged in narrating its history. Early examples of substantial efforts include the publication of the *Jahrbuch der Filmindustrie,* beginning in 1922; *Licht Bild Bühne: 30 Jahre Film* (Berlin: Licht Bild Bühne, 1924); and numerous works such as Gerhard Zaddach's *Der literarische Film: Ein Beitrag zur Geschichte der Lichtspielkunst,* diss., Breslau, 1929.

17. The best early example is Emilie Altenloh, *Zur Soziologie des Kino: Die Kinounternehmung und die sozialen Schichten ihrer Besucher* (Jena: Eugen Diederichs, 1914). Reprinted in facsimile by Medienladen, Hamburg, 1977.

18. For example, at the turn of the century the cinema commission of the Magdeburg Teachers' Association annually organized celebrations of the Battle of Sedan and the Kaiser's birthday that included short affirmative films about the army and navy. For a concise description of such activity at the turn of the century, see Dr. Samuel Drucker, "Das Kinoproblem und unsere politischen Gegner," *Die Neue Zeit* 6 March 1914: 867–72; and 13 March 1914: 907–12.

19. Siegfried Kracauer's *From Caligari to Hitler* (Princeton: Princeton UP, 1947) continues to offer one of the best critical accounts of mainstream cinema's development from 1917 to 1933. See my *Film and the German Left in the Weimar Republic* (Austin: U of Texas P, 1990) for a more detailed account of the German left's response to mainstream Weimar cinema; and Patrice Petro, *Joyless Streets: Women and Melodramatic Representation in Weimar Cinema* (Princeton: Princeton UP, 1989) for a more detailed account of Weimar cinema's address to a female audience. For a good analysis of Nazi cinema's ideological orientation, see, among others, Eric Rentschler, *Nazi Film Aesthetics: Fantasy Production in the Third Reich* (Cambridge: Harvard UP, forthcoming); Stephen Lowry, *Pathos und Politik: Ideologie im Spielfilm des Nationalsozialismus* (Tübingen: Niemeyer, 1991); and David Welch, *Propaganda and the German Cinema 1933–1945* (Oxford: Oxford UP, 1983).

20. Among others, the following studies provide information about German cinema's portrayal of history prior to and during the Third Reich: Linda Schulte-Sasse, "The Never Was as History: Portrayals of the Eighteenth Century in National Socialist Film," diss., U of Minnesota, 1985; Hans-Gerd Happel, *Der historische Film im Nationalsozialismus* (Frankfurt a.M.: R. G. Fischer, 1984); and Axel Marquardt and Heinz Rathsack, eds., *Preussen im Film* (Reinbek bei Hamburg: Rowohlt, 1981).

21. For information about the development of German cinema from the beginning to 1945, including information about the cited genres, see, among others, *Before Caligari: German Cinema, 1895–1920,* ed. Paolo Cherchi

Usai and Lorenzo Codelli (Madison: U of Wisconsin P, 1990); Curt Riess, *Das gab's nur einmal: Die große Zeit des deutschen Films*, 3 vols. (Frankfurt a.M.: Ullstein, 1985); and Jerzy Toeplitz, *Geschichte des Films*, trans. Lilli Kaufmann and Christine Mückenberger, 4 vols. (Berlin: Henschel, 1975–1983).

22. The following studies offer detailed accounts of the developing cinemas in each German state: Klaus Kreimeier, *Kino und Filmindustrie in der BRD: Ideologieproduktion und Klassenwirklichkeit nach 1945* (Kronberg: Scriptor, 1973); Peter Pleyer, *Deutscher Nachkriegsfilm 1946–48* (Münster: Fahle, 1965); Wolfgang Gersch, *Film- und Fernsehkunst der DDR* (Berlin: Henschel, 1979); and Peter Jansen and Wolfram Schütte, eds., *Film in der DDR* (Munich: Hanser, 1977). For accounts of the efforts to portray the National Socialist past, see, among others, Wolfgang Becker et al., *In jenen Tagen... Wie der deutsche Film die Vergangenheit bewältigte* (Leverkusen: Leske+Budrich, forthcoming); my *The Dialectic of Antifascism: National Socialism in Postwar German Cinema* (Berlin and New York: Walter de Gruyter, forthcoming); Eric Santner, *Stranded Objects: Mourning, Memory, and Film in Postwar Germany* (Ithaca: Cornell UP, 1990); Hilmar Hoffmann and Walter Schobert, eds., *Zwischen Gestern und Morgen. Westdeutscher Nachkriegsfilm 1946–1962* (Frankfurt a.M.: Deutsches Filmmuseum, 1989); and Anton Kaes, *Deutschlandbilder, Die Wiederkehr der Geschichte als Film* (Munich: text + kritik, 1987). Reprinted and modified in English as *From Hitler to Heimat: The Return of History as Film* (Cambridge: Harvard UP, 1989).

23. During the 1980s, the number of studies on New German Cinema grew substantially. For the purposes of this essay, reference to some of the book-length publications will suffice. Each of the cited works includes extensive bibliographical sections. See Thomas Elsaesser, *New German Cinema: A History* (New Brunswick: Rutgers UP, 1989); Eric Rentschler, *West German Film in the Course of Time* (Bedford Hills, NY: Redgrave, 1984); Klaus Phillips, ed., *New West German Filmmakers: From Oberhausen Through the 1970s* (New York: Ungar, 1984); James Franklin, *New German Cinema: From Oberhausen to Hamburg* (Boston: Twayne, 1983); Timothy Corrigan, *New German Film: The Displaced Image* (Austin: U of Texas P, 1983); Hans Günther Pflaum and Hans Helmut Prinzler, *Cinema in the Federal Republic of Germany* (Bonn: Inter Nationes, 1983); and John Sandford, *The New German Cinema* (London: Oswald Wolff, 1980).

24. The Allies' censorship decisions for films to be screened in Germany between 1945 and 1949 offer a sense of how much films from other cultures influenced the cinematic landscape. See Pleyer 427–58, for a compilation of the decisions for German, British, French, and U.S. films. As is frequently noted, the strong influence of cinema and television programming from other cultures continued throughout the postwar era. In 1989, for example, domestic films attracted 20 percent of the commercial market in the Federal Republic. Films from the United States attracted almost 66 percent. See Lothar Just, ed., *Film-Jahrbuch 1989* (Munich: Heyne, 1989) for more detailed information about cinema and television programming.

25. In her "Theory, History and German Film," *Monatshefte* 82 (1990): 294–306, Katie Trumpener outlines the extent to which American scholarship on

German cinema has embraced poststructuralist film theory. While noting a marginal overlapping in published studies with an interest in merging theory with cultural studies, she encourages much more experimentation in the teaching of German cinema. The cited issue of *Monatshefte* focuses on teaching German media and offers a variety of articles on the current status of research on and the teaching of courses about silent film, feature films from 1933 to 1945, New German Cinema, women's cinema in the FRG, cinema in the GDR, and West German television.

26. Critiques of the study began to appear almost immediately after its publication and have continued to surface periodically ever since. For early examples, see Dwight MacDonald, "Through the Lens Darkly," *Partisan Review* 14.5 (1947): 526–28; Heinz J. Furian, "Zwischen 'Caligarismus' und Realismus: Ein Beitrag zur kritischen Darstellung der deutschen Filmgeschichte," *Deutsche Filmgeschichte* 1–4 (1957) and 1–4 (1958). For a more recent example, see Michael Kessler and Thomas Y. Levin, eds., *Siegfried Kracauer: Neue Interpretationen* (Stuttgart: Stauffenberg, 1990). For other examples of recent scholarship on Weimar cinema, see Walter Schatzberg, ed. *Filmkultur zur Zeit der Weimarer Republik* (Munich: Saur, 1991); Mike Budd, ed., *Caligari: Texts, Contexts, Histories* (New Brunswick: Rutgers UP, 1990); and the special issues of *New German Critique* on Weimar mass culture 51 (Fall 1990) and Weimar film theory 40 (Winter 1987).

27. It seems possible to discern other, somewhat different implications here. One might argue, for example, that the focus on male subjectivity in crisis in Weimar culture implied the necessity to revise male subjectivity or perhaps subjectivity in general. One also might argue that what Kracauer and others found in Weimar cinema and in Weimar cultural generally was more an address to a class-specific than a gender-specific audience. Certainly women constituted a meaningful segment of the film-going public in Weimar Germany. It also is probable that lower-middle class attitudes predominated in that audience. Given commercial cinema's desire to address the largest possible audience, it seems likely that filmmakers would attempt to respond more generally to shared lower-middle-class concerns, than to those that might be perceived as distinctly male or female.

28. Of course, Petro is not the only film scholar to apply this critical approach to the study of German cinema. For other examples, see *Frauen und Film*, ed. Karola Gramann, Gertrud Koch, and Heide Schlüpmann. See also Heide Schlüpmann's *Die Unheimlichkeit des Blicks: Das Drama des frühen deutschen Kinos* (Frankfurt: Stroemfeld/Roter Stern, 1990); and Miriam Hansen, "Early Silent Cinema: Whose Public Sphere?" *New German Critique* 29 (Spring/Summer 1983): 147–84. For a thematically organized catalogue of films by and about women, see Gudrun Lukasz-Aden and Christel Strobel, *Der Frauenfilm: Filme von und für Frauen* (Munich: Heyne, 1985).

29. See the already cited volume edited by H. Aram Veeser for a collection of critical essays about this trend in textual interpretation. In contrast to the assertions of those who condemn postructuralism (see, for example, David Lehman, *Sign of the Times: Deconstruction and the Fall of Paul de Man* [New York: Poseidon, 1991]) for its apparent lack of attention to the relationship between texts and lived experience in specific sociohistorical settings, much new historicist research seeks to apply its psychosemiotic insights to histori-

cally based readings of a wide variety of discourses. Anton Kaes promotes such an approach to literary studies in "New Historicism and the Study of German Literature," *German Quarterly* 62 (1989): 210–19; and to cinema studies in his "Silent Film," *Monatshefte* 82 (1990): 246–56.

30. Eric Rentschler, "German Feature Films 1933–1945," *Monatshefte* 82 (1990): 257–66.

31. The first notable work on this topic was Willi Lüdecke's *Der Film in Agitation und Propaganda der revolutionären deutschen Arbeiterbewegung (1919– 1933)* (Berlin: Oberbaum, 1973). See also my *Film and the German Left in the Weimar Republic: From Caligari to Kuhle Wampe;* Rolf Surmann, *Die Münzenberg-Legende: Zur Publizistik der revolutionären deutschen Arbeiterbewegung 1921–1933* (Cologne: Prometh, 1982); and Helmut Korte, *Film und Realität in der Weimarer Republik* (Munich: Hanser, 1978). Of course, film scholars in the GDR also contributed significantly to documenting the film activity of the German left in the Weimar Republic. For example, see Gertraude Kühn et al., eds., *Film und revolutionäre Arbeiterbewegung in Deutschland 1918–1932,* 2 vols. (Berlin: Henschel, 1975).

32. Helmut Korte offers the clearest statement of this in *Film und Realität in der Weimarer Republik.* See especially 9–10 and 13–24.

33. KPD functionaries such as Gertrud Alexander, Alfred Durus, and Willi Münzenberg advocated cinematic correctives to what they perceived as mainstream "falsifications" of the past, calling for representations based on historical-materialist analysis but narrated with the emerging classical techniques of the "imaginary" signifier. Others, including Bertolt Brecht, Heinz Lüdecke, and Anna Siemsen began to question the influence of such a narrative strategy on reception. See, among others, my *Film and the German Left in the Weimar Republic* for an account of the developing debates about a leftist alternative to mainstream film aesthetics. Certainly, such debates were not limited to issues of film aesthetics. For information on the developing Marxist aesthetic and its expression in debates on literary and dramatic production, see, among others, Manfred Nössig et al., *Literaturdebatten in der Weimarer Republik* (Berlin: Aufbau, 1980); Walter Fähnders and Martin Rector, *Linksradikalismus und Literatur,* 2 vols. (Reinbek bei Hamburg: Rowohlt, 1974); and Helga Gallas, *Marxistische Literaturtheorie* (Neuwied and Berlin: Luchterhand, 1971).

34. In addition to the histories cited above, see, among others, the special issues of *New German Critique* on New German Cinema 24/25 (Winter/Fall 1981/ 82); on Edgar Reitz's *Heimat* 36 (Fall 1985); and on Alexander Kluge 49 (Winter 1990). See also the special issues of *October* 46 (Fall 1988) and *Text+Kritik* 85/86 (January 1985) on Kluge. For more specific information on the contributions of female filmmakers and their theoretical interests, see, among others, Richard McCormick, *Politics of the Self: Feminism and the Postmodern in West German Literature and Film* (Princeton: Princeton UP, 1991); Susan Linville, "Retrieving History: Margarethe von Trotta's *Marianne and Juliane,*" *PMLA* 106 (1991): 446–58; Ellen Seiter, "Women's History, Women's Melodrama: *Deutschland, bleiche Mutter,*" *German Quarterly* 59 (1986): 569–81; and various issues of *Frauen und Film.* Also, see the discussion of Barton Byg's essay below for information about the contribution of GDR filmmakers to this trend.

35. Corrigan, *New German Film: The Displaced Image.*
36. As cited in note 22, for example, Anton Kaes and Eric Santner have devoted booklength studies to this topic.
37. It is important to note here that the book-length project from which this essay has emerged demonstrates its author's efforts to avoid such narrative strategies and emphasizes the difficulty of accomplishing the task. See my review of the book in the *German Quarterly* 64.4 (1991) 592–93 for more detail.
38. In the final chapter of his *Stranded Objects,* Santner refers to Christa Wolf's *Kindheitsmuster* (*Model Childhood,* 1976) as a narrative model for the labor of mourning. According to his interpretation, it consists of negatively identifying totemic resources in the past, in the sense that the narrator perceives the potential for what might have been, feels sadness for what was, and locates an environment in the present that encourages the cultivation of an identity with those resources.

1

History in the Making:
Weimar Cinema and
National Identity

Thomas J. Saunders

Like the culture of which it was part, Weimar cinema enjoys a self-sustaining heritage. Whether read as a late offshoot of Expressionism, the product of a constellation of specific social and intellectual forces, or reflection of the German psyche, it remains a distinct moment in motion picture evolution. Since 1933 traditionally serves as the great caesura in twentieth-century German culture, temporal closure is usually taken for granted. Thematic and stylistic cohesion derives from focus on a select group of motion pictures. Expressionism and *Neue Sachlichkeit* provide the broad categories within which to isolate several dozen art films that testify to Weimar's idiosyncratic character and offer the raw material with which to investigate its roots and nature. Set against classical Hollywood models, Expressionist stylization, exploration of psychic interiors, reversion to Romantic motifs of magic, myth, and legend, and later experiments in social realism rivet historical interest.[1]

Historical preoccupation with Weimar's peculiarities rests more than is often acknowledged on aspirations and arguments of the 1920s. The Great War initiated an era of national cinemas, attempts to create and sustain uniquely accented national film styles.[2] Inseparable though these efforts were from the nationalism of the age, they should be interpreted less in light of popular chauvinism or xenophobia than as a drive among filmmakers to stake their claims in newly discovered territory. Like the scramble for Africa in the 1880s, occupation of identifiable filmic space guaranteed recognition both domestically and internationally. The national cinema also served as an umbrella under which to synthesize the conflicting commercial, technical, and artistic impulses of the medium. The concept admittedly remained as much rhetorical device as practical program. However, because contemporaries could not identify the features of German film without simultaneously prescribing its direction, the pursuit of a national cinema among screenwriters, critics, and filmmakers contributed to the position Weimar cinema was to assume vis-à-vis German history and international competition.

Weimar cinema emerged from the matrix of social, political, and cultural changes that constituted Germany's breakthrough to modernity.[3] It is remembered, on one hand, for experiments in modernism and, on the other hand, for highly regressive tendencies, principally the preference for historical as opposed to contemporary subjects and problems. Treatment of a Germany or Prussia that—had it ever been actual—was irrevocably gone by 1918 meant projection of national virtues or peculiarities that could locate Germany in the postwar world.[4] The search for a national cinema served a parallel function in the context of international motion picture developments after the Great War. It comprised one part of the much larger problematic of cultural identity in an era in which Germany became the intersection point of foreign cultures, principally the roaring twenties of the United States—from jazz to Charlie Chaplin—and the socialist experiments of Soviet Russia. Berlin, the heart of the world's second largest motion picture industry and the center of European culture, became a refuge to artists and intellectuals and a meeting place of cultural currents from East and West. In the second half of the 1920s it became the subject of a cultural invasion not experienced since the Napoleonic era. German cinema sought to differentiate itself in the highly competitive world of international motion picture exchange by the position it adopted toward German history.

Although Germany's exposure to foreign motion pictures proved quantitatively less intense after than before the war, it was still crucial to postwar cinematic development. Prior to 1914, Germany—though an industrial and urban giant and a major player in world trade—had a modest role on the domestic film market and a minimal one abroad. French movies dominated the international market and in company with Danish productions, Italian historical spectacles, and American westerns and slapsticks supplied German theatres.[5] However, the decade after 1910 witnessed two dramatic changes in the pattern of German cinema culture. First, production took a quantum leap forward, primarily because the war, by stimulating demand while isolating the country from most previous suppliers, yielded hothouse conditions for growth. By 1918 native output covered the bulk of domestic demand, and exporters were beginning to move into foreign markets. Second, fundamental shifts in international exchange altered the context for reception of foreign films in Germany. On one hand, serious production setbacks in other European countries left Germany for the first time the center of continental production and a potential global film power.[6] On the other hand, Germany found its place challenged at home and abroad by dual non-European revolutions.

The most frequently commemorated of these, Russia's Bolshevik revolution, gave birth to a cinematic style that for a brief period in the mid-1920s mesmerized German experts and audiences and spurred reflection on domestic production trends. The other less violent and memorable—but for the motion picture more significant—revolution was the emergence of Hollywood's global hegemony. During and immediately following the war, a seismic international shift occurred as America became the center of world motion picture production and trade.[7] Due to this preeminence, Hollywood was able in the 1920s to lure many of Germany's leading film artists across the Atlantic, invest in branch production in Germany, and threaten to Americanize German production. It thereby presented the first and most sustained challenge to Weimar cinema, and the primary impetus behind efforts to establish a distinct national product.

The foreign challenge from the ideological antipodes of Soviet Russia and the United States impinged upon artistic and commercial ambitions rooted in the previous decade. Before the war the motion picture spawned a general *Kinodebatte* that exposed the various paths which German cinema could pursue. While cinema was still primarily cheap amusement for the working classes, a young generation of authors, stage performers, and directors (many of Expressionist leanings) began to take interest in the medium and explore its relationship with art, literature, and theater. At the same time, guardians of established cultural pursuits, an assortment of aesthetes, pedagogues, pastors, doctors, and government authorities, fumed about film's cultural, moral, social, or physical dangers and campaigned to censor, tax, and/or socialize film production and exhibition. In short, middle-class Germany divided and fought for, against, and over the motion picture.[8]

The Great War, apart from laying the economic foundations of Weimar cinema, conditioned domestic parameters of its growth by affecting this *Kinodebatte* in two broad respects. First, war fostered general appreciation for the value of film in education, propaganda, entertainment, and pacification of the population, substantially reducing its cultural stigma. The prewar *Kinodebatte* acquired a new forum and emphasis. Not only did it become internalized within a substantial, articulate community of critics and filmmakers, but it also revolved around prospects for realizing film's commercial and propagandistic as well as artistic potential.[9] Second, the war figured prominently in cementing cultural, commercial, and national interests. In all belligerent nations, but perhaps most blatantly in Germany, the armed struggle was transmogrified into a contest of world views and cultural types. Statesmen couched national interests in the language of cultural superiority. Intellectuals fed this circumlocution by portraying the conflict in cultural-historical terms—a showdown between German *Kultur* on one hand and Western "civilization" and Eastern "barbarism" on the other. The result was a mode of reasoning that set Germany against the world at the level of fundamental values.[10]

For cinema interests, cultural typecasting and defense of German peculiarities dovetailed with efforts to elevate film from notoriety to respectability. The trade press attempted to consolidate the motion picture's sociocultural position by portraying it as a national institution.[11] Behind this lay obvious commercial motivation, international as well as domestic. Just as the nation's search for a place in the sun combined prestige and profit, *Kultur* and power, so its cinematic counterpart sought artistic opportunity to establish German film internationally. War justified expansion abroad in the interest of propaganda, but the impulse for expansion ran deeper. The creation of Ufa (Universum Film AG) in late 1917, in part with government funds, signified at least as much ambition to capture foreign markets as to make propaganda. General Ludendorff allegedly raged at the first production program of Ufa because it emphasized entertainment at the expense of propaganda, but the company made no secret of its objectives: its initial press statement introduced Ufa as the advance guard of German cinema in *postwar* international competition.[12]

In sum, as the republic emerged from war and defeat, German cinema assumed an increasingly self-conscious stance on the major economic, artistic, and social challenges of film development. General commercial desiderata provoked little conflict. Producers needed to attract investment and fortify a domestic position against *Kinofeinde,* tax authorities, and censors by broadening the movie-going audience. They also needed to expand their horizons beyond central Europe. What remained debatable was the strategy for achieving these goals. The ongoing *Kinodebatte* symptomized uncertainty about what constituted film and whom it was to serve. In conjunction with Germany's continued isolation from the international market—import was not officially restored until 1921—this initially left much room for speculation and experimentation.[13] Commercial and artistic impulses both coincided and clashed. Fortification of a domestic position meant overcoming middle-class antipathy toward motion pictures. The impetus thus provided for artistic experiments overlapped with the ambitions of the young filmmakers—Fritz Lang, F. W. Murnau, Paul Leni, Robert Wiene—to discover new cinematic terrain.[14] Yet how smoothly these objectives could be combined with the need to overcome foreign antipathy to Germany and to find a formula for a mass international audience remained to be seen.

Reconciliation of these artistic, cultural, and commercial objectives would have been a source of controversy even had there been no interference from without. In the event, America's presence loomed on the horizon from very early in the Weimar era, encouraging formulation of filmic objectives and identity in terms of national comparisons. Until 1921 Germany remained legally cut off from world film developments by terms of an import ban imposed in 1916.[15] But even before German experts were acquainted with American films they began to use Hollywood as a reference point. By reputation alone the American cinema presented the obvious and inescapable challenge to domestic producers.[16] Since the latter confessed their desire to make history, they faced growing pressure to create a unique cinematic product rooted in German culture. Although strictly speaking that rootedness was unavoidable, it also became a conscious, deliberate enterprise.[17]

Hollywood presented the first and most sustained invitation to self-definition, but ironically, and fatefully, Weimar was to make a dent in the American market before the reverse occurred. Late in 1920 Ernst Lubitsch's epic of revolutionary France, *Madame Dubarry* (*Passion*, 1919), created a stir in New York, and shortly thereafter *Anna Boleyn* (*Deception*, 1920) and the prototype of a peculiarly German cinema, *The Cabinet of Dr. Caligari* (1920), duplicated the feat. However fortuitous the choice and timing of their release, these films became representatives of what German filmmakers believed they could offer America and the world. Foreign acclaim fed domestic confidence that in the realm of historical spectacle and Expressionist fantasy Germany possessed unique cinematic gifts. One cornerstone was thus laid in the self-perception upon which German filmmakers were to build.[18]

Reinforcement of this self-perception came from a two-pronged American offensive in Germany. One prong was a grandiose design by Famous Players for cooperative production in Berlin. In the spring of 1921 Famous Players founded the European Film Alliance (EFA), a holding company that employed a long list of outstanding German talent, including Paul Davidson, Ernst Lubitsch, Pola Negri, Joe May, Emil Jannings, and Max Reinhardt. The American investors hoped to exploit German abilities and the German inflation to produce world-class pictures at moderate cost. EFA therefore demonstrated American respect for the expertise displayed by the first German releases in the United States.[19] However, when EFA proved a short-lived enterprise—it generated only a handful of pictures, none of which lived up to the expectations raised by *Passion*, before being dismantled as a production company in 1922—experts felt confirmed in their assumption of irreconcilable differences between the two national cinemas. They blamed the fiasco on American largesse. Fabulous salaries in dollars and the most up-to-date studios in Berlin proved more debilitating than productive. German artists could not work to American dictates. The moral of the story—at once consolation and self-fulfilling prophecy—was that American and German cinemas presented fundamentally different species.[20]

The second development of 1921 that fed perceptions of Germany's distinctive qualities was the return of American film to German theaters. Early imports consisted mainly of serialized westerns, spiced with several social dramas and slapstick shorts. Many of these were dated, dumped in Germany thanks to their novelty after the long import embargo and because the mark had already weakened to the point of prohibiting large profits. German experts remained unimpressed and, though aware that these pictures were not necessarily representative, used them to define contrasts between Hollywood and Germany. American creation of tempo, sensationalism, and comedy in westerns and slapsticks persuaded experts that Germany could not compete in these categories. By contrast, American social and historical dramas convinced critics that Hollywood could not dramatize effectively, especially in tragic situations, and that its screenplays foundered on moral or cultural conventions, like the insistence on happy endings, which undermined their credibility.[21] A rating scheme was thus developed which highlighted what were seen as essential differences between the two cinemas.

Emphasis on contrasts in reception of the first wave of American imports clearly aimed to transform the deeply rooted assumption that German and American cinema were different species into a practical program. The strategic intent was to discover effective means of competition against Hollywood. This, of course, was the thrust of Erich Pommer's later explanation for production policies of the early 1920s. Pommer, a central figure in Weimar cinema as production chief with Decla and Ufa, claimed decades after the fact that it would have been pointless to try to compete with Hollywood: artistic experimentation provided the road less traveled.[22] Although Pommer's statement rationalizes a policy which by mid-decade suffered painful eclipse and cannot by itself explain German policy, it accurately reflects contemporary desire to distinguish German cinema from Hollywood cinema.[23] Critics, screen authors, and filmmakers did generally concur on the wisdom of capitalizing on domestic peculiarities.[24] Pommer's opinion also implies, paradoxically, that Hollywood practice had already become normative, at least in a negative sense. Hollywood became the measure of what German filmmakers should not undertake and thus played a formative role in Weimar production, encouraging alternatives to its own style even when still a relatively unknown commodity. Together EFA and the early American releases in Germany therefore solidified the conviction that Germany had unique strengths on which it should continue to build. Historical authenticity, psychological consistency, the ability to breath life into myth and legend, and an eye for the uncanny and bizarre: these were gifts Hollywood lacked, gifts that could be exploited to challenge Hollywood.

To give Hollywood credit for stimulating the creation of what are today seen as Weimar's representative films is neither to argue for the primacy of foreign policy nor to deny the indigenous factors in their production. Nor is it to suggest the existence of an industry-wide policy of deviation rather than imitation: the German cinema did not represent a monolithic block, united in nature and purpose.[25] The problem of Germany's filmic identity vis-à-vis Hollywood is considerably more complex and refractory than either generalization will allow. The cry for self-cultivation arose in part to counter what contemporaries perceived as German eagerness to imitate Hollywood, for everyone recognized the United States as a tantalizing market. Moreover, woven into presumed differences of national cinema cultures were unresolved questions in the domestic *Kinodebatte*. The technical, artistic, and commercial boundaries of the medium remained in considerable flux. What constituted a motion picture and whom it was to serve could not yet be stated definitively. That these questions remained open encouraged on one hand, differentiation and experimentation. A specifically German film language could conceivably establish itself as a viable option to Hollywood. That Hollywood had already established a hegemonic position on the world market encouraged, on the other hand, the process of borrowing and assimilation. America had already demonstrated a successful route to domestic and international success; an alternate path might become a dead end.

Seen in this light, the dilemma faced by Weimar cinema was whether, as Edward Buscombe recently formulated it, "a revolt against Hollywood is indeed a revolt against the cinema."[26] In other words, did there exist or could there be fashioned a workable alternative to Hollywood? According to Buscombe, filmmakers may respond to this query in one of three ways: by imitating to try to compete on equal terms, by cultivating national traditions and peculiarities, or by exploring alternative film discourses.[27] But in practice these three options are not neatly separable. In the case of Weimar cinema, films about Prussia and prewar student life presented one possibility. But they never enjoyed uncontested dominance. To imitate or preserve distinctiveness, a problem applicable to any culture under siege from powerful neighbors, permitted no categorical answer. The bulk of what today passes as Weimar cinema blended the options just outlined, drawing on native cultural traditions, borrowing techniques from Hollywood but experimenting with modes of filmic discourse that deviated from Hollywood trends. This combination seemed to promise uniqueness and perhaps also competitive strength against Hollywood and effective use of film as an artistic and public medium. Thus the challenge posed by Hollywood—whether to borrow or to strike out in novel directions—called less for an either/or than a new synthesis.

Central to this synthesis, and therefore to national orientation, was definition of cinema's inherent properties. Understanding of the medium was still sufficiently fluid in the early 1920s to permit conflicting claims on its nature and purpose. Cinema became a battlefield of competing artistic and economic ambitions. On this battlefield the position adopted toward American motion pictures had enormous significance. As American movies began to appear in German theaters in 1921, *Die Weltbühne* featured a debate that pitted champions of Hollywood against defenders of German film. At stake was the relative value of what were identified as the strengths of American and German movies respectively. American simplicity, naturalness, sensationalism, contemporaneity, and tempo rivaled German fantasy, stylization, logic, historical sense, and profundity. The disputants agreed on the qualities assigned the respective national cinemas but disagreed on which corresponded to the inherent character of film. Each side justified its national choice by claiming correspondence between that choice and the unwritten laws of the medium. Thus the argument over national orientation became wrapped up in a struggle to stamp the motion picture with a natural, artistic pedigree.[28]

In 1921 the link between defining a national cinema and grasping the nature of the medium had a somewhat unrealistic air. American movies were just starting to see release in German theaters. But the cold hard fact of Hollywood's international monopoly had already begun to make itself felt. Indeed the threat behind the pro-American argument in the *Weltbühne* debate was the potential of Hollywood to extend that monopoly in Germany. For a brief period in which German exports reverberated powerfully in the United States and Hollywood's exports to Germany failed to impress, Germany's prospects for shaking that monopoly appeared favorable. But optimism proved short-lived. Even before America released its representative films in Germany, there came reports that the sensational breakthrough of German film in the United States had quickly lost momentum.[29] Just as runaway inflation intensified dependence on foreign earnings, the American market began to close to German pictures.[30]

Once a new currency was introduced in late 1923, a painful stabilization crisis ensued, dramatizing an already enormous drop in overall production. Simultaneously, American companies, attracted by a currency with a firm value in dollars, began to flood the German market with their films. The most ominous aspect of the American flood was the possibility, now dawning in Germany, that Hollywood embodied more than just one nation's way of understanding and exploiting the medium. American film appeared poised not only to dominate Germany financially but also to eradicate the promise of distinctiveness that domestic cinema had already shown. At this juncture the somewhat theoretical issue of 1921 and 1922 seemed a matter of life and death, and the question of national direction acquired fresh relevance.

Whether Hollywood would extinguish domestic filmmaking or force its conformity to American models depended in the final analysis on what type of films audiences in Germany and abroad could be persuaded to consume. If America succeeded in winning German audiences with its filmic formula, questions of an independent German cinema would become academic. American inroads on the German market therefore sharpened awareness of the relationship between cinematic properties and public attitudes or preferences. Initially, many German experts were at a loss to pinpoint why American films captured audiences abroad and skeptical that they could do the same in Germany. When the early imports generated unmistakable audience enjoyment, critics pleaded extenuating circumstances. Disappointed by the banality and repetition of the subject matter, they credited popular interest to the sheer novelty of American films, the breakneck tempos they boasted, and the prosperity and happiness they portrayed at a time when inflation was ruining the German economy.[31] Few expected Hollywood to wear well in Germany. However, by 1922 and 1923 they began to identify more at work in these pictures than gloss, furious action, and happy endings. American filmmakers possessed an uncanny knack for seducing the audience whether or not they had profound statements to make. Brisk tempos, natural acting, superior lighting, and polished visual dialogue characterized that knack. At its heart lay an instinctive grasp of film as image, motion, and rhythm, that is, as the child of an urban, industrial age marked by the pullulation of visual stimuli.[32]

Although strictly speaking not novel, this recognition had hortative implications for domestic producers. Since German cinema had already established an identity rooted in the pre-industrial—exotic, historical or mythical settings, exaggerated acting and ponderous tempos—it implied that American, not German, film corresponded to the natural laws of the medium. No sooner, however, had experts begun to ponder the lesson from Hollywood than evidence started to multiply that German, indeed European, audiences were tiring of the American formula. The American challenge therefore generated contradictory impulses. Hollywood's medium-specific qualities implied the need to revise domestic strategies, while public disenchantment indicated that the American formula alone would not suffice. Here then was motivation to persist in quest of a new synthesis. In fact, in the crucial period of 1923 to 1925 the search for a national cinema became a favored strategy by which to revive domestic production. Ironically, the rationale for it came mainly from the American example.

In addition to a basic course in filmic instinct and adroitness, Hollywood provided an object lesson in cultural self-confidence. Even after 1924, when critics increasingly bewailed American dramaturgic and moral idiosyncracies, they still insisted that Hollywood's success abroad rested on the unique national culture which found expression in its product. In their opinion American moviemakers created not for some hypothetical global audience but for their compatriots. They did not deny Hollywood's global ambitions or strategic cleverness in gauging and satisfying international tastes, but they insisted on the uniqueness of the American product. Whether westerns, comedies, social dramas, or even historical epics set in the Old World, Hollywood's films were unmistakably American. In treatments of European or classical history the inability to step outside American space and time created amusement or disgust among European viewers. But according to German critics, when presenting their own history or current domestic circumstances, American filmmakers achieved unrivaled authenticity and impact. They thereby demonstrated repeatedly that the national film did best on the international market.[33]

The lesson then was to borrow expertise but otherwise to cultivate one's own garden. Where to draw the line between borrowing and cultivating admittedly created some difficulties. At mid-decade a number of prominent critics argued that domestic production had failed to maintain separation because it had drawn false conclusions from American success. Misreading the American achievement as a case for gearing production to the international market, German producers had tried to create films to please a public whose tastes they could only infer from American movies. This contravened three principles allegedly taught by American achievements. First, Hollywood produced for its own market, not for Europe or any other part of the globe. Second, neither America nor any other country had any use for poor copies of American films made in Germany to an artificial notion of international taste. Third, although film was an international medium, it of necessity drew upon and reflected distinct national cultures. No filmmaker could erase national peculiarities without emasculating his work. German attempts to do so invariably flopped.[34]

Given what some contemporaries judged domestic entrapment by a false internationalism, even at mid-decade, at the close of what has been dubbed the golden age of German silent cinema, national film identity remained confused. To be sure, when experts named pictures they considered representative, a pattern of sorts emerged. Generally speaking, their choices corresponded to the consensus reigning in current scholarship. Titles vary somewhat but essentially trace the path from *Passion* (1919) and *The Cabinet of Dr. Caligari* (1920) through *Der Golem, wie er in die Welt kam* (*The Golem, How He Came into the World*, 1920), *Der müde Tod* (*Destiny*, 1921), and *Scherben* (*Shattered*, 1921) to *Die Nibelungen* (1924) and *Der letzte Mann* (*The Last Laugh*, 1924), thereby following the careers of prominent directors or authors—principally Robert Wiene, Ernst Lubitsch, F. W. Murnau, Fritz Lang, Carl Mayer, and Paul Wegener. How these added up to a national cinema is a question that historians continue to debate. Contemporaries chose to unify this assortment of historical epics, Expressionist dramas, and chamber plays by traits as much or more psychological as filmic. For them, German films valued Romanticism as a means of self-exploration, displayed motivational depth in their dramaturgy, focused on "depth of feeling," "the innerwardness of emotional life," and essence rather than appearance.[35] Yet even if relevant to the early 1920s, by mid-decade these cliché-ridden self-appraisals offered little encouragement to the quest for national film identity. At issue was not just what could be judged nationally and filmically representative but what could serve as a signpost to future development.

The classic films, however distinctive, provided extremely dubious foundations for further production, especially under the circumstances of American inroads because they had very uneven commercial records, at home as well as abroad. Expressionist features had never been box office favorites, Lubitsch had emigrated to the United States in 1922 (the historical spectacle had in any case worn somewhat thin), and chamber dramas appealed by definition to limited audiences. The German industry did have popular alternatives. Sentimental dramas—Rhine (or Danube), wine, and song—farcical treatments of prewar military life, and dramatizations of the lives of great Germans of the past were very much staples on the domestic market at mid-decade.[36] These pictures shared a preference for historical and local rather than contemporary or international settings. In this regard they met the requirements of national orientation. Nonetheless, the champions of national cinema could not, generally speaking, endorse them. Disqualified artistically by kitschy plots and in part undistinguished filmic properties, these pictures also infrequently met the export test. Even when devoid of chauvinism, they offered an image that could expect little resonance abroad, especially in the United States. Military films, for example, however harmless, would scarcely endear Germany to foreign audiences.[37] Thus both as film and as subject, the movies that generated domestic enthusiasm appeared inadequate to Germany's motion picture identity.

Contemporary sensitivity to the historical bent of Germany's popular movies was enhanced at mid-decade by a new artistic paradigm—*Neue Sachlichkeit*—and a new filmic model—the Soviet cinema. *Neue Sachlichkeit* represented Germany's coming to terms with the social, technological, and political realities of the world created by the war. Its sources were multiple and multinational. Its chief foreign inspiration was the United States, the land of Fordism, Taylorism, pragmatism, and unlimited possibilities. America was at once a novel force on the global stage, thus an enormous cultural threat, and a model offering rational, technocratic, and non-Communist solutions to pressing social, economic, and cultural problems.[38] Soviet cinema, with its dynamically charged recreations of the masses in revolt, would appear the polar opposite of such matter-of-factness. Yet the passionate artistic vision of Soviet film was likewise driven by confrontation with a world in transformation. However stylized and unhistorical early Soviet pictures appear today, for contemporaries they displayed breathtaking realism. Soviet cinema thereby reinforced concern to give filmic form to current, concrete issues.[39] The result, as carefully documented by Rainer Berg, was growing commitment to realistic filmmaking and the concomitant politicization of Weimar cinema.[40] Exposure to Soviet motion pictures and the adoption of contemporaneity and *Sachlichkeit* as guiding principles for Weimar filmmakers/critics also shifted the focus of the pursuit of national film identity.

Hollywood's revival on the German market in 1921 had been leisurely and somewhat disappointing. Soviet Russia's film debut came with the force of a bombshell. Although Willi Münzenberg's International Workers' Aid organization had previously imported several films from Russia, the Berlin premiere of Sergei Eisenstein's *Battleship Potemkin* (1925) in April 1926 constituted a cultural watershed. The bitter struggle it unleashed between left and right, involving censors, state governments, and the Reichswehr, marked a crucial stage in the politicization of the Weimar cinema. But with or without the political uproar, this film was recognized immediately for what scholars continue to designate it, a milestone in film history. Contemporaries of all political persuasions but the extreme right paid tribute to its unprecedented mass scenes, compelling images, and irresistible cutting rhythms.

Eisenstein's cinematic bombshell and the political passions it inflamed have been the most visible and regularly remarked facet of Germany's early encounter with Soviet film.[41] But this picture, and many of the Soviet releases that followed, also forced the champions of national cinema to rethink their strategies. In retrospect it is clear that Russia's revolutionary cinema proved, like German Expressionism, more impressive than popular, and a short-lived, unrepeatable phenomenon. But for German experts, disillusioned by the inability of domestic producers to withstand American inroads, the cinematic force of the Soviet alternative prompted soul-searching and some recrimination. Why had first Hollywood and then Russia given birth to distinctive filmic styles that shook the world, while German peculiarities found occasionally brilliant but inconsistent cinematic expression?

To answer this question and thereby offer a key to domestic revival, contemporaries sought to fathom the Soviet achievement. As in critical commentary on Hollywood, their attention focused on the relationship between cinema and society in national context. Responses to the classic Soviet films (*Potemkin* [1925], *Mother* [1926], *The End of St. Petersburg* [1927], *Ten Days That Shook the World* [1927]) reveal—amidst praise for shot composition, acting, technical innovation, and departure from standardized plot structures—deep enthusiasm for realism, objectivity, and honesty. Moreover, they infused *Sachlichkeit* with specific meaning. Russian filmic power and success resulted, so they claimed, from rootedness in a national culture, from the connectedness between the filmmaker and the sociocultural context within which he worked. Herein too lay the authenticity and impact of Russian acting. Even opponents of the political messages delivered by Soviet films admired their ability to bring to life what they took to be the current spirit and will of the Russian population—Soviet filmmakers captured in images the revolutionary ideal and dynamism of the Russia created in 1917.[42] In the words of Axel Eggebrecht, *Potemkin* emerged "organically from the spiritual orientation of the new Russia."[43]

Battleship Potemkin was of course a historical film. However, German experts argued that its potency derived from its tie to the present. Certainly the otherness of Soviet motion pictures, partly presupposed and partly perceived, played a crucial role in formulation of this argument linking history, artistic creation, and society. It drew attention to the political and social values embedded in cinema and to the connection between social context and the creative process, ideology, and cinematography. Otherness did not (no more than with American movies) necessarily preclude German appreciation. As long as the themes treated proved generally accessible, viewers did not need to endorse the ideological message therein. Charlie Chaplin, for instance, could be seen as everyman precisely because he simultaneously epitomized and was a product of American culture.[44] Similarly, experts lauded Sergei Eisenstein as a brilliant technical innovator who created with the camera a powerful universal language but also believed that his technique was inseparable from the aspirations and promise of the early socialist state. At stake then was not merely the genius of a director or performer but the coherence of the world view within which the performance was set. By the second half of the decade several of Germany's most acute critics decided that domestic cinema failed to establish a firm profile opposite Hollywood and Moscow because of deep flaws in recent German history and the absence of a coherent social framework.[45]

There were, of course, numerous and conflicting ways to account for German setbacks. If some observers blamed Erich Pommer and the highbrow art films, others cited Hollywood's financial or historical advantages and refusal to import German films or blamed the great inflation and German attempts to capitalize on it by imitating Hollywood.

But exposure first to Hollywood and then to Soviet cinema encouraged conceptualization on national lines, shifting attention to the social and historical prerequisites of characteristic motion picture styles. From this perspective it followed that forces nationally determined but exogenous to the cinema posed the central dilemma for domestic production and reception. Reformation of German cinema necessitated a different national history and fundamental social change. The more pressing the need for a national film identity, the less favorable appeared its prospects of realization.

The primary symptom of the German dilemma was the reluctance of domestic filmmakers to deal with current issues. Historians have seen in the flight from the present to myth, romanticized depictions of prewar university or military life and moments of national greatness either political motivation, escapism doubly potent because fed by unpleasant postwar realities, or evidence of thwarted social ambitions.[46] Contemporaries recognized at least the first two of these but also interpreted the refusal to treat current circumstances as a sign of uncertainty on the part of native producers vis-à-vis their audience. That reflected in turn the absence of unspoken assumptions bonding moviegoers to each other and to the filmmaker. As one observer argued, because Germany lacked stable and generally held social and moral conventions, thus a meaningful present, cinema either had to retreat into the past or fabricate something entirely new. In the absence of a consistent, representative world view, highbrow art films and popular historical films presented detours to creation of a national cinema.[47]

Although some commentators emphasized the political component of Germany's troubled present, the contrasts drawn with the United States and Soviet Russia suggested more far-reaching problems.[48] The eminent theater critic, Herbert Ihering, established a national cinema spectrum that placed Hollywood and Russia, *The Gold Rush* (1925) and *Battleship Potemkin*, at opposite poles. American filmmakers produced *Volksfilme* because they addressed what he called a unified *Amerikanertum*. The Soviets did likewise thanks to a dominant sociopolitical world view. In both cases cinema belonged organically to the national milieu from which it came. Germany, by contrast, had created individual pictures of outstanding quality but had no *Volksfilm* because the country was torn apart politically, intellectually, and artistically.[49] Film reflected, in other words, the ideological and social confusion of the nation. Wolfgang Petzet, a determined advocate of realism as the key to effective cinema, likewise assigned confused ideological underpinnings the primary role in German failings vis-à-vis Hollywood and Russia. Even realism—he took Walter Ruttmann's *Berlin, Symphonie einer Großstadt* (*Berlin, Symphony of a Metropolis,* 1927) as illustration—needed to be informed by some larger purpose. The specific ideological content mattered less than the fact of ideological commitment. Petzet saw Soviet cinema as confirmation of the principle that all art required relationship to some overarching value system. The key then to Soviet impact was neither montage nor direction of masses nor technical mastery but *Gesinnung,* a quality of almost religious character not amenable to industrial manufacture. German production lacked this ideological conviction and therefore continued to present an amorphous face.[50]

These general sociocultural theories of the German film problem found striking empirical confirmation in the one domestic picture of the second half of the decade with unmistakable claims to international stature. *Metropolis* (1926) illustrated to the point of caricature, according to champions of national identity, the ideological confusion that permeated German production. With the advantage of hindsight, Fritz Lang and Thea von Harbou's vision of the future may be dismissed as a late flower of Expressionism, unrepresentative of Weimar production in the era of *Neue Sachlichkeit;* its narrational vagaries can be overlooked in favor of its visual encoding of sexual/technological anxieties; its financial dimensions, requiring production decisions related as much to the American as the domestic market, demand that it be read as a heavily Americanized motion picture.[51] But for contemporary zealots of realism, *Metropolis* was an answer to Hollywood and Russia that epitomized Weimar's cinematic dilemma. In cost, dimensions, makeup, and message it offered embarrassing testimony to Germany's social and cultural confusion. Ostensibly set in the future, it regressed not only to the alchemist's den of the middle ages but also to the catacombs of the early Christian era. Superficially about the triumph of the human intelligence, it presented human beings who incited workers to attack machinery like the Luddites and who were too stupid to foresee the consequences. Taking up the burning issue of the present, the social question, it proved incapable of providing a serious answer to it.[52]

What most appalled critics was that Ufa and Fritz Lang drew all the wrong lessons from Germany's position between East and West. *Metropolis* stole from every possible world view and artistic current to offer something for everyone. The blend of German Romanticism and stylization, Soviet mass scenes and revolutionary fervor, American technology, piety, and happy ending created what Herbert Ihering called a "Weltanschauungsfilm ohne Weltanschauung."[53] In short, the film's lack of temporal sense—past, present, or future—its inability to present believable characters, and its utter helplessness in the face of the social question reflected the frantic search of German production for coherence and direction. And all of this was highlighted rather than masked by the fact that the film was staged with a cinematic brilliance that gave nothing to Hollywood or Russia.[54]

In the face of this grand smorgasbord the call for realism intersected with the search for a distinctive national cinema. Realism offered a prophylactic against filmic and ideological eclecticism that sabotaged German cinema identity. Furthermore, treatment of real-life issues in their natural settings promised to tap the artistic energy exuded by American and Soviet cinema and make possible the emergence of German film art as opposed to an international potpourri. While *Sachlichkeit* was modelled by both America and Russia, once adopted in a German setting it could distinguish domestic from foreign production. Realism therefore provided the formula with which to permit borrowing from Hollywood without Americanization, i.e., loss of identity, and by which to learn from Soviet revolutionary films without compulsion to adopt their ideological vision.

If the symptom of German inability to face the present and cope with the strains of modernization was production of films set in the prewar world, realism presented a rational cure. Realism appeared, moreover, to promise to restore the popular as well as artistic potential of the Weimar cinema.[55] But it could by no means function as a cure-all. Béla Balázs noted that the "realist dogmatists" tended to create a substitute religion, ignoring the fact that *Sachlichkeit* could present a flight from disturbing realities to self-seeking aestheticism.[56] Much more problematic was the ability of realism to function as a bridge to unite a fractured society and with it filmmaker and audience. If cinematic realism, properly understood, depended on a coherent world view, which

Germany seemed to lack, transformation of the sociocultural base was the logical prerequisite to overhauling the cinematic superstructure. Contemporary diagnoses of social and ideological fragmentation offered little hope that filmic strategies alone could yield a national cinema.

Weimar cinema did, of course, spawn impressive explorations of current themes and issues. From the proletarian pictures of Gerhard Lamprecht—*Die Verrufenen* (*The Discredited*, 1925) and *Die Unehelichen* (*The Illegitimate*, 1926)—to Walter Ruttmann's *Berlin, Symphony of a Metropolis*, G. W. Pabst's *Die freudlose Gasse* (*The Joyless Street*, 1925), and *Die Liebe der Jeanne Ney* (*The Love of Jeanne Ney*, 1927) to the more explicitly political *Mutter Krausens Fahrt ins Glück* (*Mother Krausens Journey to Happiness*, 1929) and *Kuhle Wampe* (1932), general if somewhat erratic progress was made to the goal of realistic motion picture production. But growing focus on matters of current relevance exposed rather than solved the problem of national film identity, surfacing the latent political tensions in Weimar cinema and polarizing production and reception.[57] In short, realistic motion pictures drove home the artificiality of consensus in postwar German society. They did so, moreover, without matching the outstanding Soviet films in artistic consistency and impact or seriously jeopardizing Hollywood's international hegemony. Like the earlier Expressionist experiments, too highbrow for the most part to be widely popular in Germany, they also failed to create commercial breakthroughs abroad.[58]

The concept of a German national cinema provided an important intellectual nexus between the economic and cultural demands of the postwar years but foundered on internal contradictions. Immediately following the war, extension of the import ban and runaway inflation granted German filmmakers considerable freedom to explore alternate film paths. As pressure mounted to challenge Hollywood and succeed on foreign markets, as it became increasingly clear that the artistic films were dubious or disastrous box office material, and as American films flooded the domestic market, room to maneuver narrowed. Nonetheless, the rationale for creating a distinctive product remained intact. What did change was the leitmotif of the search. Whereas historical or fantastic motifs characterized the representative films of the early years of the Republic, the catchword from mid-decade was realism. Soviet imports drove home the lesson about national distinctiveness even as they proved that the motion picture belonged essentially to the contemporary world. Thus first Hollywood and then Russia challenged German cinema to find a consistent form at once filmic, popular, and distinct.

The ambition to establish a national film identity incorporated both an artistic vision and the desire to shake the world. For a younger generation of artists and intellectuals it justified experimentation.[59] Had the box office favorites in Germany succeeded abroad and only disappointed the aesthetes, the character of German national film identity would have been readily solved. However, the logic of international market forces, the struggle to compete abroad, made the search for national identity more than a self-serving slogan. Incorporated within it were ambitions to find for Germany a formula comparable to Hollywood's for gripping audiences around the globe. America's hegemony and Russia's brief invasion fostered endeavors to develop a countercinema.

The search for a program with which to make cinema history exposed the historical and social obstacles to translation of an artistic vision into a coherent national film identity. National identity remained rooted in prewar values and aspirations because the simplest way to avoid the social and ideological divisions, which historians have ever since associated with the Weimar Republic, was to bring the past to the present as social and political cement. At the same time, the plea for realistic filmmaking enlisted film in the Herculean task of reforging Germany's fragmented social and historical consciousness. There was then no consensus on the German national film. What began as experimentation aiming to widen the horizons of the cinema, commercially and artistically, assumed conflicting and in part utopian features. The national cinema was a significant device for conceptualizing cinematic goals. It did not effect the synthesis of art, technology, commerce, and society that for domestic and international reasons was its aim.

Notes

1. Cf. Siegfried Kracauer, *From Caligari to Hitler* (Princeton: Princeton UP, 1947); Paul Monaco, *Cinema and Society* (New York: Elsevier, 1976); Lotte Eisner, *The Haunted Screen*, trans. Roger Greaves (London: Thames &

Hudson, 1969); George Huaco, *The Sociology of Film Art* (New York: Basic Books, 1965); Thomas Elsaesser, "Social Mobility and the Fantastic," *Wide Angle* 5 (1982): 14–25 and the same author's "Film History and Visual Pleasure: Weimar Cinema," *Cinema Histories. Cinema Practices,* ed. Patricia Mellencamp and Philip Rosen (Frederick, M.D.: University Publications of America, 1984) 47–84; Andrew Tudor, *Image and Influence* (London: George Allen & Unwin, 1974) 152–79; John Barlow, *German Expressionist Film* (Boston: Twayne, 1982).

2. Monaco 68, 74. On the concept see Edward Buscombe, "Film History and the Idea of a National Cinema," *Australian Journal of Screen Theory* 9/10 (1981): 141–53; Philip Rosen, "History, Textuality, Nation: Kracauer, Burch, and Some Problems in the Study of National Cinemas," *Iris* 2 (1984): 69–84.

3. On Weimar see the standard works of Peter Gay, *Weimar Culture* (New York: Harper & Row, 1968); Walter Laqueur, *Weimar* (London: Weidenfeld & Nicolson, 1974); Jost Hermand and Frank Trommler, *Die Kultur der Weimarer Republik* (Munich: Nymphenburger, 1978).

4. For more on the themes and typologies see the contribution in this volume by Jan-Christopher Horak.

5. See the summary by Bruce Murray, "An Introduction to the Commercial Film Industry in Germany from 1895 to 1933," *Film und Politics in the Weimar Republic,* ed. Thomas Plummer et al. (New York: Holmes & Meier, 1982) 23–33; Roger Manvell and Heinrich Fraenkel, *The German Cinema* (London: Dent, 1971) 3–7.

6. See Alexander Jason, *Handbuch der Filmwirtschaft* (Berlin: Verlag für Presse, Wirtschaft und Politik, 1930), I, 61; and in general on expansion Jürgen Spiker, *Film und Kapital* (Berlin: Volker Spiess, 1975) 18ff.

7. On Hollywood's new role see Peter Bächlin, *Der Film als Ware* (Frankfurt a.M.: Fischer, 1975) and Kristin Thompson, *Exporting Entertainment* (London: BFI Publishing, 1985).

8. On the film debate see the collection of original material edited by Anton Kaes, *Kino-Debatte* (Tübingen: Niemeyer, 1978), and two recent full-length analyses: H.-B. Heller, *Literarische Intelligenz und Film* (Tübingen: Niemeyer, 1985); Manuel Lichtwitz, "Die Auseinandersetzung um den Stummfilm in der Publizistik und Literatur 1907–1914," diss., Göttingen, 1986. Also useful is Gary Stark, "Cinema, Society and the State: Policing the Film Industry in Imperial Germany," *Essays on Culture and Society in Modern Germany,* ed. Gary Stark & Bruce Lackner (Arlington: Texas A&M UP, 1982) 122–66.

9. The enthusiasm for film as the solution to artistic and human conundrums can scarcely be overestimated. Cf. Thomas Elsaesser, "Two Decades in Another Country: Hollywood and the Cinéphiles," *Superculture,* ed. C. W. E. Bigsby (Bowling Green: Bowling Green UP, 1975) 200–201.

10. The classic summary is Hermann Lübbe, *Politische Philosophie in Deutschland* (Basel: B. Schwabe, 1963) 173–238.

11. See for instance W. Friedmann, "Die deutsche Kinematographie im Weltkriege," *Der Film* 11 March 1916; M. Jacobi, "Der Triumph des Films," *Der Film* 6 October 1917; "Die Kriegsdienstleistung des Films," *Kinematograph* 24 March 1915.

12. The press statement is quoted in the dissertation by Annemarie Schweins, "Die Entwicklung der deutschen Filmwirtschaft" (Nürnberg, 1958) 34–35.

Cf. Jan-Christopher Horak, "Ernst Lubitsch and the Rise of UFA, 1917–1922," thesis, Boston, 1975, x–xi.

13. Elsaesser, "Film History" 69–70.

14. Self-realization on the part of creative persons was central to this development. See Elsaesser, "Film History" 75.

15. The ban never operated hermetically. An estimated 250 foreign films entered Germany in 1919 and 1920. Hans Traub, ed., *Die UFA* (Berlin: UFA-Buchverlag, 1943) 45.

16. On this see my unpublished dissertation "Weimar, Hollywood, and the Americanization of German Culture, 1917–1933," (University of Toronto, 1985) 39–40.

17. Elsaesser, "Film History" 68, stresses the self-conscious attempt to import middle-class cultural values into an uncultured medium. One might add that Peter Gay's description of Weimar culture—the outsider as insider—fits the circumstances of this self-conscious artistic elite.

18. A summary of the American response is found in Graham Petrie, *Hollywood Destinies* (London: Routledge & Kegan Paul, 1985) 7–10.

19. On EFA see Jan-Christopher Horak, "Ernst Lubitsch" 106–8.

20. For instance Fritz Olimsky, "Tendenzen der Filmwirtschaft und deren Auswirkung auf die Filmpresse," diss., Berlin, 1931, 43; Leopold Schwarzschild quoted in Ilona Brennicke & Joe Hembus, *Klassiker des deutschen Stummfilms* (Munich: Goldmann, 1983) 246–47; "Der Untergang der EFA," *Film-Kurier* 23 November 1922.

21. Saunders 69–71.

22. Huaco 35–36.

23. Cf. Pommer's contemporary statement, "Internationale Film-Verständigung," *Das Tagebuch* 3 (1922): 993–95.

24. See, for instance, the observations of the director Joe May, "Wir und ihr Film," *Das Tagebuch* 3 (1922): 1217.

25. German production was characterized by the existence of multiple smaller firms alongside the larger corporations, permitting both diversity and specialization. Monaco 29–30.

26. Buscombe 141.

27. Buscombe 143–49.

28. The debate, initiated by Hans Siemsen, can be followed through numbers 4,6,9,11,13,15,17 of *Die Weltbühne* (1921). A summary is in Saunders 59–67.

29. Q. Fixlein, "Filmwirtschaft: Auslese des Schlechtesten," *Das Tagebuch* 2 (1921): 1026–27; H. Siemsen, "Deutsch-amerikanischer Filmkrieg," *Die Weltbühne* 1 September 1921: 219–22.

30. Cf. the American impressions of the distributor Rudolf Berg, "Amerika und der deutsche Film," *B. Z. am Mittag* 11 June 1922; the director of National Film, Hermann Rosenfeld, "Amerika und die Amerikaner," *Kinematograph* 29 July 1923; and the director of Phoebus, E. H. Correll, "Das amerikanische Problem," *Kinematograph* 19 August 1923.

31. The well-known Danish director Urban Gad claimed the secret was optimism. See "Warum siegt der amerikanische Film?" *Lichtbildbühne* 20 August 1921.

32. See the review by Max Prels of the Fox feature, *The Queen of Sheba* in *Kinematograph* 6 August 1922; Wolfgang Martini, "Vom Wesen des ameri-

kanischen Films. Vom Wesen des Films überhaupt," *Süddeutsche Filmzeitung* 14 September 1923; A. K. Rosen-Lohr, "Der amerikanische Film in Deutschland," *Film-Kurier* 14 January 1922.

33. Heinz Michaelis, "Was wir von Amerika lernen können," *Film-Kurier* 28 November 1923; Herbert Ihering, "Der letzte Mann," in his *Von Reinhardt bis Brecht* (Berlin: Aufbau, 1961), II, 487–88; A. Hollermann, "Welche Filme kommen zur Weltgeltung," *Germania* 28 June 1925; Richard Muckermann, "Nationaler oder internationaler Film?" *Film-Rundschau* 3 & 10 July 1928.

34. According to the well-known literary critic and screen writer Willy Haas German filmmakers had surrendered their individuality to try to please America, had coaxed performers to sit, walk, talk, and eat like Americans, and then discovered that American audiences had little interest in their films. See his "Die Amerikaner beleidigen uns . . !?" *Film-Kurier* 5 November 1924; "Mehr Selbstbewußtsein," *Film-Kurier* 22 October 1925. Cf. Herbert Ihering, "Zwei Waisen im Sturm der Zeit," *Von Reinhardt bis Brecht*, I, 448–51; cf., "Der internationale Film," *Film-Kurier* 23 November 1923; Heinz Michaelis, "Wahrer und falscher Internationalismus im deutschen Film," *Film-Kurier* 5 January 1923. None of these mentioned names or titles, but Haas claimed that authors had been hobbled for years by producers who insisted that their work had to succeed in America.

35. See *Film-Kurier:* Herbert Lewandowski, "Die Seele des deutschen Films," 16 July 1923; Heinz Michaelis, "Was wir von Amerika lernen können," 28 November 1923 and "Der Weg des deutschen Films," 1 January 1924; Paul Ickes, "Die 'allzu penible' Dramaturgie," 9 May 1923. Against this backdrop Kracauer's emphases appear very much those of the 1920s.

36. Although no nationwide box office statistics were published, a *Film-Kurier* poll instituted in 1925 gave contemporaries a rough guide to the types of German films that pleased domestic audiences. Cf. *Film-Kurier* 6 February 1926, 9 April 1927, 16 May 1928, 1 June 1929.

37. Willy Haas, "Der deutsche Film," *Film-Kurier* 24 February 1925, called military films a silent confession by German producers of inability to speak to a foreign audience.

38. Helmut Lethen, *Neue Sachlichkeit, 1924–1932* (Stuttgart: Metzler, 1970) 19–56.

39. John Willett, *Art and Politics in the Weimar Period: The New Sobriety* (New York: Pantheon, 1978) 97–102.

40. Rainer Berg, "Zur Geschichte der realistischen Stummfilmkunst in Deutschland—1919 bis 1929," diss., Freie U Berlin, 1982. French, British, and Swedish motion pictures appeared in German cinemas but played a role subordinate to American and Soviet imports.

41. See the material collected in Gertraude Kühn et al., eds., *Film und revolutionäre Arbeiterbewegung in Deutschland 1918–1932* (Berlin: Henschel, 1975), I, 323–69; Willett 142–45; Berg 159–66.

42. See, for instance, the unsigned review of *Potemkin* in *Die Räder* 7 (1926): 229, and the review by Roland Schacht in *Der Kunstwart* June 1926: 191–92; Rudolf Arnheim, "Pudowkins 'Mutter'," *Kritiken und Aufsätze zum Film* (Frankfurt a.M.: Fischer, 1979) 188–89; A. Rosen, "Drei andere russische Filme," *Die literarische Welt* 11 March 1927: 7.

43. Axel Eggebrecht, "Film im April," *Die Weltbühne* 11 May 1926: 737—my translation. Siegfried Kracauer called *October* a powerful testimony to the

substance of the Russian people and the living revolutionary consciousness of its leaders. See his *Kino* (Frankfurt a. M.: Suhrkamp, 1974) 78.

44. See my "Comedy as Redemption: American Slapstick in Weimar Culture," *Journal of European Studies* 17 (1987): 253–77.

45. Effective translation of social reality into film presented then only the second half of the equation. Cf. Buscombe 150–51.

46. Eisner 75; Kracauer 52–53; Elsaesser, "Social Mobility."

47. Otto Kaus, "Guter und schlechter Kitsch," *Film-Kurier* 28 July 1924. Cf. E. G. M., "Russische Filme," *Hamburger Echo* 16 May 1926, who took *Caligari* as a symptom of German remoteness from reality.

48. Cf. Axel Eggebrecht, "Filmdämmerung?" *Die Weltbühne* 9 February 1926: 227–30; Hans Georg Brenner, "'Die Filmkrisis'—und kein Ende," *Neue Bücherschau* 6 (1928): 308–10: "The German cinema has no world view, not even a clearly reactionary one. Therefore it has no face, no class and—no audience" (my translation).

49. Cf. Herbert Ihering, "Filmwende?" *Von Reinhardt bis Brecht*, II, 512–13; and "Panzerkreuzer Potemkin," *Von Reinhardt bis Brecht*, 517–19. In the first of these Ihering distinguished between the American *Publikumsfilm* and the Russian *Volksfilm*. For more on this distinction see his review, "Die Mutter," *Von Reinhardt bis Brecht* 526–28.

50. See Wolfgang Petzet, "Drei Filme," *Der Kunstwart* 41 (1928): 202–3; and "Der Stand des Weltfilms," *Der Kunstwart* 42 (1928): 116–21. Cf. Hans Georg Brenner, "Von Chaplin bis Pudowkin," *Neue Bücherschau* 6 (1928): 202–5; Felix Seherret, "Die Russen," *Westfälischer Allgemeine Volkszeitung* 22 September 1927; Lothar Holland, "Film in Not," *Hamburger Echo* 13 July 1929; and the debate between Walter Benjamin and Oscar Schmitz, "Eine Diskussion über russische Filmkunst und kollektivistische Kunst überhaupt," *Die literarische Welt* 11 March 1927: 7–8.

51. The latter receives partial treatment in Enno Patalas, "Metropolis, Bild 103," *Der Stummfilm. Konstruktion und Rekonstruktion*, ed. Elfriede Ledig (Munich: Schaudig, Bauer, Ledig, 1988) 153–62. On the former cf. John Tulloch, "Genetic Structuralism and the Cinema," *Australian Journal of Screen Theory* 1 (1977): 3–50; Andreas Huyssen, "The Vamp and the Machine: Technology and Sexuality in Fritz Lang's *Metropolis*," *New German Critique* 24/25 (1981/82): 221–37; Patricia Mellencamp, "Oedipus and the Robot in *Metropolis*," *Enclitic* 5 (1981): 20–42.

52. Cf. two blasts from the left: Axel Eggebrecht, "Metropolis," *Die Weltbühne* 18 January 1927: 115–16; Hans Siemsen, "Eine Filmkritik, wie sie sein soll," *Die Weltbühne* 14 June 1927: 947–50. Also see Willy Haas, "Zwei grosse Filmpremieren," *Die literarische Welt* 21 January 1927: 7; Roland Schacht, "Der Metropolisfilm der Ufa," *Der Kunstwart* 40 (1927): 341–43; *Die Räder* 8 (1927): 98; F. Wald, "Film-Silvester," *Deutsche Allgemeine Zeitung* 31 December 1927, who in looking back over the year selected *Metropolis* as the embodiment of a mistaken attempt to create the universal film.

53. Herbert Ihering, "Der Metropolis-Film," *Von Reinhardt bis Brecht*, II, 523–24.

54. Cf. Fritz Lang's views in "Wege des großen Spielfilms in Deutschland," *Die literarische Welt* 1 October 1926: 5–6; Eugen Gürster, "'Metropolis' oder der Weltanschauungsfilm," *Der Kunstwart* 41 (1927): 43–46.

55. Roland Schacht emphasized the weakness of German filmmakers in this department. See for instance "Buster Keaton und der Prinz Achmed," *Der Kunstwart* 39 (1926): 315–17; "Das Problem der deutschen Filmproduktion," *Der Kunstwart* 40 (1927): 416–19. Cf. Rudolf Arnheim, "Das Ende von St. Petersburg, nebst Randbemerkungen und Seitenblicken," *Kritiken und Aufsätze* 197–202.

56. See his contribution to the debate initiated by Kurt Pinthus: "Die Film-Krisis," *Das Tagebuch* 9 (1928): 759–61.

57. See Rainer Berg cited in note 40.

58. *Die Verrufenen* did prove a popular hit in Germany. See *Film-Kurier* 6 February 1926.

59. H. -B. Heller 50–53.

2

Lubitsch's Period Films as Palimpsest: On *Passion* and *Deception*

Sabine Hake

Prologue

"The representative of the Republic pay[s] tribute to a queen, even if only a historical one."[1] Initially this description referred to an unusual encounter between President Friedrich Ebert and actress Henny Porten on the set of *Anna Boleyn* (*Deception*, 1920). Lubitsch himself, the master of effects, had invited the leaders of the recently proclaimed Weimar Republic to attend the shooting of the spectacular coronation scene. With Ebert observing the masses from a safe distance and painter Lovis Corinth busily sketching Henny Porten for a planned portfolio,[2] four thousand extras in historical costumes pledged allegiance to English royalty in a grandiose setting that, down to the last details, brought Tudor London back to life. Merging in the imaginary the longing for a monarchy lost, its magical resurrection as cinematic spectacle, and the everyday reality of a republic unable to control its masses, Lubitsch's splendid settings indeed evoked a more perfect world in which individual desire and historical greatness were still one. However in order for the desired effect to take place, these particular German concerns had to be displaced into other national historiographies and thus expelled from the domain of historical consciousness.

Contemporary critics responded instantly to this incidental encounter of past and present and embellished its sparse details with the more lustful ingredients of public scandal. In his contribution to the historiography of classical German cinema Curt Riess fantasizes: "The unemployed have recognized the ministers. This seems to be the ideal opportunity for a political rally. Instead of forming for the coronation procession, they slowly approach the members of government with their spears. Instead of cheering Jannings and Porten, they boo the representatives of the republic. Then they shout in unison: 'We want jobs!' "[3] According to Riess's account, everybody anxiously left the studio. Only Henny Porten, the undisputed darling of the German people, stood like a fortress, tied down by the weight of her golden brocade train. Other, and probably more accurate, renditions of that day mention less dramatic

From the set of *Anna Boleyn* (*Deception*, Ernst Lubitsch, 1920), President Friedrich Ebert and actress Henny Porten during the filming. Courtesy of the Stiftung Deutsche Kinemathek.

details. They point to the bleak social conditions, the reminders of which threaten to destroy the visual perfection of the historical disguise: "Under those colorful, culture historical rags many shabby frocks become visible. The misery of the big city breaks through the picturesque exterior. A large contingent of extras seems to have been recruited from the army of the unemployed, and it was probably not easy to keep everything together.[4]

Whereas the visitors on the set of *Deception* still recognized the extras as human beings who lived in a miserable but at least discernible present, a later Lubitsch film, the oriental tale *Das Weib des Pharao* (*The Loves of Pharaoh*, 1921), allowed the critics to abandon politics entirely for the aesthetics of a mass direction that could be accomplished only on the film set. Having witnessed the shooting of the masterfully choreographed battle scenes, Hans Wollenberg could not help alluding to the glory of Prussian militarism, one of the period film's hidden sources of inspiration: "Issuing of orders: Lubitsch instructs the squadron leaders. Then a signal, a fanfare. . . . From the hills, men pour down in streams, from all valleys resistance rises, the rattling of vehicles, cavalrymen with tight reins, curved weapons, centuries erased: a veritable mirage."[5] As one might expect, the conditions of production left their mark on the finished product. The militaristic spirit returned to the surface in the spectators' patriotic reactions—evidence of the reciprocity of cinematic production and reception. One of the elated viewers of *Madame Dubarry* (*Passion*, 1919), the film that marks the beginning of Lubitsch's involvement with the period film, felt compelled to make the following statement: "Ladies and gentlemen! We have just witnessed what revolution really means, what kind of atrocities it is capable of. Therefore: Down with the revolution! The Emperor must come back!"[6] But the specter of militarism also prompted more liberal-minded critics like Kurt Pinthus to ask polemically: "Do you, Master Lubitsch, have ambitions to become the Ludendorff of the film, because your name also begins with the two letters Lu?—Remember what disasters Ludendorff created because he believed too much in the direction of the masses."[7]

Surrounded by such speculations Lubitsch's period films entered the stage of film history. As the first German films fully to take advantage of historical subject matter, *Passion* and *Deception* were instrumental in establishing the period film as a form of popular entertainment that successfully combined profitability with social respectability and artistic innovation.[8] Unfortunately, Lubitsch's innovative work in the genre has failed to inspire the kind of critical work that would do justice to its prominent status in the classical German cinema and, moreover, illuminate its deceptive play with history, narrative, and spectacle. The strong emphasis on narrative that, until very recently, dominated film criticism in Germany has excluded from close analysis films that rely heavily on visual spectacle.[9] Focusing on textual characteristics like plot construction, character development, and narrative motifs, film critics and historians either have neglected to take into account questions of historical reception or they have interpreted the genre's dramatic constellations as the direct expression of a fatalistic world view, in the process ignoring other cinematic means of representation. The period film could then be disregarded as escapist entertainment: sentimental and nostalgic at best, politically reactionary at worst. For the same reasons, the underlying assumption of a hierarchical relationship between form and content, which also includes the unquestioned belief in the identity of narrative and meaning, has prevented important insights into the genre's textual and visual strategies, including its political overdetermination. Thus the central question concerning the period film—that is, the blurring of the boundaries between past, present, and future—has been subordinated to the perspective of each theoretical framework instead of being taken as the vantage point for all further inquiries.

The project of this essay is to contribute to the critical work that illuminates the place of Lubitsch's period films in the cultural network of early Weimar culture. In the following section the domestic and international marketing and reception of *Passion* serves as the main example. In the subsequent section set design and mass choreography are highlighted as the two means of representation that provided a projection screen for Lubitsch's own obsession with eroticism and the contemporary audience's longing for larger-than-life heroes and grandiose historical spectacles. I will argue that *Passion* and *Deception,* not dissimilar to a palimpsest, allowed for the experience and the expression of such highly contradictory feelings as mourning, self-love, and revenge.

Both films accommodated the audience's need for sensationalism, chauvinism, and megalomania and thus gave meaning to the most diverse personal and national scenarios. Taking advantage of the multitude of voices that surrounded these two films and paying special attention to the critics' exaggerated rhetoric, then, may actually lead to the site where their truth is unwittingly spoken. With this in mind, I wish to begin by reconstructing the historical conditions of reception, for they alone make possible the analysis of cinematic texts that thrive precisely on ambiguity.

Politics, Economics, and the Nature of Lubitsch's Period Film Production

Passion and *Deception* were part of the process of economic concentration that began with the founding of the Ufa film studio (Universum Film AG) in 1917. Unlike studios such as Pathé, Fox, or Goldwyn, Ufa was not only controlled by economic and political interest groups (with the Reich and, later, the Deutsche Bank as major share holders) but also participated actively in political decisions.[10] During the postwar years, Ufa built a reputation with films that stood out through the sheer scale, volume, and technical mastery of their material assets; important technological innovations, skilled cinematographers and technicians, and the unparalleled availability of cheap labor contributed significantly to this development. Distinguished by their high production values, these films proved instrumental in the studio's attempt to regain access to the international market and, in particular, to challenge the growing influence of the American film industry.

Riess reports that "the mark of the Ufa film was the authenticity of style, the precision with which decor, props, and costumes were designed and executed, in short: that everything was right."[11] Dimitri Buchovetzki (*Danton*, 1920), Richard Oswald (*Lucrezia Borgia*, 1922), and Richard Eichberg (*Monna Vanna*, 1922) were other leading Ufa directors who succeeded in the genre of the period film, but only Lubitsch really mastered it by bringing together elements from the history play, mass spectacle, and drawing-room comedy. During the course of only three years, Lubitsch directed five feature-length film comedies—

among them *Die Austernprinzessin* (*The Oyster Princess*, 1919), *Die Puppe* (*The Doll*, 1919), and *Die Bergkatze* (*The Mountain Cat*, 1921)— as well as four period films: *Passion, Deception, Sumurun* (*One Arabian Night*, 1920), and *The Loves of Pharaoh*. Because of his background in slapstick and farce, he was able to add a touch of irony to an otherwise humorless genre and to compensate for the grand scale of history with his famed visual puns and innuendos. Of course, Lubitsch was also very fortunate to work with a team of experienced collaborators, consisting of actors Emil Jannings, Pola Negri, and Henny Porten, scenarists Norbert Falk and Hanns Kräly, cinematographer Theodor Sparkuhl, set designer Kurt Richter, and costume designer Ali Hubert. All of them contributed to the phenomenal success of *Passion* and *Deception*.

Ufa's struggle for economic control and international recognition found an adequate expression in the spectacular settings in which the new Lubitsch films were shown. The excesses of production continued in the particular conditions of reception, thus making the experience of cinema a social event and an aesthetic pleasure. On 19 September 1919, the Ufa-Palast am Zoo, soon to become Berlin's leading moving-picture theater, opened with the premiere of *Passion*. Following a musical pot-pourri and a dramatic prologue, the screening was accompanied by a full orchestra playing a musical score especially composed for the occasion. As was expected, *Passion*—because of what critics referred to as its "conscious use of all cinematic means"[12]—met with almost ecstatic reactions, from then on bringing forth a steady flow of dividends as well as critical acclaim. The film did so by creating excess in a situation of need, desire in the presence of want, and thus provided the much-needed experience of self-assurance that alone could heal the nation's narcissistic crisis in the aftermath of World War I. Its potlatch of commodities and emotions was in fact so convincing that critics time and again set out to praise the osmotic relationship between the screen's imaginary world and the auditorium's architecture, as if to exorcize completely the realities of political instability, mass unemployment, food rationing, and inadequate housing through the exuberant celebration of this other site: "The spacious auditorium of the former Palasttheater is perfect as a movie theater, with its discreet color schemes (the broad balconies in violet and gold, the circles in green and gold) contributing to a very tasteful interior design. Constructed like an amphitheater, this new Ufa theater, the Ufa-Palast am Zoo, provides excellent vision from every seat."[13] Kracauer would later ostracize this synaesthetic collaboration between films and their framework of presentation as "elegant surface splendor" and "the total artwork of effects (*Gesamtkunstwerk*)."[14]

Brought into being through Ufa's expansionist politics and nourished by the cinema's cultural ambitions, Lubitsch's period films provided a context in which fears could be articulated, anger expressed, and desires fulfilled—even if only in the imagination. At the center of these projections and identifications stood the question of national identity. The films functioned, and were meant to function, like a living proof of the professionalism that distinguished the rising German film industry from its European competitors, especially those in France and Italy. The intended promotional effect involved two kinds of arguments; one centered around the films' international orientation, the other around their participation in the redefinition of a German identity. The underlying tensions between these two arguments, however, must be seen as a function, rather than shortcoming, of the dream of national empowerment through international recognition. The period films at once reflected and reinforced the contradictions typical of a society in transition. On one hand, they attested to the atmosphere of (relative) political and economical stability that made such large-scale projects possible in the first place. The German film industry, according to this perspective, was a force to be reckoned with, both as regards international film markets and technological innovation. By introducing new cinematographic techniques and by perfecting the creative possibilities of frame composition, dramatic lighting, and mass choreography, Lubitsch's contribution to the genre in particular set new standards that were soon emulated everywhere. On the other hand, his films gave new meaning to the nationalist and, in fact, imperialist dreams of the old empire. This less obvious aspect manifested itself primarily on the level of film reception and involved a complicated negotiation between textual and contextual elements. Here the genre's formal characteristics provided the structure to which different interpretations could attach themselves. Combining historical spectacle and gripping melodrama, films like *Passion* and *Deception* satisfied people's longing for escapist entertainment. The beautiful historical settings displaced the country's monarchist heritage into aesthetic categories; thus audiences were able to enjoy its blessings without really coming to terms with its failures. Less directly, the authentic historical stories (or, to be exact, their impression of authenticity) celebrated the values of authoritarianism, as they afforded audiences the opportunity to experience strong leader figures without suffering under their actions; hence the genre's conservative orientation.

While the historical impulse reflected an intense involvement with the past, it also gave expression to experiences—the violent transition from a monarchy to a republic, the replacement of traditional bourgeois culture by mass culture—that were often equated with modernity and its deliberate rejection of history. Even the struggle for self-realization associated with modern mass society resurfaced in the settings of the past, though in more hidden ways. In their fixation on great personalities, Lubitsch's period films glorified the kind of individualism, complete with weaknesses and eccentricities, that was promoted by modern society but that could no longer be experienced without the help of consumer goods, including films. Thus the protagonists came to represent emotional dispositions rather than historical characters; their transgressions were perceived in direct relation to the restrictions and limitations of Weimar society. Similarly, through the strong emphasis on eroticism, very contemporary concerns—the changing attitudes towards sexuality, the emancipation of women—could be projected onto history's other times and places. Here it was the spectacle of a seemingly unrestrained, aggressive sexuality that compensated for the instability of sexual identities in reality.[15] As can be gathered from these sketchy remarks, the historical material produced, through the mere impression of historicity, a wide spectrum of emotional and intellectual reactions that made the genre very appealing to contemporary audiences, no matter in which century or country the stories were set or which historical personages were involved. By confirming the individual's central position in narrative, indeed by highlighting his or her significance in the hostile confrontation between individual and masses, Passion and Deception reconciled totalitarian and individualist tendencies, forcing them into a unified whole. Through their epic thrust and monumental scope, the period films again made history and, through the preference for other national histories, this attempt again involved daring acts of transgression and appropriation. This process was made possible through the promotional campaigns and critical reviews that placed the films within the larger context of nationalist and internationalist discourses and that ultimately determined their meaning.

Not surprisingly, the domestic and international reception of Lubitsch's period films took place within very different contexts and focused on very different issues. The language of film criticism, with its many metaphors of warfare and conquest, is very revealing here. The reception of *Passion* in German newspapers and cultural journals often sounded like an imaginary continuation of the First World War, with film now assuming the role of the avenging angel. In a way, the vision of German films invading the motion-picture theaters of Paris, London, and New York compensated for the traumatic war experience, the collapse of the Reich, and the humiliating conditions of the Versailles peace treaty. Reviews with headings like "The Monarchy—Victorious at the Movies," "The Entente in Tempelhof," "Paris in Berlin," and "The Fear of the German Film" bear witness to these fantasies of revenge. The German trade press, in particular, used the international success of Lubitsch's period films to indulge in a renewed sense of national pride. Aggressive self-confidence accompanied the marketing strategies for *Passion*, as is evidenced by the eloquent writings of film journalists and promotion specialists who followed its triumphant itinerary through the major international moving-picture theaters. The New York correspondent of the *Lichtbild-Bühne*, for instance, informed his readers: "This experience clearly shows what kind of a splendid weapon film could become in Germany's struggle for international recognition. It demonstrates how the film industry could be used as an important asset in improving our trade deficit."[16] It was with unambiguous malice that some film critics even urged the French film industry to accept the fact "that a defeated, impoverished, exploited, and insulted Germany has passionately thrown herself into film production, thereby creating a means through which to conquer the world market."[17] Another critic had visions of a cinematic *Endsieg* (final victory): "Then we can gladly exclaim: America, you are defeated!"[18] According to these polemics, *Passion* not only confirmed the technological superiority associated with the label "made in Germany" but also assured its audiences at home that the authoritarian foundations of Wilhelmine society had survived the onslaught of all disintegrating modernist tendencies. Evidence thereof was to be found in the film's mass scenes which, supposedly, proved the inherent incompatibility of the terms "German" and "revolution." For some critics *Passion* even offered an alternative image of the masses—or mass society, as it were—that emphasized integration instead of conflict, order instead of chaos, while at the same time focusing on the virtues of individualism rather than the threat of deindividualization. The spectacle of Lubitsch's film masses, they claimed, satisfied precisely those private and collective fantasies of heroism that had no place in modern mass society but were nonetheless necessary to its functioning—as individual fantasies. Thus it was as a result of the tension between the logic of privation and compensation that the imaginary masses of *Passion* came to participate in the nation's quest for a new/old identity.

While German critics emphasized the nationalist agenda of Lubitsch's period films, the international reception of *Passion* began with denial. Because of the still-prevalent anti-German sentiments that surfaced in frequent references to the "boches" and "huns" of the film industry, Ufa had planned to market *Passion* as an Italian film but then decided to advertise it in Paris as the work of a director from Vienna, in London that of a Swiss, and in New York that of a Parisian; these avoidance strategies also explain *Variety*'s reference to its Polish director, Emile Subitch.[19] And indeed, Lubitsch's films belonged to the first wave of foreign films that entered the American market, a process often referred to by critics as the "foreign invasion."[20] *Passion* became the first German film to be shown after the war, and it played for months at the Capitol, New York's largest motion-picture theater. The prospect of unlimited profitability even made it to the headlines of the American trade journals: "German-Made DuBarry Picture, Sold Here for $40,000, Worth $500,000, US Rights Went Begging, 106,000 Saw Photoplay in First Week, $10,000 Estimated Daily Receipts."[21] Given this favorable reception, the promotion campaign for *Deception* already focused on Lubitsch as a major asset. The trade journal *Motion Picture World*, for instance, advised its exhibitors: "Make a heavy campaign on this and make the title the smallest part of the appeal. Drive on the fact that this is a story of Henry VIII made by the same masterhand that drew the story of DuBarry in *Passion*. That's the big selling point: not another *Passion* but another play by the same master of stagecraft."[22] Inspired by the film's innovative character, some American critics went so far as to call Lubitsch "the German Griffith" and "the great humanizer of history on the screen."[23] While such enthusiastic remarks clearly prepared the ground for Lubitsch's later negotiations with American film studios, they also prove without doubt that his choice of a particular period or setting was perceived as secondary in light of the mastery with which he integrated the historical subject matter into a coherent, psychologically motivated narrative.

Without doubt, the representatives of the German film industry were as interested in increasing the number of films that could be exported as their American counterparts were afraid of the foreign competition. Like the majority of American critics, they saw Lubitsch's period films as big entertainment, not as examples of historical revisionism—a fact, however, that did not preclude the films' enlistment in the debates on national identity. Here the notion of the period film as an explicitly German genre deserves further scrutiny. Its implications were spelled out with great clarity in a controversy over *Deception* involving film critic Hans Wollenberg, film scenarist Hanns Heinz Ewers, and Lubitsch himself. The debate began with Ewers who, in response to Wollenberg's favorable review of *Deception,* had publicly accused Lubitsch of catering to foreign tastes. In his view, *Deception* ("This film will never be an international success") had to be regarded as an artistic failure and a political scandal, for it expressed the film industry's total disregard for Germany's national myths. The increasing preference for alien story material, Ewers held, created an unhealthy mixture of racial stereotypes and national characteristics that would eventually bring about the eradication of all differences. Demanding that "we have to grow our own cabbage and must leave the neighbor's field alone,"[24] Ewers probably had in mind films like his own *Der Student von Prag* (*The Student of Prague,* 1913), a fantastic film with motifs taken from German popular myths and fairy tales. The full thrust of Ewers's argument becomes clear in his concluding remarks on what he defines as the true German spirit. "The only thing that can keep the German industry in competition is the idea as such: the idea that gives to film what belongs to it, that cultivates its own fields and unlocks its last potentials!"[25] This unifying idea, of course, was the idea of nationalism that remains hidden under the rhetoric of eternal values and pure beauty. In a public response to Ewers's polemic, Lubitsch reaffirmed his commitment to the international perspective of world cinema and, under the motto "The history of all nations belongs to the world," called for the creative use of national characteristics in the peaceful encounters between all peoples and nations. "In my opinion the international success of the German film is connected to the necessity that it stands on its own feet and offers something that is different from foreign productions."[26]

Given these different perspectives, Ufa's decision to take a well-known episode from French history for the story of *Passion*—and English history, in the case of *Deception*—may have been influenced by Madame DuBarry's reputation as one of history's quintessential seductresses—and, accordingly, of Henry VIII as the ultimate philanderer. But in the final analysis, the producer was less interested in historical accuracy than market domination. With economic expansion the key factor, it remains unclear to what degree and in what ways the period films, as films, served explicitly political purposes. As noted above, the reviewers in the German trade press frequently abused the international success stories in order to emphasize film's contribution to the nationalist project. A strong German film industry, they claimed, could be essential to Germany's new rise to political power. This argument, while nationalist in its fantasies of economic expansion, was based on the premise of total marketability and, hence, cultural internationalism; it stood in sharp opposition to the speculations about the chauvinistic attitudes that some ideologues found in, or expected from, the period film. Such ideas remained limited to the cultural sphere where they developed a life of their own, thus almost becoming the genre's evil double. Some heated discussions took place between those who wanted to use the films as anti-French or anti-British propaganda, those who opposed connections between film and politics on principle, and finally those who questioned the relevance of the entire controversy. The oppositional categories of self and other introduced by the rhetoric of nationalism produced so many different configurations that the boundaries between text and context almost disappeared. Seen in this light, *Passion* and *Deception* could indeed be interpreted along the lines of national histories, whether such approaches were intended or not; the films assumed political significance simply through the political discussions that surrounded them. Though Lubitsch's interest lay primarily in exploring the interplay of political power and eroticism, his films could indeed be perceived as highly charged political scenarios, thus almost becoming what they were not. Only in this context do *Passion* and *Deception* ransack the histories of the former enemy nations for sensational story material. Only from this perspective do the films appropriate specific emotional constellations for their own narratives of national identity. It is precisely this extreme accessibility to ideological inscriptions that makes their blatant misrepresentation of historical facts not a shortcoming but a great advantage in an unscrupulous attack on the historical imagination.

This process took place in three intersecting spheres: the sphere of cultural tastes, political attitudes, and psychological dispositions. To begin with, films with a historical setting were promoted by Ufa and other studios as a way of attracting middle-class audiences who were always eager to combine entertainment with education. History provided the film industry with an almost inexhaustible supply of stories and allowed set and costume designers to demonstrate their latest accomplishments. Therein lay the genre's innovative power; therein lay its hidden modernity. As a way of turning the cinema into a showcase for German craftsmanship and technical know-how, the period film confirmed the audience's belief in technological progress and political empowerment, in spite of its apparent quaintness. The growing interest in historical narratives also made possible a compromise between the elements of spectacle that reminded audiences of an earlier, more primitive cinema and the demand for psychological motivation and narrative coherence that accompanied the cinema's elevation to middle-class culture. Bowing to the tight economy of cinematic representation later brought to perfection in the classical Hollywood cinema, the period film provided visual spectacle but did so within a psychologically motivated narrative. The result was a product that looked convincingly high-class but that still accommodated the petty-bourgeois longing for lurid stories and spectacular settings. While the old flickers were rapidly disappearing, their spectacular elements found a new home in the period film, which satisfied the desire to forget oneself in the pleasure of looking— but according to the new rules.

Moreover, the period film lured audiences into another world that appeared at once as a counterdesign and a reflection of the present one. *Passion* and *Deception* in particular displayed the kind of material surplus—the extras, the settings, the props and costumes—that was lacking in reality. While the fear of the masses inspired the glorification of ruthless individualism, the fascination with their power found an outlet in the many mass scenes. In the process, the political origin of these dispositions was reduced to a psychological level and thus obscured. By subordinating politics to eroticism films like *Passion* made sure that nobody in the audience linked its revolutionary backdrop to the daily demonstrations that took place in Berlin, as some Ufa trustees had originally feared, asking, "Don't we encourage people's revolutionary tendencies?"[27] Rather, the film encouraged the rejection of daily politics altogether and validated existing regressive tendencies. The spectators could withdraw from reality, flee into imaginary worlds, and act out their grandiose fantasies on the projection screens of the motion-picture theaters. Not surprisingly, many critics praised the period film as the ideal medium through which to forget the present and escape into the grand passions of distant times, heroic men, and seductive women. That this desire for forgetting was bound to be appropriated by political developments seems only logical, given its origins in politics.

Finally, the period film made it easier for audiences not only to avoid confrontation with the present but to displace its historical significance, and with it the question of history, into the imaginary worlds of cinema. This strategy of denial must be seen as a direct reaction to Germany's most recent past and its legacies. In fact, the memory of the war and the technological innovations made possible through military cinematography were frequently mentioned in discussions about the genre's formal qualities. Eugen Tannenbaum, for instance, detected close affinities between the First World War and the process of genre formation. The war, he argued, was the true father of the cinema, and its influence lived on in the period film's strong affinities with political spectacles. "Only the war, by inspiring and increasing our appreciation of the adventurous, the unrestrained, and the passionate has given back to the cinema what belonged to it in the first place: sensations, crimes, attacks, chases."[28] Similar thoughts, though from a more critical perspective, have been expressed by Kracauer who, in *From Caligari to Hitler*, relates the preference for skewed camera angles, bizarre closeups, and rapid editing to the war experience.[29] In his opinion, audiences had become accustomed to the sight of lacerated body parts on the battlefields; this experience in turn made possible film's new aesthetics of fragmentation. As is evidenced by such remarks, which are often more a reflection on the characteristics of film in general than of a particular genre, the period film stood at the forefront of a process that ultimately resulted in the fictionalization of politics and the politicization of fiction. This process changed the interpretation of German history, for everything that had to do with collective memories was gradually being replaced by industrially produced fantasies. Foreign national histories in particular fell prey to the film industry's almost cannibalistic hunt for appropriate story material. Conversely, the main protagonists and periods of German history were often excluded from this unavoidable mutilation and falsification. Because of its absence from the thematic register of the period film, German history could therefore be imagined as purer, stronger, and superior; its domain remained the historical film that strove for more historical accuracy and usually abstained from erotic subplots.

Lubitsch's period films inspired a wide range of often conflicting interpretations and stood at the center of an ongoing debate on national identity. Caught between the call for a strong nationalist film culture and the need for films with international appeal, film critics used *Passion* and *Deception* to address issues that had more to do with economic and political questions than with their inherently aesthetic qualities. Traces of this instrumental approach can be found in the trade press, the daily newspapers, and the cultural journals, all of which presented the films' domestic and international reception in terms of empowerment. However, the genre of the period film was far from being indeterminate; its generic characteristics only invited such multiple inscriptions. Given their implication in Ufa's schemes of economic expansion, Lubitsch's films accommodated the desire for power through the skillful use of historical narratives and visual spectacle, while at the same time satisfying the audience's need for eroticism, including the eroticism of power. Understanding this complicated relationship between textual and contextual elements requires a closer look at the films themselves.

The Convergence of History and Narrative in Lubitsch's Architecture and Mass Choreography

Statements like "world history from the keyhole perspective"[30] or "backstairs view[s] of history"[31] not only summarize the prevailing view on Lubitsch's period films but attest to the continuing low regard for the genre as a whole. Opinions were less unified at the time of their first appearance on the stages of film history. In the case of *Deception,* most critics either praised the film as a colorful historical tableau— "a part of Old English history condensed into powerful images"[32]—or dismissed it as a dressed-up tale of power and sexual desire: "joy and pain of beautiful Queen Anna . . . [the first wife] goes into exile, Anna to the scaffold. The laughing Priapeian king lies in the arms of a third."[33] These differences in opinion could be dismissed as typical of a film criticism based exclusively on taste. However, especially when one recalls the extreme complexity of early–post–World War I German culture—the context in which Lubitsch's period films were first received— it becomes clear that the conflicting opinions about the films demonstrate their nature as texts to which individuals from various perspectives could ascribe multiple levels of meaning. This accessibility to interpretation was a direct result of the conflation of story and history, and closely related to that, the function of architecture and mass choreography in Lubitsch's period films.

In *Passion* and *Deception,* the story is set into motion through a series of transitions between the world of individual desire (Jeanne Vaubernier's beauty, Henry VIII's philandering) and national politics (the French Revolution, England's breaking away from the Church of Rome). By focusing on the tensions between the two spheres, Lubitsch pursues old and new interests. With their strong woman protagonists and their complicated love triangles (Armand/Jeanne/Louis XV; Norris/ Anna/Henry VIII), both films develop further the intricacies of Lubitsch's early comedies, most obviously by adding a touch of playfulness and frivolity. But in light of their suggestive equations between power, desire, and death, they also capitalize on the tragic grandeur that the bourgeois settings of the comedies failed to provide. The combination of comic and tragic elements, as well as the constant moving back and forth between the public and the private sphere, requires a unifying force that holds together these disparate elements: this force is provided by the women characters. Accordingly, *Passion* is structured around the figure of a young, attractive milliner, Jeanne Vaubernier (Pola Negri), who has affairs with a number of influential men (the young Armand, the Spanish ambassador, the senile Count DuBarry) and eventually becomes the mistress of Louis XV (Emil Jannings). Thrown into the center of insidious political schemes rather than actively participating in them, Madame DuBarry acquires great power but is eventually punished for her social climbing by the revolutionary tribunals. In the end, she dies on the guillotine. Similarly, *Deception* tells the story of a lady-in-waiting at the English court, Anna Boleyn (Henny Porten), who attracts the attention of Henry VIII (Emil Jannings) and is chosen to replace his old wife, Catherine of Aragon. Yet she, too, fails to bear him the desired heir to the throne, and Henry turns to a new favorite, Jane Seymour. Convicted of adultery, Anna also dies on the scaffold.

Both films tell stories of male desire and female victimization played out against the backdrop of great historical events. "Because of Woman" ("Um des Weibes willen")—this programmatic intertitle from *The Loves of Pharaoh*—describes perhaps most accurately the underlying obsession with the erotic and with woman as the primary object of desire, an obsession that runs through all Lubitsch films. Because desire has such an equalizing effect, the individual traits of *femme fatale* Pola Negri (in the role of the sensual Parisienne) and plain Henny Porten (as the innocent English maiden) are little more than a function of the particular eroticism attributed to their specific historical periods: refined perversion in *Passion;* healthy lust in *Deception*. With death often perceived as the last moment of truth, the differences manifest themselves most strongly in their respective death scenes. Pola Negri struggles with her hangmen to the last minute, while Henny Porten walks toward the scaffold with great dignity. Consequently, the spectator is spared her death through a discreet fade-out.

Referring precisely to these narrative structures, Lotte Eisner's comment on *Passion* seems to leave no questions unanswered: "But a king manicuring his mistress or artlessly pinching a pretty wench is hardly Unadorned Reality, and even less History As It Was Lived."[34] Arguing along similar lines, Kracauer claims: "Instead of tracing all revolutionary events to their economic and ideal causes, it [*Passion*] persistently presents them as the outcome of psychological conflicts. . . . *Passion* does not exploit the passions inherent in the Revolution, but reduces the revolution to a derivative of private passions."[35] Consequently, Lubitsch's spurned lover turned revolutionary becomes a revolutionary out of unrequited love. The correspondences between story and history, however, are not that simple. They require, above all, a closer look at the individual's position in the historical and fictional texts, including a greater attention to his or her participation in the configurations of visual spectacle.

As has been argued above, history provided Lubitsch with an inexhaustible source of visual styles, moods, and settings. This emphasis on the historical effect—on historicity, in other words—explains the ease with which he moved back and forth between episodes from Western history (*Passion, Deception*) and more mythological periods such as Ancient Egypt in *The Loves of Pharaoh* or Persia in *One Arabian Night*. Though the choice of a particular historical setting appears to have played no decisive role, except for reasons irrelevant to plot construction, narrative films always need a center, a point of convergence, around which to organize their stories/histories. In bourgeois society, this position is most frequently occupied by an individual who must be at once unique—distinguished by power, beauty, or noble character—and fully interchangeable.[36] The story of *Passion*, for instance, is held together by the figure of a beautiful woman; but her presence at the center of the narrative does not necessarily imply her centrality to the historical process. Jeanne Vaubernier, though an inhabitant of prerevolutionary Paris, looks and behaves like a typical twenties flapper in historical disguise. The character's control of the narrative stands in sharp contrast to the actress's distance from history. Through the means of visual spectacle, Lubitsch overcomes these tensions between history and narrative and creates a false authenticity based on set and costume design. The remaining discrepancies between the woman's narrative position and the historical setting, however, prove more than anything that the historical effects in Lubitsch's period films take place outside of narrative. They are, above all, linked to visual representation and must be examined accordingly.

The undeniably strong investment in history that gives the period film cultural respectability manifests itself primarily in visual, that is, architectonic, painterly, and choreographic terms. This is no coincidence. According to critic Hans Siemsen, films—and, one might add, the period films in particular—provided the most appropriate vehicle for the transformation of history into spectacle, as they "belatedly raced through Germany's development from 1870 and 1913. Now everything looks like those ostentatious representational buildings of the Wilhelmine golden age (*Glanzepoche*): with fake and real columns, marble, capitals, domes, towers, staircases, mosaics. Like the Emperor Wilhelm Memorial Church: showy and expensive, yet boring and shallow."[37] Reflecting on the vast possibilities opened up by new media like photography and film, most critics welcomed such developments. In their opinion, the period film was a modern version of the nineteenth-century historical novel; hence its social and cultural relevance. Given the increasingly visual orientation in mass society, some even claimed that "in communicating the spirit of an epoch, film was probably the more convincing medium."[38] Indirectly, critics were referring to the advent of modernism, which had called into question the very possibility of historical representation and introduced more fragmented narratives, as well as a more disturbing investigation of questions of subjectivity. Relegated to the margins of high culture, historical narratives found plenty of new applications in the cinema: in the form of new genres, through set and costume design, as motion-picture theater architecture. At the forefront of this process stood the period film, which provided the unified vision through which the onslaught of modernism, as articulated by the literary and artistic avant-gardes, could be annulled, as in a magic trick. This convergence of narrative and history, however, was only possible through the means of cinematic spectacle.

Lubitsch, who always took great pride in the authenticity of his sets, the well-researched historical costumes, and the large numbers of extras excelled in holding together present and past, story and history with his use of set design. As early as 1916, he expressed interest in the ways set design contributed to a film's visual appeal. However, he also was well aware of the dangers involved when quality was sacrificed for quantity. As Julius Urgiss reports in a portrait of the director: "He, too, agrees that the decor has to be first rate, meaning beautiful and authentic. But considerations of design should not predominate; they should not, as is often the case, become the major concern."[39] Trained in the intimate scale of ethnic comedy, Lubitsch knew how to avoid the pitfalls of historical spectacle. His goal was to offer an alternative to the Italian monumental film. "I tried to break with the operatic style of the fashionable Italian school. I wanted to invest my historical protagonists with human features. I put as much emphasis on the intimate personal nuances as on the mass scenes. I combined both strands by finding a logical connection between them."[40] As a result, Lubitsch demanded the most detailed attention to all aspects of film production, including the latest trends in modern stage design and acting styles. "The more prominent the decor, the more we must pay attention to detail."[41] With his family background in clothing manufacture, even he at times submitted to the sensual appeal of silk, velvet, damask, ermine, lace, and brocade and fell prey to the splendid effects created in the interplay of light, movement, and precious materials; Porten's sixteen and Janning's ten magnificent costumes for *Deception* offer ample proof of his infatuation with textures. And isolated moments like the opera ball sequence in *Passion*—with its ebb and flow of soloists and chorus—demonstrate that sometimes there was even room for the tableaulike spectacles known from the earliest examples of the genre.[42]

Lubitsch's period films shared their strong emphasis on set design and hence on *mise en scène* with other films of the early twenties. The classical German cinema depended, more than other national cinemas, on the innovative work of its set and costume designers. Technical and artistic developments in set design contributed significantly to the success of the Expressionist cinema but also influenced the period film, the Prussian film, and, in treating landscape as architecture, the mountain drama. The result was a "metaphysics of decor" that, while meant to support story and characters, often dominated all other cinematic elements. Kurt Richter, the set designer for *Passion* and *Deception*, frequently sacrificed historical accuracy for the kind of "higher truth" conveyed by a specific atmosphere. For *Passion*, he chose the Rococo charm of the palace at Potsdam rather than the monumental splendor of Versailles. On the set of *Deception*, he employed up to fourteen foremen, two hundred carpenters, and four hundred sculptors and plasterers, thus treating set construction with a perfectionism usually reserved for more permanent structures. Anybody visiting the Ufa lot at Tempelhof during shooting would have been enthralled by a fascinating assemblage of fictional spaces. "The temples of *One Arabian Night* are still up, standing side by side with the contorted houses of Old Prague. A bewildering mixture of the most diverse styles, a peaceful community of palaces, churches and clay huts."[43] In the middle of this pell-mell of historical periods, Richter re-created entire sections of London, with Westminster Abbey alone standing twenty-eight meters high.

Passion and *Deception* also reveal the expertise with which Lubitsch and Richter approached different stylistic periods. Their pre-revolutionary Paris, for instance, conveys a distinctly urban atmosphere, with its picturesque quarters, narrow streets, and quaint market places. The film's spatial organization—a reflection of the narrative—follows a woman's rise from the plain milliner's shop of her humble origins to the light-flooded salons and luxurious bedrooms of the royal palaces that are filled with treacherous mirrors, silk screens, embroidered brocade curtains, and satin sheets and surrounded by geometrical pleasure gardens, rose cottages, and long alleys. After the uprising of the urban masses, Jeanne DuBarry is forced to return to the places of her past, as is suggested by the bleakness of her prison cell and, finally, the crowded market place that becomes the site of her execution. The spatial dramatics of *Deception*, too, are set into motion by a woman's beauty, her entrance ticket into the privileged world of male power. The film opens with the isolated figure of Anna as she glances onto the open sea during her passage to England but is soon taken over by the claustrophobia associated with spatial confinement and male domination. The body of the king, portrayed masterfully by Jannings with his enormous proportions, controls every setting and every moment, just as the somber Tudor palaces and churches add a distinct touch of tragedy that is only momentarily relieved during a few scenes set in the bucolic English countryside. Thus while the light-flooded interiors in *Passion* set the stage for a more playful kind of eroticism, the dark corners, closed doors, and treacherous windows of *Deception* clearly denote entrapment and death. This tyranny of space finds a most appropriate form of expression in a number of unusual masking devices, including the Gothic archlike framing of the archbishop of Canterbury.

As a result, set design, in combination with lighting and props, provides the stage on which the historical narratives come into their own. The architectural structures predetermine the social interactions that take place in and between them. Comparable perhaps to the phenomenon of petrifaction, space functions as the memory trace of past events and the inescapable mold for future ones.[44] The calculated spatial designs, the graphic interplay of light and shadow, the geometric patterns created by different forms and materials, and finally the painterly compositions of individuals and spaces attribute a kind of significance to the visible world that, in contrast to the transitoriness of desire, ultimately confirms the hegemony of structures, both architecturally and socially. It is therefore not through variations on the "cherchez la femme" motif but only through the metaphorical investment of *mise en scène* that Lubitsch's period films can be adequately understood.

The representation of the masses, who appear both as an extension of and challenge to the power of set design, underscore this preoccupation with *mise en scène*. As the subject of similarly fleeting relationships, they must be seen as its natural extension—an architecture in process—and its counterpoint. Appearing in changing states of ossification and liquefaction, the masses simultaneously threaten and protect the status quo of society and of narrative as well. To be sure, many extras are endowed with individual characteristics that distinguish them in the crowd and give each of them a personal story. Helma Sanders-Brahms has pointed to this quality. "And these mass scenes reveal once again how much more humanly than most of his colleagues this director thinks and works. . . . It is his love for human beings that makes him appear both overly critical of and highly sympathetic toward the individual."[45]

Thus the masses in Lubitsch's period films represent both the sum of those acting in solidarity and a mere reflection of the main protagonists. They are too formless to acquire real significance within the narrative but also too differentiated to function merely as an ornament. Here Reinhardt's theater productions with their spectacular mass scenes, the confrontation between individual and masses, and the dramatic lighting effects clearly exerted a strong influence that can be traced to such details as the gesture of the raised arm borrowed from the 1910 production of *Oedipus Rex*.[46] Also similar to Reinhardt's stage productions, the films frequently situate the main protagonists within empty spaces that highlight their singularity but at the same time anticipate their downfall. It is precisely this empty space that is claimed by the revolutionary masses of *Passion*, first during the verbal confrontation between the incensed mob and the frivolous court society and later through the chaos brought about by the revolutionary tribunals and public executions. *Deception* even contains a scene where this empty space is literally invaded only to be immediately restored to its original state. Shot from a high angle, the scene shows the forecourt of Westminster Abbey as it slowly fills with people gathering for the infamous coronation scene. Once Henry VIII and Anna Boleyn leave the cathedral, the masses move toward the royal couple, angrily demanding the return of the old queen, Catherine, and her daughter. Suddenly the king's pikes enter the frame and, through the ordering devices of their halberds, reconstitute the old spatial order.[47]

In the Lubitsch universe, the masses' triumph in *Passion* and their defeat in *Deception* have the same political implications since the narrative and visual function of the masses must be sharply distinguished from each other. Only the spectacle of movements counts, not their origin or direction. While the masses fail to contribute to the advancement of the story, they safeguard the continuing existence of narratives centered around the individual precisely by renouncing narrative representation. Mediating between history and desire, they protect the dominant order but also are able, at every given moment, to reverse this order and introduce another state of representation, namely that of spectacle. In other words, the masses in *Passion* and *Deception* function both as doubling devices within the films' elaborate spatial designs and as living proof of the individual's central position in narrative and, henceforth, in history. Yet in performing that role, they continue to pose a threat to these solidified spaces, a threat that is signified by their constantly changing appearance as unified body or heterogeneous crowd in the respective historical and narrative frameworks. Such instability on the level of representation may ultimately undermine their significance altogether and replace revolutionary thrust with irresponsible individualism. This has been the most frequent charge issued against Lubitsch. However, the stubborn insistence on individual desire that links the period films to his film comedies could also be seen as the point of departure for forms of historical representation that take such desires seriously.

Conclusion

History or myth, narrative or spectacle, mass ritual or drawing-room eroticism—Lubitsch's period films elude easy definition. But perhaps that elusiveness is also part of the inherent affinities between history and cinema. This analysis has shown how Ufa's interest in big profitable productions, the numerous discourses that accompanied the reception of *Passion* and *Deception*, and Lubitsch's preoccupation with eroticism and spectacle provided points of resistance to the genre's exploitation by the much less ambiguous scenarios of mass deception. Rather than being a means of manipulation, Lubitsch's films participated in and granted access to conflicting inscriptions and meanings and therefore must be thought of as a site of production rather than a mere product of dominant culture or conservative ideology.[48] Thus it may actually be more productive to conceive of the period film as a form of coming to terms with the past (*Vergangenheitsbewältigung*), that is, to theorize it in post-Wilhelmine rather than prefascist terms, as Kracauer has proposed. The critical discourses that surround films like *Passion* and *Deception* make them part of an ongoing debate on national identity and reveal the continuities, rather than the teleological moments, in the history of film. Similarly, the stories and settings bear too many traces of the immediate past and present to be reduced to their anticipatory qualities. With this in mind, a reassessment of the period film in terms of its mediation of past and future would not only open up the debate around the historical nature of cinema but also contribute to the understanding of narrative, spectacle, and visual pleasure as its major constituting elements.

To return to the image invoked at the beginning: The momentous encounter of Ebert and Porten on the set of *Deception* undoubtedly belongs to the much-maligned literary form of the anecdote. Nonetheless, precisely the triteness of the situation brings to the fore the powers that hold together such seemingly disparate temporalities. As the anecdote reveals, the genre's underlying operating principle, the encounter of real-life and fictional rulers, can be thought of as a metaphorical representation of its libidinal investments. Reality is invaded by an obsessive desire for fictionalization; representation turns away from the exigencies of the present and instead raids the archives of history in order to satisfy an insatiable need—not for remembering but for forgetting. Such speculations are supported by a photograph taken during the coronation scene. The remarkable group portrait casts together actors for yet another drama of public relations as they conscientiously smile into the camera: German president Ebert, Ufa director Davidson, scenarist Kräly with some officials in dark suits, actors Porten and Jannings in historical costumes, and, towering above everybody, the inattentive Lubitsch in casual attire. Given the complex strategies of meaning production that intersect with the genre's formulaic structure, Kurt Pinthus's half-serious campaign "Henny Porten for President!"[49] then indeed points to the overwhelming success of that other scene, the scene captured in this particular photograph.

Notes

Madame Dubarry (Passion, 1919). Director: Ernst Lubitsch, for Projektions-AG Union. Script: Norbert Falk, Hanns Kräly. Camera: Theodor Sparkuhl. Sets: Kurt Richter. Costumes: Ali Hubert. With Pola Negri, Emil Jannings, Reinhold Schünzel, Harry Liedtke, et al. Length: 6864 ft. (2280 m). Release: 18 September 1919. The film is set in prerevolutionary Paris and narrates some of the events that led to the French Revolution. Jeanne Vaubernier (Pola Negri), a young attractive milliner, begins an affair with the Spanish ambassador, Don Diego. Soon after her lover, the student Armand de Foix (Harry Liedtke), kills the ambassador in a jealous rage, Jeanne becomes the favorite of Count DuBarry (Eduard von Winterstein). At court, she attracts the attention of Louis XV (Emil

Jannings) and, while legalizing her relationship with DuBarry, becomes the king's favorite. However, her life of luxury and power comes to an end with the king's sudden death and the public uprisings that culminate in the storm on the Bastille. DuBarry is convicted by a tribunal headed by her former lover and dies on the guillotine.

Anna Boleyn (*Deception*, 1920). Director: Ernst Lubitsch, for Projections-AG Union. Script: Norbert Falk, Hanns Kräly. Camera: Theodor Sparkuhl. Sets: Kurt Richter. Costumes: Ali Hubert. With Emil Jannings, Henny Porten, Aud Egede Nissen, Paul Hartmann, et al. Length: 8379 ft. (2793 m). Release: 14 December 1920. The story is set in sixteenth-century England during the rule of Henry VIII. The young Anna Boleyn (Henny Porten) arrives in England to live with her uncle, the Duke of Norfolk. A blossoming romance with the young Norris (Paul Hartmann) develops. Anna is introduced at court and becomes lady-in-waiting to the queen, Catherine of Aragon. Henry VIII (Emil Jannings) pursues the young woman with great persistence and, in defiance of papal laws, divorces Catherine and marries Anna. This leads to England's break with the Roman Catholic church. After Anna gives birth to a daughter, Henry loses all interest and turns to her lady-in-waiting, Jane Seymour (Aud Egede Nissen). Anna, who still loves Norris, becomes the victim of court intrigues. Accused of adultery, she dies on the scaffold.

---

1. L. K. F. [Lothar Knut Fredrik], "Der Reichspräsident bei *Anna Boleyn*," *Film-Kurier* 1 November 1929. All translations are mine unless noted otherwise.
2. See Herbert Eulenberg, *Anna Boleyn: Originallithographien von Lovis Corinth* (Berlin, 1920). Note also Paul Eipper who, in *Ateliergespräche mit Liebermann und Corinth*, confirms the incident reported by Riess; reprinted in Helga Belach, *Henny Porten: Der erste deutsche Filmstar 1890–1960* (Berlin: Haude & Spener, 1986) 63–69.
3. Curt Riess, *Das gab's nur einmal* 1 (Munich: Hanser, 1977) 89.
4. L. B. [Ludwig Brauner], "*Anna Boleyn*, Ein neuer Großfilm der Union," *Der Kinematograph* 10 October 1920.
5. H. W. [Hans Wollenberg], "Pharao an der Oberspree," *Lichtbild-Bühne* 6 August 1921. Compare another eyewitness: "This crowd, how colorful, how fateful, a truly impressive sight, masterfully directed, and probably irresistibly fantastic on the screen." "Die Schlacht in den Gosener Bergen," *Der Film* 7 August 1921.
6. "Sieg der Monarchie im Kino," *Vorwärts* 21 January 1920.
7. Kurt Pinthus, "Lubitsch in Ägypten" (1922), *Lubitsch*, ed. Hans Helmut Prinzler and Enno Patalas (Munich: Bucher, 1984) 101. For a brief historical assessment of Lubitsch's mass direction, see Lorenzo Codelli, "Lubitsch der Massenregisseur," *Positif* 292 (June 1985): 23. For an account by Lubitsch himself, see also "Wie mein erster Großfilm entstand," *Lichtbild-Bühne, Luxusnummer* "*30 Jahre Film*" (1924).
8. Alternative terms include historical film (*historischer Ausstattungsfilm*) and costume film (*Kostümfilm*). The term *period film*, however, seems most suited to accommodate the dynamics of the genre, including its strong

Sabine Hake

emphasis on spectacle, the highly personalized approach to history, and the problematic conflation of history, style, and eroticism.

9. Siegfried Kracauer, *From Caligari to Hitler: A Psychological Study of the German Cinema* (Princeton: Princeton UP, 1947) has provided the model for this kind of film criticism. Examples include standard film histories like Ulrich Gregor and Enno Patalas, *Geschichte des Films* (Reinbek: Rowohlt, 1976), as well as close textual readings of particular films, such as Helmut Korte, "Der Einsatz der nationalen Propaganda—Beispiel *Madame Dubarry* (1919)," *Film und Realität in der Weimarer Republik* (Munich: Hanser, 1978) 70–83. More recent studies have taken mass psychology (Le Bon, Durkheim, McDougall, Freud) as a point of departure for understanding the representation of masses in the period film. See Markus Amann, "Massenpsychologie und Massendarstellung in Film," diss., Munich, 1983.

10. For a historical account of Ufa politics and Lubitsch's work for Ufa, see Jan-Christopher Horak, "Ernst Lubitsch and the Rise of Ufa 1917–1922," thesis, Boston U, 1975. Also see Ursula Hardt, "Erich Pommer: Film Producer for Germany," diss., U of Iowa, 1989.

11. Riess 102.

12. "*Madame Dubarry*," *Vossische Zeitung* 21 September 1919.

13. L. B., "*Madame Dubarry*," *Kinematograph* 24 September 1919.

14. Siegfried Kracauer, "Kult der Zerstreuung: Über die Berliner Lichtspiel-häuser"(1926), reprinted in *Das Ornament der Masse*, ed. Karsten Witte (Frankfurt a.M.: Suhrkamp, 1977) 311, 312 and in English as "The Cult of Distraction," trans. Thomas Y. Levin, *New German Critique* 40 (Winter 1987): 91–96.

15. For historical background information, see Renate Bridenthal, Atina Grossmann, and Marion Kaplan, eds., *When Biology Became Destiny: Women in Weimar and Nazi Germany* (New York: Monthly Review Press, 1984). For the relationship between women's emancipation and the cinema, see Miriam Hansen, "Early Silent Cinema: Whose Public Sphere?" *New German Critique* (Spring/Summer 1983): 147–84; and Patrice Petro, *Joyless Streets. Women and Melodramatic Representation in Weimar Germany* (Princeton: Princeton UP, 1989).

16. "*Madame Dubarry* in Amerika," *Lichtbild-Bühne* 12 November 1920: 20.

17. K. K., "*Madame Dubarry*—ein deutscher Sieg," *Lichtbild-Bühne* 10 April 1920: 27.

18. Artur Liebert, "*Madame Dubarry:* Der Aufschwung des deutschen Films," *Der Film* 10 September 1919: 46. Years later, in a book published by the union of German motion-picture theater owners, this rhetoric was forcefully repeated by another critic who praised the period film as an effective weapon of national propaganda. See Alexander von Gleichen-Rußwurm, "Kino und Weltgeschichte," *Das deutsche Lichtspieltheater in Vergangenheit, Gegenwart und Zukunft*, ed. Rudolf Pabst (Berlin: Prismen-Verlag, 1926).

19. The title *Passion* was chosen to avoid confusion with a recent Fox release of *Madame Dubarry*. The English title for *Anna Boleyn, Deception*, then only continued in that tradition of catchy one-word titles while at the same time referring to the film's melodramatic mood. In reviews of *Passion* (*Exceptional Photoplays* 1 [1920]: 13) and *Deception* (*Exceptional Photoplays* 5 [April 1921]: 3–4), critics frequently spoke out against these sensationalist titles.

20. Alfred Kuttner, "The Foreign 'Invasion,'" *Exceptional Photoplays* 1 (1921):

1–2. See also Walter P. Eaton, "The German 'Invasion,' " *Freemen* 3 (1921): 208–9.

21. *New York Times* 23 December 1920: 28.

22. "*Passion*," *Motion Picture World* 30 April 1921. See also the reviews of *Passion* in *New York Times* 13 December 1920: 19 ("one of the pre-eminent pictures of the day"). For a short discussion of the American reception of *Passion*, see Lewis Jacobs, *The Rise of the American Film* (New York: Teachers College, 1968) 305–6.

23. Herman G. Weinberg, *The Lubitsch Touch. A Critical Study*, 3d rev. ed. (New York: Dover, 1977) 38. Also note Lubitsch's public letter praising Griffith's *Orphans of the Storm*, "Lubitsch Praises Griffith," *Film Daily* 5 (1922): 1.

24. Hanns Heinz Ewers, "*Anna Boleyn*," *Lichtbild-Bühne* 18 December 1920: 24.

25. Ewers 24.

26. Lubitsch, "Lubitsch contra Ewers," *Lichtbild-Bühne* 25 December 1920: 29.

27. Riess 77.

28. Eugen Tannenbaum, "Der Großfilm," *Der Film von morgen*, ed. Hugo Zehder (Dresden/Berlin: Rudolf Kaemmerer, 1923) 61. For more theoretical reflections on this relationship, see Paul Virilio, *War and Cinema: The Logistics of Perception*, trans. Patrick Camiller (London: Verso, 1989).

29. Reviewing *One Arabian Night*, the critic Ernst Benzinger once complained bitterly that its story was constantly disrupted by spectacular cinematic effects. This uneasy tension between continuity and segmentation, according to Benzinger, was symptomatic of narrative cinema and largely responsible for its failure as a form of storytelling. His argument is worth quoting at length. "The excellent, poetic film *One Arabian Night* looks as if shredded, cut, and reassembled into an endless multitude of short and all too short images and flashes of images. They pass before they even appear on the screen, thereby violently arresting and interrupting the flow of the story. Without cause, logic, reason, or inner connections, they utilize the most diverse perspectives, long shots, medium shots, silhouettes and close-ups in order to bring together different locations. They reproduce every conceivable mood and position, no matter whether this is possible or not—with the result that no reasonable pleasure can arise." In Ernst Benzinger, "Schaufilm oder Spielfilm?" *Das Tage-Buch* 13 November 1920: 1333.

30. Gregor and Patalas, *Geschichte des Films* I, 48.

31. Edward Wagenknecht, *The Movies in the Age of Innocence* (Norman: U of Oklahoma P, 1962) 202.

32. W. P., "Filmschau *Anna Boleyn*," *Vorwärts* 16 December 1920.

33. My., "*Anna Boleyn*," *Vossische Zeitung* 16 December 1920.

34. Lotte Eisner, *The Haunted Screen*, trans. Roger Greaves (Berkeley: U of California P, 1973) 82.

35. Kracauer, *From Caligari to Hitler* 49. Kracauer's remarks in *From Caligari to Hitler* offer a useful point of departure for further inquiry, despite their blindness to the many levels of cinematic representation. He sets out by revealing the economic, social, and psychological conditions that stood behind the genre's success and that are responsible for its nihilistic philosophy of history. In so doing, he uses it as supporting evidence for the existence of protofascist sociopsychological tendencies in the classical German cinema.

Sabine Hake

According to that narrative, the period film anticipates the coming submission of the masses under the tyranny of the autocratic leader. Compare his very different analysis in an essay called "Die Photographie" (1927, "Photography"). "Photography provides a continuity of space; historicism strives to fill a continuity of time. Historicism is concerned with the photography of time. Its time-photography would correspond to a monumental film that fully depicted all events as they are connected in time." Kracauer, "Die Photographie" (1927), *Das Ornament der Masse* 24. Compare, again, his comments on the inherent limitations of the historical film in "Der historische Film" (1940), *Kino: Essays Studien Glossen zum Film*, ed. Karsten Witte (Frankfurt a. M.: Suhrkamp, 1974) 44–45 and in *Theory of Film: The Redemption of Physical Reality* (New York: Oxford UP, 1960) 77–78.

36. David Hull, for instance, has argued that every narrative needs such a center in order not to fall apart. "The notion of central subjects is crucial to the logical structure of historical narrative. Assuming for the moment that history could be analyzed completely into a single set of atomistic elements, there are indefinitely many ways in which these elements can be organized into historical sequence. The role of the central subject is to form the main strand around which the historical narrative is woven." David Hull, "Central Subjects and Historical Narratives," *History and Theory* 14.3 (1975): 255.

37. Hans Siemsen, "Die Filmerei," *Die Weltbühne* 17.1 (1921): 103.

38. Kurt Pinthus, "Aus dem Tagebuch, *Anna Boleyn*," *Das Tage-Buch* 31 December 1920.

39. Julius Urgiss, "Künstlerprofile: Ernst Lubitsch," *Der Kinematograph* 30 August 1916.

40. Jerzy Toeplitz, *Geschichte des Films* I, trans. Lilli Kaufmann (Munich: Rogner & Bernhard, 1977) 214. Contemporaries, on the other hand, often noted the inspirational influence of the Italian and American monumental films, for instance Léon Moussinac in his *Naissance du cinéma* (Paris: J. Povolozky, 1925) 129.

41. "Ernst Lubitsch über Film, Filmkunst und sich. Ein Interview," *Film-Kurier* 19 January 1920.

42. The DuBarry novel, published in conjunction with *Passion*'s release, contains a lengthy sequence where Jeanne and her lover Jean DuBarry meet, for one last time, in the middle of a devastating fire in the Paris opera. See Hanns Steiner, *Madame Dubarry* (Berlin: Buch-Film Verlag, 1919).

43. "*Anna Boleyn* in Tempelhof," *Film-Kurier* 27 July 1920.

44. Commenting on the prominent status of architecture in Lubitsch's period films, Dieter Bartetzko has argued that the passionate debates about trends in modern public architecture during the twenties were, in fact, debates about new spaces for a new society. With Lubitsch and Lang as initiators of this trend, Bartetzko claims that their emphasis on set design and choreography even set the mood for the monumental architecture of the Third Reich. See Dieter Bartetzko, *Illusionen in Stein: Stimmungsarchitektur im deutschen Faschismus. Ihre Vorgeschichte in Theater- und Filmbauten* (Reinbek: Rowohlt, 1985). On architecture, silent German cinema, and the "Ausstattungsfilm," see also Helmut Weihsmann, *Gebaute Illusionen: Architektur im Film* (Vienna: Promedia, 1988), esp. the chapter "Raumplastiken," 60–99.

45. Helma Sanders-Brahms, rev. of *Madame Dubarry*, Prinzler and Patalas,

96

Lubitsch 135. A comparison to the distinct strategies of quantification and ornamentation that characterize the representation of the masses in the work of Joe May and Fritz Lang may serve to illuminate their ambivalent status in the early work of Lubitsch. With such highly successful monumental films as *Veritas Vincit* (1918) or *Das indische Grabmal* (*The Indian Tomb*, 1921), May shamelessly indulged in the conspicuous consumption of men, animals, and materials, as Riess has rightly pointed out: "Joe May has brought more extras onto the screen. But they remained extras under his direction. They play around in the background, they walk across the screen making noises that nobody hears" (102). Without even a rudimentary story line, May's big productions lacked the technical perfection as well as the operatic pathos that at least distinguished the Italian monumental film as high spectacle. Lang's mass choreography, on the other hand, submitted the human body to the rules of a geometry that rendered insignificant all distinctions between individuals and objects and that obliterated all differences in favor of pure form. Clearly the architectural and social formations in Lang's *Die Nibelungen* (1924) and *Metropolis* (1927) owe much to the exploration of *mise en scène* begun by *Passion* and *Deception*. But for him, man existed only as a part of geometrical configurations, as a cog in the wheel of anonymous political machineries. Compared with the films of May and Lang, Lubitsch's period films, then, offer a third possibility. In contradistinction to May, Lubitsch always returns to the individual gesture. His extras are not a mere backdrop but, as individuals, create an atmosphere of diversity and heterogeneity—perhaps a hidden comment on the historical process as such. At the same time, Lubitsch's ironic approach to the historical material is also sharply set against Lang who also uses stylization but under the influence of a very different notion of history.

46. Eisner was the first to discern connections. "In *Madame Dubarry* the revolutionary masses clamoring around the guillotine for the death of the former favorite raise their right arms, a formalized movement frequently seen in German films whenever a crowd of extras has to express fury of exultation. Reinhardt gave these gestures to the classical chorus in his production of *Oedipus Rex*, performed in a Berlin circus in 1910. They lose all value in the majority of German films in which inspiration has deteriorated into mere technique," Eisner 86.

47. Gilbert Seldes praises that scene for masterfully involving "every correct principle of the aesthetics of the moving picture." Gilbert Seldes, *The Seven Lively Arts* (New York: Harper, 1932) 336. In more general terms, the reciprocal relation between structure and structuration in Lubitsch's mass scenes has also been commented upon by British critic Claire Lejeune: "but Lubitsch had a way of manipulating his puppets that gave multitude, and in contrast, loneliness, a new face. No one before had so filled and drained his spaces with the wheeling mass, rushing in the figures from every corner to cover the screen, disposing them again like a whirlwind with one single figure staunch in the middle of the empty square," C. A. Lejeune, *Cinema* (London: Alexander Maclehose, 1931) 64.

48. In that sense, Jean-Louis Comolli has argued: "It is my hypothesis that the cinematic representation of History defies Fiction although it holds only through it. In such a paradoxical situation, both required and prevented, irresistible and imprisoned, historical fiction becomes a kind of analyser

which pushes to their most revealing limit the conditions of exercise and stakes at play in all cinematic fiction." Jean-Louis Comolli, "Historical Fiction: A Body Too Much," *Screen* 19.2 (1978): 42.
49. Pinthus, "Henny Porten als Reichspräsident," *Das Tage-Buch* 15 October 1921.

3

Imagining History:
Weimar Images of
the French Revolution

Marc Silberman

I

In his "Theses on the Philosophy of History" Walter Benjamin writes about history as "the subject of a structure whose site is not homogeneous, empty time, but time filled by the presence of the now."[1] Benjamin's aim in the "Theses" is to distinguish between two kinds of historical understanding, historicism and historical materialism, and his implicit point of reference is to Marx's *The Eighteenth Brumaire of Louis Bonaparte*. In the introduction to his analysis of the failure of the July Revolution, Marx paraphrases Hegel concerning the inevitability of repetition in history and goes on to remark that this understanding of the past as repetition positions us in an imaginative relation to the present.[2] Hegel, Marx, and Benjamin were inspired in their historical research by the fact that we focus on the past because of something that interests us in the present.

History might consist of past events, of a record of those events, of a causal or temporal chain of events, of accounts of such events, and of explanations of such accounts. In any case, history is constructed in a formal way. It is not the physical past, available in an unproblematic way for inspection and analysis; it is an imaginary construct. As such, historical discourse shares with narrative the organizing principles of causality, continuity, and explanation. Both are concerned with the what, the what for, and the for whom. If politics takes precedence in historical representation, then a conflictual perspective dominates, where conflicts arise from transformations in power relations or resistance to changes in the control of power. This explains why a great deal of historical writing seems to have an aesthetic dimension, with the beauty of a well-wrought drama organized around a development, a crisis, and a resolution. Moreover, the relations of power in this kind of representation—be it historical or fictional—are condensed or contracted into providential persons who advance the course of events. The personalization or subjectivization of events prevents denial by virtue of the immediacy of emotional identification, and at the same time it engenders the blindness necessary for managing or containing the contradictions inherent in any imaginary or formal construct.

In spite of the cinema's reputation for concrete, physical reality, it seems to succeed better in presenting oneiric error than in telling the truth. Thus the cinema cannot provide knowledge of but only a relation to history. Every film is rooted in particularities of place: its socioeconomic, political, and cultural place of production. As a product of that place, the film offers an interpretation, a new interpretation saturated by various operations and practices. Film analysis, in particular the analysis of the historical film, assumes an awareness of what past it reflects or criticizes. Moreover, it requires an accounting of how the film's modes of presentation relate to the place of production, to the society from which it emerges, and to the specific representational forms at its disposal. Film analysis, then, proceeds to establish more or less implicitly its own historical narrative. Siegfried Kracauer attempted, for example, to demonstrate how the cinema functions as society's discourse about itself by examining unconscious homologies and allegorical relations between film characters or plot resolution and political developments in the Weimar Republic. Yet, films are not a palimpsest in which one reads the secret workings of a nation's subconscious. Similarly the cinema does not directly reproduce social relations. Because the past is not immediately accessible and does not consist of some kind of generally accepted wisdom, the film narrative engages a process of construction. This imaginary transformation of social relations through narrative restructures the past. Both the film narrative and the historical discourse, then, must be (re)-constructed after the fact and with a view toward their socially stratified reception.

This perspective can be expanded within a rather limited framework by considering three related historical films, the only three extant films about the French Revolution produced in Germany during the Weimar Republic: Ernst Lubitsch's *Madame Dubarry (Passion,* 1919), Dimitri Buchovetzki's *Danton (All for a Woman,* 1921), and Hans Behrendt's 1931 remake of *Danton*.[3] Each film was produced during times of rapid social change when the terrain of history and its discourses were becoming politically threatening: the end of the Great War and the subsequent November Revolution in 1918, the collapse of the Kaiserreich in the course of the twenties, and the upheaval of the Great Depression in the early thirties. Typically they construct an image of revolution that has little to do with the politics that set the events to work in France in 1789. Rather they maintain it as an autonomous signifier that triggers a plot crisis at times of extreme tension when it seems impossible to regulate narrative antagonisms. In other words, here the French Revolution acts not as a real event but as the discursive representation of a specific category of historical process. Aggravation of conflict, rupture, irreversible and precipitous change all combine in this representation to rearrange the process of history retroactively by shifting the relations of power.

Of course, the French Revolution is one of those signifiers that calls up a great number of prejudices owing to its historical distance and to the diverse utilizations given it by tradition. During the nineteenth century the dominant German view regarded the revolution (and its aftershocks in 1830, 1848, and 1871) as an intellectual conspiracy charac-

terized by anti-Christian and antimonarchical tendencies.[4] The Great
War only reinforced the negative image of France, and Clemenceau's
postwar policies concentrated against France the hostility of the entire
German political spectrum from Spartacists and Communists to extreme
right nationalists. Under these conditions, images of or fictional narratives about the French Revolution produced in Germany must be situ-
ated in the broader framework of discourses about change, which were
so central in the constitution of the consciousness of the present during
the Weimar Republic, especially at its beginning and end.[5] Concern with
state authority and order, with constitutional rights and dictatorship,
with class structure and political rivalry finds expression in the collapse
of the French monarchy and the Jacobin revolution as well as in the lived
experience of the German Republic. More to the point, the central
questions of the French Revolution also went right to the core of the
republican idea in prefascist Germany: is change possible without destruction? is renewal possible without chaos? The three films do not pose
these questions explicitly, let alone offer answers. In their historical
discourses they elaborate conflicts with imaginary resolutions that reveal
opposed interests and point to the site of contestation where the power
struggle for change and renewal was being waged.

II

The fact that the plot of Lubitsch's *Passion* draws on the historical
event of the French Revolution for its narrative framework seems to be
more a coincidence than a calculation of political or overt ideological
significance.[6] History is here displaced to the margins, and historical
ornament—especially dress, gesture, and decor—becomes essential for
the needs of the *mise en scène*. From the genre of the historical costume
film, Lubitsch adopts the primacy of effect: not reality but artifice dominates the film's visual style. At the same time, the film draws details from
the traditional, social drama's plot structure that were familiar to the
contemporary audience: a conflict between rich and poor in which the
former are portrayed as lazy and decadent and the latter as honest but
exploited. Like all his films from the German period (until 1922) *Passion*

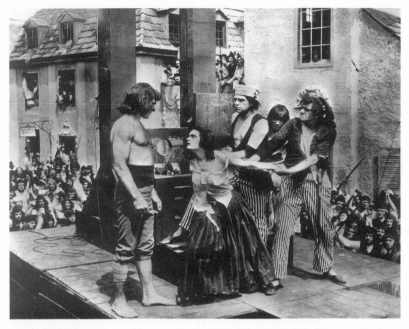

From *Madame Dubarry* (*Passion*, Ernst Lubitsch, 1919), Pola Negri as Madame Dubarry. Courtesy of the Stiftung Deutsche Kinemathek.

engages the relations of the powerful to their subjects. The fictional plot revolves around sexuality and desire where male obsessions are counterposed to female objectification through spectacle and display. It is no accident that the narrative opens in a dress shop. Lubitsch, the son of a Berlin textile merchant, had discovered in his earlier slapstick comedies the clothes store as a model for relations of exchange and continued to invoke it well into the forties.[7] The protagonist Jeanne's meteoric rise from the position of seamstress into the world of wealth and noble titles depends on her beauty as exchange value and her eroticism as promise of untold pleasures. She makes explicit the connection between the store and patriarchy. Both are ideological edifices that are inscribed with relations of power and rely on a system of repressive authority. The first shots in Madame Labille's store portray Jeanne as an energy that must be tamed so that the store's commodity circulation can function. This same energy, however, will enable Jeanne to cross all social thresholds. The dress shop, itself a world of costume and masquerade, is the ideal point of departure, then, for a film narrative that will focus on woman as the site where appearance and spectacle intersect in an interrogation of patriarchal social structures.

Jeanne is first shown in her love relationship to the student Armand, who will later become a nodal point for issues of class and patriarchal conflict. The plot's structure in the first half of the film, the prerevolutionary phase, traces a series of exchanges between him and his rivals. The first in this sequence is Don Diego. Along with all the other aristocrats, he is associated with wastefulness and libertine sexuality. Indeed, these are precisely the social class attributes against which the ascendent bourgeoisie historically forged its notion of productivity and refined its practice of repression. Jeanne triggers the conflict between Armand and Diego when she must decide whose invitation to accept for Sunday afternoon. In the first of several role-playing situations that allow Jeanne a measure of control, she introduces a game of chance by counting the ribbons on her bodice to determine the winner. Chance and desire do not coincide, however, when Armand wins this game, so Jeanne begins to count once again, reversing the order in Don Diego's favor and giving in to desire and curiosity.

This "decision," this assertion of female sexuality, activates a chain of encounters in which Jeanne, the medium of circulation, mediates male desire. First, during her intimate tête-à-tête with Don Diego, she must quickly hide behind a screen when Count Dubarry interrupts them. She catches his eye and inflames his desire when he sees her in a mirror as she throws kisses to Don Diego. Jealous Armand later quarrels with and stabs Diego at the opera ball, leaving Jeanne in the arms of Dubarry as he is led off to prison. Dubarry wins Jeanne's affection with gifts of jewelry and becomes her protector, but soon his money runs out. His schemes to instrumentalize her beauty for his own ends bring her quite by accident into the presence of King Louis XV, who also becomes interested. Dubarry is persuaded to relinquish his mistress to the king in return for a generous financial compensation, and Louis, like all the other men, falls victim to her beauty and exuberance. To stifle court criticism, he pays to have her married to Dubarry's dissipated brother for his noble title—Countess Dubarry—and formally introduces her to the royal court.

Jeanne enters a hierarchical social organization as object, exchanged and used by men as a kind of currency in the circulation of male desire. Her positioning as the absolute object of the commodity form is based on her appearance, on characteristics of excessive beauty, ornament, costume, and masquerade. The narration's intricate play of point-of-view shots and gazes visually foregrounds Jeanne both for the spectator and for her male lovers as the site of male fascination, binding specularity (being looked at) to sexuality (femaleness) within the explicit terms of patriarchal desire. She is appearance on display, framed or sometimes masked in a way that heightens the voyeurism. The play of appearance allows Jeanne, however, to negotiate the social organization as subject because it confuses the very absoluteness of the distinction between subject and object. Thus, in her excessiveness she is the object of the male gaze, but she cannot be contained by it. She learns in the course of the film to appropriate and control the look, transforming it into a transitive power for flaunting her own desire, which can disrupt social barriers and level thresholds of difference. She entices men to seduce her, functioning not only as object of the gaze but also as an agent who uses it.[8] At the same time, Jeanne's power rests in her ability to complicate if not reverse the spectator/spectacle opposition of patriarchal discourse. Women's desire unsettles (men), and the disorientation caused by the collapse of power relations enables Jeanne in an emblematic sense to cross a social and sexual boundary. Increasingly the spectator watches not only the object Jeanne (framed by the camera, looking in mirrors, pinned down by a male gaze) but also the subject Jeanne looking at men or at men being seduced by her beauty, so that the men too become objects of spectacle. The look, then, emerges as the most forceful language of communication, an ideal vehicle for seduction in a silent film about female power.

In her innocence Jeanne confirms patriarchal logic, but at the same time she is the outsider who violates it when she becomes the most powerful woman in France through the absolute commodification of her body. Lubitsch's female protagonist is a strong, aggressive woman whose strength derives not from manipulative calculation but from a kind of instinctual talent for artifice and the play of appearances. Appearance becomes a real factor in this constellation, and the film's conflict is carried out between this scandalous power of female artifice and the representatives of social order who fall prey to its seduction. Jeanne, the simple girl of the people, rises to the position of the king's mistress and learns how to master power. Her assumption of the master's role makes manifest the vulnerability of male control when exposed to the fascination of the erotic and, because this is not a comedy, explains why she must be eliminated at the end of the film.

History finally catches up with the love story, transforming excessive desire into the immediate meaning effect of aggravation, rupture, and erasure contained in the sign "French Revolution." Jeanne tries to extend her control not only over the king but also over her first love, Armand. The past cannot be reactivated, however. It has a tendency to return with a vengeance as a symptom of that which was repressed. When Armand discovers that his beloved Jeanne has become Countess Dubarry, the king's mistress, he rejects her, gives himself up to helpless weeping, and becomes a leader of the mass rebellion. His repression of desire and rejection of sexuality allows him to identify fully with the bourgeois revolution. Jeanne, in short, comes to symbolize in her very power the most vulnerable point in a moribund system of authority and identity based on exchange. And male aggression is played out on Jeanne, the site where the stability of the entire system is threatened. Arrested by the police, Armand gains his freedom from the king's finance minister on the condition that he join him—in an ironic parody of class collaboration—to drive out the excessive female sexuality threatening the country (Jeanne). Later Jeanne is dragged before the revolutionary tribunal where Citizen Armand now reigns as judge. Although her imploring look can still awaken his desire, he condemns her to death, but—closing the circle of attraction and (self-) destructive repression—he makes one last, desperate attempt to help her escape from her prison cell. Discovered by his comrades, he is shot and Jeanne beheaded on the guillotine while the crowd cheers.[9]

Lubitsch's film was a box-office success that addressed the growing and increasingly socially stratified cinema audience in postwar Germany. Familiar plot elements from popular genres, fascination with the wealth and decadence of the aristocracy, the opportunities to exploit visual spectacle: all were formulaic elements designed to appeal to the viewing dispositions and imagination of the traditional proletarian cinema public on whom certainly the social dimension of this voyeurism was not lost. Concurrently the possibilities of identifying with Jeanne's social mobility as well as Armand's indefinite class position (as student, lieutenant in the king's guard, citizen leader of the revolution, chair of the revolutionary tribunal) and the projected triumph of bourgeois rationality offered a petty-bourgeois public fantasies of economic and political power that were, in the real context of revolutionary Germany in 1919, just beginning to assert themselves. Lubitsch's balance of extravagance and suggestiveness (in acting, visual images, plot reversals), always just at the edge of the probable and the proper, promised something to both audiences. The film further raises questions about the patriarchal discourse on woman as amoral, unknown and unknowable, a disintegrative force. Jeanne is specifically the hyperbolized figure of excessive female sexuality, ignoring or negating all (socially) acceptable boundaries. Her desire is uncontainable and ultimately fatal (to her and the society around her), yet at the same time, its promise makes her the most desirable object to possess. Thus, male/female gender differences offer another potential stratification or split in spectator identification.

Passion recognizes both political revolution and patriarchy as discourses. Lubitsch is not interested in the French Revolution as event or historiography. As a representation of the French Revolution, the narrative is of course wrong in its details, privileging the anecdotal over the central events and collapsing the political into the play of eroticism and vanity. Yet, it is an imaginary construct for interrogating power strategies as a process of realigning sexual roles and sexual repression among the bourgeoisie, a process that was well underway in Germany after the collapse of the Wilhelmine Empire and the defeat of the war in 1918. Less a denunciation of social revolution either in the form of the historic French Revolution or of the revolutionary activities in Germany in 1919, *Passion* is an anticipatory critique of emergent bourgeois social life.

The two *Danton* films of 1921 and 1931 are less rich visually,

Marc Silberman

narrationally, and in their *mise en scène* than Lubitsch's *Passion*. In contrast to Lubitsch's film, which focuses on the struggle of the bourgeoisie against the monarchy and its decadence, the *Danton* films concentrate solely on the republican phase of the revolution, beginning with the king's trial and beheading. This allows them to elaborate the opposition between the two notions of freedom and violence, represented by Danton and Robespierre respectively. Whereas it was possible, then, to situate *Passion* in the immediate context of rupture and dislocation of Germany's November Revolution, the later films are concerned with a critique of the bourgeois revolution in a postrevolutionary phase. Both Buchovetzki's silent film and Behrendt's early sound film are adaptations of Georg Büchner's 1835 dramatic fragment *Dantons Tod* (*Danton's Death*), and it would not be farfetched to suggest that both films probably trace their roots back to well-known Berlin theater productions of this play.[10] As in Büchner's play, the conflict in these two films is structured around two diametrically opposed views of the revolutionary process and set against the background of its imminent collapse. Danton, a vital man of expansive gestures and powerful presence, finds in the revolution's political achievements the confirmation of individual freedom and wants to enjoy it as his right to indulge in sensual pleasures. Robespierre, more in the tradition of Rousseauistic puritanism, sees the idea of the revolution threatened on all sides, including by Danton's anarchic individualism, and insists on protecting and defending the people's will, even if it entails violence against them.

Buchovetzki's *All for a Woman* reveals Lubitsch's influence in the scenic dramaturgy, both in some framing and masking tricks and in the organization of mass scenes.[11] Although it was considered a success—especially the acting by Emil Jannings in the role of Danton and by Werner Krauss in the role of Robespierre—and although it established Buchovetzki's reputation as a director of historical films, it betrays all too clearly the derivative stage source.[12] *Danton* cannot be compared to the Expressionist auteur films by directors like Wiene, Murnau, Leni, and Lang with their integration of set design, lighting, *mise en scène*, and embedded narratives. There are nonetheless definite traces of Expressionistic acting. Krauss, who of course had played Caligari, uses the familiar rigid gestures and exaggerated, slow movements for his Robespierre character. Dressed in a tightly cut, black frock coat buttoned to the neck with a grotesquely high collar that seems to prop up his head, his body has that unreal quality of a marionette, conveying the precise sense of a neurotic tyrant who only knows self-denial.[13] Other actors in the film use this style at most intermittently. In his climactic defense before the revolutionary tribunal, for example, Jannings's frozen poses, frenzied movements, and distorted facial features are reminiscent of Caligari when he breaks down in the asylum, while Camille and Lucile Desmoulins's fearful gestures recall Francis and Jane in *The Cabinet of Dr. Caligari.*

Following a brief exposition, which dramatically introduces the main characters with irises or wipes and summarizes with a few titles the fundamental stand-off between the antagonists, the narrative unfolds in a fairly linear manner. Danton withdraws from politics to become a bon vivant and to chase women (intertitle: "I want to live!"), while Robes-

From *Danton* (*All for a Woman,* Dimitri Buchovetzki, 1921), Emil Jannings as Danton and Maly Delschaft as Julie. Courtesy of the Deutsches Institut für Filmkunde E.V.

pierre and his friends intrigue against him. After several delays and attempts at reconciliation, Robespierre has Danton and his friends arrested, tried, convicted, and finally guillotined. Counterposed to the antagonists are the masses for whom they both speak: Robespierre as the stern authority who will commit any crime for and against them to defeat the enemies of the revolution and Danton as the popular leader who is paternalistically arrogant and contemptuous toward them. Thus, although Danton initially offers a positive figure of identification, his excess and political irresponsibility mark him, like Robespierre, as an untrustworthy leader of the revolution. Meanwhile, the revolutionary justice demanded by the masses is brutal and vengeful. Aroused by Robespierre's and St. Just's denunciations, they rush to Danton's house. There, standing high on his balcony, Danton intimidates them with an angry scowl and deflects their rage by recalling his revolutionary feats (intertitle: "Did you forget that it was Danton who toppled the tyrant?"). The crosscutting between high shots of the threatening, then subdued, then excited crowd packed into the narrow street and low shots of Danton's towering figure conveys the impression of a mob at the mercy of their emotions and deformed by hate.

Lubitsch was praised for the powerful choreography of the mass scenes in *Passion,* which he achieved by combining the camera's cinematic properties with some of Max Reinhardt's techniques for the disciplined movement of groups on stage. In the early opera ball sequence, for example, the carefully timed rhythm of camera distances (long, medium, close) and the variation in camera angle (from low to bird's-eye shots) reveal a complexity and richness in the creation of on-screen and off-screen space that was entirely new in the German cinema. Even more striking is the movement of crowds within the frame. Circular, snaking, or lateral lines moving in opposite directions create a maelstrom effect of dancers at the ball, and in some shots the layering effect of crowds on the dance floor and groups in the theater loges above, or later of crowds in public squares and flags waving on poles above, intensifies the dynamization of space. In the court scenes and street scenes, Lubitsch effectively employs motion along a diagonal axis from the top to the bottom of the frame (or vice versa) to energize the space. In the scenes of revolutionary violence and at the guillotine the combination of groups moving

110

simultaneously back and forth with waving fists conveys a further sense of the mass dynamic. Obviously Buchovetzki had learned from Lubitsch as well as Reinhardt. A long, high shot of the masses endlessly streaming from the front exit of the National Convention looks like flowing lava from an erupting volcano, the effect intensified with moving shadows cast by high powered spots on one side of the enormous portal.[14] The tribunal sequence creates a theatrical stage space divided into three sections: a grandstand in the back filled with the masses, a raised, fenced platform for the accused in the center, and a long table near the foreground where the judges sit with their backs toward the camera. Once again Danton is able to control the restless crowd with a gesture of his hand, with his laughter, with his passionate defense until St. Just cleverly announces that bread is being distributed in the streets. The mob exits in a tight group, abandoning Danton and his friends to their accusers.

The representation of the masses as a mob both in *Passion* and in *All for a Woman* characterizes an attempt to articulate the place of the people, of the citizenry in the historical process of political change. The elaboration of cinematic techniques for creating images of the masses goes hand in hand in Germany with the need to invent "the people" as political subjects. The way such cinematic representations imagine the people as a political group actualizes fears about the estrangement of the individual in modern political life and expresses real ambivalence toward mass revolutionary action. Usually shown in delimited spaces (narrow streets, enclosed squares, the grandstand of the tribunal, the gallery of the convention), this pre-Eisensteinian mass declares itself as such only when it breaks out of its assigned space as a result of the mobilization of emotions. Especially in *All for a Woman*, the masses are not a collective but a crowd of people always seen in long shots. The anonymous group acts like a drill team taking cues, charging forth like an unleashed fury or calmly sitting in ordered rows. The masses never speak as "we," nor are they even quoted as a group, but rather they are spoken to or for by the leaders who are opposed to the crowd as its adversaries. Equally opposed to the masses are the nobility and royalty, who are at the same time highly eroticized in their behavior and in the *mise en scène*. Buchovetzki underscores this point with a Pygmalion subplot involving

Babette, a "representative" of the people who, like Jeanne in *Passion*, is transformed from an impoverished beggar into an elegant mistress by Count Hérault. His aggressive, almost sadistic examination of the helpless girl through his lorgnon (a masked shot slowly pans up along her body as if she were pinned down like an insect by his look), the struggle to dress her in a tight-fitting dress (she is virtually tied into it), and the closeup of the maid's grotesquely moving mouth telling her how to behave are object lessons on the price poor people must pay if they opt for an alliance with nobility. Consequently, when the mob enters Hérault's house at the end, Babette throws off her finery almost without remorse and gleefully joins in the plundering.

What position of identification is offered to the spectator, then, if neither the masses' emotionalism nor the nobility's sadistic eroticism, Danton's individualism nor Robespierre's dictatorship of terror guarantees an acceptable relation to power? Unlike Büchner's play, where the women—Danton's wife Julie, Camille's wife Lucile, and the prostitute Marion—offer countermodels to the alienation experienced by all the male characters, here the representatives of mind and might suggest the only utopia that might offer an alternative to self-destruction. Danton's friends Westermann, the military general, and Camille, the poet, both argue—albeit unsuccessfully—for reconciliation between the opposing factions, a motif that anticipates by five years Fritz Lang's famous handshake in *Metropolis*.[15] They define a space in which the bourgeois subject can escape the violence done to individuals, a space projected beyond the Manichean confrontation of Danton's irresponsible inactivity and Robespierre's desperate actionism. The skepticism toward class struggle and revolutionary violence as well as the yearning for political change contained in such gestures of reconciliation actualizes the ambiguous relationship to the young Weimar Republic that many spectators must have shared at a time when it was still under attack from armed right-wing armies (the *Freikorps* groups) and the fragmented energy of the left wing.

Like Buchovetzki's *All for a Woman*, Hans Behrendt's *Danton* of 1931 covers the events from the collapse of the monarchy and the beheading of the king to Danton's execution and focuses the conflict around antithetical personality traits of the two Jacobin leaders, although

From *Danton* (Hans Behrendt, 1931), Fritz Kortner as Danton. Courtesy of the Deutsches Institut für Filmkunde E.V.

Danton is less a libertine and Robespierre more thoughtful.[16] If anything, the narrative is here even more closely tied to the dramatic opposition of the former's humanistic virtues as counterposed to the latter's purist demagogy. It defines the very organizational principle of the screenplay's five-act structure in which the core of each act consists of a series of sequences in parallel montage explicitly contrasting Danton and Robespierre. Consistent with this theatrical organization are other typical symptoms of filmed plays: the indulgence toward Fritz Kortner's opulent acting style in the role of Danton, the understated, subdued rhythm of the editing, and the almost ascetic use of the camera. Moreover, as an early sound film it exhibits the nagging difficulties with microphones and sound balance, especially in the scenes with large groups.

Despite the similarities between *All for a Woman* and *Danton*, Behrendt sets his accents differently, and these shifts relate to some of the changes that had taken place in Germany during the ensuing ten years of republican politics. First, whereas Buchovetzki situates his figures within the discourse of freedom—a political accomplishment of the newly founded Weimar Republic—and two views of power that promise

113

to guarantee such freedom for the unreliable masses, Behrendt's figures experience the gray melancholy of everyday bourgeois life. For them freedom, or the promise of revolutionary change, seems to be no more than a historical reminiscence. Hence, both Danton and Robespierre are shown grappling with the omnipresent threats to the revolution, and the narrative gives as much space to Robespierre's arguments for the revolution's right to defend itself as it does to Danton's determination to make compromises at every turn. Second, although for Behrendt, too, the power struggle between the antagonists is a central structural element, it is not this internal strife among the Jacobins that threatens the revolution but rather its external enemies.[17] They are frequently introduced only anecdotally; but taken together they constitute a recurring motif that traces a fateful web of dangers: economic exigencies, military treason from within, the united power of Europe's monarchs, the clerical critics, the nobility's plotting against the convention (including Marat's murder), and the bourgeoisie's unscrupulous exploitation of the revolution for profit. Thus, Behrendt's narrative articulates sympathy for the idea of revolution and even confirms the historical necessity of change, but at the same time it recognizes the failure of the revolution to fulfill its promises.

The third and perhaps the most crucial distinction between the two Danton films concerns the role of the masses. Unlike *All for a Woman*, here the people hardly appear as a collective group, and when they do—plundering the palace, in the galleries of the convention, on the square in front of the guillotine—it is a relatively small and static group. Behrendt presents instead personalized members of the people, individuals who speak with the voice of the masses and enter into dialogue with the leaders while always maintaining their distance (sometimes indicated by bars or fences separating them). The most important of these figures is the old retiree who repeatedly nags each leader of the revolution with his question: "Who is going to pay my monthly pension of one hundred francs now?" This is the voice of the people, the voice of reason that can be the first to yell "Down with the king" in response to Danton's accusations against the royal house's irresponsibility but also the voice of those who live the daily social reality beyond grand power politics. It represents the perspective of "common sense," often linked to shots of leaders filmed from low angles and marked by the camera immediately in the opening sequence as that of the spectator's point of view, yet it is also the voice to which each of the leaders—Marat, Danton, Camille Desmoulins, and Robespierre—turns a deaf ear because he has some more important business to attend to.[18] Other minor characters also carry this "perspective from below." In the second scene Robespierre shows more concern for the way his housekeeper irons his shirts than for her anxious questions about the future of the revolution, and later Danton brushes aside some common soldiers who enthusiastically support him because he is more interested in flirting with one of the noble women in prison. Other scenes point to the gulf between the leaders and the people. Camille fires up a group of peasants with a call to storm the Tuileries and then sits down for a glass of wine in a café as they run off, and Robespierre's posted proclamation announcing a curfew, food and alcohol rationing, and the end of prostitution only draws cynical comments from two citizens.

Filmed during a time when the middle and lower classes in Germany were suffering the catastrophic consequences of the world market crash, the narrative's unremittingly pessimistic view evoked by the "common people" toward the demagogy of its various political and military leaders moves in the direction of a hope already widely held among the petty bourgeoisie.[19] It is the reverse side of the coin that believed the problems of the Weimar Republic could be solved if only a strong, benevolent leader were to appear who could unify the nation. Two details illustrate this central point. Immediately after Danton makes the crucial mistake of supporting General Dumouriez, a young officer requisitioned for office duty because he was considered unfit for field service asks Danton to reverse the order. His name: Bonaparte. Later, during the negotiations for a compromise, the Duke of Coburg insists that in Germany no one understands anything about revolution, to which Danton responds by paraphrasing Schiller's *Robbers:* "Put me in front of a few guys like myself and I'll make Germany into a republic!" The anecdotal reference to a mix-up that almost blocked Napoleon from his glory as well as the reference by a French Jacobin to the tradition of Schiller's heroic idealism are both examples of the desperate wish that in the absence of a general political will, some other, more radical solution might restore stability. Exactly two years after the premiere of Behrendt's *Danton*, the onset of the Third Reich shifted radically the coordinates for the public discussion in Germany about the process of political change and its power relations.

III

The historical film is a form of narrative discourse about the past. It is the cinematic genre that under the pretext of retelling the past seeks to reorganize social relations in the present. The "present," here refers to the history that takes place as the process of construction; the "past" refers to that which is constructed as object by the film text. In both cases my attention is only secondarily engaged by the facts, by the extradiscursive real. The cinematic world is not congruent with the real; rather it picks and chooses. It redistributes and resignifies elements of the real to create its own reality: one-sided, subjective, incomplete, in a word—imaginary. Insofar as a film works with or addresses the imagination, it has its own logic, its own system of coherency and way of seeing. For this reason, the primary concern in the analysis of the historical film should not be to measure its fictions against history, to judge its mimetic quality, or to evaluate its accuracy. Imitation and repetition based on a pseudoscientific notion of exactitude traditionally lead to an idealist abstraction of history where it is no more than a theme that commemorates the past. On the contrary, the historical film constructs memory as a political position through the organization of an image of the past. Its effect is in the showing, the imagining, not in the accuracy of the facts shown.

My interest in these three films about the French Revolution produced during the Weimar Republic is directed at the concatenation of history, the past and the present in an imaginary relation. In each case I ask myself what variables and choices function in the cinematic construction of the past. The organization of the images, the characters, the narrative structure all contribute information that helps us determine how people living during the twenties imagined their relation to their own time. Thus, it should be evident that what these films mean concerns me less than how they produced meanings at a specific, historical juncture. It is not a question of the events of the revolution itself, but how they are perceived, integrated, and communicated in the cinematic text. Each film presents a critique of the long-overdue bourgeois revolution in Germany from a perspective that articulates both hopes and doubts associated with rapid, violent change. The symptomatic skepticism toward historical agency, the suspicion that no adequate historical subject exists to carry the revolution, describes an imaginary relation that can be made intelligible only by inserting the films back into history. As such these films provide a privileged example of how the cinematic discourse of history is not constructed in the past but in the present political relations of the spectator to history and to the history represented in the film. This imaginary construct is not, however, a reflection of history but a reaction in it. It is the extension of something real in the relation to history, an expression of the desire to transform one's relation to reality.

Notes

1. "Die Geschichte ist Gegenstand einer Konstruktion, deren Ort nicht die homogene und leere Zeit, sondern die von 'Jetztzeit' erfüllte bildet." Walter Benjamin, *Illuminationen* (Frankfurt a.M.: Suhrkamp, 1961) 276; English translation by Harry Zohn in Walter Benjamin, *Illuminations* (New York: Schocken, 1969) 261.
2. Karl Marx, *Der achtzehnte Brumaire des Louis Bonaparte*, in *Politische Schriften* (Stuttgart: Cotta, 1960) I:270.
3. There are no existing copies of three other German films set in the French Revolution: *Charlotte Corday* (Friedrich Zelnik, 1919), *Marie Antoinette* (Rudolf Meinert, 1922), and *Revolutionshochzeit* (*Revolution Wedding*, A. W. Sandberg, 1928).
4. For an overview and sources on the reception of the French Revolution during the nineteenth century in Germany, see Beatrix W. Bouvier, *Französische Revolution und deutsche Arbeiterbewegung: Die Rezeption des revolutionären Frankreich in der deutschen Arbeiterbewegung von den 1830er Jahren bis 1905* (Bonn: Neue Gesellschaft, 1982).
5. Other public discourses on revolution during this time include, for example, the Expressionist obsession with "Aufbruch" or revolt (see Silvio Vietta/Hans-Georg Kemper, *Expressionismus* [Munich: Fink, 1983]), the model of the Russian October Revolution (see the rich literature in Georg P. Meyer, *Bibliographie zur deutschen Revolution 1918/1919* [Göttingen: Vandenhoeck & Ruprecht, 1977], esp. 31–34) and the popular war literature associated

Marc Silberman

with Freikorps values (see Klaus Theweleit, *Male Fantasies*, 2 vols., trans. Stephen Conway et al. [Minneapolis: U of Minnesota P, 1987–89]).

6. Ernst Lubitsch, *Madame Dubarry* (Passion, 1919)
   Producer: Carl Moos, Projektions-AG Union, Berlin
   Screenplay: Fred Orbing (=Norbert Falk), Hanns Kräly
   Cinematography: Theodor Sparkuhl
   Set decoration: Kurt Richter, Karl Markus
   Costumes: Ali Hubert
   Music: Alexander Schirmann
   Cast: Pola Negri (Jeanne Vaubernier/Madame Dubarry), Emil Jannings (King Louis XV), Reinhold Schünzel (Choiseul, Finance Minister), Harry Liedtke (Armand de Foix), Eduard von Winterstein (Count Jean Dubarry), Karl Platen (Guillaume Dubarry), Paul Biensfeldt (Lebel, King's Chamberlain), Magnus Stifter (Don Diego, Spanish Envoy), Willy Kaiser-Heyl (Commander of the Guards), Elsa Berna (Duchess Gramont), Fred Immler (Duke Richelieu), Gustav Czimeg (Duke Aiguillon), Alexander Ekert (Paillet), Marga Köhler (Madame Labille), Bernhard Goetzke, Robert Sortsch-Plá.

7. For example in the 1916 *Schuhpalast Pinkus* (*Pinkus' Shoe Palace*) and the 1940 *The Shop Around the Corner.*

8. The notion of the gaze has been an important element in theorizing female spectatorship and identification in the cinema, especially among feminist-oriented critics. The seminal article in this context is Laura Mulvey's "Visual Pleasure and Narrative Cinema," *Screen* 16.3 (Autumn 1975): 6–18, with her later addendum "Afterthoughts on 'Visual Pleasure and Narrative Cinema' Inspired by *Duel in the Sun*," *Framework* 15/16/17 (1981): 12–15. Other important contributions include Annette Kuhn, *Women's Pictures: Feminism and Cinema* (London: Routledge and Kegan Paul, 1982); E. Ann Kaplan, "Is the Gaze Male?" *Women and Film: Both Sides of the Camera* (New York: Methuen, 1983); Mary Ann Doane, "Film and the Masquerade: Theorizing the Female Spectator," *Screen* 23.3/4 (September/October 1982): 74–88, as well as her *Desire to Desire: The Woman's Film of the 1940s* (Bloomington/Indianapolis: Indiana UP, 1987). The collection *Female Spectators. Looking at Film and Television*, ed. E. Deirdre Pribram (London: Verso, 1988), includes some challenging analytical examples that indicate the complications and possibilities of theorizing the gaze.

9. Some versions of the film include a last scene where the executioner shows Jeanne's severed head to the crowd and then throws it to them like a football. See, for example, the summary by Helma Sanders-Brahms in *Lubitsch*, ed. Hans-Helmut Prinzler and Enno Patalas (Munich: Bucher, 1984) 132–36.

10. I am referring to Max Reinhardt's 1916 production at the Deutsches Theater, which ran for almost three years until spring 1919, and to Karl-Heinz Martin's 1929 production at the Volksbühne. Reinhardt staged *Dantons Tod* once again at the Grosses Schauspielhaus in December 1921 and apparently was interested for that reason in Buchovetzki's film version which was released in April 1921. He also staged Büchner's drama in 1929, both in Vienna and in Munich, but it is unclear to what extent Behrendt was familiar with these productions. Gustav Gründgens, who plays Robespierre in the 1931 film version, acted the role of St. Just for Reinhardt's 1929 staging. It might be of interest to note that *Dantons Tod* was not premiered until 1902 in an unsuccessful Berlin theater production and really entered stage history only

with Leopold Jessner's Hamburg production in 1910. During the Weimar Republic, however, especially during the second half, it was among the most popular German classics in the theater, with eighty-nine different productions between 1919 and 1933. Büchner did not come into his own as an important German writer until the Expressionists discovered in him a kindred soul, and one measure of the growing popular access to *Dantons Tod* was its publication for the first time in 1919 in an inexpensive Reclam edition. The only other play about the French Revolution that could compete with Büchner's during the Weimar Republic was Romain Rolland's *Danton*, written in 1900 (in *Théâtre de la révolution* [Paris: Ollendorff, 1923–24], translated into German by Wilhelm Herzog in 1921 and not to be confused with Rolland's later, 1938 version in which Robespierre becomes a much more sympathetic character). Reinhardt's staging of the Rolland play ran at the Grosses Schauspielhaus from February 1920 to September 1921 during the filming of Buchovetzki's *Danton*, and in his 1929 productions of Büchner's play he actually incorporated some of the speeches from Rolland's version. For the reception of the Büchner play, see Wolfram Viehweg, *Georg Büchners "Dantons Tod" auf dem deutschen Theater* (Munich: Laokoon, 1964), and for dates and casts of Reinhardt's theater productions, see Heinrich Huesmann, *Welt-theater Reinhardt: Bauten, Spielstätten, Inszenierungen* (Munich: Prestel, 1983).

11. Dimitri Buchovetski, *Danton* (*All for a Woman*, 1921)
    Producer: Wörner Film, Berlin
    Asst. dir.: Richard Gerner (Deutsches Theater)
    Screenplay: Dimitri Buchovetzki, based on Georg Büchner's play *Dantons Tod*
    Cinematography: Arpàd Viràgh
    Set decoration: Hans Dreier
    Cast: Emil Jannings (Danton), Werner Krauss (Robespierre), Ossip Runitsch (Camille Desmoulins), Ferdinand von Alten (an aristocrat), Eduard von Winterstein (General Westermann), Charlotte Ander (Lucile Desmoulins), Maly Delschaft (Julie), Hilde Wörner (Babette), Hugo Döblin (Henriot), Friedrich Kühne, (Fouquier-Tinville), Robert Scholz (St. Just), Albert Florath (provocateur), Else Lorenz (provocateur).

12. The fact that Buchovetzki called on Richard Gerner from the Deutsches Theater as his assistant director only confirms this point. The uncinematic script would also suggest that Carl Mayer did not cowrite the screenplay, as has sometimes been claimed but never substantiated.

13. A photograph of Bruno Decarli playing Robespierre in Reinhardt's first Berlin production of Büchner's *Dantons Tod* would suggest that Krauss adapted his own marionette style from that interpretation. See illustration 5 in Viehweg, n.p. Krauss himself played St. Just opposite Decarli in the same stage production.

14. Buchovetzki adapted both the lighting and elements of the stage design from Reinhardt's 1916 *Dantons Tod* production for this scene and for the tribunal scene. See the sketches in Ernst Stern and Heinz Herald, *Reinhardt und seine Bühne: Bilder von der Arbeit des Deutschen Theaters* (Berlin: Eisler, 1918) 86–91, as well as the description of the lighting and set in Ernst Stern, *My Life, My Stage* (London: Gollanz, 1951) 161–63.

15. I characterize Camille as a poet not because of any historical evidence (in

fact, he was a journalist) but because his major act in the film is to compose and sing a satirical song directed against Robespierre and his circle. Although the song element appears nowhere in either Büchner's or Rolland's Danton plays, it is crucial not only in the Buchovetzki and Behrendt films but even in *Passion*. In all three, the people (the masses) are moved to agitate when they hear a revolutionary song, a fact that seems to indicate at least on the part of the filmmakers an unusual insistence on the power of music and poetry!

16. Hans Behrendt, *Danton* (1931)
    Producer: Allianz-Tonfilm, Berlin
    Screenplay: Heinz Goldberg; dialogue: Hans José Rehfisch
    Cinematography: Nikolaus Farkas
    Set decoration: Julius von Borsody
    Costumes: Theaterkunst Kaufmann
    Sound: Birkhofer and Metain
    Editing: G. Pollatschek
    Music: Arthur Guttmann
    Cast: Fritz Kortner (Danton), Lucie Mannheim (Louise Gély), Gustav Gründgens (Robespierre), Alexander Granach (Marat), Gustav von Wangenheim (Desmoulins), Werner Schott (Saint Just), Hermann Speelmans (Legendre), Georg John (Fouquier-Tinville), Ernst Stahl-Nachbaur (Louis XVI), Walter Werner (Malesherbes, the king's defender), G. H. Schnell (Duke of Koburg), Ferdinand Hart (General Dumouriez), Carl Goetz (retiree), Till Klockow (Cornelia, Robespierre's housekeeper), Friedrich Gnass (executioner Sanson), Maria Foresku, Hugo Fischer-Koeppe, Gustav Pütjer, Bernd Aldor.

17. One could go so far as to identify the antagonists with contemporary Weimar positions: Danton, the moderate socialist who stresses individual freedom, and Robespierre, the left socialist with radical demands for equality as the basis of freedom.

18. Behrendt may have adapted the idea of the "perspective from below" from Karl-Heinz Martin's 1929 production of *Dantons Tod* at the Berlin Volksbühne. In that production two executioners discuss the revolution from the peasants' point of view in a scene added at the beginning. Similarly, Martin's use of ominous drum rolls to punctuate scene changes resurfaces frequently as a sound transition in *Danton*. For a description of Martin's staging of the Büchner play, see Viehweg 120–42. Incidentally, like Martin's stage script, Behrendt's screenplay includes texts from Romain Rolland's *Danton*, and the interruptions with commentary by the common people during Louis XVI's trial also follow Rolland's model.

19. For a commentary on the ideological issues at play behind the notion of the "conservative revolution" that would sustain the status quo, see Jost Hermand and Frank Trommler, *Die Kultur der Weimarer Republik* (Munich: Nymphenburger, 1978) 101–7.

4

Eros, Thanatos, and the Will to Myth: Prussian Films in German Cinema

Jan-Christopher Horak

Picture the following scene in a German B-movie: Two young lovers, hardly acknowledging their host, stare at each other across the dinner table. The party receives a message; the young man becomes agitated. He runs into the garden, gripped by the thought of the holy oath binding him to his fraternity brothers: "The first call of the *Führer* will find us at his side." His eyes no longer shining with love or tenderness but radiating fanatically, he is obsessed with the coming rebellion against the French army of occupation. Lightning strikes once, twice, three times, ever brighter in accompaniment to his thoughts: "Who can keep his hands folded in his lap, like a coward? The people are rising, the storm unleashed." His lover pleads with him not to leave her, not to go to war, not to sacrifice his life needlessly, but the vision of dying a hero's death for the *Vaterland* has seized him completely. Reflecting his inner turmoil, the storm reaches an orgiastic peak. Thanatos has conquered Eros.[1]

This scene from the bio-pic, *Theodor Körner—Ein deutsches Heldenlied* (*Theodor Körner—A German Hero's Song*, Carl Boese, 1932), is typical of fascist cinema in the Weimar Republic and the Third Reich. It propagates a fanatic patriotism, renunciation of individual happiness, total commitment to the state, the valiant and unflinching heroism of teutonic men, and the honor and rapture of a death for the German *Volk*. Eros conquered by Thanatos represents the life and death instinct, intertwined and always present, according to Freud. Likewise, this narrative of sexual sublimation, of the organism surrendering to a death wish, of self-sacrifice for the *Vaterland*, is a common feature of Prussian films.

Theodor Körner presents an episode in the history of Prussia. However, it is neither Prussia, nor Prussian history at stake here but rather a mythological Prussia in the service of fascist ideology. *Theodor Körner* depicts the "wars of independence" against Napoleon and the "heroic" death of a twenty-year-old poet whose nameless reincarnation will appear in the snow-covered ruins of Stalingrad to sacrifice himself just as unconditionally for Germany. As in countless other *Preussenfilme*, a genre particular to German cinema, Prussian history is instrumentalized to create a myth, a myth of Prussian virtue and Prussian invincibility. This myth is to be perceived as both a sustaining element of German national consciousness and as a vision of what is yet to come and thus communicates the authoritarian and patriarchal ideology of Nazi fascism. Though produced before Hitler's ascension to power in 1933, *Theodor Körner* can be seen as a typical example of narrative and iconographic structures that are common to the genre.

While the transformation of Prussian history into myth was well under way in nineteenth-century German poetry and popular literature, produced for the most part by second-rate, ultranationalist writers, German commercial cinema quickly appropriated both its narratives and ideology. Isolated in World War I from the French competition, which had dominated film distribution before 1914, German film producers rushed to make patriotic films, getting rich in the process. However, it was the incredible financial success of Arzèn von Cserèpy's four-part epic, *Fridericus Rex* (1922–23), that defined the genre of the Prussian film. No less than ten films about the legendary Frederick the Great followed between 1927 and 1942, while elements of the genre are visible in more than three hundred films.[2] The genre's other favorite historical periods were the Napoleonic wars and the unification of Germany under Bismarck. All three periods spawned a rich popular literature that continued into the twentieth century. These eras represented milestones of German nationalism, its victories under Frederick, humiliation at the hands of the French republican code, and rebirth in the second *Kaiserreich*.

After 1933 Prussian films drew historical analogies to imply that the Third Reich constituted the next reawakening in German national power. Its heroes were invariably military men who had fought valiantly on the battlefields or other great men who through their deeds had contributed to the growth of national consciousness. "Great men" also meant the exclusion of women, who are practically invisible in this most patriarchal of genres. After the fall of the Third Reich in 1945, the Prussian film lay dormant for a few years, only to be revived in the Federal Republic in the 1950s, during the period of reconstruction and rearmament under the wing of NATO.[3] Less authoritarian than their predecessors, Prussian films under Adenauer nevertheless retained elements of fascist ideology, now cloaked in patriotic anti-Communism and conservative Christian-Democratic ideology, but were no less patriarchal.[4]

While it is true that during the Weimar Republic it was primarily film producers connected to nationalist and protofascist financiers, especially Ufa, who produced Prussian films, liberal and Jewish producers also favored the genre because of its immense popularity and profitability. In some rare cases—for example, Gerhard Lamprecht's *Der Katzensteg* (*The Cat's Walk*, 1927), based on a well-known Hermann Sudermann novel—producers actually attempted to turn the genre ideologically against itself, articulating pacifist and antimilitarist statements. The most famous example of this kind was certainly *Mädchen in Uniform* (*Girls in Uniform*, Leontine Sagan, 1931), a film that not only attacked an archaic, authoritarian mode of Prussian education but also the tenets of patriarchy underlining that system.[5]

The Prussian film is the genre most heavily invested in patriarchy, more so than any other European or American genre, including the Western and other male action films. More radically than other genres, the Prussian film addresses a male subject, while denying the existence of female subjectivity. Not only are women consistently removed from the narrative as figures of identification, but their gaze also is supplanted by a male one.[6] Woman's desire, as positioned in narratives of heterosexual eroticism and sexual union, is consistently denied and ultimately eliminated, through the privileging of narratives of male bonding and aggression.

In this essay I would like to focus on those generic structures in Prussian films that repeatedly construct a discourse on love, sexuality, duty, and death. My metanarrative of Prussian films is as follows: (1) love story develops in which woman is revealed to be in conflict with the male hero's aspirations; (2) the hero realizes that his true duty lies in his sacrifice to the nation; (3) through the group dynamics of male bonding the hero experiences true brotherhood; (4) the hero finds the strength to embrace his fate as a martyr. Such a metanarrative aspires to trace the trajectory of the Prussian male's sexual sublimation from a renunciation of heterosexual union via an only barely repressed homoeroticism to an ultimate death wish. By positioning the male subject in this drama of Thanatos, Prussian films—especially those produced in the Third Reich—prepared young men for their imminent death on the battlefields, and thus represent an overt ideological manifestation of fascism.

Fascism—particularly German fascism—is a political and social organization of society based on authoritarian rule, a virulently aggressive form of laissez faire capitalism, imperialist expansionism, and absolute patriarchy.[7] The elimination of a democratic opposition in Germany in 1933 through legal (the *Notstandsgesetze*) and extralegal means (concentration camps) meant not only the end of Weimar democracy but also the end of any kind of political or social (labor unions) opposition to the elites in the military, judiciary, and business communities. While the ruling class reaped economic benefits from the uninhibited exploitation of labor, and from the confiscation of Jewish capital—made possible through the racist Nuremberg Laws (1935)—ordinary Germans were asked to fill their stomachs with the symbols of Nazi German power.

Conversely, individual desire, in so far as it pertained to middle- and working-class Germans, had to be eradicated in favor of the state. Self-sacrifice to the point of self-annihilation was propagated to be the highest ideal of the individual.

All social formations under fascism, i.e., their representations, function merely as guarantees for the survival of the state.[8] While men are asked to fight and die for the higher good, women are to produce cannon fodder.[9] As Wilhelm Reich argues in *The Mass Psychology of Fascism*, within the structures of an authoritarian and aggressively imperialist regime, the role of woman is limited to that of childbearer, while her desire as a sexual being is repressed.[10] To allow sexual desire free reign would be equivalent to allowing for individual need against the interests of the state, i.e., the ruling elite. Thus, public representations in fascist societies repress sexual desire and deny subjectivity in the interest of authoritarian ideals. The process of sublimation addressed here, as Susan Sontag points out, is characteristic of fascist art in general. "The fascist ideal is to transform sexual energy into a 'spiritual' force, for the benefit of the community. The erotic is always present as a temptation, with the most admirable response being a heroic repression of the sexual impulse."[11] The abandonment of sexual desire and heterosexual union promises a higher, spiritual form of bliss within the body of the national *Gemeinschaft*. The individual body is robbed of its physicality and sensuality, coopted into an idealized, fetishized *Übermensch*, integrated in the geometry of fascism's masses. Eternal life is promised through ethereal union with the body politic. The cataclysm of a hero's death supplants sexual orgasm as the pinnacle of human emotion.

Central to Prussian films made before 1945, then, is the creation of a national mythology whose primary purpose is to trigger aggression and by extension a collective death wish. How is the male viewer positioned in these dramas of death? Sigmund Freud never really worked out his own concept of Thanatos in any detail, but he did return time and again to the question of the relationship between Eros, Thanatos, and aggression.

In his 1920 essay, "Beyond the Pleasure Principle," Freud first postulated the existence of two primary instincts, which he labeled Eros and Thanatos.[12] These two instincts were said to be interrelated, one striving toward life, the other toward death. In "The Libido Theory" (1923) Freud elaborated on this hypothesis, arguing that the two instincts worked essentially in silence, both being common to the human organism. "The erotic instincts and the death instincts would be present in living beings in regular mixtures or fusions; but diffusions would also be liable to occur."[13] In "New Introductory Lectures on Psycho-Analysis" (1933) Freud returns to the dualistic concepts of Eros and Thanatos, life versus death, pleasure and inorganic stasis.[14] But it is in his 1940 essay, "An Outline of Psychoanalysis," that Freud most clearly defines Thanatos as a primary instinct aimed at the return of the organism to an inorganic state, producing secondary instincts, connected to aggression and sexual energy. Of particular interest to this discussion of Prussian films, is Freud's understanding of the Thanatos drive as producing psychological derivatives *only* when directed towards the external world. "So long as that instinct operates internally, as a death instinct, it remains silent; it only comes to our notice when it is diverted outward as an instinct of destruction."[15]

In Prussian cinema the Thanatos drive is directed outward when the male group enters battle against all odds. Based on Freud's theory, then, we can see how the genre addresses the Thanatos drive, positioning the male subject in a drama of self-denial and self-destruction.

However, it is the fanaticism of the Prussian male—Theodor Körner burning white hot for a martyr's death—that offers an explanation for the victory of Thanatos over Eros. In his discussion of "Libidinal Types" (1931) Freud suggests that three different personality types exist: erotic, narcissistic, and obsessional, the last type being most closely associated with fanatical desire of any kind.[16] While Freud himself never connected the obsessional type to aggressive behavior, seeing that personality type in a more positive light ("upholders of civilization"), Freud's student, Ludwig Eidelberg, explicitly relates obsessional behavior to Thanatos. "The three libidinous types represent different mixtures of eros and thanatos. In the erotic type, the eros component predominates; in the narcissistic type, the two components are approximately equal; in the obsessional type, the thanatos component dominates."[17] Eidelberg goes on to state that the obsessional type experiences aggressive pleasure when the subject overcomes or conquers the object of desire, in contradistinction to sexual pleasure that involves the gratification of subject and object.[18] In other words, while erotic pleasure (and by extension visual pleasure) depends on the engagement of male and female desire, alternatively subject and object, aggressive pleasure postulates a (male) subject who subjugates an object.

As the metanarrative of Prussian films (constructed below) demonstrates, Prussian films not only codified Nazi fascist ideology to address an exclusively male subject but more specifically valorized obsessional libidinous types, fanatically dedicated to duty, willing to sublimate their erotic economies in favor of an aggressive Thanatos drive.

While German cinema, under the centralizing forces of Ufa, instituted a Hollywood-style, producer-controlled studio system, German popular films very quickly internalized the conventions of classical narrative to construct the subject.[19] As products of a popular genre, Prussian films therefore often utilized standardized narrative conventions rather than the experimental forms of German Expressionism. For example, the erotic attraction between lovers is often first signaled through the gaze. Closeups and eyeline matches visually isolate the hero and heroine from their environment, allowing the subject to experience voyeuristically the private, often silent moment of the lovers. Through the gaze, the subjects are positioned in a drama of blooming love, promoting identification with the lovers as well as visual pleasure through the "never-ending alternation of its two sides: active/passive, subject/object, seeing/being seen."[20] In *Theodor Körner*, for example, the fleeing poet meets the actress Toni Adamberger at a crossroad. Stepping on the running board of her carriage, his gaze lingers, despite the danger. It is love at first sight, unspoken, but nevertheless clearly evident through the codes of the look. In *Trenck* (Heinz Paul, 1932), Amalie, the sister of Frederick the Great, passes Lieutenant Trenck in the gardens of Sanssouci, then turns around to look into his eyes. Not a word is spoken, but that night he enters her private chambers.

But these scenes of mutual sexual attraction, codified in the male and female gaze, shot and reverse shot, eye-to-eye match-editing, only seemingly address the female subject, only seemingly enunciate audience desire for heterosexual union. In reality, woman is only momentarily the object of the male gaze, a body frozen in his vision, a temporary diversion from his true desire, which will in fact denounce erotic attraction. This actual state of affairs in the Prussian film is visualized in . . . *reitet für Deutschland* (*Riding for Germany*, Arthur Maria Rabenalt, 1941), in which the hero, Rittmeister von Brenken, falls in love with a painting of a woman in a deserted villa. Not her real physical presence, which would bring her corporal sexuality into play, but her image seals their fate when they meet. She will become an asexual *Hausfrau*, content to support his duty and mission for the greater glory of Germany, invisible in the background, no more physical than her image on the wall.

The painted portrait of the young woman, an image of German womanhood, firmly inscribed by the patriarchal order, connotes the true position of women in the erotic order. Frozen in the male gaze, woman is perceived as a sensual object only temporarily igniting man's desire. While male heroes continue to pursue work, careers, and military orders, women are defined in relation to men, their identities and purpose in society a function of men's desire. In virtually every Prussian film, e.g., *Der höhere Befehl* (*The Higher Order*, Gerhard Lamprecht, 1935), *Robert Koch* (Hans Steinhoff, 1939), *Das Fräulein von Barnhelm* (*Fraulein von Barnhelm*, Hans Schweikert, 1940), *Der große König* (*The Great King*, Veit Harlan, 1942), and *Kolberg* (Veit Harlan, 1945), the heroines remain stereotypes, daughters or sisters waiting to find a husband. Those women who have their own profession before meeting their lovers usually give them up to support their men.

Wives in Prussian films exist only to serve their respective husbands, allowing their spouses the freedom to pursue their careers while sacrificing their own desires. This image of the caring and apparently asexual wife is an ideal of fascist patriarchy that sought only to identify womanhood with motherhood.[21] Denying any sexual desire in the mother, fascist cinema played the jealous son, unwilling to acknowledge the power of the father.[22] In *Kadetten* (*Cadets*, Karl Ritter, 1941), the heroine Sophie plays the role of *Ersatzmutter* for the young military school cadets, her virtually asexual relationship to the hero a function of his role as father figure/*Führer* to the boys. *Das Flötenkonzert von Sanssouci* (*The Flute Concert at Sanssouci*, Gustav Ucicky, 1930) is an object lesson in sacrifice, involving a young wife who must recognize that her courier husband's first allegiance is to King Frederick II. Directed by a loyal member of the Nazi party, the film presages in many respects the social ideal for women in the Third Reich: chaste, self-sacrificing, humble, the producer and keeper of little Aryans for the *Vaterland*. Frederick (as portrayed by the actor Otto Gebühr, who acted the role countless times) repeatedly plays the stern father of his troops, the *Übervater*, a role Adolf Hitler was to inherit.

The irony of the initial construction of the subject through the erotic gaze lies in its creation of desires, which the narrative must subsequently subvert in the interest of ideology. Not only must the female subject be placated but also the erotic desires of the male subject must be suppressed. This is accomplished by constructing the "erotic woman" as a negative stereotype, while the self-sacrificing and desexualized woman/mother is presented as a positive social force, if only through her invisibility. The male subject's erotic desire, on the other hand, is revealed to be a weakness the state cannot afford.

The initial definition of the heroine as love object for the male gaze ties the image of woman to her erotic appeal. This allows at least theoretically for the release of the woman's desire, which is then revealed to be a trap for the male. Female eroticism, contained in the image of her physical body, blurs the hero's vision, seducing him. Private desires begin to undermine the male's sense of duty, causing him ultimately to betray the higher order. In keeping with fascist iconography, the women most willing to demand their erotic due are actresses and other "loose" women, who are denounced in the narratives as predators.

In *Die Affäre Roedern* (*The Roedern Affair*, Erich Waschneck, 1944), the hero mistakenly leaves secret plans in the Austrian Embassy because he feels he must defend his actress mistress's honor. Roedern thus brings upon himself a major scandal, which leads to arrest and conviction on charges of treason. *The Great King* features the bravest soldier in the regiment, whose warbride causes him to be reprimanded repeatedly for insubordination. Interestingly, the foot soldier's relationship is characterized as oversexed, just as working-class characters in all Nazi films would be.

A similar narrative is developed in *Der alte und der junge König* (*The Old King and the Young King*, Hans Steinhoff, 1935) although in this case erotic entrapment is homoerotic. In the love relationship between the young Frederick II and his friend, Lieutenant Katte, Katte takes the role of the female seducer. Pursuing such feminine activities as the making of music and the reading of French literature, Katte helps Frederick to desert his father's house. Only after Katte has been executed by order of King Frederick William does the crown prince accept his duty to serve the stern father, who simultaneously embodies the state. In all the Frederick films, the real king's connection to Voltaire and the French Enlightenment is repressed in favor of the image of Frederick as Prussian general and founder of the German military state. On the other hand, Frederick's known homosexuality is barely disguised.

Frederick the Great's father, Frederick William I coined the phrase known to every German child, "Learn to suffer without complaint." The concept of duty to the state is absolutely central to Prussian films, driving their narratives forward to the point of closure. Duty and sacrifice subvert the subject's erotic desire. To stray from one's duty, to allow oneself to be seduced by desire, is equated with a loss of self-value and honor in Prussian films.

The Frederick films overtly manifest the connection between duty and the state. *Fridericus Rex* presents a Frederick faced with a string of military defeats who nevertheless carries out his duties until victory is at hand. *Der Choral von Leuthen* (*The Hymn of Leuthen*, Carl Froelich, 1933) repeats the tale. In *Die Tänzerin von Sanssouci* (*The Dancer of Sanssouci*, Friedrich Zelnik, 1932), the king's secretary, in secret mission, must commit treason, thus subjecting him to undeserved vilification. In *Heiteres und Ernstes um den großen König* (*Light-Hearted and Serious Things about the Great King*, Piel Jutzi, 1936), a servant betrays his master to the king, thus saving the Prussian army from certain defeat. Finally, in *The Great King*, Frederick once again fights the Seven Years War, a lonely, suffering, but loyal servant of his people, his image now consciously drawn to parallel that of the *Führer*, Adolf Hitler.

To fulfill one's duty will always demand suffering; it invariably implies the repression of personal desire and the acceptance of the state as master of one's life. The family as a social unit is relegated to the space beyond the frame, i.e., narratives of family relations and love are nonexistent. Scenes in which Frederick is shown in the circle of his family are virtually excluded. In *Trenck* Frederick uses a family dinner merely to give orders to his sisters in regard to state business while turning a deaf ear to his sister's desires. In *The Great King* he cannot even tear himself away from his duties when his son is on his death bed; the son dies without seeing the father. His wife the queen complains in the film, "He never needs me, neither in bad times nor on good days." As supreme commander of the military, Frederick's soldiers are his family.

Other German bio-pics are also little more than morality tales of Prussian honor and duty.[23] The families in these films are invisible except for brief establishing shots. The role of the women is limited to being props for their husbands' aspirations. For example, Robert Koch and his assistant neglect wife and child to discover the origin of tuberculosis in *Robert Koch*. In *Riding for Germany* von Brenken swears to restore Germany's honor on the equestrian course, forcing him to sacrifice both his family and his estate. As a result, the possibility for female subjectivity in Prussian films is severely limited since women are not only eliminated from the narrative as figures for identification, but their domestic space, the home—so prevalent in American melodramas as a space for the play of woman's desire—is also rendered invisible.[24]

Surprisingly, notions of love and duty hardly changed in the Prussian films of the postwar German Federal Republic. The narrative of *Königliche Hoheit* (*Her Royal Majesty*, Harald Braun, 1953) centers on a young duke torn between his duties and his love for a young American woman. While the values of his strict Prussian tutor are shown to be problematic (when they are not "humanized") the film also presents the tutor as a positive figure: necessarily strict if order and honor are to be maintained. *Königin Luise* (*Queen Luise*, Wolfgang Liebeneiner, 1956) can hardly be differentiated from Liebeneiner's overtly fascist films. Queen Luise takes her duty to the state seriously, suffers defeat at the hands of the French with her people, and ultimately tries to negotiate a truce with Napoleon. The rapprochement with the French can be seen in the interest of postwar cooperation, while at the same time there are intimations of threats from the "East," i.e., Russia, giving the film an anti-Communist, pro-NATO slant. The film's relationship to authority is blatantly patriarchal and fascistic.

In those films where men succumb to their personal desires, the narrative eventually leads them to a realization of their primary goals. Usually the male hero's sexual desire precipitates some kind of catastrophe that leads not only to the personal misfortune of the hero but also causes harm to the state. For example, when von Schlüter's tower crumbles in *Andreas Schlüter* (Herbert Maisch, 1942), he realizes his duty to the king. In every case the personal defeat of the protagonist is ultimately evaluated as a victory of Prussian reason over the feminine irrationality of love and desire. Furthermore, man's sexual desire is shown to be both a function of female egoism and her ability to prey on male narcissism. As a sign of submission, the hero invariably accepts the *raison d'état*, which seemingly caused him so much personal pain, because the threat of womanhood is shown to cause even greater damage.

The sexual desire of the male is sublimated in his heroic sacrifice, ending the threat of erotic entanglements in the interest of social order. Duty is repeatedly characterized as a spiritual value far higher than the carnal seductions of the flesh. Heterosexual love is likewise devalued because the needs of the *Gemeinschaft* are more important than the fulfillment of personal desire. "There is no happiness without performance of duty" says the hero in *Kameraden* (*Comrades*, Hans Schweikert, 1941). The sublimation of erotic desire, however, is problematic since the repression of heterosexuality brings with it the specter of homoerotic bonding. In an authoritarian, patriarchal state, the comradeship of men, not the love between men and women, becomes the primary interpersonal relationship.[25] Serving the needs of the state and society is with few exceptions seen to be a male activity. The goals of men in Prussian films are defined as executed by groups of men whose modes of interaction are guided by strict codes of conduct and who as a matter of honor support each other. Institutions in which such male bonding occurs are perceived to be the primary pillars of society and state, while the exclusion of women from the centers of power is a policy consistent with patriarchy. In film the Prussian military becomes a microcosm for the military state that was the Third Reich. Military discipline and duty are moral constants that serve not only the army but the whole state. *Kameradschaft* is deemed an absolute necessity, not only for the survival of the individual but more importantly for the whole group, i.e., party, i.e., state. As Hans Scheugl notes in *Sexualität und*

Neurose im Film, "Eroticism is transferred to a male partner, which becomes most apparent in the male-bonding organizations of the Party."[26] The homoerotic moment of transgression bubbles just under the surface, through the repression of heterosexual desire.

The recognition of male duty forces his separation from the female love object who had previously seduced him with her desire. Prussian men invariably leave their lovers to go to war, to be with other men. The topos of the dutiful Prussian in the community of other males is highlighted by its iconographic opposite: the stereotype of the feminine male and the transvestite woman. The effeminate man in Prussian films is presented frequently in the company of women, is a connoisseur of literature and music, is often a francophile, despises military virtues, and is usually willing to commit theft or treason for his own advantage. *The Flute Concert at Sanssouci* has a French-speaking merchant seducing the wife of the king's courier through his recital of poetry. Effeminate Frenchmen also make appearances in *The Dancer of Sanssouci, Fraulein von Barnhelm, Comrades,* and *The Roedern Affair*. While Prussian men prove their honor in battle, these feminine men are shown to be cowards.

Those few women who wish to gain access to the exclusive society of men in battle do so surreptitiously by dressing and passing as men. A secondary character in *Theodor Körner,* Eleanore von Prohasky joins the *Freikorps* disguised as a boy. She subsequently falls secretly in love with Körner and nurses him back to health after he receives a war wound. She never reveals her sex or desire, choosing instead to worship Körner silently, her self-sacrifice in accordance with Prussian military virtue. Likewise, *Schwarzer Jäger Johanna (Black Ranger Johanna,* Johannes Meyer, 1934) features the Prussian equivalent of Joan of Arc as its central character, a heroine who cuts off her hair and wears the uniform of the Prussian *Freikorps*. When she is taken prisoner, she refuses to betray the names of any of her coconspirators, although faced with a firing squad, proving herself an honorable *Kamerad*. Having a woman as independent as Joan would however have been intolerable to the fascists, so she too is chasing the man she loves. The sexual ambiguity of her relationship to Korfes, the cross-dressing visual evidence of homoeroticism, becomes even more apparent diagetically when Korfes falls in love with the (wo)man in uniform, whom he had previously ignored in skirts. In *Theodor Körner* the "boy" Eleanore lays down in the woods with the young poet who tries to comfort her/him. Again the underlying homoeroticism is visualized.

The irony of these two generic character types, the effeminate man and the woman-as-soldier, is that once fascism was in place, the ideological system could not allow for their inherent ambiguities. While Joseph Goebbels indeed managed to organize a relatively insular and efficient propaganda machine, state ideology could never quite contain the sign systems through which it was made intelligible. It is also true that while the censors in the heads of filmmakers, as well as Goebbels's own, missed little in terms of dangerous political and social content, they were not ubiquitous. Thus, while homosexuality was officially declared a criminal offense in Nazi Germany, punishable after 1935 with imprisonment in concentration camps, gayness is still visible in Prussian films, as both a negative and positive stereotype. Cross-dressing is also not uncommon in other German genres, such as comedies and operettas, where it comes out of the theatrical tradition of *Hosenrollen*. One might assume that the context of reception for a German audience was more naïve. On the other hand, the experience of 1920s Berlin, as well as the 1934 Röhm-Putsch, precludes naïveté on the part of the filmmakers. It is more likely that the narrative, no matter how carefully constructed and censored, could not ultimately contain the homoerotic excess produced by the visual images.

In Prussian films of army life, the homoerotic moment is no less evident, despite attempts at repression. The pent-up sexual energy of the male group is channeled into ritualistic oaths of allegiance and aggressiveness toward the enemy. In *Theodor Körner* and countless other films, young men swear a personal oath to each other and to their cause, binding them in loyalty till death. Soldiers, says an officer in *Kolberg*, the last of the Ufa's monstrous *Durchhaltefilme*, are married to war. When faced with a hopeless battle in which death is a certainty, as in almost all of the Frederick films, the boys march together, side by side, eyes glazed, happily to their doom. To sacrifice one's life for the life of a *Kamerad* is the highest honor in the Prussian code of conduct.

However, it is in the Frederick films that the homoerotic moment is most clearly brought to the surface. Frederick is always more interested in men than women, whom he perceives as nothing more than necessary evils. In *Fridericus Rex* he mourns his dead generals more than his family: "Schwerin, Winterfeld, Katte. All of them have left me." The scene is repeated almost word for word in *Trenck*. Seeing Trenck in a mirror, he smashes it, jealous that Trenck is in love with his sister. While Frederick's court whispers of the privileges Trenck is enjoying, the king confesses to Trenck, during a ride on horseback, that he is reminded of his youth, a clear allusion to his relationship to Katte, which is taken up in *The Old King and the Young King*. Frederick's relationship to his wife is unambiguously stated in *The Flute Concert at Sanssouci*, where he hardly acknowledges her, while the ladies of the court characterize him as *weiberfeindlich*, i.e., misogynist.

Thus in the character of Frederick, two gay stereotypes make an appearance. On one hand is the soft, physically weak, flute-playing, French-literature-reading effeminate, on the other the aggressive, masochistic, self-sacrificing general in love with victory or death. It was Frederick as the supposedly asexual supreme commander of his men, that the fascists wished to propagate, often drawing direct parallels to the *Führer*, Adolf Hitler. Fritz demands in all of his films that his men fight to death. Thus, the repression of Eros ends in the unleashing of an aggressive Thanatos.

A Prussian U-boat commander in *Morgenrot (Dawn,* Gustav Ucicky, 1933) says, "We Germans maybe don't know how to live, but we certainly know how to die." Lotte Eisner quotes Clemenceau, who once noted that the Germans have a taste for death the way other nations do for life.[27] From Kleist to the German Romantics to Wagner's "Liebestod," German poets have described death in loving terms. In *Theodor Körner,* Eleanore speaks of her desire to sleep and never awake, while Körner himself writes, "outside my door dear death waits." Frederick II in *Fridericus Rex* wishes to find peace in death.

But it is only after the advent of the fascist film in 1933 that death on the battlefield is propagated as state ideology. In Prussian films from the Nazi era the death wish is ubiquitous. The Prussian hero of *Flüchtlinge (Refugees,* Gustav Ucicky, 1933) says that "to die for something is best of all." A hero's death is fetishized in Nazi literature, film, and music as a privilege of the Aryan *Übermenschen*. As the Nazi film historian Oskar Kalbus formulated it, "The idea is not foreign to us, but rather quite contemporary. Working, fighting, dying for a higher goal, the effort of one for all, the one unifying belief in the liberating power of the supreme sacrifice."[28] The dematerialization of the physical body into the power of the state allows death to serve as a passage into eternity. Being killed in action is presented as a glorious cavalry charge into the heavens rather than as a bloody, lonely, and dirty fate.

The *Freikorps* in *Körner* decide, true to their oath of loyalty, to break out of the encirclement by the French or die together. Korfes states in *Black Ranger Johanna* as the troops prepare to attack vastly superior force, "Even if we fall, we will have proven that there are men in Germany willing to die for their country." In *The Great King* Frederick demands a "wall of corpses" to hold up the enemy. In *Cadets* young teenagers defend a fortress alone against seasoned Cossacks, eerily presaging the Hitler youth of the last days of World War II, who faced tanks with small arms. Time and again in Prussian films, the troops are placed in a hopeless military situation, but still they fight to the end rather than retreat. Death or freedom, death or victory, the choice is always absolute and final. "The people arise, the storm is unleashed." Theodor Körner's words, quoted in Goebbels's 1943 speech on "total war" and again in *Kolberg*, thus become those of a martyr for a whole nation fixated on Thanatos.

Before the credits roll, however, the martyrs of the battlefield are promised eternal life in the collective memory of the nation. Death is articulated as an event of liberation and spiritual release. Prussian films end either with the survivors marching, orderly and refreshed, after the battle, cheered on by the masses, or with a column of ghostly martyrs, marching through the heavens, their invincibility in death signified by smiling faces. Death, the return to an inorganic state also guarantees the survival of the higher order, the state. In *Robert Koch* this relationship is made overt when Koch's assistant dies for the cause. With his master at his side, Fritz's eyes glaze over in peaceful death. Heavenly music on the track is accompanied by celestial images of flowing chiffon, followed immediately by the sound and images of Robert Koch's victory against his "democratic" opponents in the Imperial Parliament, equating Fritz's death with victory of the higher order. Likewise, the men, i.e., Fritz and Robert Koch, are bound in death, fanatically committed to their mission, while Fritz's wife is nowhere to be seen. Unlike American films, where the death of a hero is often punctuated with crosscutting to the female loved one, Prussian films only allow for male subjectivity.

The Prussian male, whether a simple foot-soldier or Frederick the Great himself, is marked as obsessional, as fanatically committed to the state. It is thus possible to read the metanarrative in Prussian films as a trajectory from the erotic to the thanatonic, from an erotic libidinal economy to a libido driven by aggression and obsessed with death. Given such a metanarrative in Prussian cinema, we can see how fascist ideology promotes the creation of obsessional libidinal types, who are fanatically dedicated to duty, willing to sublimate their erotic libidinal economies in favor of an aggressive thanatos drive, and ultimately bringing the supreme sacrifice for *Volk* and *Führer*.

In Prussian films, a fascist ideology of death functions to position the male spectator in a spectacle of self-sacrifice, destruction, and death, ultimately preparing him to face his own moment of decision in the world war to come.[29] Women remain invisible, both as figures of identification and as subjects. The success with which Nazi Germany's producers of canon fodder turned little Hitler youth into suicidal shock troops is a matter of historical record. To what degree German youth had internalized the slogans of Prussian films, such as *Heldentum* (heroism), *Kameradschaft, Verzicht und Opferbereitschaft* (renunciation and sacrifice), is demonstrated in a German cinema reception study of 1943. The popularity of Prussian films with German teenage boys is justified time and again in connection with such terms.[30] The consequences of the successful ideological campaign in Prussian films and other film genres that glorified German military might were still visible in 1945, when after the war had already been lost, gangs of so-called *Werwölfe*, mostly boys and young men in their teens, hid in the woods, sworn to continue a guerrilla war against the Allies in the name of Adolf Hitler, himself already a martyr for a nation obsessed with death.

Notes

1. This is a completely revised version of an essay originally published in German, under the title: "Liebe, Pflicht und die Erotik des Todes," *Preussen*

im Film, ed. Axel Marquardt and Heinz Rathsack (Reinbek: Rowohlt, 1981) 205–18.

2. Axel Marquardt and Heinz Rathsack, eds., *Preussen im Film* (Reinbek: Rowohlt, 1981) 234.

3. See Ulrich Gregor, "Verdrängung, Satire und Innerlichkeit. Preussen im Film nach 1945," Marquardt and Rathsack 39–54.

4. For more on the continuities in themes and personnel between Third Reich cinema and the FRG, see Claudius Seidl, *Der deutsche Film der fünfziger Jahre* (Munich: Heyne, 1987).

5. Heide Schlüpmann, "Momente erotischer Utopie—ästhetisierte Verdrängung. Zu *Mädchen in Uniform* und *Anna und Elisabeth,*" *Frauen und Film* 28 (Juni 1981): 28–31.

6. For an introduction to issues involving female subjectivity and the gaze see Constance Penley, ed., *Feminism and Film Theory* (New York: Routledge, 1988), particularly Laura Mulvey's essays, "Visual Pleasure and Narrative Cinema" and "Afterthoughts."

7. See Reinhard Kühnl, ed., *Faschismustheorien* (Reinbek: Rowohlt, 1979), Ernst Nolte, ed., *Theorien des Faschismus* (Königstein: Athenäum, 1979).

8. The literature on theories of fascism is voluminous. One of the best sources is still: Franz L. Neumann, *Behemoth: The Structure and Practice of National Socialism* (New York: Oxford UP, 1942; New York: Octagon, 1963).

9. See Claudia Koonz, *Mothers in the Fatherland: Women, the Family, and Nazi Politics* (New York: St. Martin's, 1987).

10. Wilhelm Reich, *The Mass Psychology of Fascism* (New York: Farrar, 1970) 105.

11. Susan Sontag, "Fascinating Fascism," *New York Review of Books* 6 Feb. 1975, reprinted in Bill Nichols, ed., *Movies and Methods* (Berkeley: U of California P, 1976) 41.

12. Sigmund Freud, "Beyond the Pleasure Principle," *Standard Edition of the Complete Psychological Works of Sigmund Freud,* vol. 18 (London: Hogarth, 1955) 36–43.

13. Sigmund Freud, "Two Encyclopedia Articles: B) The Libido Theory" (1922), *Collected Papers,* vol. 5 (London: Hogarth, 1953) 135.

14. Sigmund Freud, "New Introductory Lectures on Psycho-Analysis," *The Standard Edition,* vol. 22 (London: Hogarth, 1964) 96, 107, 115.

15. Sigmund Freud, "An Outline of Psycho-Analysis," *The Standard Edition,* vol. 23 (London: Hogarth, 1964) 135.

16. Sigmund Freud, "Libidinal Types" (1931), *Collected Papers,* vol. 5 (London: Hogarth, 1953) 248.

17. Ludwig Eidelberg, *An Outline of Comparative Pathology of the Neuroses* (New York: International UP, 1954) 35.

18. Eidelberg 36.

19. See David Bordwell, Janet Staiger, and Kristin Thompson, *The Classical Hollywood Cinema: Film Style & Mode of Production to 1960* (New York: Columbia UP, 1985).

20. Christian Metz, *The Imaginary Signifier: Psychoanalysis in the Cinema* (Bloomington: U of Indiana P, 1982) 94.

21. For an American view on this subject see Gregor Ziemer, *Education for Death: The Making of a Nazi* (New York: Oxford UP, 1941). See also Jan-

Christopher Horak, *Anti-Nazifilme der deutschsprachigen Emigration von Hollywood 1939–1945* (Münster: MAKS-Publikationen, 1984, 1986) 236–54.

22. See Andrea Huemer, *Von der "ewigen Hüterin" und einem Steuerungsinstrument des "Unbewussten": Frau und Film—Frau im Film als Objekt der nationalsozialistischen Propaganda*, diss., U of Vienna, 1985 (Vienna Institut für Theaterwissenschaft; 1985).

23. For an analysis of another fictionalized Nazi biography, see Jan-Christopher Horak, "Luis Trenker's *The Kaiser of California*: How the West Was Won, Nazi Style," *The Historical Journal of Film, Radio and Television* 6.2 (1986): 181–88.

24. See Mary Ann Doane, *The Desire to Desire: The Woman's Film of the 1940s* (Bloomington: Indiana UP, 1987) 70–95.

25. On this point see Klaus Theweleit, *Männerphantasien 2 Männerkörper—zur Psychoanalyse des weissen Terrors* (Reinbek: Rowohlt, 1980) 328. Also available in English translation, *Male Fantasies. Vol. 2: Male Bodies: Toward the Psychoanalysis of the White Terror*, trans. Stephen Conway et al. (Minneapolis: U of Minnesota P, 1989).

26. Hans Scheugl, *Sexualität und Neurose im Film* (Munich: Hanser, 1974) 227. Author's translation.

27. Lotte Eisner, *The Haunted Screen: German Expressionism in the Cinema* (Berkeley: U of California P, 1969) 89.

28. Oskar Kalbus, *Vom Werden Deutscher Filmkunst, 2. Teil, Der Tonfilm* (Altona-Bärenfeld: Zigaretten=Bilderdienst Altona=Bärenfeld, 1935) 104.

29. This agenda of the Propaganda Ministry was even more explicitly articulated in the German newsreels. See David Welch, *Propaganda and the German Cinema, 1933–1945* (Oxford: Clarendon, 1983).

30. "Die Stimmung der Jugend," A. U. Sander, *Jugend und Film*, Sonderveröffentlichung Nr. 6 von *Das Junge Deutschland* (Berlin, 1944), reprinted in Gerd Albrecht, ed., *Film im Dritten Reich* (Karlsruhe: SCHAUBURG Fricker & Co. OHG + DOKU-Verlag, 1979) 156–88.

5

Leni Riefenstahl's
Feature Films
and the Question
of a Fascist Aesthetic

Linda Schulte-Sasse

In labeling a text "Nazi" or "fascist," critics often restrict their criteria (to the extent these are articulated at all) to content-based motifs such as the valorization of a *Führer* or leader figure, the exaltation of nature, the glorification of the military and of death, or the negative portrayal of racial (especially Jewish) groups. Although these motifs clearly pervade National Socialist culture, one can question whether, on one hand, they are present in all of Nazi culture and whether, on the other hand, they are unique to that culture. Already in the thirties and forties Bertolt Brecht and Walter Benjamin offered analyses of Nazi culture that went a step further by concentrating on structural in addition to thematic tendencies. Both thinkers address nazism's attempt to break down the boundaries between the aesthetic and real life and the mobilization of technology for this purpose. Brecht enlists a metaphor, political discourse as theater, to describe nazism's destruction of the public sphere; Benjamin describes the same process as an "aestheticization of political" life, engineered as spectacle *for* but also *by* the masses.[1] National Socialism, like other forms of fascism, is of course far too heterogeneous and inconsistent to be reduced to any single strategy or set of motifs. Nevertheless, Brecht's and Benjamin's theorization of National Socialism points to the impossibility of understanding fascism without addressing its structural tendencies, without examining modes of address in its artistic and political texts as well as the institutionalization of these texts. This is not to suggest that predominant textual motifs are not important, only that they are inextricably connected to textual strategies and, in particular, to processes of aestheticization.

Yet rather than offering the consolation of a neat taxonomy separating a fascist text from a nonfascist text—and thus allowing contemporary critics to place National Socialism at a comfortable distance—a structural approach to the fascist aesthetic likewise opens up a Pandora's box. The reason is that it automatically raises the same two questions, as do content-based definitions, only with greater urgency. First, do the majority of narrative texts produced during the Third Reich qualify as fascist texts in any strict sense? Do they, in other words, break down the boundary between the aesthetic and life and thereby lead the spectator into an aestheticized activism? Second, do various contemporary (non-Nazi) phenomena that live off the same tension between reality and the imaginary and likewise attempt to transgress the boundary between the imaginary and the real then qualify as fascist? The latter is particularly disconcerting in its implicit suggestion that fascism, if understood in a structural sense, may be alive and well in American political discourse, which is increasingly determined by the dissemination of aestheticized images, and in many other phenomena in contemporary societies currently discussed as features of postmodern societies. Since 1945 the terms *Nazi* and *fascist* have been used so restrictively as to shed little light onto nazism's success in evoking a collective identity in its constituents, or so loosely as to signify a historically useless catchword for whatever its user opposes (and allowing this user to mythify the self as a romanticized opponent of the hegemonic order).

Before offering some tentative answers to these questions in the final section of this essay, I would like to reconsider the notion of fascist aesthetics using the quintessential articulator of the Nazi film aesthetic, Leni Riefenstahl, as my point of departure. I intend to examine, however, not her celebrated propaganda vehicles but her two feature films, *Das blaue Licht* (*The Blue Light*, 1932) and *Tiefland* (1954), as works that occupy the grey zone between films whose content, production, and distribution history render them clear examples of "Nazi propaganda" and films clearly dissociated from National Socialism or its antimodern precursors. The two films challenge rigid criteria of taxonomy since neither can be branded a "Nazi" film in a specific chronological sense, nor can they be absolved from such a labeling since they feature Riefenstahl as director, producer, and acting "star" and since they belong to the suspicious mountain film genre Susan Sontag labels "an anthology of proto-Nazi sentiments."[2]

The process from inception to release (or rerelease) of *The Blue Light* and *Tiefland* spans a period from the early thirties to the fifties; whatever their appeal, in each case it pre- and postdated the Nazi regime.[3] *The Blue Light,* on which the leftist filmmaker and critic Béla Balázs collaborated,[4] originally had its premiere in 1932 and was released a second time after the popular success of Riefenstahl's *Olympia* in 1938. Since the original film negatives were eventually lost, Riefenstahl gathered outtakes, redubbed the voices and again released the film in 1952. *Tiefland's* origin is even more controversial since it was produced during the war and employed Gypsies held in concentration camps. Riefenstahl originally planned a film version of Eugen d'Albert's 1903 opera of the same title in 1933. Although she began filming in 1940, various circumstances, including political upheaval, demands on her by the Nationalsozialistische Deutsche Arbeiterpartei (NSDAP), and illness delayed the completion of filming until 1944. She was not able to finish editing *Tiefland* until after the war and after she had undergone "denazification." Finally the film was distributed by Allianz in 1954, when it enjoyed "some critical success."[5]

Public response to the two films has ranged from an adulation of Riefenstahl's genius for "sheer pictorial beauty"[6] to a condemnation of the films as transparent expressions of Nazi ideology. This disparity is consistent with the general assessment of Riefenstahl as either a genius victimized by her times or as a diabolical manipulator. Perhaps because of this ambivalence she has been the object of a singular fascination among the public and scholars alike, as indicated by the use of such epithets as "legend," "fallen goddess," and "deceptive myth" to describe her. The controversy surrounding Riefenstahl can be summarized in two alternative positions: the minimizing of her Nazi connection based on an endorsement of the transhistorical sanctity of the artistic sphere[7] and, on the other hand, the insistence—articulated most vocally by Siegfried Kracauer and Susan Sontag—that her entire career displays a direct connection to Nazi aesthetics and ideology, including her feature films with their romantic anticapitalism and semiotically charged use of landscape.[8]

For obvious reasons 1933 cannot be treated as a magic year in which all earlier art forms were aborted, and much can be learned by exploring nazism's indebtedness to generic traditions, both literary and filmic, as Kracauer's and Sontag's critique suggests. Like the latter, I consider the exculpation of Riefenstahl as an apolitical artist merely in search of pristine beauty ludicrous. Nevertheless, restricting the issue to the terms of a binary opposition—whatever side one chooses—does not bring one much closer to grasping fascist textual strategies in a way that transcends an individual case. I prefer to eschew a personalized debate on the exaltation or excoriation of an individual and search for criteria in assessing the films that allow both for historical specificity and problematic continuities. In doing so I will propose an operative distinction between a fascist text and the more general category of a modern[9] narrative that is informed by a certain type of antimodern nostalgia as a means of addressing whether—despite the thematic and cinematic continuities between Riefenstahl's fiction films and her Nazi propaganda vehicles—the former in fact contain inherently fascist traits. I will argue that while Nazi art and rhetoric is pervaded by a nostalgic longing for an ideal located in a vaguely defined past, this category does not suffice to distinguish it from other artistic forms.

Junta's Impenetrable Otherness: *The Blue Light* as a Modern Text

The Blue Light, the first film Riefenstahl ever directed, closely adheres to the mountain film genre in which she had previously worked as an actress and dancer, most frequently under the directorship of Arnold Fanck.

The mountain girl Junta (Leni Riefenstahl) is considered a witch by the villagers of Santa Maria in the Italian Dolomites since she is the only one able to scale Mount Cristallo without falling to her death. The village has already lost numerous young men to the lure of the mysterious blue light that emanates from the mountain with every full moon. The Viennese painter Vigo (Mathias Wiemann) comes to the area and, attracted to Junta, begins living in the primitive mountain retreat she shares with the shepherd boy, Guzzi. One evening Vigo follows Junta up the mountain to the source of the light, a crystal grotto. Hoping to secure financial prosperity for Junta and for the impoverished village, he directs the villagers to the grotto, where they mine the crystals. Later, discovering her grotto ravished, Junta falls despondently to her death. The villagers continue living in prosperity and revere her memory.

In a recent essay, Eric Rentschler carefully examined the complex history of the film's various incarnations.[10] The original 1932 version surrounded Junta's tale with a frame story set in the present, in which the villagers tell her legend to a visiting honeymooning couple. Riefenstahl's reconstruction of the film in 1952 omits the frame. Thus, if one examines the evolution of *The Blue Light*, one ends up with two stories: one about Junta herself and one explicitly about the modern world's relationship to her. The frame accompanying the original version creates, as Rentschler analyzes, a tension between a modern present and a past lost to modernity. Although the modern couple is deeply affected by Junta's legend, a distance remains between the couple's present and Junta's nostalgic world. The appearance of the modern honeymooning couple is particularly conclusive since the elision of the couple's gender distinctions through the aviator jumpsuits they wear and the woman's positioning at a car's steering wheel suggests a decadent Weimar culture with its threat to patriarchy, for which Junta's tale serves as "a needed corrective."[11] Yet the scene is more than just a commentary on Weimar decadence; it also provokes a critical commentary on a modern relationship between the imaginary and the real, for the imaginary reconciliation embodied in the story of Junta could hardly survive in the real world of modernity.

The loss of the frame in the 1952 version may de-emphasize the distance between the real and the ideal but need not erase it since there still remains a disjuncture between Junta's legend and the timeless present to which her legend is addressed. With or without the frame, the film depends on a sense of loss of an other space that somehow used to be. Yet both versions offer the observer (within or outside the text) subjected to modern pressures a compensatory pleasure in savoring that loss. Whereas the 1932 version appears evaluative in its perspective, the later version reflects a tragic, Spenglerian view of the struggle between the elemental and civilization, between a nonalienated union with nature and forms of alienation engendered by exchange value: The demise of Junta's realm appears lamentable but virtually inevitable. It seems the 1952 version cannot decide whether to be an anticapitalist narrative or not. Crucial to the film's ambivalent position is the sympathetic painter Vigo, who among the film's characters comes closest to providing a figure of spectator identification. He, like the spectator, is an outsider from a secularized world, and with him we explore the enigmas posed by the narrative: Who are the lost boys? Who is Junta? Why do they fear her? When Vigo shifts from observer to agent in the narrative; i.e., when he provides the villagers with the knowledge with which they can demystify nature in the service of instrumentality, he does so with the sincere conviction that the material gain will benefit Junta as well, promising her she will "no longer have to go around in rags and barefoot!" Without the sympathetic Vigo, the weight of negative semantic markers[12] would fall decidedly upon the villagers (i.e., civilization), whose cruelty to Junta is portrayed as a kind of mob behavior, which, coupled with their repression through cultural mores, institutionalized religion, and superstition, colors the spectator's sympathetic response to their fear for their sons' lives. The society seems *gleichgeschaltet*, with the villagers displaying synchronized movement, as when three black-clad old women turn simultaneously to exchange hostile gazes with Junta. An irony lies in the fact that Vigo, the figure most responsive to the freedom from cultural repression that Junta represents, is simultaneously the figure whose actions destroy nature and Junta with it. Because of Vigo's dominant role, the story fails to provide an unambiguous space (either in the anticapitalist or the nostalgic, modern vein) from which the narrative trajectory can be evaluated. It also provides a commentary on the ambivalent role of the intellectual and the artist as agents in modern societies since their intentions rarely coincide with the effect of their intervention.

I would like to consider whether either of these versions is a fascist narrative or in fact merely a modern or romantic narrative characterized by a tension between an instrumental, modern reality and something that is other, be it nature, woman, or art, and by a nostalgic longing for that other as a space of reconciliation, a space of redemption lost to modernity. Thinkers from Immanuel Kant to Max Weber to Jürgen Habermas have described modernity as compartmentalized with different realms of praxis, and since the eighteenth century the realm of the aesthetic has been treasured for offering an imaginary space of solace free from commerce, alienation, and the *agonia* of modern life. A constitutive aspect of fascism on the other hand is that it attempts to dissolve the boundary between the institutionally separated spheres of modern reality and provides a space of reconciliation, albeit a *Schein*—or illusory reconciliation *within* reality. The space of reconciliation otherwise offered by the aesthetic is expanded to penetrate all aspects of life. As Benjamin suggests with his category of the "aestheticization of politics," the compartmentalization of modernity is broken down, the aesthetic sphere begins to permeate others, including that of politics. It seems to me that despite nazism's undeniable exploitation of the structure of modernity (and specifically its exploitation of romantic motifs), *The Blue Light*—in both of its versions—exemplifies a modern and not a fascist structure in which Junta remains an inaccessible other ultimately lost to Vigo and to the spectator who occupies Vigo's fictional space. In other words, although *The Blue Light* shares thematic and stylistic traits with many Nazi films (and other artistic forms), it lacks structural elements characteristic of a fascist discourse. While the same can be said of many films produced during the Third Reich, others have at least moments in which the boundaries between the aesthetic and the real begin to dissolve.

A central example for the preservation of the imaginary as imaginary in the film is the metaphor of the blue light that can never be captured, i.e., made real within modernity but can only be destroyed by modernity. Underlying the light metaphor are two allusions that support the interpretation of the film as a modern text. It can be read first as a demonic natural force reminiscent of the *Tannhäuser* legend in which young men are lured to their deaths in the Venusberg. For the villagers, Junta is nothing less than a demonic and destructive Venus whose eroticism threatens their social order; the innkeeper can be likened to a kind of Eckhart figure attempting to protect his offspring from the lure of dissolution (*Entgrenzung*). Just as Eichendorff's *Marmorbild* contrasts Venus with the madonnalike Bianca, Riefenstahl's editing frequently juxtaposes Junta with Lucia, a young woman who represents domesticity and containment of eroticism, suggested by the contrast between the head scarf that tightly binds her hair and Junta's free-flowing hair. Yet the demonization of Junta is restricted to the point of view of the villagers, i.e., society, and the film's exposition strongly aligns the spectator with Junta as the victim of an internally repressed people constantly shown closing windows to shut out the light of the full moon, and thus the danger of eroticism or the dissolution of boundaries. The scene in which Junta is conspicuously left outside while the villagers enter the fortifying vessel of the massive town church illustrates how the community's Christian bonding serves to ostracize those outside the social order.

Second, the blue light with its obvious allusion to Novalis's blue flower, represents a general romantic longing or *Sehnsucht*, linked to woman.[13] This *Sehnsucht* springs from an awareness of lack, creating a desire that eludes fulfillment and in being "mined," to borrow Rentschler's term, is destroyed. The film displaces Junta, as object of desire, to the space of representation and thus upholds the gap between the real and the imaginary other that is constitutive of the modern. As discursive phenomena, Junta and the blue light remain a focal point of nostalgia standing in for a fulfillment, for a presence that can never be achieved. The romantic motif of language within the film augments Junta's inaccessibility. She understands the signs of nature, recoiling from Vigo after reading an apparent message in a crystal, but fails to comprehend Vigo's language, just as she utterly lacks comprehension of his world. Vigo appears to possess some insight into this modern structure when he remarks that "it couldn't be more beautiful" if they were able to communicate via language.

Stylized poses, filters, shadows, and other cinematic techniques work throughout the film to equate Junta with a *Sehnsucht* for that which is always already beyond the reach of the pedestrian being. Vision becomes a weapon with which Vigo captures Junta when he paints her, when he watches her sleep, and finally when he finds her corpse: "In a subjective shot that aligns the camera's gaze with that of the onscreen artist, we see how the male look virtually metamorphoses Junta's countenance."[14] Rentschler draws parallels between the vampire in Murnau's *Nosferatu* (1922) and Vigo sucking the lifeblood out of Junta. While this reading is accurate, it should not be overlooked that Vigo's appropriation of Junta is simultaneous with his loss of her, and the final closeup shot of Vigo shows a tear rolling down his cheek. Vigo's role as the textual representative of the viewer's subject position reinforces the nostalgic, aestheticistic effect of this text; an effect that undermines a purely fascist appropriation of the narrative. (It is interesting in this context that Riefenstahl's defense of her Nazi past consists in likewise restricting herself to the utopian space of the aesthetic. She insists that her art was untouched by any motivation other than the pursuit of beauty. "Whatever is purely realistic, slice-of-life, which is average, quotidian, doesn't interest me . . . I am fascinated by what is beautiful, strong, healthy, by what is living. I seek harmony.")[15]

Tiefland and *The Blue Light:* Two Modernist Narrative Traditions

As is implicit in its title, *Tiefland* has in common with *The Blue Light* the basic antimodernist constellation of civilization opposing nature. Yet *Tiefland* shifts the source of narrative conflict and aligns the spectator more decidedly with one set of values.

The shepherd Pedro (Franz Eichberger) comes from the mountains into the lowlands with the skin of a wolf that he killed with his bare hands. He sees the Gypsy girl Martha (Leni Riefenstahl) dancing in the tavern of Roccabruna and falls in love with her. Marquis Don Sebastian (Bernhard Minetti) also sees Martha and proceeds to make her his mistress. Don Sebastian is hated in the entire region for his exploitation of the peasants, whose water source he has rechanneled to supply the cattle he raises. He also has large debts with the mayor and is thus forced to marry the wealthy mayor's daughter. In order to keep Martha at his disposal, he marries her to Pedro. When in the night of both marriages Don Sebastian comes to be with Martha, Pedro kills him exactly as he had killed the wolf. Pedro and Martha return to the mountains.

As a means of contrasting the structure of *Tiefland* with that of *The Blue Light*, I would like to draw upon Jürgen Link's analysis of what he calls "the social psychological drama." This genre, which dates back to the mid-eighteenth century and includes both popular narratives and "high" art, is constituted by varying relationships between two central factors: social class and "natural human qualities."[16] Link conceptualizes these two factors as axes of a matrix, with each character in a given drama located somewhere in the matrix according to his/her specific combination of class and character: "aristocracy and evil," "bourgeoisie and virtue," etc. He analyzes how in later forms of the social psychological drama the ever-increasing dominance of the "natural human" axis at the expense of the social axis coupled with the simplification of the former to a basic plus/minus "heart" scheme has led to a devolution of the genre to kitsch, which fulfills a socially affirmative function in its avoidance of social contradictions. In other words, modern popular narratives tend increasingly to define their characters simply as "good" or "heartless," neglecting the complicating relations between character and social class addressed by a Schiller or Lessing.

Tiefland can likewise easily be conceptualized in terms of the axes of social class versus "natural human qualities," betraying an indebtedness to the paradigm of the bourgeois tragedy and its historical descendents in popular literature (see figure 1). As in the bourgeois tragedy, the forces driving the narrative action forward are located largely on the axis of social class, while spectator sympathy or rejection is elicited largely on the human axis. Each character can be easily located on a basic scale from "good" to "evil," a constellation carried to an extreme by the verbal motif of the devil linked with Don Sebastian and underscored by his physiognomy and behavior (defiance of moral laws). Moreover, social power and good human characteristics tend to be in inverse proportion to each other. *Tiefland* bears out what Link cites as another trend in the devolution of social psychological drama to kitsch: the reduction of unstereotypic combinations of traits that permit the appearance of an ambiguous figure such as Schiller's Lady Milford, who is unchaste but still good.[17] Instead, Riefenstahl's film displays the most typical combinations possible: the lecherous, evil aristocrat, the honest miller, the pure shepherd. With its traditional binary oppositions *Tiefland* is far less ambiguous

Configurations Matrix to TIEFLAND

Axis of social qualities	"good" / + heart						"evil" / - heart					
	– Calculating				+ Calculating		– Calculating				+ Calculating	
	blind to calculation		aware of calculation				blind to calculation		aware of calculation			
	+erotically attractive	-erotically attractive	+erotically attractive	-erotically attractive	-erotically attractive	+erotically attractive	-erotically attractive	+erotically attractive	-erotically attractive	+erotically attractive	+erotically attractive	-erotically attractive
"high" +Aristocracy											Don Sebastian	Camillo (Don Sebastian's Administrator)
–Aristocracy											Mayor's Daughter Amalia	Mayor
+bourgeois												
–bourgeois (peasants)				Miller, Natario, Old Woman, other peasants								
outside social community **"low"**	Pedro Martha			Nando (old shepard)								

Axis of 'natural'-human Qualities

1. Configurations Matrix to *Tiefland*. A diagram of the relationships in *Tiefland* illustrates how the film reproduces a configuration dating back to the bourgeois tragedy, albeit in reductive, sentimentalized form. The predictable inverse relationship between possession of social power and positive human qualities leads to typical, black-and-white characterizations. The dominance of binary oppositions makes for easy resolution (whether happy or tragic) of conflict. An element *not* generally found in the enlightenment tradition is the glamorized portrayal of figures whose enigmatic origins and life-style place them outside the social order.

than *The Blue Light* in its assignment of value; the former belongs more unabashedly in the tradition of sentimental anticapitalism, linking wealth one-sidedly with materialistic values.

The same matrix does not work as well for *The Blue Light* (see figure 2). Despite the occasional tendencies of the villagers toward mob behavior, all characters are located on the left (plus "heart") side of the matrix. Thus although the narrative elicits a strong sympathy for the mistreated Junta, no character is depicted as evil, and the constellation plus/minus "heart" so central to popular narratives does not determine *The Blue Light*. Social class as a power factor is virtually absent, hinted at only in the factor of plus/minus "enlightenment" (connoting instrumentality, practicality, and progress, as opposed to naïveté or superstition), which implies formal education and exposure to a rationalized, secularized society. Instead the characters are identified by their place on two central scales: one ranging from "superstition" to "enlightenment"; the other from "alienation from nature" to "mystical union with nature." The relationships between the two are arbitrary; the most "enlightened" figure, the artist Vigo, also has a greater feeling for nature than do the superstitious villagers.

In its valorization of "virtue," its happy ending, and its triumph of heart over social class, *Tiefland* adheres more closely to a model—however sentimentalized—of enlightenment literature than to a model of romantic literature; *The Blue Light* with all its ambiguities tends toward the latter. Its story culminates not in the tragic loss of a utopian space as does the earlier film but in its fulfillment (happy ending). Nevertheless, since the fulfillment offered by the text is a displacement into the imaginary and since it again relies on the tension between social modernity (inside and outside the text; i.e., including the viewer's modernity) and the mountain sanctuary to which the lovers flee, *Tiefland* also typifies a modern rather than a fascist narrative. Despite the significant differences between *The Blue Light* and *Tiefland*, both exhibit a modern structure in their narrative and cinematic privileging of one spatial sphere, the mountains, and of woman. The special status they assign to the mountains and to woman is analogous to the status of the aesthetic in modern societies as the sphere untouched by banalities and duplicities of everyday life.

Configurations Matrix to THE BLUE LIGHT

Axis of social qualities			"good"				"evil"
			+ heart				- heart
			+ mystical union with nature		- mystical union with nature		
			+erotically attractive	-erotically attractive	+erotically attractive	-erotically attractive	
"high" +bourgeois	+ education/ enlightenment				Vigo (feeling for nature)		
	+ superstition/ naivité						
-bourgeois (peasants)	+education/ enlightenment						
	+ superstition/ naivité				Tonio (innkeeper's son) Lucia (his wife)	Innkeeper other villagers (tendency to mob behavior)	
outside social community "low"	+ education/ enlightenment						
	+ superstition/ naivité		Junta	Guzzi (pre-pubescent)			

Axis of 'natural'-human Qualities

2. Configurations Matrix to *The Blue Light*. The characters from *The Blue Light* cannot be relegated to diagonally opposite ends of the matrix as in *Tiefland*, since the former, with its indebtedness to the romantic tradition, operates with ambiguities rather than binary oppositions. All characters are essentially good, although the villagers display narrow-mindedness and sadistic mob behavior, and Vigo unintentionally destroys Junta. (The arrows represent tendencies within the characters or tendential developments within the plot.) Social class disappears as a narrative factor, except as reflected in the degree to which characters display an enlightened attitude. The failure of the narrative to focus on good versus evil, but rather on irreconcilable differences, eliminates the possibility of a clear-cut resolution to conflict as in *Tiefland*; instead, the basic tragic conflict is resolved when one set of values (nature) is nostalgically subjugated to another (instrumentality). The film contains a contradictory tension *within* the plus "heart" realm that would be impossible in a "social psychological drama" such as *Tiefland*.

Each film involves essentially two narrative spaces with only one figure (Vigo/Martha) capable of traversing several spaces relatively unscathed. The spatial constellation of *Tiefland* is actually triadic if one considers not only the opposition mountain-lowlands but the split within the lowlands between the spaces of aristocratic intrigue, predominantly the marquis's stone fortress, and the peasant spaces, predominantly the mill. Although bound by social laws and lacking the pristine freedom of the mountains, the latter represents a positive force of community imbued with a closeness to nature; indeed, the mill is the locale in which the eventual union of Martha and Pedro occurs.[18]

The exhilirating effect of the mountain scenes in *Tiefland*, which usually begin with an expansive low-angle, open-air shot of backlit mountains, cumulus clouds, and soaring birds, depends largely on their position in the film's syntax. The effect of the scenes intensifies because of their stark deviation from the aura of constraint permeating the lowlands. The scene in which Don Sebastian first appears, for example, stresses visually the literally weighty force of social class. It begins with a long shot of the stone fortress, followed by a cut to the interior. The camera travels in a circular motion around the large room before revealing the marquis in an oversized chair behind an oversized table. The camera's self-conscious dwelling on the marquis's massive surroundings points not only to the linkage between the emptiness and coldness of the stone fortress and his character but to his confinement in his stone prison and aristocratic coding. Throughout the film the castle scenes are marked by a preponderance of barriers: the lattice work on the large doors and windows suggests imprisonment; even Martha's fourposter bed is draped by fabric that seems to imprison her while Don Sebastian constantly reminds her of his obsessive power over her. When Don Sebastian seduces Martha, we see only their shadows, dominated by the shadow of a lattice-framed door in the background, suggesting a spider web in which Martha is enmeshed.

Both films enlist the semantic traditions of water and wine in delineating their spatial distinctions. Massive waterfalls figure prominently in the nature scenes, suggesting Freudian connotations of natural sexuality and serving as backdrops for the innocent eroticism of the *Naturkinder* Junta and Pedro. In *Tiefland* water also becomes a significant narrative motif as the natural, God-given life-force of the farmers, withheld unnaturally by the despotic Don Sebastian.[19] The scene in which workers divert the natural flow of the water away from the farmers recalls the picks that decimate Junta's crystal grotto in *The Blue Light*. No shot in either film clearly reveals the faces of the workers; if visible at all, they are shown from a distance or take the form of a shadowy silhouette. Each scene highlights closeups of picks and shovels, giving the impression that instruments work independently and implying an abstract representation of modernization, of instrumental forces at work.

Tiefland self-consciously aligns wine with the maligned wealthy classes and with sexuality. Don Sebastian signals his rejection of the mayor's rich daughter by insisting on drinking water rather than wine with her. His insistence, by contrast, that Martha drink wine with him constitutes his first sexual innuendo in a stylized seduction scene culminating in Martha's hand knocking over the glasses and spilling the red wine as the marquis carries her off. The spilled wine becomes a visual metaphor of Martha's violation, standing in for the blood of a virgin. The shot recalls a similar strategy from *The Blue Light*, when the plundering of Junta's grotto is followed by a jump cut to a circle of male hands joining in a toast. Again red wine spills conspicuously on the tablecloth below, suggesting at once deflowering and death, as Junta is sacrificed to instrumentality.

The redemptive space indistinguishable from woman in *The Blue Light* is inhabited in *Tiefland* by a male, Pedro, who shares a number of characteristics with Junta (as well as with the prepubescent shepherd boy Guzzi). Both share a mystical union with nature coupled with an absolute oblivion to the ways of the world. They also share an unconscious eroticism that exercises considerable influence over others. In *The Blue Light* the repressed villagers channel this erotic attraction into a hostility absent in *Tiefland*, where Pedro is an object of playful female desire, as in the scene when he is positioned conspicuously at the end of a long rectangular table, at a distance from an audience of giggling peasant girls leering at him. Significantly, both Junta and Pedro are shown sleeping in strikingly similar poses: their bare chests highlighted by an almost celestial lighting, their erotic, restless movements suggesting an innate sensuality.

Despite his unambiguously male diegetic role as the agent who eventually appropriates Martha, Pedro is in some ways femininized. He is a nurturant figure when he, like Junta, serves milk (providing the third element in the wine-water motif chain) or when he nurses the unconscious Martha, rendering him almost a male counterpart of Klaus Theweleit's "white nurse."[20] The softness of his features and curly blond hair suggest femininity, especially in contrast with the sharp, Mephistophelian features of Don Sebastian (cf. also the obvious male sexual overtones in the nickname of "wolf" the peasants give Don Sebastian, as well as is his steer, from which, as the story stresses, he does not profit materially,[21] versus Pedro's association with the lambs he is forever rescuing). An undifferentiated, not-yet-modernized society can be portrayed as androgynous.

The wholesome Pedro nonetheless lacks the qualities of enigmatic otherness that characterize Junta and that are essential to the structure of modernity, for he is too well integrated with the peasants as representatives of "civilization." His relative social integration makes sense with regard to gender, for it is woman who has been "a receptacle for all kinds of projections, displaced fears and anxieties . . . brought about by modernization."[22] The role of enigma in *Tiefland* is again reserved for woman; Martha, like Junta, functions as a disturbance or what Teresa di Lauretis calls a "mythical obstacle."[23] They are similar in their positions as total outsiders (Junta is called a "witch"; Martha "the stranger"), in their murky origins, and in their lack of civilized training. Just as it remains inexplicable how Junta mastered mountain-climbing, Martha "never learned" to dance but has it "in her blood." Both exercise a mesmerizing effect on others, on children and adults alike. Moreover, it is Junta and Martha who are the specularized objects on which the films' titillating effects depend. Although Martha is specularized throughout the film, nowhere is this more crucial than in the tavern dance scene, which bears ample evidence of how the innocence of Riefenstahl's characters "contrasts with the less than innocent strategies of [her] camera" in depicting woman "as an erotic presence and a seductive force."[24] The scene begins as Pedro passes the tavern and peers through the window (traversing with his eyes a barrier to erotic pleasure) at Martha's body, fetishized by a series of shots fragmenting her body parts, which move sensuously with the rhythm of the music. Shots of Martha alternate with shots traveling through the crowd of lustful men, creating a frenzy that ceases only when Don Sebastian enters, closes the door behind him, thus shutting Pedro literally and figuratively out of the picture, and appropriates Martha with his masterful gaze. The scene encapsulates the narrative's central events, when Pedro hands over the wolf's skin to Don Sebastian to obtain a reward, and when Martha feverishly shoves away a spectator who lunges toward her. But most importantly, it establishes Martha/Riefenstahl as the consummate representation of desire, as much through reaction shots of dazzled men as through her Carmen-like erotic presence.

One could scarcely find in film history a more typical example of the paradigm Laura Mulvey put forth in 1975 in which the woman acts "as object of the combined gaze of spectator and all the male protagonists in the film. . . . isolated, glamorous, on display, sexualized."[25] Leni Riefenstahl was in the unusual position in film history of playing a dual role as both object of the gaze and controlling eye behind it.[26] Yet, particularly from a feminist vantage point, it is tempting to overstress the notion of a conscious decision behind Riefenstahl's self-fetishization, as Ruby Rich does when she states that Riefenstahl "was granted 'permission' by the patriarchy to be privileged in its power *in exchange* for adopting its values" (my emphasis).[27] It seems to me that Rich underestimates a possible slippage between the roles of object and controller and the fact that the enunciating agency in a film is not totally identifiable with (or controlled by) the director or writer but located in a larger ideological apparatus.[28] Moreover, precisely readings delineating the affinities of Riefenstahl's early and late work to fascist aesthetics imply that she had adopted such values well before Hitler seized power. I am suggesting that—her opportunism notwithstanding—Leni Riefenstahl's project may not have been deliberate complicity with patriarchy "in exchange" for privilege but that an internalized acceptance of woman's role as object permitted her narcissistically to enjoy fetishizing her own body. John Berger has discussed the split self-engendered in women by western culture as comprising a female side that is surveyed by others (analogous to Mulvey's object of the male gaze) and a male side that constantly surveys the self being surveyed (analogous to the male looker)[29]—yet only with the help of relatively recent feminist analysis has the complicitous function of these contradictory roles been articulated. I believe Leni Riefenstahl's film practice exercises this very dual role, that it does not necessarily play along with but naturalizes and relishes the objectified role of woman in patriarchy.

Through her own fetishizing camera work Riefenstahl/Martha remains, like Junta, an allegory of desire. Although Don Sebastian renders her an object of exchange (first with a Gypsy, then with Pedro), she nonetheless remains an elusive object of desire for him. Just as Junta is appropriated by male vision at the end of *The Blue Light*, Martha is finally appropriated by Pedro, again in a manner consistent with Mulvey's original paradigm: "as the narrative progresses she falls in love with the main male protagonist and becomes his property, losing her outward glamorous characteristics, her generalized sexuality, her show-girl connotations; her eroticism is subjected to the male star alone."[30] As suggested by Mulvey's description, Martha's "redemption" comes at the expense of her eroticism (at least for the pleasure of the viewer) but likewise at the expense of sexual vitality in general. The exorcism of this vitality is achieved as Pedro kills the "wolf" Don Sebastian (i.e., bestial and merely possessive sexuality) to obtain his reward and complete the circular closure of the narrative. The film's final scene is a long, backlit pastoral image of Martha and Pedro walking in the mountains, turning so that they are walking with their backs to the camera, as in the romantic tradition of painting,[31] into a celestial beam of sunlight. The scene despecularizes both figures, who blend into the overwhelming natural background and at the end of the scene are barely distinguishable. As they pass by, their gazes focus neither on each other nor on the camera but on space, giving them a glazed, exalted look, a look oblivious to the spectator and to the modern world below.

The trajectory of *Tiefland* carries Martha from a state of unnatural oscillation among spaces to a "Heimat," a space of reconciliation where she cannot be contaminated by the alienation of civilized existence; indeed, where her earlier social stigma (embodied in the villagers' mocking laughter) no longer matters. The unity of redemptive space and woman as the other of modernity, initially present but lost in *The Blue Light*, is achieved in the course of *Tiefland*. Instead of the real woman being rendered an icon as when the live Junta becomes ossified in the form of a photograph, in *Tiefland* the icon of woman fused with nature (as in Pedro's vision of Martha's face projected against the clouds) is rendered reality within the text. Yet a consistent alignment of the spectator's position with Pedro (suggested by Mulvey's model) would oversimplify the dynamics of the film since it finds its satisfying resolution in the distant projection of a unified male and female. The ending sublates gender, as woman's nostalgic function gives way to that of the united couple enshrined in a state of premodern harmony. This is not to say that the film in any way disrupts a patriarchal discourse but that Pedro's/ the spectator's desire for Martha gives way to the spectator's desire for the harmony they as a unit represent. The final composition, which shows the couple's backs to the camera, allows them to function as a (united) surrogate viewer for the spectator, who looks into the distance with them. Yet they remain decidedly at a distance inaccessible to the spectator; thus, as in *The Blue Light*, the space of reconciliation remains imaginary, distant from the lowlands of the narrative and of the spectator, which are necessarily characterized by alienation and social divisiveness. Hence the space of solace offered by each film is defined as a geographic one—following the mountain film genre—and as a temporal one. The films' mountain regions preserve an unalienated existence that—as a projected, imaginary state—cannot be located in any specific time or place but in a distant and imprecise past characterized most crucially by its freedom from the modern pressures against which conservative movements from the mid-nineteenth century through the Third Reich reacted.

The Step to a Fascist Aesthetic

Is there, as Kracauer and Sontag suggest, a linear route from glaciers to *Gleichschaltung;* that is, does the fascination with the elemental common to these and other mountain films bear a direct relation to Nazi ideology? Of the two films discussed, *The Blue Light* comes closer to a fascist aesthetic precisely in the ambiguity with which it regards the relationship between instrumentality and idealism, between the rational and the sentimental. Through its refusal to negate either position (to relegate either to the "minus heart" side of the matrix), the film flirts with the possibility of transgressing the institutional boundary between the imaginary and the real posited at the beginning of this essay as constitutive of a fascist aesthetic. Or, more precisely, it does not reproduce the split of the real and the imaginary on the diegetic level in order to reconcile this very split at the end, as do popular narratives that are more narrowly modern. By refusing reconciliation on the diegetic level (which would displace the possibility of such a reconciliation into the imaginary), the film seems to insist on a mimetic evaluation of reality because that which comes close to a unity with nature is doomed to be destroyed. It is Junta's "mors ex machina" (Jürgen Link) that prevents the text from offering a merely imaginary reconciliation of modern tensions, although the ideal thus retreats to a nostalgic distance, remaining, to use Lacan's term, an *objet a*. This ultimately is a critical commentary on modernity—a commentary that could easily be associated with a search for a "real" redeemer. *Tiefland*, on the other hand, with its roots in a sentimentalized enlightenment tradition, maintains a greater distance from a fascist aesthetic since it clearly upholds its separation of the rational and sentimental. At the risk of imputing a certain intention to the film, I would suggest that *Tiefland* reflects the ideology of the newly founded Federal Republic of Germany with its rationalistic orientation. Such a structure depends on the complementary relationship of a rationalized reality and the possibility of an imaginary retreat to sentimentality through art and specifically through narrative. Even with the heinous production history of *Tiefland*, the imaginary reconciliation offered by the film fully accords with the function of the sentimental in a society based on an enlightenment tradition (whatever the historical origins of the film).

I would thus question strongly whether there exists a necessary connection between films of the mountain genre and National Socialism—despite the recurrence of these motifs in Nazi art and the fact that in the context of the Third Reich and its precursors, the films reinforced a dangerous antimodernism, and could thus be mobilized to function as part of a broad propaganda apparatus. The step from *The Blue Light* or *Tiefland* to *Triumph des Willens* (*Triumph of the Will*, 1935) with its (in)famous opening scene rendering Hitler a celestial and all-pervasive presence emerging from the clouds is indeed a logical one. The crucial difference is that *Triumph of the Will* clearly does transgress the boundaries of the imaginary, merging the political and the aesthetic and permitting the individuals attending the rally and those reliving it through the technological apparatus the experience of a collective decentering or *Entgrenzung*. National Socialism would, of course, have been unthinkable without all the genres, movements, and images from which it borrowed; it builds on a foundation of modernism and uses nostalgia to "colonize the fantasy life" (Rentschler) of its constituency. But it goes beyond this by trying to introduce the imaginary into the public sphere, by conflating the imaginary with modern reality, as Riefenstahl's narrative films—even *The Blue Light*—do not. To be sure, *The Blue Light* exhibits, as Rentschler points out, the "kitsch of death," which Saul Friedländer considers the bedrock of Nazi aesthetics.[32] Yet the "kitsch of death," while indeed a favorite topos and image in Nazi films, is derivative of other movements stressing the search for decentering experiences, such as European aestheticism. Examples of a "kitsch of death" not associated with nazism are Heinrich Mann's *Göttinnen* (1903), whose protagonist, Violante d'Assy, dies in a state of intoxication or *Rausch* having become a work of art, or the popular nineteenth-century icon of the dead girl from the Seine. Again, National Socialism turns the "kitsch of death" experience into something real, inspiring and organizing people to march intoxicated into their own deaths; it dissolves the distinction between the imaginary and the real, translating the mass ornament into a mass event. Whereas traditionally the instrumental is opposed to decentering experiences, it is here that I see the category of the instrumental as crucial: the mass experience of intoxication (*Rausch*) can only be orchestrated with careful planning. The transgression of the separate realm of the aesthetic or, more precisely, the introduction of the aesthetic into reality, requires an *actual* mediation of the instrumental and decentering experiences in a new mode of the political.

To return to the questions posed at the outset regarding the degree to which a structural definition of a fascist text overlaps with the historical phenomenon of National Socialism: The first question was whether the majority of entertaining film narratives produced during the

Third Reich can be considered fascist texts, if this is to mean anything more than having been produced under fascist rule. An attempt to suggest that all Nazi films *should* be fascist leads to the dead end of regarding the Nazi takeover in 1933 as a sudden break or historical aberration, as a cultural revolution more radical than has ever occurred in history. It would lead us back to the Hull and Leiser positions over which most scholarship on Nazi cinema has advanced considerably.[33] Apart from the fact that propaganda minister Goebbels's film policies favored a high proportion of entertainment films over directly political films, it would have been indeed unique if an entire narrative tradition had been overturned in a mere twelve years.

However, without getting involved in the quagmire of categorizing Nazi films as "P" (political), "H" (*heiter* = comedies) or "E" (*ernst* = serious) as did Gerd Albrecht in the late sixties,[34] I would suggest that a reasonable percentage of Nazi feature films do have at least moments that dissolve the boundaries between the imaginary and real life and aestheticize the political through extradiegetic references. Accessible examples are *Wunschkonzert* (*Request Concert*, Eduard von Borsody, 1940), with its transcendence of physical space and its spiritual reunification of a dispersed German community through the memory of the 1936 Olympics (which it presents through documentary footage) and through the radio, or *Die große Liebe* (*The Great Love*, Rolf Hansen, 1942), where the spectacles Zarah Leander orchestrates fulfill a similar function. Although they make no direct reference to events outside of their textual boundaries, any of the "genius" biographic films produced in the early forties could likewise transgress the imaginary since all construct aestheticized images of Germany's cultural past to create a sense of collective identity in the present, to inspire the spectator to celebrate the consciousness of being German—a consciousness that can be carried beyond the theater. While the merging of the aesthetic and the real in the preceding examples fosters an illusory harmony, the same strategy can function to fortify opposition to an other, as in *Jud Süß* (*Jew Süß*, Veit Harlan, 1940), with its concluding exhortation, "keep our race pure." Steve Neale has suggested how the exhortation breaks the boundaries of classical narrative closure and connects the imaginary with the world of the spectator: "it aligns the subject as in a position of struggle vis-à-vis certain of the discourses and practices that have been signified within the text, and signified in such a way as to mark them as existing outside and beyond it."[35] Neale's definition of propaganda can be linked with the Benjaminian analysis of how fascism erases boundaries in that it posits as fundamental for the propagandist text the attempt to rupture textual boundaries in contrast to the classical realist text, which marks closure as closure and demarcates "a definite space and distance between the text and the discourses and practices around it. [Propaganda] is . . . a continual process of marking the discourses and practices signified within the text as existing outside it, and as existing outside it in conflict."[36]

The second automatic question was whether the term *fascist*, if understood in a structural sense, can be extended to include contemporary phenomena that blur the distinction between reality and the imaginary. Such an application is problematic, given the inflationary and hence trivializing manner in which the term has been wielded, particularly in the sixties and seventies. Again, let me stress that National Socialism represented the intersection of far too many historical, economic, social, and psychological factors to permit a simplistic analogy with any other historical conjuncture. Nevertheless, it is worth considering structural similarities between National Socialism's attempt to aestheticize political life and the tendencies in a wide range of discourses in contemporary societies today to generate a sense of public euphoria and well-being, usually through images and sounds produced by the electronic media. Just as in *Triumph of the Will*, reality was staged for the purpose of spectacle, current political acts are likewise staged for aesthetic reproduction, with the difference that today's political spectacles can be conveyed instantaneously.[37] This increasing dependency on spectacle and imaginary dissolution extends from political imagery and televised news to commercials, televised religion, sports events like the Olympics, rock concerts, and music videos. It works to undermine reasonable debate and foster an intermittent state of anesthesia or what Brecht called "sleepwalking." Particularly in the cases of political discourse and televised religion, pervasive imagery elides the distinction between public icon and private friend, with the effect of affirming faith in a leader figure. Although there could scarcely be two political figures with a more different leadership style than the demagogical hysteric Hitler and the relaxed, intimate, pseudopal Ronald Reagan, the similarity of Reagan as an actor and Hitler's training by an actor points to the importance of aesthetic illusion for the success of both men, expressed by Brecht in a reference to Hitler easily applicable to Reagan (or most any other modern politician).

> Let's observe above all the way he acts while delivering his big speeches that prepare or justify his slaughters. You understand, we have to observe him at that point where he wants to make the public feel with him and say: yes, we would have done the same thing! In short: where he appears as a *human being* and wants to convince the public that his actions are simply human and reasonable, and thus to give him their blessing. That is very interesting theater![38]

A crucial difference is that while modern political leaders, particularly in the United States, reinforce a sense of euphoric membership in a collective (one which is strongly invoked in selective moments such as the seizing of hostages or other acts subsumable under "terrorism"), this collective is paradoxically characterized by an ideology of individualism that generally precludes the kind of unqualified subservience that characterized Hitler's constituents. Moreover, in the United States the aestheticization of politics tends to engender political passivity (reflected in extremely low participation in elections) rather than the activism that characterized National Socialism. Although an allegation that any modern society today repeats the National Socialist experience would be absurd, many and precisely the most technologically advanced societies exhibit processes of aestheticization that foster a public so homogenized as to realize the Nazi notion of *Gleichschaltung* beyond its potential in the 1930s and 1940s. Such a conception of fascist tendencies may allow us to address a continuity that is more problematic than ever.

Notes

1. See, for example, Brecht's "Der Messingkauf," *Gesammelte Werke* 16 (Frankfurt a.M.: Suhrkamp, 1967): 501–657; Benjamin's "Kunstwerk im Zeitalter seiner technischen Reproduzierbarkeit," *Gesammelte Schriften* 1 (Frankfurt a.M.: Suhrkamp, 1908): 471–508 (English translation, "The Work of Art in the Age of Mechanical Reproduction," *Illuminations* [New York: Harcourt, 1968]) and "Pariser Brief," *Gesammelte Schriften* 3: 482–95.

2. "Fascinating Fascism," *Under the Sign of Saturn* (New York: Farrar, 1972) 76.
3. Riefenstahl planned both a ballet version and a remake of *The Blue Light* in England with Pier Angeli and Lawrence Harvey in the roles of Junta and Vigo respectively. Neither came about.
4. Riefenstahl expunged his name from the credits of later releases of the film.
5. See Francis Courtade and Pierre Cadars, *Geschichte des Films im dritten Reich* (Munich: Hanser, 1975) 240–41. For a detailed account of the film's arduous production history, see David B. Hinton, *The Films of Leni Riefenstahl* (Metuchen: Scarecrow, 1978) 83–106, Renata Berg-Pan, *Leni Riefenstahl* (Boston: Twayne, 1980) 163–75; or Riefenstahl's *Memoiren* (Munich: Alfred Knaus, 1987) 216–20, 354–71, 515–19. Jean Cocteau prepared French subtitles for the film.
6. Marguerite Tazelaar in the *New York Herald Tribune* 9 May 1934; as quoted in Glenn B. Infield, *Leni Riefenstahl: The Fallen Film Goddess* (New York: Thomas Y. Crowell, 1976) 34.
7. Cf. for example Kevin Brownlow's comments "Art transcends the artist . . . politics and art must never be confused . . . these old adages are forgotten instantly when the name of Riefenstahl is raised. And it is our fault. We have ourselves been the victims of insidious propaganda" *Film* (London) (Winter 1966/67): 14–15, as quoted in Eric Rentschler, "Fatal Attractions: *The Blue Light*," *October* 48 (Spring 1989): 47–68.
8. See *From Caligari to Hitler* (Princeton: Princeton UP, 1947) and Sontag's "Fascinating Fascism."
9. I would like to clarify my use of the term *modern*, lest it be confused with *modernist*, a term often used to refer to a type of text whose content and form are conceived in opposition to bourgeois culture. By "modern" I mean instead a narrative structure for which a gap between the real and the imaginary is constitutive. The resultant nostalgic, romantic mood of many modern texts is not characterized by an awareness of and critical reflection on the gap between the aesthetic and reality (thus *romantic* does not refer to early German romanticism, which indeed had a limited awareness of this gap). I, of course, do not mean to classify modern texts as a whole but to point to a recurrent prototype found in high culture and especially prevalent in popular culture.
10. "Fatal Attractions," see note 7. I am indebted to Rentschler's article for many insights regarding *The Blue Light*. Indeed, my own essay began in its earliest stage as a conference response to Rentschler's reading of the film.
11. Rentschler 63.
12. A. J. Greimas's term *semantic markers* (*Structuralist Semantics: An Attempt at a Method*, trans. Daniele McDowell and Alan Velie [Lincoln: U of Nebraska P, 1983]), has been applied by Jürgen Link and others in charting the structure of a narrative according to the positive and negative traits of its characters. Plus and minus signs signify possession or lack of qualities: "plus materialistic" typically combines with "minus heart," for example.
13. Cf. Rentschler's description of the crystal grotto as "womblike," 64.
14. Rentschler 62.
15. *Interviews with Film Directors*, ed. Andrew Sarris (Indianapolis: Bobbs, 1967) 394.
16. "Von 'Kabale und Liebe' zur 'Love Story'—Zur Evolutionsgesetzlichkeit

eines bürgerlichen Geschichtentyps," *Literarischer Kitsch*, ed. Jochen Schulte-Sasse (Tübingen: Niemeyer, 1979) 121–55. All translations from the essay are my own.

17. Link 138.

18. The peasants in *Tiefland* take on allegorical dimensions as forces of nature at the film's conclusion. With their black capes flapping ominously in the stormy wind, the village men function like a Greek chorus, observing and prodding Don Sebastian to his fate.

19. Water assumes a different connotation when Martha is first admitted to Don Sebastian's castle, and a subjective shot leads through massive gates to a symmetrically placed fountain, against which she is subsequently positioned. The fountain with its playful waste of water channeled into an ornamental design again serves as a contrast to the natural flow of water in the mountains and also suggests a kind of recreational sexuality, calling to mind the sexual romping of Freder and a playmate around a similar fountain in Fritz Lang's *Metropolis* (1927).

20. *Male Fantasies*, vol. 1, trans. Stephen Conway et al. (Minneapolis: U of Minnesota P, 1987), esp. 90–199, "The White Nurse."

21. Indeed, Don Sebastian's obsession with the steers reveals a "sick" egotism (riddled with erotic implications) since his financial destitution is at least in part a result of his failure to permit his serfs the use of water on his drought-stricken farmlands, which would enable them to pay their dues. He puts the peasants in a classic double-bind situation: threatening to drive them off the land if they fail to pay their dues and withholding the means with which they could do so.

22. Andreas Huyssen, "Mass Culture as Woman: Modernism's Other," *After the Great Divide* (Bloomington: Indiana UP, 1986) 52.

23. *Alice Doesn't* (Bloomington: Indiana UP, 1984) 103–57.

24. Rentschler 64. To be sure, Junta's gesture of throwing a half-eaten apple at Vigo's feet is a narrative act suggesting the *conscious* adoption of a role as Eve-like temptress.

25. Laura Mulvey, "Visual Pleasure and Narrative Cinema," *Screen* 16.3 (Autumn 1975): 13.

26. Perhaps for this reason Riefenstahl has been no less fetishized by some critics than by the camera. Cf., for example, Glenn Infield's description of her attending the premiere of *Triumph of the Will*, "Wearing a white fur coat and a low-cut gown that revealed her ample breasts, Riefenstahl smiled and waved to the cheering throng"—this in a book written in 1976 and criticizing nazism's "antifeminism." *Leni Riefenstahl: The Fallen Film Goddess*, 3.

27. "Leni Riefenstahl: The Deceptive Myth," *Sexual Stratagems: The World of Women in Film*, ed. Patricia Erens (New York: Horizon, 1979) 208.

28. See, for example, Kaja Silverman, *The Acoustic Mirror* (Bloomington: Indiana UP, 1988) 11.

29. *Ways of Seeing* (London: BBC and Penguin, 1972) 45–47.

30. Mulvey 13.

31. See Rentschler's article for a discussion of Riefenstahl's (and the mountain film's) indebtedness to romantic painting, especially that of Caspar David Friedrich. "Like Friedrich, Riefenstahl transforms landscapes into emotional spaces, granting to exterior nature an interior resonance," 51.

Linda Schulte-Sasse

32. *Reflections of Fascism* (New York: Harper, 1982). See Rentschler, 59.
33. I am referring to some of the earliest studies on Nazi cinema: David Stewart Hull's *Film in the Third Reich* (Berkeley: U of California P, 1969) and Erwin Leiser's *Nazi Cinema*, trans. G. Mander and D. Wilson, (New York: Macmillan, 1974).
34. *Nationalsozialistische Filmpolitik: Eine soziologische Untersuchung über die Spielfilme des dritten Reiches* (Stuttgart: Enke, 1969).
35. "Propaganda," *Screen* 18.3 (Autumn 1977): 31.
36. "Propaganda" 31.
37. For some interesting analyses of modern political spectacles in the form of "Gesamtkunstwerk," see Eric Rentschler, "The Use and Abuse of Memory: New German Film and the Discourse of Bitburg," *New German Critique* 36 (Fall 1985): 67–90 or Jochen Schulte-Sasse, "Electronic Media and Cultural Politics in the Reagan Era: The Attack on Libya and Hands Across America as Postmodern Events," *Cultural Critique* 8 (Winter 1987/88): 123–52.
38. "Der Messingkauf" 563.

6

Television as History:
Representations of German
Television Broadcasting,
1935–1944

William Uricchio

Walter Benjamin's "Das Kunstwerk im Zeitalter seiner technischen Reproduzierbarkeit" ("The Work of Art in the Age of Mechanical
Reproduction") appeared in the *Zeitschrift für Sozialforschung* several
months after the Reich Broadcasting Company announced "the world's
first regular television service."[1] The near simultaneity of the appearance
of a new mass medium and an implicit critique of its cultural inscription
marks a striking conjunction. Given the massive cultural role television
subsequently assumed, and Benjamin's relative marginalization to a small
circle of intellectuals, it seems astonishing that his essay achieved a much
higher profile in cultural memory than did the considerable developments of German television broadcasting between 1935 and 1944.

Benjamin's discussion of a cultural shift to reception in a state
of distraction, and with it his prescient observations regarding mass
aesthetics and politics, stands as but one of a spectrum of discourses

surrounding the emergence of television. In Germany in particular, the diversified and often conflicting administrative units and personalities responsible for television broadcasting were quite articulate about their visions of the medium. Whether the socialist wing of the Nationalsozialistische Deutsche Arbeiterpartei (NSDAP) or friends of corporate capitalism in the Postal Ministry, whether through the persuasive interests of the Propaganda Ministry or the martial interests of the Air Ministry, whether governmental entities or multinational electronics corporations, all contributed to a vision of television—its organization, programming, and potential impact—which reveals as much about the state of the medium as the historical assumptions in which this vision was embedded. Internecine warfare among these interests spawned numerous debates and policy positions, some of which were publicly promoted through the press in Germany and abroad. Yet, despite abundant discourse, despite the widespread involvement of public and private institutions, somehow the very existence of German television broadcasting in this early period has slipped from popular memory. The ease with which the British and Americans lay unchallenged claim to that always tenuous position of "first" in their assertion of primacy in regular public television broadcasting stands as but one manifestation of this situation.[2]

This essay traces several strands of the discourse emerging from the period, using the patterns of evidence on German television together with elements of its ongoing representation as reflections of broader historical concerns. The story of television's development appears intertwined in a complex web of determinants. Sorting them out offers the potential to reveal the medium as a site of contestation and cultural paradox, while reflecting back upon the character of the ever-changing national, technological, and economic historical paradigms through which it has been represented. Whether during the Third Reich or the Cold War, these perspectives have continued to shape public access to the events surrounding television between 1935 and 1944, accounting in large part for their curious omission from contemporary studies. This essay will thus sketch out and problematize concepts of German history as inscribed within the cultural configuration and representation of early German television in trade journals, the popular press, scholarly essays, and other texts.

German television before 1944, as a medium of representation and transmission, dealt tangibly with images of history and thus its programming might seem to provide more direct access to concepts of German history than discourse about it. Whether enveloping events such as the 1936 Olympic Games in the aura of the "world historical," or broadcasting feature and *Kulturfilme* with explicitly historical subjects, television continually demonstrated its potential as an agent in the construction of popular memory. The transmitted sporting events, films, news, drama, and public affairs programs that made up the typical German broadcast day all would seem to resonate with the fullness of the historical moment, but two factors motivate this essay's focus on discursive practices.

First, virtually no intact programming from 1935 through 1944 exists. The little that has been discovered—several clips and compilation films for broadcast—while useful for the pursuit of specific topics, largely precludes systemwide analysis.[3] Second, while television was well publicized and while receivers were promised at reasonable prices, estimates suggest that only between two hundred and one thousand sets were actually available. Despite the steady expansion of the program day, German television fundamentally lacked an audience. For the most part, the German public had much greater exposure to the discourse about television than any direct experience of the medium.

Although textless in a traditional sense, the many contradictions pervading German television's national and international development together with the patterns of its historical treatment suggest television's relevance as metatext, as a lens on the broader patterns of German history. The kinds of questions that can be raised about early German television, and our evidence-based access to them, may be used to reveal the assumptions and functions of the surrounding institutional and technological discourse. Much more so than in the case of cinema with its relatively long-term international organizational and representational practices (encouraging analytic focus on individual films and reception as the site of specific historical concepts), television's brief history prior to 1944 and its unique institutional status encourage this metatextual approach.[4] Divided among three ministries, struggled over by national and multinational corporations, and driven on by ideologues of various

William Uricchio

inclinations, technological visionaries, and bureaucrats, television existed at the nexus of an array of forces central to the epoch's development. Television's proximity to the agents of the state and capital that helped to define the Reich, in turn, fueled postwar interpretive strategies. More often than not, historical television found itself contextualized within a series of specific ideological discourses. Thus, critiques of the Reich as aberrant capitalism or as a deviant (totalitarian) state apparatus appeared on the level of discussions of television, in the process, invoking and inscribing Germany's ongoing history.

This essay, then, seeks to approach the discourse surrounding television, both within the Third Reich and since, as a representation of German history in its own right. To this end, the central role played by concepts such as nationalism and technology in discursive practice will be explored, providing a parallel and counterpoint to the thematic representations in film and television content discussed elsewhere in this volume. Nationalist rhetoric in particular played a significant and often overarching role in the otherwise disparate motives of the many constituencies struggling for control of pre-1944 broadcast efforts. The political interests of different factions within the NSDAP, the careerist motives of individuals in the scientific, governmental, and corporate communities, and the economic interests of multinational corporations all legitimized themselves in their embrace of broadly nationalistic goals. Moreover, although the nuances of nationalism changed in the course of the country's postwar physical bifurcation, the concept's dominant role in representations of early television remained unchallenged. Indeed, on both sides of the divide, differing configurations of nation helped to express the ideological distinction of the "other" Germany, both in the sense of the Third Reich and of opposing sides of the wall.

Yet in the postwar years, nearly a decade of television broadcasting, and with it a set of rather impressive advances, slipped from popular memory. The complexities of television's development within the Reich, the often contradictory available evidence compounded by the postwar division of archives, and the broader problem of accommodating divergent concepts of history and explanatory paradigms all contributed to the near loss of a past that laid the foundation for the soon pervasive "new" medium of the 1950s.

170

The Struggle for Control

The discourses and developmental patterns surrounding television's appearance in Germany chart not only a limited range of broadcast-specific interests, but reveal the interworkings among individuals, ministries, and national and multinational corporations in the perception and formation of a new mass medium. The terms in which this new medium appeared, as Benjamin suggested, fundamentally challenged the project of human agent-oriented history and the role of rational discourse within it. As we shall see, broadcasting authorities advocated group viewing of television specifically to preclude the array of audience negotiations that they felt atomized home viewing encouraged. Moreover, the discursive framing of television crystallized an equally telling shift in the conception of technology. In place of the Enlightenment principle of science as a means to the common good of humanity, technology appeared as a tool in the service of the German nation. Whether by implanting the image of the *Führer* in the hearts of his people, proclaiming the superiority of German technology, or using television guidance systems for torpedoes and missiles, a discursive tradition that had remained vital, despite nationalistic challenges to it in the nineteenth century and at the start of the twentieth century, had emphatically ended.

On 22 March 1935, *Reichssendeleiter* (Director of Broadcasting) Eugen Hadamovsky declared, "Today National Socialist broadcasting, working together with the Postal Ministry and German industry, begins as the first broadcasting system in the world with regular television programming. One of man's boldest dreams has been realized."[5] By pointing to the shared mission of government and national industry, Hadamovsky's address accurately located the dynamic that propelled German broadcasting into the forefront of international activity. While some very real benefits emerged from this conjunction, it also resulted in fundamental contradictions particularly for the German electronics industry.

Rapid advances in cable technology, in the live transmission of images (used in the 1936 Olympics), and in receiver technology were promoted and heavily marketed in the annual public broadcast exhibitions to both domestic and foreign markets. Each of the major electronics companies developed a wide variety of home receivers and displayed them with appropriate hype to a market ready for the future. Despite initial intercorporate competition, the government extended its coordinating function, evident in new politico-economic formulations of socially sanitized monopoly-capitalist production such as the *Volkswagen* and *Volksempfänger*, to television, and in so doing, mapped the route to prosperity for the major electronics concerns. Nationalism was good for business.

The electronics industry fully expected purchases of home television receivers to parallel the levels already experienced by radio. In 1937 Germans held over eight million radios—by far the heaviest concentration on the continent—and this was merely the midpoint of a campaign to place "a radio in every German house."[6] Yet by 1939, only two hundred home television sets had been sold.

Extrapolating from its experience with radio, the German electronics industry had every reason to believe that it would experience massive television sales. Although it became increasingly clear that Germany's industrywide standardization (the down side of the government's coordination [*Gleichschaltung*]) would limit profit margins and the competitive distribution of capital, most large industries already had experienced the benefits of state regulation and consequent reduction of intercorporate competition during the First World War. Moreover, at least within the electronics industry, stock ownership patterns and board of director memberships demonstrated widespread integration of ownership and control, facilitating intercorporate cooperation and financing.[7] But while the government encouraged this development, its role was not without contradiction.

Government regulation and coordination facilitated technological development and norms, but they quickly ran counter to industry expectations. Elements within the government, and particularly those with NSDAP affiliations, appeared to have had a very distinct concept of television's form and social function. Tensions between the two dominant plans for television, i.e., industry's and the party's, both garbed in the protective cloak of national interest, played themselves out most explicitly in ministerial disputes. The government regulated television, like radio, through several channels including the Postal Ministry (*Reichs-*

postministerium [RPM]), the Reich Broadcasting Company (*Reichsrund-funkgesellschaft* [RRG]), the Propaganda Ministry controlled Broadcasting Chamber (*Reichsrundfunkkammer*), and ultimately Goebbels's Ministry for Enlightenment and Propaganda (*Reichsministerium für Volksaufklärung und Propaganda*). The Postal Ministry, long allied with the electronics industry, acted in a manner consistent with its counterparts in Britain and the United States and mandated television's technical standardization.

But the Propaganda Ministry, with its much closer affiliation to the NSDAP, asserted a distinct development plan, suggesting audience homologies somewhat closer to film (centralized, public screening) than radio (decentralized, private listening). The propaganda theory then in vogue, strongly supported by Hadamovsky and Goebbels, favored the efficacy of group reception as a means to ensure consistent interpretation and minimize aberrant negotiations of meaning. And so initially, to the dismay of the corporate community, public television halls seating between forty and four hundred people emerged as the primary reception forum (an approach not dissimilar to that used in the Soviet Union at the time).

The development of this conflicting strategy—preparation for a strong home receiver market on the part of industry versus the government's push for a mass viewing environment—emerges from a number of changing factors. These include the aforementioned propaganda theories; the early "socialist" tendencies of National Socialism (supporting public viewing until receiver cost was affordable to the masses); changing technical standards (180 lines through 1937 and 441 lines in 1938 and after); and the shifting role of multinational corporations in political policy throughout the National Socialist period; together with the initiating mission of German television broadcasting. Again, Hadamovsky, "Now, in this hour, broadcasting is called upon to fulfill its greatest and most sacred mission: to plant the image of the *Führer* indelibly in all German hearts."[8] While the business community apparently had no reservations about this mission, its implementation posed substantial problems. By the late 1930s, as the technical situation finally stabilized around a 441 line norm, industry together with the Postal Ministry moved ahead with plans for consumer sector receivers. Ironically, just as mass production orders for television receivers were issued, the shift to a war economy together with the restrictive broadcast laws of 1939 precluded the mass production and marketing plans so evident in the corporate record and at the Berlin television exhibitions.[9]

As previously suggested, Hadamovsky's inaugurating speech accurately located the dynamic that propelled German television broadcasting by pointing to the "shared mission" of the government and national industry. The exact nature of that mission, however, remained unclear. Expressions of solidarity, protection, and mutual support bound governmental and corporate interests together. However, equally distinct tensions between the government and the private sector, apparent in the national coloration of multinational trade concerns, interministerial policy struggles, and the perception of and lobbying for various models of television's organization, also pervade the period.

As a result of the Postal Ministry's and particularly Hans Bredow's interest between 1926 and 1934, the government provided heavy subsidies for television's technical development (together with related technologies of cable, telephone, wired and wireless image transmission, and amplifier development).[10] These subsidies reflected the ministry's long-standing concern with and structural involvement in communications technologies, a level of involvement evident before the turn of the century and one frequently articulated in terms of potential military applications. Patents such as Paul Nipkow's 1884 electronic telescope and Dieckmann's 1906 facsimile transmission device—both directly related to early television systems—manifested a dimension of televisual communication consistent with and of relevance to supravening national concerns.[11] The Enlightenment project of science and technology for the common good fell under siege well before the formation of the party that would eventually epitomize its collapse.

Based on Postal Ministry correspondence with the Finance Ministry (*Reichsfinanzministerium*) during the Weimar Republic, national security seems to have been a motivating factor in the government's expenditures on the development of related technologies. Among the assertions that emerged, two dominate subsequent discourse. First, assumptions regarding hard information transfer fundamentally unify the sense of these technologies, their national security potential, and their consequent character, coordination, and control through governmental agencies (ultimately the RPM). Second, governmental subsidy of the massive research and development costs for these technologies in domestic firms, and the subsequent privatization of the results at the point of commercial application suggest the special nature of the government's relationship to private corporations.[12] This type of supportive integration for the mutual benefit of industry and the state set the pace for subsequent developments, including continued governmental subsidies, regulations, and ultimately, coordination with the NSDAP agenda.

The intrusion of a set of somewhat more economically autonomous players complicated the Postal Ministry's inroads into selected portions of the domestic electronics industry. From 1921 through the early 1930s (with a particular flurry of activity brought on by the stabilizing of the mark through the Dawes Plan in 1924), U.S.-based multinational corporations played an important role in the German economy. German businesses floated over $826 million in bonds in the United States, and many American firms invested heavily in German companies, entering into partnerships or establishing subsidiaries, including Dow Chemical, Ford, General Motors, I. E. DuPont, and General Electric.[13] The multinational patent base of many technologies also encouraged a broad pattern of license and patent-sharing agreements, evident in television technology with companies such as Baird, RCA, Farnsworth, and International Telephone and Telegraph.[14] Fernseh A.G., one of Germany's two largest television companies, was founded in part by Baird International Television (in partnership with Robert Bosch, Zeiss Ikon, and D. S. Loewe) and shared patents with Farnsworth.[15] Other television companies had equally complicated relations: Lorenz (and its related conglomerate, Standard Elektrizitäts Gesellschaft [SEG]) was a wholly owned IT&T subsidiary, and Telefunken (with its parent companies, Siemens and AEG) was tied to RCA's license system.

Despite this fabric of multinational interconnections, the inauguration of regular public broadcasting in March 1935 appeared in a nationalistic light. Although receivers remained generally unavailable and although service began on an already obsolete standard (180 lines), the government initiated broadcasting specifically to beat the British for reasons of both national interest and German exports.[16] The commercialization potential of a new technology brought with it the possibility for rapid expansion absent in more traditional sectors, and an established interest group eagerly awaited an opportunity to profit by it. As international trade and popular press reception indicate, not only Germany but other countries as well tended to nationalize fully multinational technology and therefore profits. But this nationalistic discourse also masked the ownership and licensing patterns of multinational corporations such as IT&T and RCA, which were able to sustain profits in diverse markets despite increasing international hostilities.

The apparent tension between multinational developments (the necessity of patent sharing, attempts to integrate new markets, and so on) and national interest emerged in several ways. The world economic crisis of the late 1920s certainly encouraged multinational investment, as did an awareness of the international realities of technologies such as the telephone and telegraph.[17] Moreover, growing evidence indicates that early National Socialist economic policy was receptive to development, driven more by attempts to restore business confidence with promises of modernization and financial security than by threats of foreign war. Like autobahn construction and car production, developments in television provided a propaganda coup for the government while bolstering the confidence of the domestic business community (electronics in particular).[18] The state saw exports as critical to economic survival and thus structurally encouraged national expressions (and sales) of the new technology through subsidies and tax incentives, even when dependent upon others' patents.[19]

The Postal Ministry sponsored elaborate marketing opportunities through the annual broadcast exhibitions and the heavily publicized televising of the 1936 Olympics.[20] Foreign press received special consideration, and great care went into providing state of the art communications facilities. Perhaps more importantly, the Postal Ministry encouraged competition among the various electronics firms and multinational licensing affiliates, effectively holding out the prize of national conversion to the winner's standard. Thus, the Olympics served as a battleground for Fernseh/Farnsworth and Telefunken/RCA, all the while demonstrating "German" television to the world.[21] In sharp contrast to the policy of secrecy that veiled parallel British and sometimes American developments, Germany seemed to take the initiative, positioning itself to leap ahead into the international market.

The start of war in 1939 substantially complicated the picture, enhancing the protective coloration of multinationals. Structural constraints such as the British, German, and American trading-with-the-enemy acts, the American freezing acts, and the roles played by various offices of alien property custodians resulted in curious contradictions.[22] Licensing agreements and patent exchanges between German electronics corporations and American firms such as IT&T continued after 1941, and IT&T retained control of its subsidiaries (including 28.3 percent of the Focke-Wulf military aircraft company) and even expanded its operations in Germany during the war.[23]

The explicit shift to military applications of television technology after 1939 might seem to have inhibited multinational corporate activities. But, given the previously mentioned long-standing and close relationship of the electronics and telecommunications industries to national security interests, such developments came as no surprise to the multinationals. The contradictions that emerged in this period constitute a repressed chapter in the history of multinationals, helping to account for the complexity and sensitivity of the situation in the postwar period.[24]

Within Germany, a complex set of overlapping jurisdictional claims and disputes characterized the government's involvement with television after 1933. The Postal Ministry, for example, encountered television through its own matrix of intraministerial agencies including the *Deutsche Reichspost*, the *Reichspostzentralamt* (RPZ), the *Forschungsanstalt der DRP*, and through its role in the Reich Broadcasting Company. Interministry relations held more potential for serious conflict. From its inception in 1933, the Propaganda Ministry was embroiled in a chronic fight with the Postal Ministry over shares of radio license income and ultimately control over the Reich Broadcasting Company (a struggle that ultimately caused the collapse of the Reich Chamber Broadcasting).[25] Even on the petty level of rent payments for the television halls, disputes emerged between the Postal Ministry and the NSDAP, the latter refusing to pay for the few halls it controlled. An extreme, though telling, eruption among several ministries followed Hitler's awarding of overall control of television to Reich Air Minister

Goering in July 1935 (a transfer of power carefully kept from the press).[26] The Postal Ministry and Propaganda Ministry both protested vigorously,[27] and despite Goebbels's attempts to strike a side-deal with War Minister Blomberg, by December a new directive divided responsibility among all the players.[28] The Postal Ministry was given responsibility for technical development and transmission; the Propaganda Ministry, programming; and the Air Ministry, defense applications.[29] Additional parallel and often overlapping jurisdictions were established by the Nazi party through the *Gau* system, and the division of power was further complicated by the organizational affiliations of various labor groups.

One of the clearest tensions to emerge in this matrix of overlapping jurisdictions and interests regarded the exhibition of television and involved the Postal and Propaganda Ministries. Although involved in an ongoing series of disputes over income and cost sharing, their struggle masked a deeper division. Staffed by career specialists who had long-standing relationships with the industrial sector, the postal authorities coordinated technical developments and, until 1933, controlled broadcast fees. By contrast, recently empowered party members dominated the Propaganda Ministry and cut into the Post's turf and fees with their party-specific agenda. Goebbels and Hadamovsky typified the latter.[30] Moreover, as Germany's leading propaganda theorists, both concurred that mass reception of propaganda was most effective, and Hadamovsky consequently encouraged the public character of television's reception. The electronics industry, and with it the Post (ever dependent on license fee revenues), pressed for the widespread proliferation of individual home receivers, consistent with that of radio's development.

The widely divergent interests and strategies of the various constituencies among and within the ministries, together with the complications fostered by the different factions of the NSDAP, point to the inadequacy of unified national interest as an explanatory paradigm for the historical development of television. "Führer" and "Vaterland" were certainly invoked at any given opportunity, but the record suggests that politicians and industrialists were motivated by self-interest rather than any commitment to the nation or the common good. Nationalistic discourse about television deviated from the Enlightenment principles of the common good by providing protective coloration to the narrow interests of bureaucracies and individuals.

In terms of the medium's physical development, many of these same factors—national and multinational industrial interests, governmental agencies, and rapidly shifting technical standards, together with the pressures of the world economy—suggest a number of possible causal factors. Serious disputes on any one of these levels might have been sufficient to delay television's standardization and deployment. Conversely, appropriate pressures from one or another sector may have been able to consolidate interests.

Closure, when it came, was marked by the emergence of a technical standard and the convergence of the major electronics firms. As in Britain with the competing Baird and EMI/Marconi systems, Germany initially faced the Fernseh (Farnsworth/Baird patents) and Telefunken (RCA) systems, the technical grounds for the delay in receiver production. The situation was complicated by a nationalistic tenacity regarding mechanical systems (the Nipkow disk), given both the high state of refinement it reached as a result of exacting engineering and manufacture (high vacuum technology) and its status as "purely German."[31] Nevertheless, Zworykin's iconoscope emerged as the superior technology, and in 1937, 441 lines formally appeared as the German standard.[32] Through the coordinating function of the RPZ and the RRG, all of the competing electronics manufacturers, despite their previous and ongoing corporate and license agreements, converted, thus clearing the way for the cooperative mass production of receivers. Approval of designs for the low-cost *Fernseh-Volksempfänger* [the "people's television receiver"] were held-up until late in 1938, a delay that would seem to have cost the electronics industry dearly. As noted, soon after the RPM issued its first large order, the war began, and production of consumer receivers slowed to a near stop. Despite apparent stasis, research, planning, and programming continued to develop rapidly. Work on a nationwide cable system continued, and the program day, which had averaged 3 hours a day until 1938 (excluding the Olympics) reached 6.5 hours in the early 1940s (including 1.5 hours live).[33] Access to receivers remained limited largely to functionaries, with many of the available private sets being diverted to use in military hospitals and recreation centers. Television viewing rooms remained the predominant public venue, and research continued in the area of large beam video projectors and high-definition systems of 1,029 and even 2,000 lines.[34]

Significantly, post-1939 research and development stressed explicit military application. Reconnaissance (hence, the interest in high definition), television-guided missiles, bombs and torpedoes, as well as spin-offs such as heat-seeking missiles and related technologies underwent rapid development paralleling developments in the United States. Based on a preliminary analysis, both the production levels and profit margins of the German electronics industry's involvement with the military greatly exceeded their efforts (and perhaps potentials) in the civilian sector.

Television as History

Even a gloss of television's development in Germany reveals a matrix of contradictions complicating the roles and relationships of technological research, national and multinational industrial development, and state economic coordination. In some senses a testament to the remarkably diverse and often conflicting appeals and interests encompassed by the Third Reich, television stands as but one of many instances whose very development inscribes and reifies the complexity of a historical moment. While useful as a comparative model to alternative and better documented media systems, the extremity of the German situation also serves to highlight relationships and tensions present in the broader scheme of modern German history.

German television appears distinctive both because of the NSDAP's attempts to dominate the medium as a mode of party-specific agitation (most evident in the activities of the Propaganda Ministry) and because of the explicit coordination of private and public sector efforts in the introduction and promotion of television (through the Postal Ministry). As such, it might appear that the social production of German television, together with television as a means of production within that social framework, share a highly specific and nationally circumscribed set of referents. Certainly this perspective offers useful possibilities, particularly in the light of a reconsideration of Germany's pre-1939 economic policy. The idiosyncratic particularity of the German case, in turn, could be seen as motivating the marginalization of this moment of broadcast history in subsequent discourse.

In contrast to these positions, however, closer investigation of the underlying structural unities binding the German experience to parallel developments in other national markets—the United States and Great Britain for instance—permits the contours of a broader technological-economic system to appear. The multinational character of television's research and development, the patterns of its technological transmission (patent sharing and licensing agreements), its place in the fabric of early twentieth-century economic growth, coupled with the explicit industrial involvement of RCA, IT&T, AEG, and so on, all suggest a set of common denominators that call into question concepts of historical process that focus almost exclusively on the nation state and national loyalties. Moreover, in the shift to the far more profitable military application of television technology and in the maintenance of at least some explicit multinational corporate connections involving weapons systems throughout the war substantial contradictions to the received view emerge.

Although a wide range of factors appear to account for Germany's development of television, cultural configurations further complicate the nation's status in broadcast history. The relationship between period reception and consequent historical representation provides valuable insight into the shifting history of mentalities in the postwar period. The diversity of the available record and the selection process whereby historical questions and methods frame particular strands of that record as relevant reveal the broadly ideological role played by television as a cultural entity and as an object of study.

Of the many possible expressions through which the process of German television's concrete historical representation can be traced, a start can be made by examining the public reception of several constituencies as distinguished by their relationship to the medium. An account of the approaches taken by the domestic and foreign popular press, the trade press, and the industry through their published reports and circulated opinions throws one dimension of the basic contours and nuances of the situation into comparative light. Of course, such an approach at best suggests the general public orientation of the institution making the utterance and of necessity misses the fuller range of social forces and the consequent plurality of discourses (many of which have already been mentioned).[35] But as an indication of public positioning, this approach provides at least the broad contours of reception while constituting the type of evidence to which subsequent generations of historians have had ready access. Thus I will sketch the view of television presented to the general public through newspapers, to the electronics trade and professionals through their journals, and to the corporations through reports in order to reveal one set of television's public contours. For reasons of expediency, German and American reception during 1935 will be used to map out the spectrum of responses.

The heavily publicized start of public broadcasting in 1935 may have lacked a viewing public, but it nonetheless appealed to mass audiences through extensive and intensive press campaigns. A spectrum of attitudes emerged in the popular press, and 1935—the year Germany introduced its public television service—provides a nodal point in the representation and configuration of perceptions.[36] Within Germany, with its already centralized press service, Reich Broadcasting Company press releases and hyperbolized commentaries heralded the nation's technical achievement as proof of a new direction in both industrial and consumer sectors and as evidence of the fruitful collaboration of state and industrial interests. Television as evidence of Germany's technological superiority, as a vindication of its new economic order, as tangible proof of the benefits of the Reich permeated domestic press coverage. Multinational affiliations, relatively prominent in the trade press, rarely appeared in popular reports, although the visits of American and British scientists sometimes received attention as further proof of Germany's lead in the field. The public nature of exhibition often appeared as evidence of an egalitarian policy by which free television service was provided to all until receivers reached a sufficiently affordable level (the latter proposition always posited in imminent terms).

The popular press in Britain and the United States often exhibited a similarly nationalistic tone in television discussions. The *New*

York Times repeatedly mentioned German attempts to attain parity with American standards rather than British, despite the absence of formal or even licensed experimental American broadcasting. Nevertheless, the centrality of United States patents and the assertions of its technological superiority appeared regularly.[37] In addition, a recurrent tendency to privilege British over German developments dominated the popular press, despite the fact that in some cases the British technology at issue had not actually been seen by the reporter (and the reviewed German systems were acknowleged to be both varied and available).[38]

An awareness of competition and its dangers also entered the discourse. The importance and rapid growth of radio in Germany was regularly noted and used to forecast projected developments in television.[39] Often, German developments were cast in what might be described as motivational terms, as a headline from the *New York Times* emphasized, "Germany rushes work on TV system: Berlin doesn't intend to be outdone by London in the matter of television."[40] J. Royal, vice president of the National Broadcasting Company, exaggerated the medium's impact in Germany relative to the United Sates market as part of a broader attempt to stimulate federal licensing agreements, saying, "Television is rapidly becoming a national pastime in Germany."[41]

In contrast to this nationalized and competitive discourse about the historical development of television in Germany, both the German and international professional trade press—at least until declarations of war—dutifully reported technical innovations both from the perspective of patent and license sharing agreements and from that of new manufacturing techniques. The *Journal of the Royal Television Society*, for example, devoted substantial space to detailed descriptions of and debate about the annual broadcasting exhibitions in Germany, carefully comparing available receiver models and studio technique and frequently lamenting the British penchant for secrecy. Visiting delegations of engineers reported on their findings, and generally the trade literature reveals a pattern of respect for German engineering and technological craft but dismay about their (initial) retention of mechanical systems and programming.[42]

For its part, the German trade press—and particularly Telefunken and Fernseh A.G.'s technical journals—disseminated the details of the latest patent acquisitions from their American or British affiliates while addressing their own progress. A revealing source for the close cooperation among multinationals, the German professional trades provide a rich evidence base until their termination with the start of total war in 1941. The German trades differed from their British and American counterparts only in the specificity of their occasionally nationalized discourse particularly evident in the historical grounding of developmental issues. Thus, for example, discussions of the prominent place of Paul Nipkow and Manfred von Ardenne in television's evolution and their continuing role in the medium's development appeared only in the German context.

While reflecting the interests of the multinational electronics and telecommunications industry, corporate discourse presents serious research difficulties because of the generally private nature of its expressions. Nevertheless, selected elements of the record appear in government files, corporate officers' memoirs, reports to stockholders, and postwar litigation records.[43] Remaining within the sample year, 1935–36, American industry generally focused on Germany's technical achievements. British efforts received much closer attention because their programming developments and receiver marketing strategies more closely paralleled American plans.[44] German programming, in addition to the differences emerging from its avowed political function, was also linguistically marginalized.

David Sarnoff's 1936 report to the Federal Communications Commission, *The Future of Radio*, noted that "other nations are accepting the standards and methods of RCA engineers and are applying them to the solution of their own television problems."[45] Sarnoff's reports to RCA's stockholders, however, were more explicit, with statements of annual patent income reaching levels of $20,166,545.06 (minus reserve for patents of $11,503,333.79 or $8,663,211.27) in 1934.[46] Within the United States, at least, television's competitive implications for radio seemed to occupy a sizeable part of the available 1935 record.

Meanwhile, industry executives and technicians carefully documented developments in England, Germany, Japan, Argentina, and the Soviet Union, pursuing market openings and remaining fully abreast of technological transformation and application. Marked by Federal Communications Commissioner Sykes's wait-and-see approach, the industry seemed to monitor Germany, like England, as a testing ground for the early battles of Farnsworth and RCA technology.

Even from this brief sketch of television's popular, trade, and industrial reception during 1935, television's cultural configuration, complicated by the matrix of intersecting structural reasons previously suggested, appears in often conflicting terms. Yet if nothing else, discussion of Germany's developments at least penetrated the populations addressed by these various journals. Given this sort of public presence, how can we account for the postwar marginalization of developments in pre-1945 German television? What range of interpretations have been made of this record (together with the much fuller available evidence base) and to what extent do they inscribe concepts of German history? A glance at the postwar reconfiguration of discourse suggests the broad contours of a response. The process of television's cultural reconfiguration implicitly problematizes the relationships among technology, industry, and politics while revealing one strand in the ongoing construction of history.

The postwar representation of German television reflects the range of material constraints, such as archival access, and perhaps more importantly, ideological assumptions upon which our current interpretations rest. Three developments exemplify the spectrum of the subject's dominant historical representations: (1) immediate postoccupation intelligence reports, (2) scholarship emerging from the Propaganda Ministry archives in the FRG, and (3) scholarship based upon the Postal Ministry archives in the GDR. The divergence among these approaches helps to throw into relief some of the assumptions evident in current research. At the same time, these approaches are bound together by a use of history that implies common interest and common historical development in opposition to a threatening other. Most often defined as fascistic, the depiction of the other often has resonated with the other Germany.

One source of information on the immediate postwar state of German television and a close overview of its brief history appears in the American FIAT (Field Intelligence Agency, Technical Division), British BIOS (British Intelligence Objectives Subcommittee), and joint American and British CIOS (Combined Intelligence Objectives Subcommittee) reports. Working largely in the service of industry, both as a source of patent war booty and as a base for patent infringement litigation, these studies emerged from extensive interviews and investigations held as closely as possible to actual military seizure of enemy property. Employed by the United States Department of Commerce and the British Board of Trade, FIAT/BIOS/CIOS interviewers tended to be civilian specialists temporarily on leave from companies such as RCA and IT&T. In many cases the record shows that the interviewers were well acquainted with the German engineers and technicians they interrogated through prewar contact. Their interviews confirm the directions of technical activity as well as levels of production for the German television industry. Given the post-1941 termination of many German trade publications, this evidence is of vital importance. For example, BIOS Report No. 867 reported that Fernseh's Obertannwald facilities employed 750 persons and that Telefunken's factories were producing up to 300 mini-cameras for missile installation per month with semiskilled female laborers, thus suggesting both the scale and orientation of television-related production late in the war.

A distinct pattern of competitive investigation emerges in the BIOS, FIAT, and CIOS files. BIOS reports often note that equipment had been removed by the Americans prior to British investigation, and the function of CIOS was largely to coordinate and make sure that each knew or had access to what the other was doing. Given the competitive nature of the commercial interests both FIAT and BIOS served and the profit potentials in seized technologies, this tension appears hardly surprising. While corporate interests covered by a veneer of nationalism appear throughout the reports, all three note that their Soviet counterparts played the game more seriously. For example, the Soviets are reported not only to have dismantled and shipped east a Blaupunkt factory involved in television receiver manufacture but to have shipped the entire staff as well.[47]

The reports that emerged systematically failed to address organizational issues or multinational patent sharing agreements, focusing instead primarily on technical issues. Consistent with their charge, these studies isolated technology from either politics or industrial development. But the very nature of the investigations, together with their close correlation to the efforts of corporate intelligence and job recruiters, speak clearly to the underlying issue. Thus while explicitly providing valuable documentation of otherwise lost technological development, the FIAT/BIOS/CIOS reports implicitly testify to the continuing symbiosis of what Eisenhower called the "military industrial complex." The sense of other that emerges from these reports is compounded by the ease with which the investigators distanced themselves from parallel (and often corporately interlocked) activities. In the process, an overriding vision of history as fundamentally self-serving appears with remarkable clarity.

Postwar German scholarship on early television reflects the ideological and physical bifurcation of the FRG and GDR. While more often than not emerging from a conscious national perspective, the published research seems remarkably free of the self-interest that marked both pre-1944 accounts and the BIOS/FIAT/CIOS reports. Yet, arguably, the project of constructing a national history, of selectively valorizing or criticizing developments in television's brief history, inexorably intertwines broader issues of continuity and change in national identity. Thus, limited access to the archival record compounded by (and at times coincident with) broader ideological patterns of understanding the recent past reveal certain tendencies. In the light of the momentous changes now occurring in Germany's identity, in the context of the breakdown of the structural barriers that have limited scholars from both Germanies, these patterns seem more striking than ever. Structural constraints emerge in part from the consequent division of Germany's archives, with the Propaganda Ministry's files for the most part located the FRG, and the Postal Ministry's files in the GDR. Given the previously discussed divergent interests and constituencies of both ministries, the implications of this division are profound. For heuristic purposes, the discussions that follow attempt to portray the broadest contours of the scholarship that has typified West and East block approaches to German television until the last decade. By comparing various scholars' accounts of Germany's failure to develop a market in consumer sector television receivers, we can quickly differentiate their perspectives. Emphasizing the common thrust of various researchers necessarily sacrifices important nuance and distinctions, but at the same time, it suggests shared responses to limited evidence bases and supravening ideological contexts, revealing larger historical patterns.

First, Gerhard Goebel's 1953 study, "Das Ferneshen in

Deutschland bis zum Jahre 1945," stands as a rare early and respected West German example of an attempt to synthesize the archival evidence bases of both ministries. Despite a fabric of references that overlaps with much of the GDR scholarship, however, Goebel uses the material primarily to gather technological data rather than to discern organizational implications in a manner common to many other western scholars of the period. Based upon close investigation of the patent record, trade journals, technical reports, and interviews Goebel traces the evolution of German television technology. Although his overview includes program scheduling and analysis and suggests the economic contours of the industry, his orientation generally coincides with the technical interests of the Postal Ministry (in which he served) without recourse to its archives or internal paperwork and as such remains grounded in its public reception. Thus as a measure of the Postal Ministry's legitimate realm of concerns, Goebel's influential work suggests the centrality of technological evolution—invention, modification, and refinement—as the factor primarily responsible for Germany's delay in mass producing receivers.

Heinz Pohle's 1956 study and Winfried Lerg's 1967 analysis both tend to rely on periodicals and public record, like Goebel's work, with minimal reference to archival sources.[48] Thus, for example, by relying on trade publications and newspapers, both interpret the events surrounding the 1935 jurisdictional disputes that resulted in the Air Ministry's temporary control of television from a perspective largely consistent with that of the Propaganda Ministry. Perhaps more significantly, however, by relying on German periodical literature, they replicate the perspective of the Propaganda Ministry. By combining the hyperbolic tone of the Propaganda Ministry with the realities of television's technical development, they essentially argue that the delay in home receivers emerged from the industry's premature start in 1935. By moving ahead too soon at the behest of the Propaganda Ministry, industry actually set itself back, never to recover. Both authors hint at the Propaganda Ministry's *de facto* subversion of capitalist interests, but neither cites specific evidence.

The archival record now available in the FRG tends to confirm this perspective. The Propaganda Ministry files deal tangibly with television, but given the division of responsibility for television and the evident conflicts of interest established by 1935, this perspective provides only one piece of a complicated matrix of concerns. In correspondence with the perspectives of some western historians, the Propaganda Ministry's records indicate a concern with persuasion in programming that reinforces the notion of a seizure of power. Although evidence is certainly available in western archives to counter this position (copies of selected Postal Ministry correspondence to the finance office or chancellory, for instance), the Postal Ministry's corporate perspective and sensitivity remain only marginally represented.

By contrast, efforts emerging from the GDR as exemplified by the work of Manfred Hempel produced work based on the Postal Ministry archives, providing a critically important complement to western scholarship. Through the Postal Ministry, Hempel had access to the day-to-day workings of state and corporate interrelations, thus permitting a focus on the history of multinational investment, interindustry battles, and the process of industrial-state coordination. Hempel accounts for early German television's failure to attract a public by documenting the infighting between Telefunken and Fernseh (and their respective multinational backers), compounded by both companies' rapid abandonment of low-cost television developments for much higher profit military production. Thus the maintenance of full-scale television research and development (despite dropping the consumer market) together with the rapid technological expansion to related technologies appears in terms of corporate profit. Like his counterparts in the FRG, Hempel's access to his archival base permitted him to affirm the GDR's Marxist perceptions, in this case, the linkage of fascism with monopoly capital. The same argument would be difficult to mount with access only to the Propaganda Ministry files.

As Cold War tensions subside and reactive positions, pro and con, to corporate continuities with the National Socialist past fade, the history of television continues to reflect the changes. Since the late 1970s, shifts in focus, access, and method have partially eroded this bifurcation. Erwin Reiss's work largely popularized some of Hempel's ideas in the West.[49] And thanks to the efforts of individuals such as Friedrich Kahlenberg, Angsar Diller, Knut Hickethier, Manfred Hempel, Winfried Lerg, Siegfried Zielinski, and groups such as the Studienkreis Rundfunk und Geschichte and the media study group at Siegen, the period has seen closer attention directed to issues such as reception, programming, relations between television and film, television genres, and close textual analysis in those few cases where texts exist.[50]

Conclusion

The patterned production of evidence within the period of 1933 to 1944 remains a highly complicated affair. Competing forces within individual ministries, coupled with interministerial disputes, all overlaid by the often contradictory interests of the party and individual national and multinational corporations, have simultaneously produced a highly diversified and complex evidence base.

Several factors further skew the evidence. First, multinational involvement, often masked as national for protective reasons (particularly after the declaration of war to evade trading-with-the-enemy legislation), has clouded the evidence base. The material gathered by allied investigators in the immediate postwar period essentially served corporate interests: consolidating markets, updating patent pools, and locating new specialists. The rapid emergence of the cold war and the consequent reestablishment of old Allied-Axis corporate ties and quick rehabilitation of many Nazi collaborators in the West, together with the limited access to information or evidence in GDR archives, further complicates the picture. But more than anything else, the division of the archives along ministerial lines, particularly given television's development pattern in Germany, accounts for the character of the research effort. The division, of course, has to some seemed fortunate, given the ideological perspectives on both sides of the border, confirming visions of the National Socialist epoch as anticapitalist, overregulated, propagandistically driven dictatorship in the West, and as monopoly-capitalist, crisis-averting contradiction in the East.

Throughout the development of early German television, the role played by multinational corporate capitalism both prior to and during the war—a relationship that persists in the present—continues to be masked by a series of nationalistic discourses. As the television case demonstrates, investment, ownership, patent and license agreements, as well as the nature of, for example, telecommunications technology, assured steady technological transfer, whether productive or destructive. Despite this, or perhaps because of it, analysts have on the whole chosen to work with cultural configurations of national dimensions. Only the most explicit intrusions of national-based programming into other nations seem consistently to attract attention to multinational issues. But the underlying economic-technological identity of television within its fully multinational and monopoly-capitalist framework requires much more careful address.

The discourses surrounding the development of early German television and its subsequent representation reveal as much about the emergence of a technology as about the construction of historical perceptions. The history of National Socialist television's inscription in a set of nationalistic, technological, and economic discourses, particularly considering the effective excision of this cultural moment from popular memory, raises fundamental questions about our ability to come to terms with the Third Reich and Germany's fate in the intervening years.

Notes

1. German television broadcasting service was declared public on 22 March 1935; Benjamin's article appeared in volume 5, number 1 of the 1936 issue.
2. See William Uricchio and Brian Winston, "The Anniversary Stakes," *Sight and Sound* Autumn 1986: 231–32. British broadcasting began in 1936, terminating with the start of war in 1939. Public American broadcasting, despite early technological leads, was delayed until 1939 and even then proceeded only on an experimental license.
3. Despite the paucity of available evidence, attempts have been made to examine television texts in terms of production and exhibition. Friedrich P. Kahlenberg, for example, has examined a surviving Ufa made-for-television compilation film in "*Von deutschem Heldentum:* Eine Film-Kompilation für das Fernsehen aus dem Jahre 1936," *Mitteilungen: Studienkreis Rundfunk und Geschichte* January 1979: 21–27, trans. and reprinted as "*Von deutschem Heldentum:* A 1936 Compilation Film for Television," *Historical Journal of Film, Radio and Television* 10.2 (1990): 187–92, and Knut Hickethier, on the basis of scripts and interviews, has examined the production of television dramas "The Television Play in the Third Reich," *Historical Journal of Film, Radio and Television* 10.2 (1990): 163–86.
4. This is not to suggest that television emerged without reference to longer-term cultural practices. Theater, cinema, and in particular radio provided explicit homologies to which television referred. But despite representa-

tional and organizational communalities, the discourse surrounding television as television is relatively distinct.

5. *Mitteilungen der Reichsrundfunkgesellschaft*, 460 (30 March 1935). Unless otherwise noted, all translations are the author's.

6. Radio audiences increased dramatically through the joint efforts of the government and industry. Between 1 May 1932 and 1 May 1939, the number of listeners increased from 4,177,000 to 12,500,000. See Heide Riedel, *60 Jahre Radio: Von der Rarität zum Massenmedium* (Berlin: Deutsches Rundfunk Museum, 1983) 61–65.

7. Corporate directorships, then as now, relied upon pooling leading figures from banking, the government, and related corporations. In addition, informal advising circles made up of corporate leaders and government officials met regularly in order to coordinate activities. For detailed instances of both, see the Kurt von Schroeder interrogations National Archive (NI–247).

8. *Mitteilungen.*

9. The RPM divided its first consumer-targeted receiver production order for over 10,000 sets among the five largest television manufacturing companies: Telefunken, Fernseh, Lorenz, Loewe, and Tedake. The Post Ministry provided a 25 percent subsidy (RPM files, 9 March 1939). Declaration of hostilities effectively stopped production. Immediate postwar intelligence suggests that of this initial order, only between 600 and 1,000 sets were actually produced (British Intelligence Objectives Subcommittee, Report No. 867). Curiously, these events paralleled developments in the United States. The FCC established its VHF broadcast standard of 525 lines in 1941, finally permitting mass production of receivers. However, America's entry into the war that same year put an immediate stop to commercial production. See Brian Winston, *Misunderstanding Media* (Cambridge: Harvard UP, 1986) 13.

10. See Bundesarchiv RPM correspondence (R48/4343, 4344); by 1934, the Post's annual television research and development expenditures reached about 500,000 RM with an additional 400,000 RM in ancillary expenses provided specifically for television's refinement (RPM correspondence to RFM, R2/4903).

11. For a discussion of the multinational technological and conceptual origins and developmental pattern of early television technology see Winston, *Misunderstanding Media* and Gerhard Goebel, "Das Fernsehen in Deutschland bis zum Jahre 1945," *Archiv für das Post- und Fernmeldewesen* 5 (1953): 259–393.

12. Typically, the government subsidized research and development costs and with the perfection of technologies permitted the industries involved to control the resulting patents. This level of integration accounts in part for the extraordinary cooperation both among industries and between industry and state. For a fuller study of this integration see, Manfred Hempel, *Der braune Kanal* (Leipzig: Karl Marx Universität, 1969) and Manfred Hempel "Die Entstehung und Entwicklung der Television in Deutschland bis zur Zerschlagung des Hitlerregimes," *Mitteilungen des Postmuseums Berlin* 3/4 (1970): 33–75.

13. For an overview of these investments from the perspective of an industry apologist, see Robert Sobel, *IT&T: The Management of Opportunity* (New York: Times Books, 1982).

14. See, for example, IT&T's corporate history by Sobel. The range of corporate interconnections covered the ideological spectrum. On 5 May 1937, the

New York Times announced that Moscow television reached an agreement regarding RCA devices—the same period in which its patents were shared with Telefunken.

15. Baird dropped out after a few years, and Loewe dropped out in the mid-1930s. This was a period of intense capital demand, with an estimated corporate expenditure of 20 million RM up to 1939 (with profits from exports and the German Post coming in at about 8 million). By contrast, Telefunken's expenditures are estimated at 15 million RM and the other companies totaling 8 million (Goebel cited in Fritjof Rudert, "Fifty Years of Fernseh, 1929–1979," *Bosch Technische Berichte* 6.5/6 [May 1979]: 28–58, here, 29). By 1938, just as profitability was showing signs of turning around, Zeiss-Ikon also dropped out, leaving Fernseh a Bosch subsidiary, which it remains today.

16. Bundesarchiv RPM/RRG correspondence to RFA R2/4903 1934–35. The British announced a proposed start-up date in fall 1935, allegedly prompting the German move in spring.

17. IT&T's investment behavior is instructive. By 1930, IT&T owned or controlled subsidiaries on every continent. See Anthony Sampson, *The Sovereign State of IT&T* (New York: Stein and Day, 1973).

18. Detailed analysis of specific industries has begun to alter the view that National Socialist economic policy was unsystematic and reactive, relying primarily on public works, rearmament, and war. See, for example, R. J. Overy, "Transport and Rearmament in the Third Reich," *Historical Journal* 16 (1973): 389–409 and R. J. Overy, *The Nazi Economic Recovery: 1932–1938* (London: Macmillan, 1982).

19. Emil Lederer points out that by September 1939, some 73 percent of Germany's trade was with the industrialized world. See his "Gegen Autarkie und Nationalismus," *Kapitalismus, Klassenstruktur und Probleme der Demokratie in Deutschland 1910–1940*, ed. Jürgen Kocka (Göttingen: Vandenhoeck & Ruprecht, 1979) 199–209. Although the economy was assisted by Schacht's public works and expenditures programs (mapped out by Strasser in 1932), growth of the export sector was critical. In April of 1933, Hitler pointed out the West's mistake in providing industrial development to previously undeveloped parts of the world together with its implications for the German economy (see Peter Krüger, "Zu Hitler's 'nationalsozialistischen Wirtschaftserkenntnissen,'" *Geschichte und Gesellschaft* 2 [1980]: 263–82; here, 274). Expansion into new areas was a key strategy (see Lotte Zumpe, "Weltwirtschaftslage und faschistische Außenwirtschaftsregulierung," *Jahrbuch für Wirtschaftsgeschichte* 4 [1978]: 201–7; here, 203ff), and television was ideal in this regard.

20. The broadcasting exhibitions reported annual admissions of over 300,000. Olympic television appeared in up to 25 television halls, including one in Potsdam and two in Leipzig (one of which seated nearly 400 people). Programming was increased from the usual 3 hours per day to over 8 hours, and attendance was put at 162,228.

21. Although the 1936 Olympics served as a public testing ground for both RCA and Farnsworth systems, the Postal Ministry apparently perceived the RCA system as superior and supported national conversion to the RCA standard before actual coverage of the games.

22. United Kingdom Trading with the Enemy Act, 1939; United States Trading with the Enemy Act, 1917, amended 1940, 1941, etc.; Executive Order No.

William Uricchio

8389 of 10 April 1940, etc., Martin Domke, *Trading with the Enemy in World War II* (New York: Central Book Co., 1943).

23. Despite trading-with-the-enemy legislation, multinational corporations were uniquely positioned to maintain their investments. IT&T provides an unusually well-documented case. Its CEO, Sosthenes Behn, cultivated close relations with the Reich, and IT&T was one of the first foreign companies to be declared "German," thus exempt from the Reich Custodian of Alien Property. Although a series of investigations were begun by the Department of Justice and the FBI, by the start of the cold war, IT&T's complicity with the German state was reframed. Day-to-day control of its German operations was seen as outside IT&T's direct control. Nevertheless, testimony by IT&T's German directors Westrick and Schroeder conflicts with postwar corporate testimony on this issue. See, for example, Schroeder interrogations, National Archive, NI–234, 15 November 1945 and NI–235, 16 November 1945. Regarding patent exchanges, German trade journals regularly reported on the patent developments of and licence agreements with their American affiliates such as RCA until total war caused the suspension of their publication. Close parallels in American and German television weapon patent development after this blackout suggest that information flow continued.

24. On the surface at least, close parallels exist between Telefunken and RCA's developments of television surveillance planes, television-guided and heat-seeking missiles, and so on. Their correspondences mark an area of ongoing research. IT&T's involvement with war-related technologies and industries is more fully documented.

25. Documented in the Bundesarchiv RFM files, R2/4903.

26. *Reichsgesetzblatt* T. 1 No. 88 (12 July 1935) 1059.

27. Reich Chancellory papers, Bundesarchiv, R43II/267a.

28. *Reichsgesetzblatt* T. 1 No. 136 (11 December 1935) 1429–30.

29. Given the awareness of military applications evident even in the fax transmissions of the late 1920s, this latter allocation is not surprising. By the early 1940s, development of television-guided missiles, torpedoes, unmanned surveillance planes, and related technologies such as radar and heat-seeking missiles were under military directive. See Combined Intelligence Objectives Subcommittee (CIOS) Report No. 28–41, No. 31–1, No. 31–8; British Intelligence Objectives Subcommittee (BIOS) Report No. 867; Public Records Office (London) AIR MIN files 40/1656, 40/2000.

30. See, for example, Hadamovsky's *Der Rundfunk im Dienste der Volksführung* (Leipzig: R. Noske, 1934) and *Propaganda und nationale Macht* (Oldenburg: G. Stalling, 1933), English translation, *Propaganda and National Power* (New York: Arno, 1972).

31. This mechanical technology was occasionally judged by the British as superior to their electric systems in terms of image clarity, and the Germans were able to push it far beyond expected limits to a 729 line image, see Ernest H. Traub, "Television at the Berlin Radio Exhibition, 1937" *Journal of the Television Society*, 2d Ser. 2.11 (December 1937): 289–97.

32. 15 July 1937.

33. Programming consisted of *Kulturfilme* and shortened feature films, sports, news, weather, and so on. The program day for Friday, 28 July 1939 consisted of the following:

12:05	"Blitzlichter"
13:00–13:30	(Pause)

13:30	"Musikalisches Zwischenspiel"
14:00	"Das Deutsche Rote Kreuz"
15:00	"Das schöne Deutschland"
15:45	"Altwiener Bilder"
16:50	Einführung in die Veranstaltungsreihe "Sport und Mikrofon"
17:45	"Aus der Werkstatt des Rundfunks"
18:35	"Ein Traum im Puppenladen"
19:15–20:00	(Pause)
20:00	Nachrichten, Wetter
20:15	"Interessantes aus aller Welt"
20:25	Zeitdienst
21:00	"Altwiener Bilder"
22:00–22:20	Nachrichten, Wetter, Sport

34. For a fuller discussion of German technical advances, see the BIOS, CIOS, and FIAT reports.

35. Space constraints preclude a discussion of attitude formation and reception in the 1920s and early 1930s, during which, among other things, television's utopian dimension predominated. See Monika Elsner, Thomas Müller, Peter M. Spangenberg, "The Early History of German Television: The Slow Development of a Fast Medium," *Historical Journal of Film, Radio and Television* 10.2 (1990): 193–220.

36. The patterns of reception in popular, trade, and industrial discourse obviously constitutes a huge area of study which this article can only introduce.

37. Coverage regarding the start of German television service is typical. See, *New York Times* 30 June 1935, 2 February 1935, 27 April 1935.

38. *New York Times* 4 September 1935. A related set of assertions addressed the lag in U.S. television deployment relative to Germany and Britain in positive terms. Following assertions from American industry, Judge E. O. Sykes of the FCC was reported to have told the British, "If you start television over there before we do here, we'll wait and profit by your mistakes." (*New York Times*, n.d., 1934, from N. E. Kersta papers, File 2a, Pennsylvania State U.)

39. Typical of these reports is a *New York Times* assertion from May 1935: "nevertheless, the important role which radio plays in Germany's political scheme will tend to accelerate television."

40. *New York Times* 26 July 1935.

41. *New York Times* 25 August 1935.

42. See, for example, Ernest H. Traub, "Television at the Berlin Radio Exhibition," *Journal of the Television Society*, 2d Ser. 2.3 (December 1935): 53–61. Traub's detailed reports appeared as an annual feature of the journal.

43. The industry's reception of German television is the subject of my ongoing research and thus is presented in tentative terms. Compare my "Rituals of Reception, Patterns of Neglect: Nazi Television and Its Postwar Representation," *Wide Angle* 11.1 (February 1989): 48–66.

44. From its formal start in 1936, the British program day appeared substantially more developed than its German counterpart. Moreover, with sales of receivers amounting to some 10,000 sets in the same period that Germany sold between 200 and 1,000, Britain provided a better model.

45. David Sarnoff, *The Future of Radio: A Report to the FCC* (New York, 15 June 1936).

46. N. E. Kersta papers. File 1b. Pennsylvania State U.

47. The technological advantages that potentially could be gained, together with issues of staff recruitment from among German engineers and footholds for subsequent corporate reconfiguration in Germany, were huge. Corporations sent their own investigators, often through military channels. IT&T's CEO, Sosthenes Behn, arrived in France in 1944 wearing battle fatigues, and two of his vice presidents—who months earlier enjoyed corporate positions in New York—appeared as high-ranking army officers. See Sampson (an IT&T critic) and Sobel (an IT&T supporter) for essentially overlapping testimony on this point.

48. Heinz Pohle, "Wollen und Wirklichkeit des deutschen Fernsehens bis 1943," *Rundfunk und Fernsehen* 1 (1956): 59–75 and Winfried Lerg, "Zur Entstehung des Fernsehens in Deutschland," *Rundfunk und Fernsehen* 4 (1967): 349–75.

49. Erwin Reiss, *"Wir senden Frohsinn": Fernsehen unterm Faschismus* (Berlin: Elephanten, 1979).

50. In this regard, see the special early German television issue of *Historical Journal of Film, Radio and Television*, 10.2 (1990), which includes an array of essays representing new work on the subject.

7

Generational
Conflict and Historical
Continuity in GDR Film

Barton Byg

Functions of Cinema in the GDR

The waves of young people leaving the German Democratic Republic in 1989 and the ensuing political upheaval (leading to that state's demise) reflected a crisis of confidence and continuity between generations that had been evident in GDR culture for some time. For instance, Günter Erbe distinguished between the generation of GDR poets active since the early 1960s, who saw themselves as part of a great social movement to perfect socialism, and the generation born after 1945 or 1950, who had a less solid attachment to the GDR.[1] The lack of interest many young people demonstrated in the future of socialism is typified in the oft-quoted remark by the poet Fritz-Hendrik Melle (born in 1960) regarding Volker Braun. "All I can say is, that boy is torturing himself."[2] Perhaps too late to rejuvenate GDR film, however, the late 1980s also revealed a new historical continuity as GDR cinema rediscovered links to its own history and a youth culture that had been repressed. In 1987 and 1988 three films, withheld from cinemas at the time of their production, were released to GDR audiences. The films *Jadup und Boel* by Rainer Simon (1980; 1988), *Die Russen kommen* (*The Russians Are Coming*) by Heiner Carow (1967; 1988), and *Berlin um die Ecke* (*Berlin Around the Corner*) by Gerhard Klein and Wolfgang Kohlhaase (1965; 1987) mediated between recent and more distant history, reflecting the ruptures and continuities that characterized the history of socialism in the GDR. Before we look more closely at these films and their relevance to the dilemmas of GDR culture in the late 1980s, we must note that their late emergence also draws attention to various functions of the cinema that were plagued with difficulties over the four decades of Deutsche Film-AG (DEFA) history: cinema as an outlet of creative expression for the young and as a source of pure entertainment; cinema as a forum for dealing with contemporary issues; cinema as a representation of the national identity and sense of history.[3]

Fulfilling the first two of these functions has been a perpetual source of frustration for young people in socialism. Cinema has always held a special appeal for the young, and the GDR was no exception.[4] The main audience for film in the GDR was young people, aged fifteen to twenty-five.[5] Aside from music and meeting friends, going to the movies ranked as their most highly valued form of entertainment.[6] Movies, like music, are a way to participate in international youth culture, as well as a source of adventure and entertainment. Studies by GDR sociologists revealed film spectatorship to be a highly valued way for young people in the GDR to relate to their peers.[7] Films were looked to for concrete information about the world, especially young viewers' own surroundings, and for *Lebenshilfe* ("help for living").

The most prominent directors in the GDR also drew their fascination with film from their youth, but for most of them this was twenty to forty years earlier. On one hand this was a potential source of national continuity since many established filmmakers in the GDR came into conflict with official cultural policy over the years by attempting to make films in the context of international youth culture. Their own difficulties in coming to terms with the state and their own identity as GDR citizens represented a concrete link to the issues raised by young people born after the Berlin Wall was erected in 1961.[8] On the other hand, the predominance of established directors left very little room for young directors in the GDR. Because of the structure of the education system, with internship and (for men) military service before film school, directors who endured the long process of becoming qualified rarely were able to produce their first feature films before age forty. Even then, with a level of production of between fifteen and twenty films per year, there was little regular work in cinema for the thirty or so feature film directors in the country. Television offered much greater capacity, but due to its responsibility to the Central Committee rather than the Ministry of Culture, it was not flexible in the opportunities offered newcomers.

Until the late 1980s, those who completed one or more short films as students also had little opportunity to show their work to the public or at festivals abroad. Repeated suggestions that a separate studio branch and distribution program be set aside for *Nachwuchs,* in contrast to other socialist countries, led to no concrete action in the GDR. By late 1989, the only step in this direction had been the increased availability of films by film school students in the theaters of GDR film clubs and at festivals there and abroad. Film school continues to be the starting point for many young filmmakers in the united Germany. German unification and the advent of market mechanisms may offer some new opportunities to young filmmakers, particularly in television, but scarce resources and the uncertain future of state subsidies do not promise much expansion in the area of film, at least in the short run. The new freedom, however, does mean that film artists can look for work outside the former GDR.

In addition to the limitations of scale and age, socialist cultural policy inhibited the production of films that merely seek to entertain. Since many such products are looked at by intellectuals and politicians alike as an unavoidable vice, it seemed practical to import them from the United States and other countries. Indeed, countries around the world are resigned to American domination of the entertainment media market, and the GDR had little prospect of being an exception.[9]

The principal difficulty in making DEFA films interesting to youth in the GDR arose from the obstacles to treating controversial issues of contemporary life or the official view of history. The more institutions a film brought under critical scrutiny, the more committees had to approve the project at every level. The centralized review procedure, which for literature was removed in the GDR in January 1989, was left in effect until 1990 for the very expensive and public enterprise of film.[10] The number of controversial and topical films that didn't get beyond the treatment stage cannot be known, but at crucial points in the development of the GDR and its film industry, films or groups of films were withheld from release. This had the doubly chilling effect of cutting off public and artistic reception of a work and of putting the filmmakers on notice to be even more cautious in the future. One crucial example was the film *Sonnensucher* (*Sun Seekers*, 1957/58) by Konrad Wolf,[11] which dealt with the uranium miners under Soviet management in the Wismut area. The film was banned in 1959, at least initially to avoid embarrassing the Soviet Union during nuclear arms negotiations. *Sun Seekers* contains a rather romanticized view of the harnessing of the atom as well as exhortations of the Germans to go all out to help the Soviets develop nuclear capability in the late 1940s. It thus went against the international image the Soviets wished to project ten years later. Of much greater significance in the GDR however, is the fact that the film also depicted— not altogether in a flattering way—the rough-and-tumble energy of the young republic and even showed the democratic removal of a party secretary. Its disappearance for fourteen years, until the relative liberalization ushered in by the Honecker era, did leave a gap in political film culture. The significance of its absence is confirmed by its inclusion along with other tabooed topics in a controversial survey of important film influences conducted by the journal *Filmwissenschaftliche Mitteilungen* in 1965. In her response to the opinion survey, Christa Wolf suggests that the film would have been one of DEFA's most important—had it been able to prove itself.[12]

Perhaps the biggest setback in GDR cinema's effort to treat contemporary problems (or any subject for that matter) came soon after the end of Khrushchev's chairmanship, when the Eleventh Plenum of the Central Committee of the SED in 1965 shelved virtually the whole year's film production.[13] In 1979 one of the screenwriters affected, Wolfgang Kohlhaase, stated that the resulting breach of trust between the party leadership and the film community still had not healed.[14] Kurt

Maetzig, one of the few remaining filmmakers who had been among the cofounders of DEFA, expressed bitterness in a 1989 interview that his film *Das Kaninchen bin ich (I'm the Rabbit)* had still not been released.[15]

The "rabbit films" illustrate in retrospect the potential for a youth-oriented reform movement that existed in the GDR in the early 1960s; at the same time the movement shows striking similarities to the thaw that produced the Prague Spring. Since each of the films deals with some aspect of the frustrations and conflicts of young people in the socialist system, they were condemned for importing from Czechoslovakia the idea that alienation could exist in socialism and for displaying too much Western decadence and formalism.[16] In banning the films, the party was actually reversing reform impulses it had earlier explicitly encouraged in its Youth Communiqué of 1963, which had expressed a desire to increase youth support for socialism.[17]

At the end of the 1970s and the beginning of the 1980s there again seemed to be a chance for DEFA to regain its artistic momentum and its credibility with its audience. Numerous provocative contemporary films generated unprecedented public interest and discussion of their social implications. The high point of these developments was Wolf and Kohlhaase's *Solo Sunny,* which attracted a phenomenal GDR audience of over 3.5 million and stimulated unprecedented debate over unconventional aspirations in socialism.[18] Like the "rabbit films" of the 1960s, *Solo Sunny* also combined its socially critical stance with conscious adoption of entertainment conventions. From Hollywood film it borrowed a self-conscious presentation of the female star as spectacle and a ubiquitous musical theme. The period of rising expectations typified by the film, however, was also marked by increasing restriction of artists, partly in the wake of the expulsion of the singer and poet Wolf Biermann in 1976. After another wave of artists left for the West between 1979 and 1981 and Konrad Wolf died in 1982, another period of cinematic doldrums began that even the exceptional success of *Einer trage des anderen Last (Bear Ye One Another's Burdens,* Lothar Warneke, 1988) was unable to relieve. Works by new, relatively young directors and individual successes in documentary films such as *Winter adé* (1988) came too late to bring millions of young people back to the film theaters to see domestic productions.[19] Political change overtook artistic protest, and GDR audiences joined their Western counterparts as consumers in the world media market.

A less publicly visible but essential role of film in the GDR was that of national self-representation, and this resonance of film history with general history will continue to be relevant in the ongoing transformation of German culture. GDR films, like other cultural products, were partly meant to contribute to a national identity for a new generation of GDR citizens. Events of 1989 to 1991 clearly reveal the weaknesses of this sense of identity in the GDR, but the generational conflict reflected in DEFA films and their difficult history helps to explain this failure.

Unshelving Forbidden Films

The question of generational conflict and understanding, crucial to the fate of the GDR, stood at the center of three important DEFA films that were withheld from release for between eight and twenty-two years. The fact that these films finally did reach audiences in 1987 and 1988 reflects an attempt to address the crisis of historical continuity and to reclaim a repressed view of GDR history. There was little publicity of this as a unified phenomenon, partly due to the reticence of the critics and partly due to a general tendency to avoid calling public attention to course corrections, which would mean admitting that something was amiss in the previous course. As Stephan Hermlin put it in a 1989 interview, the GDR often attempted to solve problems without admitting they exist.[20]

The release of shelved films, and by implication an ensuing policy of greater openness in film production, of course runs parallel to developments in the Soviet Union. There a number of films have been released years after their production, and as a result they have received perhaps exaggerated attention, even in the United States. These films include Tenghiz Abuladze's *Pokayaniye* (*Repentance*, 1984; 1987), Alexei Gherman's *Proverka na Dorogakh* (*Trial on the Road*, 1971; 1986) and *Moi Drug Ivan Lapshin* (*My Friend Ivan Lapshin*, 1981; 1985); Gleb Panfilov's *Tema* (*The Theme*, 1979; 1986); and Alexander Askoldov's *Kommissar* (*Commissar*, 1967; 1987). Of similar significance is the posthumous acceptance of Andrei Tarkovsky as a "Russian artist" after he had defected in 1984 and died in Paris in 1986.[21] These latter two phenomena are also relevant in the GDR, where a belated reception of Tarkovsky began in the late 1980s in club cinemas and where *Commissar* was among a program of five Soviet films banned in November of 1988 and later quietly released on a smaller scale. Perhaps as a small gesture of protest, the Sektion Theorie und Kritik (Section for Theory and Criticism) of the Verband der Film- und Fernsehschaffenden (Film and Television Association) gave their critics' prize to *Commissar* as "the best foreign film in the cinema offerings of 1988."[22] After all, it was among the film offerings for a matter of days!

The three unshelved GDR films of the late 1980s focus on the following issues central to the GDR's cultural identity: the GDR's relation to pre-1949 German history and fascism, the history of GDR cultural policy that led to banning the films, and the history of socialism (especially Stalinism), which—as in the Soviet Union—has been one of the major taboos to be attacked by *Glasnost*. The fact that, unlike in the Soviet Union, the films were released before *Glasnost* became official policy in the GDR, could help explain why this process of restoring films to their place in the national film history took place quietly.

Jadup and Boel, the most recent film of the three and the only one to reach finished form, uses a subjective and psychological approach (unusual for DEFA films) to link current issues of the younger generation with unresolved problems from World War II and ensuing years. Jadup, the mayor of a small town, is played by Kurt Böwe, an actor who often selects roles of people whose critical consciousness comes into conflict with their social position. The mayor is haunted by memories of Boel, a young woman who came to the village after the war as a displaced person from the eastern provinces. She was treated as an outcast (although Jadup was secretly friendly with her) and was eventually the victim of a rape. Like the rest of the village, Jadup turned his back on her at this point. No particular effort was made to find the rapist, although people had a good idea which of the "respected" citizens it was, and Boel simply disappeared. This distant memory is juxtaposed with Jadup's contemporary problems—his lack of real commitment to his job and the boring speech that he makes every year to the assembled citizenry. He also is disturbed by the spectacle of his son Max, about fourteen years old, who is learning to become a conformist and repeating Jadup's mistake of not defending a friend who commits the "crime" of being different. In Max's case, the conflict takes place in school, where the children write essays about model socialists. Max's friend, a girl from a large poor family with a disreputable father, instead writes a scathing satire about what "big fat model socialists" the members of her family are. At a school meeting to discuss the matter, Max earnestly urges her to make an insincere retraction, as apparently most people would do. (This scene in particular evoked howls of laughter from the GDR audience.) At the end of the film, Jadup discards his customary speech and confesses his feelings about deserting Boel. The optimistic conclusion is that perhaps the son will learn not to base his life on deception and denial.

Upon its release in 1988, a review in the GDR film journal *Film und Fernsehen* did not mention the reasons for the film's initial withdrawal but instead described the situation in 1980 and the relevance of the film's social criticism.

> In 1980 contemporary topics dominated. People went to the movies because they found their problems were taken seriously there. . . .
> "Jadup and Boel" would have been the only film in 1980 on the history of the GDR. The historical dimension of the work gives it a particular significance today, now that its contemporary content already belongs to the past.[23]

This final sentence can only mean its opposite: the film could be released because its contemporary barbs appeared to be outmoded, but in fact its criticisms remained valid.

Since the reasons for censoring or banning films are difficult to document, one has to speculate about the areas where Simon would have had to make changes to get the film accepted. Most likely are the unflattering depictions of party functionaries and the education system. The latter, headed by Minister of Education Margot Honecker, was known to be particularly averse to public criticism. The content of a film is not necessarily sufficient to explain its being censored, however, since the sensitivity of party functionaries to controversy fluctuated significantly over periods of just a few months. Simon's film was to be released at a time when controversy between artists and the state had been unusually intense, and official policy was probably to avoid anything that might fuel public debates over party authority and submission to it. After Gorbachev had become Soviet leader and in the absence of a general artistic controversy, the release of *Jadup and Boel* seemed less likely to be explosive. The absence of sensation on the side of journalists merely underscores that no one wished to take the chance of either promoting a broad public controversy or provoking further state restriction.

It is perhaps telling that this unwillingness to provoke controversy even extended beyond the collapse of the SED regime. In early 1990 a reevaluation of the DEFA films of the 1980s in *Film und Fernsehen* is more of an epitaph than an investigation. Much of the article is devoted to *Jadup and Boel*, but beyond citing some of the provocative content of Simon's film, it makes no exploration of exactly who banned the film or how. It merely resignedly observes the limitations of even DEFA's most optimistic moments: "The appearance of the film *Solo Sunny* was only one side of the coin; the nonappearance of *Jadup and Boel* was the other."[24]

The frustration such restrictions caused for directors who wanted to deal with contemporary issues was expressed by Rainer Simon in an interview published in August 1989. Explaining why he chose to work on a film about Alexander von Humboldt after *Jadup and Boel*, he said:

> During the catastrophic back and forth about whether *Jadup and Boel* would come out or not, I looked for film subjects I could do. . . . It was clear to me that for now I would never be able to express what I cared about with a contemporary subject. And I was not (and am not) willing to make compromises. I can't waste precious time in life considering what is or is not possible for reasons of current politics.[25]

Whereas Simon's film had been made in a period of rising expectations when other critical films had wide resonance, Heiner Carow's *The Russians Are Coming* faced a more difficult situation in 1967. Its fate reveals that even historical topics could be controversial, especially if they touched the theme of antifascism, which was fundamental to the cultural and national identity of the GDR and the legitimacy of the state itself. Antifascist films also represent the oldest and most respected tradition of DEFA,[26] beginning even before the founding of the GDR, but its limitations were more pertinent than its achievements to the youthful cinema public at the end of the 1980s.

The early DEFA films appealed to broadly humanistic cultural values as an antidote to nazism. They had two main political aims: first, to convince their audiences that a German resistance to Nazi ideology had existed and that such an alternative still could be chosen as a basis for a new postwar society; and second, to counteract the tendency toward despair and apathy in a population still in shock from the experience of defeat.

Another important component in DEFA's antifascist films was their study of how basically honorable, ordinary people—bourgeois, petty bourgeois, or even workers—could have tolerated or supported fascism. Outstanding examples are the early films by Kurt Maetzig, Wolfgang Staudte, and Konrad Wolf. Despite these achievements, or perhaps because of them, the antifascist tradition in GDR film also has specific limitations.

Because the presentation of antifascism as a victorious alternative served a central function for national identity and legitimacy in the GDR, it also justified an intolerance of criticism of the government or questioning of its historical roots. Films avoided investigating the historical mistakes or moral shortcomings of those who resisted the Nazis, and GDR artists also scrupulously avoided depicting either the victims or the practitioners of Stalinism. Although the Communist party acknowledged "guilt" in 1945 for failing to forge a successful coalition of resistance to the fascists, concrete investigations of such failures were not tolerated. As a corollary to this, films based on such an understanding of antifascism, since they encouraged the same stance in the population, did not investigate to what degree GDR citizens or institutions actually applied the moral implications of antifascism. Since antifascism's main function was served on the level of national identification, it did not generally lead to a search for holdovers from the fascist period in the form of conformism, authoritarianism, anti-Semitism, or racism.

The problem with offering such a foundation for the antifascist identity to the population of the GDR was that it allowed for an unmediated transition from defeat in the war to identification with the victors.

In the cultural vacuum created by the repudiation of socialism in the GDR at the end of the 1980s, there has been a danger that this pattern might be perpetuated by again identifying with the victors—this time the West Germans. To avoid alienating the public, some early DEFA films also used the pedagogical expedient (employed in the 1980s as well) of presenting the antifascist resistance as victorious, which it clearly was not, except in the wake of the allied victory and the Soviet occupation. It became possible for audiences to assume that acceptance of a new (antifascist) authority was the equivalent of dealing with their own complicity (with nazism) or feelings of guilt.

The Russians Are Coming violated this convention of antifascism as the "myth of origin" in the GDR,[27] and the attacks on the film were so severe that it supposedly was destroyed when it was banned in 1967. This occurred in the aftermath of the Eleventh Plenum of the Central Committee of the SED in 1965, which had shelved virtually an entire year's film production either for being too formally experimental or showing too negative a view of socialist life. Events leading up to the Prague Spring in neighboring Czechoslovakia also gave GDR conservatives more cause to seek to restrict controversial artworks. The film survives only because its editor Evelyn Carow preserved a rough print. Extant copies are produced from this copy and not from the original negative, which was destroyed. This gives the film a peculiarly documentary look, as if it indeed were found or rediscovered footage.

The story is set in the eastern provinces of Germany at the time when the Russians occupied them near the end of World War II. Günther, a loyal and idealistic member of the Hitler Youth, desperately refuses to accept the example of the adults around him as they attempt to hide any sign of their allegiance to Hitler. The stylized approach the film takes to the time it treats raises issues of historical perspective: At the outset, while we see a group of three teenagers teasing each other on the beach, there is very little hint of the time or place. Only when the trio discovers the corpse of a soldier is it clear that a war is going on, and even then it is only much later that the film makes it entirely clear that its setting is the conclusion of World War II.

The timeless appearance of the three teenagers increases the historical irony of the film. The exposition at first suggests a harmless love triangle: A blonde suitor and a brown-haired suitor playfully vie for a girl's attention. It becomes grotesque when we discover that the blonde suitor is a Soviet prisoner who has escaped from his forced labor detail. The brown-haired Günther has learned his lessons well as a Hitler Youth. He eventually leads the local militia to where the Russian boy has fled and pleads with him to stand still. The result is that the Russian is simply shot.

The film probably was not approved for release at its completion because of the power of this irony: The "good boy," with whom many of the middle generation of GDR citizens—including party functionaries—could identify, is also at least partly a murderer. And the liberation of Germany by the Red Army, seen here from the point of view of German family and private life, sets off a crisis of authority and belief between the boy and his elders. Carow's film dares to point out that the GDR as an antifascist state did not emerge full-blown with the arrival of the Russian liberators but instead was at the outset confronted with violence, confusion, and deep unprocessed feelings of having been betrayed.

The Russians Are Coming was not the only film to return to the origins of the GDR as conflict between artists and the state intensified in the mid-1960s. *Ich war neunzehn* (*I Was Nineteen*, 1967), one of Konrad Wolf's most personal and successful films, looks at the last days of the war from the other side. Although Wolf's film is much more optimistic than Carow's, the story it tells from the point of view of an exiled German youth, returning as a Soviet soldier, also does not glorify or oversimplify the antifascist stance. Because of this "subjective authenticity"—a term borrowed from the novelist Christa Wolf—*I Was Nineteen* was a key film in helping DEFA both recover from the trauma of the Eleventh Plenum and reclaim a degree of credibility with young audiences. But *The Russians Are Coming* was prevented from complementing *I Was Nineteen* to stimulate a multifaceted discussion of the historical origins of the GDR and its antifascist heritage. Only a dedication to Konrad Wolf in its opening titles bears witness to this connection. On the other hand, however, the late release of Carow's film allowed it to resonate with the work of a young director on a similar motif—Michael Kann's 1987 film *Stielke, Heinz, fünfzehn . . .* (*Stielke, Heinz, Age Fifteen*). Kann likewise focuses on a boy in the Hitler Youth to explore the disillusionment and exploitation of a younger generation.

The power of Carow's film to connect different points of history partly rests on its avoidance of general historical references, its neorealist documentary style and its concentration on a rather private, everyday story. Our knowledge that the film too has a history of repression and liberation simply adds a level of meaning to what is already there, and the film's grainy, uneven material quality provides a physical trace of the struggle between cultural memory and ideology. It is unfortunate that virtually the only American review of the film saw it as "a ham-fisted attempt to portray the Soviets as unerring liberators" and attributed the material evidence of the film's near destruction simply to "bad production values."[28]

The third and oldest film to be rereleased also bears the most dramatic relevance to the upheavals in the GDR of 1989. The film is *Berlin Around the Corner,* directed by Gerhard Klein, one of the most consistent practitioners of the GDR's adaptation of Italian neorealism,[29] and written by Wolfgang Kohlhaase. *Berlin und um die Ecke* (the film's working title) was never completed in the turmoil of the Eleventh Plenum of 1965 and was released only in 1987 in a retrospective of Klein's work sponsored by the State Film Archive of the GDR. For its 1990 release, Wolfgang Kohlhaase and Evelyn Carow reedited the fragmentary version that the archive had screened.

The sort of debate among young people avoided by withholding *Berlin Around the Corner* is very clear, since it explicitly presents generational conflict in a contemporary (i.e., 1965) setting. Indeed, few films made after 1965 grappled with social and political issues as vividly and as directly as this film or perhaps *Sun Seekers.* In an interview in 1979, Kohlhaase recalled the importance *Berlin Around the Corner* might have had in connecting art to the contemporary concerns of young people, using terms not far removed from the attitudes of the Italian neorealists. He concluded that the wounds of the Eleventh Plenum still hadn't healed.

> In the mid-60s a number of films were finished but not shown, among them one of mine. Klein and I had intended to carry on with certain aspects of [*Berlin—*] *Ecke Schönhauser.* We had not lost any of our commitment, the ever-new questions of young people concerned us; and films, too, as we thought, and as I still believe, are a part of a publicly active moral consciousness in a socialist society. For the first time I sat there, as our film was discussed, and went away with a feeling

of revolt and an empty feeling. Today I think that for complex reasons political positions were being taken in the disguise of a discussion of art. The attempt was made to prove something using examples that didn't fit what was to be said, at least not with such clear rigor. Thus the question and the answer could never come together. For a sensitive matter, more sense of proportion was lost than was gained. Above all, a certain generation in the arts, to which I belong, came into conflicts that it seems to me have not since been overcome by a collective understanding.[30]

The generation conflict in the GDR of the mid-1960s is depicted in stark clarity in this film. The anger of the young workers, led by a Marlon Brando-like character named Olaf, played by Dieter Mann, and the proud inflexibility of the older communists are both given their due. Olaf evokes Brando in his slouching body language, grinning irony, and explosive emotions. He rides a motorcycle and wears a leather jacket. With this character the film also recalls a role played by Ekkehard Schall in Kohlhaase/Klein's 1956 film *Berlin—Ecke Schönhauser* (*Berlin—Schönhauser Corner*) and thus resonates with a body of films that belonged to the international youth culture of the 1950s.[31] The male youth culture of dance halls and chasing women also provides a counterpoint to the political and historical conflicts in the factory where Olaf and his friends work. Here the members of a youth brigade complain that they are underpaid since their higher productivity is bureaucratically transformed into higher wages for the older workers. After various confrontations and protests over this issue, the youth brigade decides to take revenge on their older colleagues by showing that the factory could really produce two hundred to three hundred percent more if people actually worked up to capacity. As the two young workers are offered an award for their initiative, they refuse it, publicly stating that their aim was to expose the fraud and hypocrisy of the factory and quit instead.

Workplace conflicts also take the form of personal conflicts between characters of the younger and older generations. Two very memorable representatives of the older generation of Communists and antifascists are played by Erwin Geschonneck and Hans Hardt-Hardtloff. The former has the role of the foreman, to whom the young workers do have a relationship of trust and admiration. He is one of the old school who treats the machines as if they were his own, shutting them off every minute they are not producing to spare them wear. He often remains in the factory after hours, looking after things, and agonizes constantly over the lack of this or that spare part. Hardt-Hardtloff plays an old Communist who at first is totally unsympathetic because of his dogmatic refusal to recognize the younger workers' point of view. It is with this character that the confrontation takes on the most powerful cinematic expression. After a particularly acrimonious conflict over graffiti by Olaf's friend— "Wir sind alle Sklaven" ("We are all slaves")—Olaf attacks the old man on his way home and bloodies his nose. The shock of this scene is allowed to sink in over a long period of silence (somewhat shortened in the 1990 editing) as the old man goes slowly up to his tiny apartment, sits down weakly, and washes off the blood. Realizing what he has done, the young man finally comes in to explain that the police have been to see him. The old man responds, "The last time they hit me, it was at roll-call. He was just as young as you—April 24, 1945." Olaf then presents the young generation's point of view: "I notice I'm not so happy as the newspapers say," and "Why doesn't anyone believe us? . . . Whenever you want to talk to somebody about it, they only say, 'Be grateful you didn't live through those days.' It sounds like an excuse." The old man reassures Olaf that his generation will have all the power soon enough. This exchange cannot be said to result in communication, however. Instead, the scene ends with Olaf noticing the humbleness of the apartment and asking questions about the old man's personal isolation.

By the end of the film, more evidence emerges that the older generation is giving way to the new when the Geschonneck character dies. In a rather unconvincing turn of the plot, his legacy is passed on to Olaf, and the film ends with Olaf developing a more responsible attitude toward life, going off with the woman he has been pursuing all along and giving his leather jacket to his younger brother.

The importance of this film in linking *Gegenwart* and *Geschichte* was stressed in a 1988 article published in West Germany by the GDR film critic Hannes Schmidt:

> Now that *Berlin Around the Corner* can be seen after many years, the question of the film's contemporary relevance poses itself anew. The film has retained an amazing freshness, poetic attraction, self-assured-

ness and consciousness of the issues. Such themes as the relation to the younger generation, honesty in everyday socialist life, the right to have a voice, in other words the concrete practice of socialist democracy, are obviously still of burning relevance today."[32]

This contemporary relevance can be found in several scenes of the film that underscore the difference between the generations and perhaps also in its wishful thinking that the middle and younger generation would be more flexible in governing because they are less marked by the fearful habits of the cold war. For example, after unsuccessfully urging the much younger party secretary to respond to the youthful provocations with an iron fist, the old Communist asks him simply and directly, "Aren't you ever afraid that we could just lose everything?" This question stands for much of the intransigence the SED exhibited over the years. But after a seemingly endless pause to clean his eyeglasses, the party secretary replies, "No, I never am." A humorous scene represents the call for more democracy that was no less relevant in the late 1980s than in 1965: At a boring meeting of the factory workers there is no response when the party secretary asks if they have any discussion. But later, when the youth brigade gives voice to its discontent and accusations begin to fly back and forth, someone quips, "See, there you have discussion."

Outlook for DEFA

The rapid collapse of party control in the GDR following Erich Honecker's resignation in October 1989 underscored the conflicts of legitimacy and historical continuity present in these three films, as well as in the "rabbit films" of 1965/66, released in 1990. The young party secretary's confidence in a democratic reform of socialism, in a film banned in 1965, was out of place after the older generation had stubbornly clung to power for twenty-four more years that ended in scandal and discredit. The inability of the succeeding generation of Communists to regain credibility and carry out belated reform by 1989 was but one result of the policies that could not tolerate public reception of such films in past decades.

This is the other side of the coin regarding the relevance of the GDR's banned films as that state reached its final crisis. Political events removed the context for the socialist reforms they represent. Contrary to a movement toward socialist democracy as invoked by Schmidt in his praise of *Berlin Around the Corner*, the result seems to be a widespread repudiation of socialism in the GDR. Thus the director Frank Vogel said there were limits to his joy at seeing his banned film *Don't Think That I'm Crying* released after twenty-five years.

> But that didn't last long before the sadness came, deep sadness, because the film really is still alive, contemporary in its message, its concerns. A depressing feeling, when a society more or less stagnates for a quarter-century, when unconditional conformity is rewarded and creativity is punished. What could have become of this land, if only. . . . But history knows no "What might have been, if only."[33]

As far as social and political reform is concerned, the banned films arrived on the scene too late to be anything other than documents of its failure. Günter Stahnke, director of *Spring Takes Time*, also speaks of the rabbit films as part of a failed attempt to improve socialism in 1965. "If we had been able to improve it then, it wouldn't be being abolished now."[34]

The release of three banned films before 1989 at least revealed that there were reform elements within the party and the cultural establishment who hoped *Glasnost* would permit a constructive airing of generational conflicts. But when German unification replaced *Glasnost* as an issue in the GDR, the creators of these films were in a strangely ambiguous position. On one hand, much of the population saw them as figures of relative power and privilege who benefitted from the policies of the past. On the other hand, there was little appreciation of their artistic achievements, their links to a distinguished European tradition, or their attempts to deal with the uncomfortable aspects of German history.[35]

The founding of a review commission, which began bringing out the rabbit films in January 1990, was an attempt to preserve the historical and cultural value of GDR film traditions for all of Germany. As the commission's head, Rolf Richter, described them:

> The films that were banned for attempting to strike a blow for liberation now provide us with a much needed perspective on the history of our society. They show this history with an impact and plasticity offered by no other source today, including historians and philosophers.

They are a window through which we see ourselves and our times more clearly. We feel the benefits offered by these films just now, but we also feel bitterness—bitterness over the loss of creative potential, imagination and critical keenness that our land suffered. The ban on these films had consequences, the full meaning of which we are beginning to understand.[36]

Speaking at the premiere of the rabbit films at the GDR Academy of Arts in February 1990, Richter went on to stress the importance of reclaiming at least some of the artistic and historical potential they represent. Despite its defeats in the past, then, GDR cinema could contribute to the sense of a national cinema in a united Germany, thus helping to create a national sense of identity that would be distinguished from popular culture products imported from the United States and elsewhere. All of the films treated here attempted to be both popular and political in a way in which imported material clearly is not. Imported culture is only political inasmuch as it represents a rejection of the status quo, but once the status quo has been rejected in its politics and not just its entertainment offerings, a need is opened up for culturally and historically specific alternatives. This need is confirmed by the high level of interest in the banned DEFA films in all parts of Germany, where they have been shown in theaters and on television.

Part of the historically specific alternative suggested by the banned GDR films is to continue the investigation of guilt and betrayal in another side of German history, the history of German socialism. As was evident for the films examined here, historical questions have contemporary implications. The meaning of antifascism must be reexamined both in the light of a critique of the Stalinist legacy and in the face of resurgent neofascist expressions; a balance must be drawn between the ideals socialism claimed for itself and the conformity and compromise that was enforced in the name of those ideals. These films showed young people being manipulated and exploited in the name of ideology. They showed them forcing their elders to face a deformed reality and refusing to accept what is passed on to them by being passive and grateful. As such they help express what is at stake in the struggle for a humane and democratic turn in German history—in both East and West—in the last decade of the twentieth century.

Notes

1. Günter Erbe, "Zum Selbstverständnis junger Lyriker in der DDR: Kolbe, Anderson, Eckart," *Studies in GDR Culture and Society* 4, ed. Margy Gerber et al. (Lanham: University Press of America, 1984) 172–73; all translations are my own.
2. Cited in Wolfgang Emmerich, *Kleine Literaturgeschichte der DDR 1945–1988*, 2d ed. (Frankfurt a. M.: Luchterhand, 1989) 426–27; the full quotation is: "Volker Braun? Da kann ich nur sagen, der Junge quält sich. Dazu habe ich keine Beziehung mehr.—Ich bin schon in einer frustrierten Gesellschaft aufgewachsen. Diese Enttäuschung ist für mich kein Erlebnis mehr, sondern eine Voraussetzung."
3. General works on GDR cinema include the following: Hartmut Albrecht et al., *Sozialistisches Menschenbild und Filmkunst* (Berlin: Henschel, 1970); ed. Rolf Richter, *DEFA-Spielfilm-Regisseure und ihre Kritiker*, vols. 1 and 2, (Berlin: Henschel, 1981; 1983); Peter Jansen and Wolfram Schütte, eds., *Film in der DDR* (Munich: Hanser, 1977); *Film und Fernsehkunst der DDR: Traditionen—Beispiele—Tendenzen* (Berlin: Henschel, 1979); Sigrun D. Leonhard, "Testing the Borders: East German Film between Individualism and Social Commitment," *Post New Wave Cinema in the Soviet Union and Eastern Europe*, ed. Daniel J. Goulding (Bloomington: Indiana UP, 1989) 51–101. On the sparse availability of DEFA films in the United States, cf. my "Cinema in the German Democratic Republic," *Monatshefte* 82 (1990): 286–93.
4. Lothar Bisky and Dieter Wiedemann, *Der Spielfilm: Rezeption und Wirkung* (Berlin: Henschel, 1985) 13–14.
5. Bisky and Wiedemann 13.
6. Bisky and Wiedemann 15.
7. Bisky and Wiedemann 17–18 and Dieter Wiedemann and Hans-Jörg Stiehler, "Kinobesucher als Gegenstand soziologischer Analyse," *Filmkommunikation in den achtziger Jahren—Bilanz und Ausblick, Informationsbulletin Jugendforschung* (Leipzig: Zentralinstitut für Jugendforschung beim Amt für Jugendfragen beim Ministerrat der DDR, 1984) 20.
8. The problem of making credible films about the issues of concern to young people was raised by a young viewer of Konrad Wolf's film *Mama, ich lebe* (*Mama, I'm Alive*, 1976), which treated the choice of national loyalties faced by Wolf's own generation. The viewer said, "You have no credibility with me, even if you tell the truth about the war, as long as you don't depict our troubles, our conflicts just as convincingly. Can't you do that or aren't you allowed to do it?" Konrad Wolf, "Von den Möglichkeiten sozialistischer Filmkunst: Reaktionen auf *Mama, ich lebe*," *Film und Fernsehen* 10.10 (1982): 69. This challenge partly motivated Wolf to direct *Solo Sunny*, a film specifically related to dissatisfied youth, and to work with the young cinematographer Eberhard Geick rather than Werner Bergmann, his partner of many years.
9. For further information on the role of Western products in GDR film offerings and other media, cf. Wolfgang Kohlhaase, "Some Remarks about GDR

Cinema," *Studies in GDR Culture and Society* 7, ed. Margy Gerber et al. (Lanham: University Press of America, 1987) 1–6 and Lothar Bisky, "Mass Media and the Socialization of Young People in the GDR," in the same volume 7–14.

10. The most thorough description of film production is Heinz Kersten, *Das Filmwesen in der Sowjetischen Besatzungszone Deutschlands* (Bonn: Bundesministerium für gesamtdeutsche Fragen, 1963). Cf. also Heinz Kersten, "Entwicklungslinien," *Film in der DDR* 38–39; the entry under "Filmwesen," *DDR Handbuch*, ed. Bundesministerium für innerdeutsche Beziehungen, 2 vols. (Bonn: Verlag Wissenschaft und Politik, 1985) I:388–90; and *Filmland DDR: Ein Reader zu Geschichte, Funktion und Wirkung der DEFA*, ed. Harry Blunk and Dirk Jungnickel (Cologne: Verlag Wissenschaft und Politik, 1990). Published documentation of the approval process for film projects and of cases of censorship was rare, however. A publication on such cases was a project of the review commission that brought out the banned films after October 1989 but did not come about in the rush to unification.

11. Cf. Karl Georg Egel and Paul Wiens, *Sonnensucher: Filmerzählung* (Berlin: Henschel, 1974) and Kersten, *Das Filmwesen in der SBZ* 103–4. Cf. also Kersten, " 'Sonnensucher' aus der Versenkung geholt," *epd Kirche und Film* June 1972: 14–15; excerpted in "Konrad Wolf," *Metropolis* (Hamburg cinema brochure) 9 (1985): n.p.

12. "Umfrage," *Filmwissenschaftliche Mitteilungen* 2 (1965): 316.

13. On the drastic intervention undertaken at the Central Committee's Eleventh Plenum, cf. Kersten, "Entwicklungslinien" 42–43 and Manfred Jäger, *Kultur und Politik in der DDR: Ein historischer Abriß* (Cologne: Edition Deutschland Archiv, Verlag Wissenschaft und Politik, 1982) 115–22. Jäger provides an excellent chronology of the vicissitudes of GDR cultural policy.

14. Hans Richter, "Gespräch mit Wolfgang Kohlhaase," *Sinn und Form* 31.5 (September/October 1979): 983–84.

15. The "rabbit films" were released soon after Honecker's resignation and received much attention in the GDR and in the West. The Academy of Arts of the GDR screened eight of them in January 1990, and they were then included in the (West) Berlin International Film Festival in that year, which for the first time was held in both parts of the city. At the festival, Frank Beyer's *Spur der Steine (Traces of the Stones)* was in the main program, out of competition. The International Forum of Young Film screened the rest: Kurt Maetzig's *I'm the Rabbit*—the source of the nickname for the banned films, Frank Vogel's *Denk bloß nicht, ich heule (Don't Think That I'm Crying)*, Hermann Zschoche's *Karla*, Günter Stahnke's *Der Frühling braucht Zeit (Spring Takes Time)*, and *Monolog für einen Taxifahrer (Monolog for a Taxi Driver*, 1962, unexpectedly added to the program), Egon Günther's *Wenn du groß bist, lieber Adam (When You're Older, Dear Adam)*, Jürgen Böttcher's *Jahrgang 45 (Born in 1945)*, and Gerhard Klein's *Berlin Around the Corner*. For a discussion of these films, cf. my article "What Might Have Been: DEFA Films of the Past and the Future of German Cinema," *Cineaste* 17.4 (Summer 1990): 9–15.

16. The 1963 Kafka Conference at Liblice, Czechoslovakia, was a high point in the debate about alienation in socialism and was an early cause of the GDR's

vehement rejections of Western-influenced critiques of orthodox Marxism. Cf. Jäger 108–10. The Kafka Conference itself is documented in Paul Reimann et al., eds., *Kafka aus Prager Sicht 1963* (Prague: Verlag der Tschechoslowakischen Akademie der Wissenschaften, 1965).

17. Cf. Dietrich Staritz, *Geschichte der DDR 1949–1985* (Frankfurt a.M.: Suhrkamp, 1985) 170.

18. Related films include *Sabine Wulff* (directed by Erwin Stranka, 1978), *Bis daß der Tod euch Scheidet* (*Till Death Do You Part*, Heiner Carow, 1978) and *Bürgschaft für ein Jahr* (*On Probation*, Hermann Zschoche, 1981). Regarding the success of *Solo Sunny*, cf. "Es ist etwas im Gange in der DDR," *Der Spiegel* 7 April 1980: 233 (interview with Konrad Wolf), and Heinz Klunker, "Sunny politisch Sorgen herzungewisse" (sic), ed. Hans Günther Pflaum, *Jahrbuch Film 80/81* (Munich: Hanser, 1980) 135–52.

19. Considerable promise has been shown by the young feature film directors Peter Kahane (*Ete und Ali*, 1985; *Die Architekten* [*The Architects*], 1990) and Michael Kann (*Stielke, Heinz, fünfzehn . . .* [*Stielke, Heinz, Age Fifteen*], 1987); Helke Misselwitz, with Heiner Carow as mentor, had the unusual opportunity to make her first feature-length film a documentary about women in the GDR—*Winter adé* (now distributed in the United States by Zeitgeist Films). In eight months of release, mostly in small theaters, the film had over 300,000 viewers. (Helke Misselwitz, discussion after screening, Amherst, MA, 9 November 1989.)

20. "Wir brauchen vor allem Glasnost" (Interview with Stephan Hermlin), *Der Spiegel* 6 February 1989: 77. Hermlin said, "Es gibt eine Praxis bei uns. Man kann sie merkwürdig finden, aber sie ist eine traditionelle Praxis: daß man eigentlich die Fehler der Vergangenheit zu korrigieren sucht, aber sie nicht zugibt."

21. Karen Rosenberg, " 'The Most Important Art': Movies in the Soviet Union," *The Nation* 21 November 1988: 526–27.

22. Cf. "Schmerzhafte Geburt einer neuen Welt" (Interview with Alexander Askoldov), *Film und Fernsehen* 17.8 (1989): 15.

23. *Film und Fernsehen* 16.11 (1988): 10. "Zeitgenössische Stoffe dominierten. Die Leute gingen ins Kino, weil sie ihre Probleme dort ernstgenommen sahen. . . . 'Jadup und Boel' wäre 1980 der einzige Film zur Geschichte der DDR geworden. Die historische Dimension des Werkes gibt ihm heute, wo seine Gegenwartsebene bereits zur Vergangenheit gehört, ein besonderes Gewicht."

24. Fred Gehler, "Aufbruch oder Niedergang: DEFA Spielfilm in den 80er Jahren," *Film und Fernsehen* 18.3 (1990): 2.

25. *Film und Fernsehen* 17.8 (1989): 2. "Ich habe während des katastrophalen Hin und Her, ob 'Jadup und Joel' kommt oder nicht, nach Stoffen gesucht, die ich machen kann. . . . Es war mir klar, daß ich vorerst bei einem Gegenwartssujet nie und nimmer ausdrücken konnte, was mich bewegt. Und zu Kompromissen war (und bin) ich nicht bereit. Ich kann kostbare Lebenszeit nicht damit vergeuden zu überlegen, was aus tagespolitischen Gründen geht und was nicht."

26. Cf. Barton Byg, "The Anti-Fascist Tradition and GDR Film," *Proceedings, Purdue University Fifth Annual Conference on Film* (West Lafayette: Purdue Office of Publications, 1980) 81–87; Wolfgang Klaue, ed., *Filme contra*

Faschismus (Berlin: Staatliches Filmarchiv der DDR, 1965); and *Film- und Fernsehkunst der DDR* 94–105 and *passim;* Bruce A. Murray, *The Dialectic of Antifascism: National Socialism in Postwar German Cinema* (Berlin, New York: de Gruyter, forthcoming).

27. *Jadup and Boel* also transgresses against the antifascist myth but does so by evoking the atmosphere left by 12 years of nazism without labeling any acts or groups as fascist.

28. Gill, "Die Russen Kommen," *Variety* 24 February 1988: 406.

29. Neorealism was an important influence in the GDR as in many other countries; GDR film criticism, however, never significantly recognized this tabooed aspect of its own history, which was consistently a part of the controversial effort to make films for young audiences.

30. Richter 983–84. "Mitte der sechziger Jahre ist eine Anzahl von Filmen, die produziert worden waren, nicht aufgeführt worden, darunter auch einer von mir. Klein und ich hatten vorgehabt, gewisse Aspekte von 'Ecke Schönhauser' weiterzuführen. Unser Engagement war nicht geringer, die immer wieder neuen Fragen anderer junger Leute gingen uns an; auch Filme, so dachten wir und so denke ich, sind Teil des öffentlich tätigen moralischen Bewußtseins in einer sozialistischen Gesellschaft. Zum ersten Mal saß ich damals, als es um unseren und andere Filme ging, in Diskussionen, aus denen ich voller Widerspruch und mit leerem Gefühl ging. Heute meine ich, daß eine aus komplexen Gründen erfolgte politische Standortbestimmung in Kostüm einer Kunstdiskussion auftrat. Es wurde etwas an Beispielen zu beweisen versucht, auf die nicht zutraf, was gesagt werden sollte, jedenfalls nicht in so schlichter Rigorosität. So konnten Frage und Antwort sich kaum begegnen. Es ist, für eine sensible Sache, mehr Maßstab verloren als gewonnen worden. Vor allem eine bestimmte Generation in den Künsten, zu der ich gehöre, geriet in Konflikte, die, wie mir scheint, nicht mehr in ein gemeinsames Verständnis gebracht worden sind."

31. These two Kohlhaase and Klein films, their 1954 film *Alarm im Zirkus,* Heiner Carow's *Sheriff Teddy* (1957) and *Sie nannten ihn Amigo (They Called Him Amigo,* 1959) and, with less justification, Kurt Maetzig's *Vergeßt mir meine Traudel nicht (Don't Forget My Traudel,* 1957) are often referred to as the "Berlin films." Internationally, a number of films had a similar atmosphere of youthful defiance bordering on nihilism, such as *The Wild One* (1953) and *Rebel Without a Cause* (1955) in the United States, *Kanał* (1957) and *Popiół y Diament (Ashes and Diamonds,* 1958) in Poland and *Letyat Zhuravli (The Cranes Are Flying,* 1957) in the USSR. It was the nihilistic tendencies to which GDR cultural functionaries reacted most strenuously, both in the late 1950s and the mid-1960s. Cf. *Film- und Fernsehkunst der DDR* 178.

32. Hannes Schmidt, "Kollision mit der Umwelt: Zu G. Kleins Spielfilm 'Berlin um die Ecke' (DEFA 1965)," *Medium* 18.2 (April/June, 1988): 69. "Jetzt, als nach vielen Jahren die Möglichkeit bestand, *Berlin um die Ecke* zu sehen, stellt sich die Frage nach der Aktualität des Films neu. Geblieben sind eine erstaunliche Frische, poetischer Reiz, Souveränität und Problembewußtheit. Daß Themen wie das Verhältnis zur jungen Generation, die Ehrlichkeit im sozialistischen Alltag, das Mitspracherecht, d.h. die konkrete Ausübung der sozialistischen Demokratie, noch immer brennend aktuell sind, liegt auf der Hand."

33. "Denk bloß nicht, ich heule," 20. Internationales Forum des jungen Films, Berlin 1990, Brochure No. 17: 2.
34. "Es ist zum Heulen," *Berlinale Tip*, 15–21 February 1990, 15.
35. This mood is reflected in the West as well. A very negative assessment of the past and future of DEFA was published by Matthias Matussek: "Honeckers Hollywood," *Der Spiegel* 19 March 1990: 258–65; a more dispassionate overview of the dilemmas and options of DEFA is provided by Wolf Donner: "DEFA: Ende oder Anfang?" *Tip* 1–14 February 1990: 14–17.
36. Cited in "Die 'Verbotsfilme' der DDR aus den Jahren 1965/66 und das 11. Plenum des ZK der SED" 20. Internationales Forum des jungen Films, Berlin 1990, Brochure No. 15: 5. "Die Filme, die verboten wurden, weil sie einen Befreiungsschlag versuchten, erlauben uns gerade jetzt einen notwendigen Blick in die Geschichte unserer Gesellschaft, so plastisch und eindrucksvoll, wie er gegenwärtig von keiner anderen Seite zu bekommen ist, auch nicht von der Geschichtswissenschaft, auch nicht von der Philosophie. Sie sind ein Fenster, durch das wir uns, unsere Gegenwart deutlicher sehen. Wir spüren den Gewinn, den die Filme gerade jetzt bringen, wir haben aber auch ein Gefühl der Bitterkeit, der Bitterkeit über den Verlust, den das Kreativitätspotential des Landes erlitten hat, über den Verlust an Phantasie, an kritischer Schärfe. Das Verbot der Filme hatte Folgen, die wir jetzt in der ganzen Bedeutung zu verstehen beginnen."

8

The Disposal of Memory:
Fascism and the Holocaust
on West German Television

Michael E. Geisler

There is a twofold irony to the fact that since 1979 every attempt
to talk about the reception of fascism and the Holocaust in West Germany
must begin with or at least make some sort of reference to Gerald Green
and Marvin Chomsky's epic *Holocaust.* First, it is ironic that the most
visible catalyst by far for West German soul-searching was not made in
Germany at all but had to be imported from the United States. The
second irony lies in the medium itself for which *Holocaust* was produced:
television. To the generation of scholars and intellectuals raised on the
Frankfurt School's summary condemnation of mass culture, television
was, and often still is, the new "opium for the masses," the hypodermic
needle through which millions of "couch potatoes" are being turned into
"videots," as Jerzy Kosinski once put it.

This complacent exclusion of television from the purview of
legitimate analysis was—briefly—shattered by the *Holocaust* phenome-

non. Although the series was broadcast over the less popular regional Third Programs (syndicated for the occasion),[1] 20 million people watched at least one episode, and more than 10 million watched two or more of the four episodes, scheduled during the fourth week of January in 1979.[2] Some 30,000 calls and thousands of letters inundated WDR (Westdeutscher Rundfunk), the ARD (Arbeitsgemeinschaft der öffentlich-rechtlichen Rundfunkanstalten der Bundesrepublik Deutschland) member station responsible for the broadcast. While there were the expected negative responses, ranging from continued denial to neofascist threats and even a bomb attack against WDR facilities, there was also genuine shock and concern about the extent to which the topic had been suppressed in West German society. Many viewers stayed up late into the night to watch the discussions following the broadcasts. Universities and evening schools established companion programs, often in the form of "Fernsehabende" (television evenings), where groups of viewers would watch the program communally and discuss their reactions. School classes put the program on their syllabus, making it the centerpiece of a discussion of fascism and the Third Reich. Faced with the strong public response, liberal journalists such as *Zeit* editor Marion Gräfin Dönhoff[3] defended the series solely on the grounds of its impact, while others, such as *Stern* editor Henri Nannen hastened to confess their complicity in the crimes (by admitting to a lack of courage to resist).[4] Even critics who had originally attacked the series for its melodramatic format changed their minds in the face of the popular discussion it engendered.[5]

In his recent study *From Hitler to Heimat: The Return of History as Film,* Anton Kaes describes the shock experienced by the traditional cultural elites,[6] when they were confronted with the fact that a product of popular culture and, even worse, a product made for a commercial station seemed to have accomplished what neither writers nor historians had been able to do: to reach out to millions of people, to generate an atmosphere of national reflection. Siegfried Zielinski summarized the general feeling of the West German *intelligentsia* when he wrote, in retrospect, "A few market-wise Americans had achieved what our public mass media had not been able or willing to do for their entire 33-year history: by focusing on the exemplary lives of two families, one representing the victims and the others the perpetrators, they had come up with a dramatic treatment of the taboo topic that moved a mass audience."[7]

The sociopolitical scenario suggested by all of this is one of a nation refusing or unable to begin the labor of mourning (*Trauerarbeit*) as prescribed by Alexander and Margarete Mitscherlich in the 1960s, a nation whose intellectuals had been found sleeping on the job (as watchdogs of the collective consciousness) by "a few market-wise Americans" who, unafraid of taboos, dared to tackle the difficult topic with a characteristically American lack of inhibitions.

However, this scenario does not correspond with reality in a number of important aspects. Since this is not primarily an analysis of *Holocaust* and its reception,[8] I shall restrict myself to sketching a few corrective remarks to the above scenario before going on to an analysis of the programs produced by West German television itself.[9]

1. Once *Holocaust* was produced, it was a foregone conclusion that it would one day be shown on German television. The only question was when and under what conditions it would be aired. In surveying the international reception of the miniseries, Zielinski has shown that once the epic had been aired in England, France, and Israel, there simply was no way the Federal Republic could have justified a decision not to go ahead with the broadcast.[10] Kaes nicely summarizes the political implications of the reception when he writes, "the *Holocaust* series seemed to be a challenge to the Germans to recognize themselves in the mirror held up by Hollywood. One advantage of the 'right' reaction would be the chance to show the rest of the world that the Germans had learned from history, that they had changed."[11]

This is just one of the factors that influenced the reception of the series in West Germany and that make the overblown claim that *Holocaust* was the sole catalyst of a long-overdue nationwide consciousness-raising so dubious. While it is unlikely that individual German viewers "performed" in a certain way to project the proper image to the international community, the network's awareness that the reception of the series in West Germany would be seen as a litmus test by others was certainly one of the reasons why the broadcast was strategically surrounded by concentric rings of accompanying documentaries and televised discussions. Banks of telephone operators were standing by, ready to respond to (and, of course, to take down) viewer's concerns, reactions, and questions. These immense preparations heated up an already intense media discussion about the broadcast so that it is safe to say that, not unlike ABC's *Day After, Holocaust* was a media event even before the first installment was aired.[12]

2. Regarding questions of observation, this setup may have significantly loaded the reception process, for we will never really know to what extent the quantity and the quality of the responses were a direct reaction to the series' narrative and its particular modes of presentation and to what extent they were preconditioned by the perceived sociopolitical importance of the event.[13]

3. Any long-term impact the series may have had was thus not predicated primarily on the text itself but on the circumstances under which *Holocaust* aired in West Germany, the institutional, national, and international "horizon of expectation" attached not to the narrative, but to the event and the way Germans would react to it. This sociopolitical aspect of the broadcast changed the conditions under which West German films, documentaries, and other television programs about fascism, the Third Reich, and the Holocaust were conceived, produced, broadcast, and perhaps received.

4. The basic argument of the advocates of *Holocaust* is that the success of the melodrama points up a major historical deficit on the side of West German television (and film). As the central mediator of public discourse, so the argument goes, West German television failed to address the issue of fascism and the Holocaust, leaving it once again to an impetus from outside to put these long-suppressed questions on the agenda of public discourse. When crosschecked against the actual body of texts produced by West German television on various aspects of the Third Reich, this implicit argument turns out to be not so much incorrect as beside the point. While it is true that the years since 1979 have seen a marked increase in West German television programs about the Holocaust, there exists nevertheless a sizeable quantity of such programs produced before, or more significantly, concurrently with *Holocaust*. (The latter, by the way, holds true for West German cinema as well). The question then that needs to be asked is not why there were no attempts at coming to terms with the fascist legacy before the broadcast-

ing of *Holocaust* but why had these (existing) German attempts failed where *Holocaust* succeeded?

I will suggest some preliminary answers to these questions by means of a brief, selective survey[14] of television texts that address issues related to the Third Reich and the Holocaust.[15] The historical contextualization of these dominant programing trends will be offset by a different reading of the *Holocaust* series (and subsequent West German television programs) against the matrix of media theory. Finally, a discussion of shifts in emphasis of television programing since 1979 will lead to a reconsideration of recent attempts at historicizing the Holocaust.

Facets of Fascism: The Discourse of Resistance

To my knowledge,[16] the earliest television program to deal directly with a major aspect of German fascism was Claus Hubalek's *Die Festung (The Fortress)*,[17] an adaptation of Hubalek's own radio play. The television play *(Fernsehspiel)* was aired in 1957 (ARD: NWRV [Nord- und Westdeutscher Rundfunkverband]), three years after the First Program (ARD) network had been completed to include the entire Federal Republic.

The Fortress tells the story of an army general in command of a town that has been turned into a fortress by one of Hitler's final, insane orders to hold the line. Although the general recognizes that there is no chance of staving off the attack and that defending the town will result in the slaughter of the civilian population, his ingrained sense of military obedience does not permit him to surrender. The town is saved by the cunning resistance of the general's aide-de-camp, who deceives his superior into believing that the "Führerhauptquartier" has agreed to capitulation.

Although quite critical in its portrayal of the German propensity to obedience at all cost, Hubalek's script also set the tone for what was to be (for the next two decades) the dominant theme in the way West German television dealt with fascism: the (German) resistance. Certainly the attempt to redeem the memory of those Germans who had taken incredible personal risks to fight the Nazi terror was a necessary act of redemptive historiography for the young Republic; and neither was it a bad idea to show German youths that there were some positive role models in recent German history and that resistance is possible and necessary even under the most oppressive political circumstances. The problem is that, until the mid-seventies, the preponderance of programs dealing with the resistance was so pronounced that a casual observer might wonder how the regime managed to stay in power with so many Germans engaged in active resistance.[18] Especially the *Dokumentarspiel*, an ambitious but methodologically questionable genre of fact-based reconstructions of historical events (not unlike the American docudrama but with greater emphasis on authenticity)[19] was prone to overemphasizing the resistance movements within the churches[20] and parts of the military.[21]

There are clear parallels here to the way the Third Reich is presented in West German high school history textbooks of the 1950s and early 1960s, where the emphasis also was on the resistance by parts of the clergy and the military. Many textbooks of the period went to great lengths to discuss the actual and planned persecution of Christian churches during the Third Reich. Some dedicated so much space to the discussion of what Hitler might have done to churches if he had had his way that very little room was left to discuss the actual victims of the regime. Only a few paragraphs were reserved for a discussion of the Holocaust.[22]

The psychological mechanisms of this discourse are fairly straightforward, yet they provide the blueprint for the German debate on fascism to the present day, even as the displacement techniques become more and more refined. What happens, essentially, is that the historical continuum that makes up the particular terrorist pattern of the Third Reich is transformed into a simple binary figure. The spectator is sutured into the text's respective enunciatory position (identified explicitly or, more often, implicitly with the position of the victims) and invited to join this "we group" in the denunciation or condemnation of a shadowy "they group" which stands for the perpetrators, the fathers, the fellow travelers, and those who want to forget what happened. This transformation holds true across classes and even across almost the entire political spectrum. We, that is the persecuted left, the resistance, the millions of

Michael E. Geisler

charter members of the "inner emigration," the churches, and, of course, the little people, the silent majority. This collective recasting, the denial by redistribution of responsibility, a process that turned practically all of Germany into a nation of victims, inflected even the most sincere attempts to come to terms with the Holocaust by means of historiography (cf. the hundreds of publications with titles like "Heidelberg [Hamburg, Bremen, Frankfurt, etc.] *unter* dem Nationalsozialismus," or *Alltag unterm Hakenkreuz*).[23] Fascism thus turns into a dehistoricized, mystical other, a vaguely defined incarnation of evil whose major raison d'être for the current debate lies in its function as a legitimizing catalyst for processes of identity formation (*Identitätsbildung*).[24] A side effect of this displacement is the marginalization of the Holocaust, effected through a process of deputization. The We group acts as a stand-in for all the victims of fascist terror, thus avoiding the traumatized confrontation with six million murdered Jews and Gypsies.

Inquiries

The continued bracketing of the Holocaust and the casting of the traumatic legacy in dichotomous schemes is characteristic of many of the television dramas produced in the 1960s and early 1970s. The creation in 1958 of the central clearinghouse for investigations into Nazi war crimes (in Ludwigsburg), the Auschwitz trials in Frankfurt (which started in the early 1960s and lasted until the mid-seventies), and the almost contemporaneous debate about the extension of the statute of limitations for these crimes marked the end of a period of almost complete silence on the Holocaust that had lasted for more than a decade. Two events had anticipated this attitudinal shift. In 1956 Alain Resnais's *Night and Fog* became the catalyst for a scandal at Cannes when the West German delegates walked out on the festival in protest. In 1957 the steadily increasing sales of *The Diary of Anne Frank* skyrocketed in the wake of theatrical adaptations in a number of West German cities. Mostly responsible for this strong reception were West German youths. For them the young victim became the focal point of a national campaign to revive the memory of the Holocaust. Alfred Grosser reports that in 1957

Erich Lüth, then press secretary of the Hamburg city council, organized an educational trip to the concentration camp at Bergen-Belsen. Instead of the expected 80 to 100 applications, he received 2,000. School classes collected money to finance the trip for their poorer classmates. In many cases, the journey was made against strong resistance from the teachers.[25] While it is probably an overstatement to argue that the new debate on the Holocaust was actually initiated by the German youth, it is clear that they appropriated it, often against strong opposition from the parent generation. The debate was thus, from the beginning through the years of the student movement and beyond, cast in generational terms. As Michael Schneider put it in his classic 1981 analysis of the historical subtext of the West German student movement, "Since the fathers had failed to indict themselves for their monstrous pasts, they were put on trial by proxy by the radicalized sons and daughters in 1968 and thereafter."[26] A look at a key television drama from the period not only illustrates Schneider's point but actually exposes the inner contradictions of the movement's approach to the problem of guilt.

Die Anfrage (*The Inquiry*, ARD:NDR [Norddeutscher Rundfunk], 1962), written by the West German author Christian Geissler and directed by Egon Monk, shows us the young physicist Köhler, who is asked by his department head to meet in his stead with a Mr. Weissmantel. Weissmantel is a German-American Jew, whose family used to own the building in which the institute is housed before they were dispossessed during the "Aryanization." Except for Weissmantel, not a single member of the family has survived the Holocaust. The encounter prompts the young physicist to set out in search of the hidden past. His quest for the suppressed history serves as a loose narrative thread, giving Geissler the opportunity to confront the viewer with a number of deeply disturbing reactions by contemporaries—all the more unsettling because most of them apparently are based in fact. However, the young man's inquiry is upstaged by his accusatory fervor, his fixation with assigning guilt. The dominant note is struck in the opening sequence. Egon Monk shows us an imaginary, empty courtroom in which a number of reverse-angle-shots are arranged to suggest the positions and perspectives of the presiding judge, the accused, and his son who, we assume, is sitting somewhere among the spectators. Overlaid is the following voice-over dialogue:

> NARRATOR: The prosecution and the defense had done their jobs on the last day of the trial. The judge now turned to the accused:
> JUDGE: Is there anything you wish to add before the court withdraws to consider a verdict?

NARRATOR: The accused nods, rises—and says nothing. It is only when he finds the face of his son among the spectators in the courtroom that he says,

ACCUSED: I am guilty. I ask the court to reject the case made by the defense for an acquittal on grounds of insanity. I was in complete command of my senses throughout the years of 1933–1945. I stand guilty as charged.

JUDGE: Would you like to explain to us the reasons for your request?

ACCUSED: I have a son. It is better for a son to have a guilty father than an insane one. You are not doing a man a favor by denying him the opportunity to be held responsible for his actions. By removing him from justice you are also depriving him of forgiveness. You are denying him the right to be human. It is important for a son to know that his father was a human being. The knowledge that his father was an imbecile will eventually destroy him. That is why I ask the court to reject the plea made by the defense.

NARRATOR: This scene, especially the father, is entirely fictitious. The following scenes, especially the fathers appearing in them, are not fictitious. This is the basis for THE INQUIRY. [Credits].

The last lines suggest that this self-implication of an imaginary father is the ideal scenario as demanded by the generation of 1968, not just of the real culprits but of their entire parent generation. This becomes apparent in the following lines of the narrator, spoken as voice-over at the end of the expositional sequence. The videotrack shows first archival footage of Nazi rallies and then documentary street scenes from contemporary (1962) life in the Federal Republic.

NARRATOR: Our inquiry comes from a generation that, in 1933, was still in Kindergarten. The inquiry is directed toward the fathers. The inquiry is necessary because the fathers do not speak. It is important for us to question those who, in those days, were doing the writing, and the talking, and the acting, and the celebrating, so as to make them admit their mistakes.

Within the context of the early 1960s, that is a reasonable enterprise. Yet it seems that behind Köhler's righteous anger lies not primarily the desire to dismantle the apologistic strategies of the war generation but more the oedipal need to take revenge on the parents, especially the fathers, not so much for actually committing the crimes as for burdening the younger generation with the inherited guilt. As *The Inquiry* (and other television dramas displaying a similar conflict) suggest, the process began long before 1968, but the teleplay also shows that the "conspiracy of silence" as Schneider calls it, has not really been broken yet. It is significant that the final lines of the expositional sequence quoted above include an explicit reference to the nonculpability of the accusing generation, immediately followed by the wholesale indictment of their parents. It is equally significant that the inquiring, accusing physicist Köhler, in the teleplay, does not question his own father (he does not seem to have one) but rather a succession of surrogate figures from his department head to his old high school teacher. Similarly, the documentary street scenes at the end reinforce the impression of a sweeping indictment that seeks to assign guilt not on the basis of individual (or, for that matter, class) responsibility but rather attacks the parent generation on a global scale.[27]

Many of the contemporary texts (i.e., of the 1960s and most of the 1970s) that deal with the issue of fascism and the Holocaust display a narrative structure similar to *The Inquiry*.[28] A young man, sometimes a projected personalized narrator, acting as his generation's representative-in-the-text[29] begins to research his immediate environment for traces of the Nazi legacy, finding in the process that his quest is not simply a historical one but that the ideology of fascism is alive (xenophobia, racism) even though the rhetoric has changed.

Paul Mommertz's *Der Pedell* (*The Superintendent*, ZDF [Zweites Deutsches Fernsehen], 1971) features a young television author commissioned to write a teleplay about Jakob Schmidt, the university superintendent who reported Sophie and Hans Scholl and their White Rose circle of student resistance to the authorities. The narrative thematizes the research efforts of the author trying to get Schmidt's friends, relatives, and neighbors to speak out about the man. He runs, of course, into a great deal of leftover NS-ideology or, alternatively, into the proverbial wall of silence. It is interesting to note that the victims of the crime he is investigating are not Jews but Gentiles—and students!

The investigation into the NS-crimes is thus displaced. The generation of 1968 rewrites the historical scenario of racial persecution as one of political persecution, casting themselves in the role of chief investigators or prosecutors (often foregrounded in the role of the projected narrator). This displacement can lead to absurd results. Toward the end of *The Inquiry*, we see documentary shots of Dachau and the death machinery—but only because Köhler shows the site to Weissmantel, a pragmatic Jew who questions Köhler's prosecutory fervor by arguing that "not one of the fathers will talk as long as he is despised." A German Gentile explaining the evils of fascism to a Jew—there is no indication anywhere in the script that Geissler would have sensed the absurdity of this proposition.

There are significant exceptions to this trend toward displacement. Some of them come from journalists or documentarists.[30] In the January 1959 issue of the television magazine *Blick in die Zeit* (*A Look at Our Times*, ARD:NWRV), Eugen Kogon, himself a victim of Nazi terror, asked a number of West German high school students what they knew about National Socialism. Three months later (4 April 1959) the ARD member station HR (Hessischer Rundfunk) broadcast Jürgen Neven-du-Mont's in-depth report on the same issue: *Blick auf unsere Jugend: Die Schüler und Hitler* (*Focus on Our Youth: The Students and Hitler*). The broadcast, which exposed the scandalous shortcomings of the West German educational system where recent history was concerned, caused a similar stir as did, nearly twenty years later, Dieter Boßmann's compilation of high school compositions about Hitler and the Third Reich.[31] Peter Schier-Gribowsky's *"Als wär's ein Stück von dir." Jüdische Mitbürger in Deutschland* (*As If It Were a Part of You—Jewish Citizens in Germany*, ARD, 1959) featured street interviews, discussions with survivors and (a rarity) with some of those responsible for the crimes.

Probably the most important among the few fictional texts of the time that addressed the Holocaust directly are Gunter R. Lys and Egon Monk's *Ein Tag* (*One Day*, ARD:NDR, 1965) and Rolf Hädrich's *Mord in Frankfurt* (*Murder in Frankfurt*, ARD:WDR, 1968). *One Day* chronicles the events on a typical day in a German concentration camp. In good Brechtian tradition (Monk actually worked with Brecht on the stage before turning to television), the text is a montage of intertitles, archival footage, and fictional sequences. It is most effective, however, when it operates with hard juxtapositions between the ordinariness of the terror and the terror of the ordinary, as in the scene where one of the guards reminds another to keep the machine gun ready; there is a rumor that one of the Jewish prisoners might try to escape and a standing promise of a three-day, special furlough for any guard who shoots an escapee. This is related in the manner of a business transaction, without any personal malice towards the prisoners; it's a job. Similarly, the dehumanizing scene in which the newly arrived inmates are shorn is complemented by the commandant's orders for the commercial resale of their hair. The sense of terror is actually stronger, more immediate in these relatively harmless scenes, even though the drama does not shy away from showing brutal beatings and murder.

Hädrich's *Murder in Frankfurt* is probably the most complex and interesting television drama of its time, and arguably one of the best German television productions to date. Hädrich intertwines three independent narrative strains in a kind of supermontage, creating an associative narrative structure based on a complex diegesis:

1. A Polish professor, a former concentration camp inmate, arrives in Frankfurt to testify at the Auschwitz trials. When he appears in court to testify against his former torturers, he finds that historical truth, as experienced by an eye-witness, is no match for the procedural maneuvers of the defence attorneys. Sad and disgusted, emotionally drained, he returns to Poland early, without bothering to wait around for the sentencing.
2. A young flight attendant spends time between flights with her friend, an actor at the Frankfurt Theater. She attends a rehearsal for a production of Peter Weiss's play *Die Ermittlung* (*The Investigation*, 1965), in which her friend plays the role of the public prosecutor. This experience prompts a discussion with her friend about the possibility of coming to terms with the past through the medium of theater and art in general.
3. The least developed plot (in traditional terms) combines archival footage of demonstrations and strikes by Frankfurt taxi drivers (following a series of taxi murders) with fictional reconstructions in which the taxi drivers demand the reinstatement of the death penalty in the Federal Republic.

Hädrich's kaleidoscopic montage freezes a moment in time yet links it clearly to past and future developments. The discussion during the theater rehearsal touches on some of the central problems of the aesthetic reflection on/of fascism and the Holocaust (e.g., when the director admonishes the actors portraying the SS-henchmen to hold back a little so as not to upstage the victims), including, quite literally, the issue of multiple specularity. The stage designer wants to put up huge mirrors around the stage, hoping that the audience will recognize themselves in the performance. In the courtroom sequences, Hädrich focuses on the question of memory. The defence's ruthless exploitation of minor inconsistencies in the professor's account, given twenty years after the event, is partly an allusion to the problems of historical reconstruction, partly an indictment—by inverse reflection—of West German strategies of oblivion. Finally, the taxi drivers' crusade for the reinstitution of the death penalty links the issue of the Holocaust to contemporary mainstream debate, showing how thin the veneer of liberal tolerance actually is.[32] It is precisely by sacrificing traditional narrative techniques that Hädrich manages to highlight the different facets of fascism that were part of the public discussion at the time, locating them in relation to each other and along the historical axis.

Monk's and Hädrich's texts are not the only ones to deal with the Holocaust before the watershed of 1979. Heinar Kipphardt's *Die Geschichte von Joel Brandt* (*The Story of Joel Brandt*, ARD:WDR, 1964) is a scenic reconstruction (in the cool, detached, simulation game-style of the time) of Eichmann's obscene offer to sell Hungarian Jews to the Allies for one thousand army trucks. Dieter Meichsner's *Wie ein Hirschberger Dänisch lernte* (*How a Man from Hirschberg Learned Danish*, ARD:NDR, 1968) and Karl Fruchtmann's *Kaddisch nach einem Lebenden* (*Kaddisch for a Living Man*, ARD:RB [Radio Bremen], 1969) inquire about the fates of those who barely escaped the inferno and those who went through it and survived, broken, physically shaken, often traumatized for life.

The programs discussed so far, including the ones not bracketing the Holocaust, have one thing in common: a tremendous sense of distance. Even *One Day*, which takes us closer to the reality of the murders than any of the other texts, maintains this distance with a veritable battery of alienation techniques, including the conscious refusal to offer anything approximating identification. Instead of assuming a position in the text, the spectator is, as it were, kept at arm's length from the diegesis. Kipphardt's screenplay, on the other hand, quickly slides from a consideration of the dehumanized proposal itself into a traditional suspense thriller, kept in motion by the question of whether or not the Allies will agree to make the exchange; *Murder in Frankfurt, A Man from Hirschberg,* and *Kaddisch* are distanced in time, or through the particular perspective of exile.

In summarizing the developments until 1979, we can say that (1) the widespread belief that West German television made no serious attempts at dealing with issues relating to fascism, the Third Reich, and the Holocaust prior to the broadcast of the American miniseries is essentially incorrect; (2) however, there is a strong tendency to displace, instrumentalize, or otherwise remove the Holocaust itself from the center of the discussion to its fringes. With most of the authors, this is not the result of a conscious refusal to deal with the issue but rather a complex and painful mental shielding process.

It is important to keep in mind that in only a few of these cases is the Holocaust completely absent from the narrative (in the sense of not being represented). Where it is not directly thematized diegetically, it is referred to through the use of archival materials, photographs, and flashbacks.[33] The problem is that being relegated to the position of referent and instrumentalized in the interest of narratives whose main concerns lay elsewhere, these sequences and photographs of mass murders and gas chambers, of torture and dehumanization became part of what Anton Kaes has called the "iconography of the Nazi era":[34] a set of disposable, interchangeable, dehistoricized images that can be inserted into any historical narrative, no matter how trivial, to give it a simulated authenticity and a sense of tragic depth.

Holocaust and the Aesthetics of Television: Another Look

The sense of distance, of detached observation that is character-istic not only of the television texts of the time but also (as Andreas Huyssen has pointed out) of the contemporary drama,[35] has to do with two other, interrelated blind spots in the West German discourse on the Third Reich: everyday life (especially just before 1933) and the psychol-ogy of the perpetrators.[36] West German cinema provides an excellent, if solitary, glimpse of the latter in Theodor Kotulla's 1976 film *Aus einem deutschen Leben* (*Death Is My Trade*), a docufiction biography of the life of Auschwitz commandant Rudolf Höss. The film, an adaptation of Robert

Merle's *La mort est mon métier,* was broadcast by West German television in February of 1979, one month after the screening of *Holocaust* (i.e., it was in production long before the broadcasting date of the American series).

But the former aspect, the reality of everyday life at the end of the Weimar Republic and during the time of the Third Reich, was not really explored on television until the late 1970s. This is the gap filled by *Holocaust.* The success of the series in West Germany (to the extent that this success is actually an effect of the narrative) is not primarily related to style (melodrama) but to its overall mode of presentation, i.e., its participation in the aesthetics of television. In contrast to film (and literature), television narrative is inextricably intertwined with its mode of reception.

In recent years, the Frankfurt-School-inspired view of mass media communication as total manipulation has been challenged by models of "aberrant"[37] or "negotiated readings,"[38] that attempt to fine-tune reception theory to include the extent to which the social setting of the act of reception influences the reception process itself. In this light, the television text appears as one of the most open narratives since its reception takes place in a setting that is, typically, singularly unconducive to truly passive reception. Even the most obstinate couch potatoes break whatever spell the narrative has by getting up to fix a sandwich or to go to the bathroom, at least during commercials, not to mention such distracted viewing experiences as watching a program while fixing dinner, feeding the kids, taking one's cues for intermittent viewing from the soundtrack, or using the remote control device to scan program offerings.[39] In contrast to the moviegoer, whose viewing experience takes place within the boundaries of what Peter Berger and Thomas Luckmann have termed a "finite province of meaning" clearly separated from "paramount reality,"[40] television watching intersects with that reality-construct itself. Obviously, this has influenced the production of television programming, especially in the United States where the necessity of inserting commercials further disrupts any spell the narrative might have. Consequently, American television (and, increasingly, television worldwide) appropriates issues, including historical ones, on the basis of what we might call "the discourse of everyday life," adapting the dominant narrative codes of the medium to its mode of reception.

Holocaust was cast in this mold. To American audiences, the horrors of mass extinction had (in the minds of media executives) to be personalized, humanized, and narrated to make them accessible on the basis of "the discourse of everyday life." This is what *Holocaust* does, especially in the opening episodes. It shows us facets of "normal" Jewish life, even under fascist rule. The exposition establishes the Weiss family as subjects (an image reinforced throughout the series by Rudi's resistance) before they become objects of the Nazi extermination policy. This is an important shade of meaning, for it undercuts to a certain extent the secondary dehumanization of the persecuted that is the result of many well-intentioned educational programs that involuntarily reduplicate the Nazi perspective of depersonalized objects in the attempt to show the magnitude of the crimes. On the other hand, the series also provides glimpses of Erich Dorf's background. Although the Dorf figure is hopelessly overloaded, and very likely inconsistent as a character portrayal,[41] there is an attempt at motivation. Dorf, who has graduated among the top 10 percent of his class in law school, cannot find a job in Weimar Germany and fears losing the respect of his wife over it. His initial involvement with the SS is nothing more than a desperate attempt at cashing in on his wife's connections. In fact, in the beginning, Dorf is portrayed as a fairly sympathetic character; this initial offer of identification is, however, drastically altered in the light of his later actions. This forces viewers to question their earlier assessment, thus helping us understand the mechanisms of cooptation.

More importantly, however, this is a great deal more than most German texts had provided, partly as a result of the various displacement mechanisms described above, partly out of fear that humanizing the perpetrators would be seen as apologia. This is probably one of the reasons why *Holocaust*, at the time, could not have been made in West Germany. The taboo *Holocaust* broke in Germany (inadvertently, for it was simply the result of the aesthetics of the medium and the culture for which it was originally produced) was precisely the embedding of the terror in the matrix of everyday reality.[42] Even though, in the later episodes, this reality recedes as the actual murders are foregrounded, the discourse of everyday life has been firmly established by then and is reinforced with every new episode because of the particular aesthetics of the miniseries. Through the format of the narrative, this genre fuses the fictional reality of the narrative with the paramount reality of the viewer's everyday experience in a much more powerful and permanent way than does the single event of a one-hour documentary or even a regular feature. In a sense a miniseries, especially one with such a tremendous resonance in mainstream discourse as *Holocaust*, actually becomes part of the personal life experience and memory of the viewer. This effect is to a large extent predicated on the series format with its constant reinforcement over the period of a week, and with ample opportunity to talk about it at home, in the schools, and at the work-place.[43]

Holocaust utilized the power of the miniseries to fuse narrative remembrance and the viewer's personal experience while drawing on a different set of memories, those of the victims.[44]

The consternation among West German media critics over the fact that the identificatory structures of *Holocaust* seemed to have set in motion the process of mourning the Mitscherlichs had demanded in 1968 is based on an underestimation of the actual role played by identificatory schemes in all cognitive processes, including the labor of mourning—and possibly on a misunderstanding of the potential role of a mass medium in this context. A genuine labor of mourning involves learning, the pro-cessing of information that—to the extent it is external to the learner's personal experience—has to be appropriated, integrated with one's own life experience if it is to influence or modify behavior and if it is to become part of memory.

It is this process of identificatory, appropriative learning that was foreshortened by the various displacement techniques and the distanced, detached documentary style of the productions before 1979.[45] Even such excellent texts as *One Day* or *Murder in Frankfurt* essentially did not provide any answers (on a personal level) for the open questions regarding the historiography of the Third Reich: (1) What was *not* done to prevent the Nazis from coming to power in 1933; what are the "roads not taken," the missed opportunities, the resistance not offered? (2) What was the emotional, psychological appeal of fascism? (3) What was everyday life like under fascist rule? (4) What constitutes the personality structure of a perpetrator or a "fellow traveler"?

Alltagsgeschichte and the Documentary

Since the late 1970s, attempts have been made to find answers to some of these unanswered questions. There is, however, still a noticeable shortage of films that try to comprehend and explain the attractions of fascism, texts that retrace the ways in which the Nazis appropriated and inverted legitimate hopes and desires, a line of inquiry mapped out by Ernst Bloch as early as 1935.[46] By contrast, some real progress has been made in the project to comprehend the mindset of the perpetrators, the fellow travelers, and the average citizens who permitted it all to happen, either because they managed to screen out their knowledge of what was going on or because they really did not know enough. This is the project of *Alltagsgeschichte* (the history of everyday life).

The progress made in this area is mostly the result of the efforts of documentary filmmakers who used the opportunity for more exhibition space provided by the shock of *Holocaust*. A good deal of groundbreaking work was done by Eberhard Fechner's interview montages (*Klassenphoto*, [*Class Photograph*] ARD:NDR, 1971; *Unter Denkmalschutz*, [*Under Landmark Protection*] ARD:HR, 1975; *Die Comedian Harmonists*, ARD:NDR, 1976; and *Der Prozeß*, [*The Trial*] Third Programs, 1984).[47]

Although methodologically problematic, Fechner's technique of intercutting the statements and responses of his interviewees so as to relate them to each other in a narrative montage has by now become a diachronic fabric of twentieth-century German social history, especially bourgeois society. At the end of the cycle (so far) stands his *Trial*, a three-part, seven-and-one-half-hour interview chronicle of the Majdanek trial, probably the last NS-trial of such proportions to be held in the Federal Republic. The broadcast date of the film is misleading because the decision to document the Majdanek trial was made by Fechner and NDR producer Hans Brecht in 1975 at the time when the trial was about to begin,[48] four years before *Holocaust* was broadcast in West Germany. Although it aired three months after *Holocaust* (ARD:SWF, [Südwestfunk], April 1979), Ebbo Demant's *Lagerstraße Auschwitz* (*Main Street, Auschwitz*) was very likely also conceived and produced one to two years earlier. Demant's interviews with three convicted Auschwitz murderers, two SS-men, and the director of the medical support staff, is perhaps the closest we will ever get to a psychography of the perpetrators. In a companion piece, *Und sie waren gleich tot. . . ! Drei Auschwitztäter sprechen* (*And They Died Immediately. . . ! Three Auschwitz Perpetrators Speak.* SWF 3 [Südwestfunk 3], 1980) that draws on the same material, Demant explains that "the conversations were intentionally held on a non-controversial level. It was only in this way that I believed I could get an authentic self-presentation of the perpetrators."

And in a press release on *Main Street Auschwitz*, the filmmaker describes his own feelings during the tapings.

> I had never before sat across from people who had killed other people. And here I was, talking to three men who had been convicted of murdering, or being accessories in the murders of dozens, in some cases hundreds of innocent people. Since I wanted something from them, I had to assume their language, had to interview them about their crimes with clinical detachment, could not accuse them, and barely contradict them. Otherwise they simply would have gotten up and returned to their cells.[49]

This is the traumatic situation that probably deterred most other filmmakers from getting too close to the center of the Holocaust: the nightmarish vision of having to empathize, or at least simulate empathy, with the murderers. Fechner and Demant personalize the terror. There are certain risks in that. One is the danger of a freakshow effect; we watch the monsters and recoil, seemingly safe in the knowledge that we could not commit such crimes. The other risk has to do with the subjects' motivation for speaking out. They have a story to tell, and where personal scripting is involved, the attempt to vindicate, to explain oneself is a natural impulse. Demant's interviewees for the most part do not deny their crimes; in fact, they even describe them in minute detail, carried away by the aura of professionalism accorded them by the television camera. But they do invoke the stereotypical sense of duty, of having followed orders. Considering the mechanisms of selective reception, this may play into some viewers' strategies of denial. However, given the historical significance of these documentaries, the risks are worth taking. More problematic is the networks' decision to marginalize both programs by scheduling them in late-night spots or the Third Programs, where only a fraction of the viewers can be reached.

Two other important Holocaust documentarists of the late 1970s and 1980s are Paul Karalus and Lea Rosh. Karalus was chosen by WDR to provide one of the companion programs to *Holocaust*. His documentary, *Endlösung: Die Judenvernichtung in Deutschland, (Final Solution: The Destruction of the German Jews*, ARD:WDR, 1979), personalizes the victims through a portrait of a survivor, the German Jew Klaus Scheurenburg, whose family has been living in Germany for eight hundred years. Scheurenburg includes in a significant psychological detail when he talks about the deep-seated longing among young Jewish boys to be part of this movement that was bent on their exclusion ("Man hat sich dazugestohlen"), a poignant facet also briefly alluded to in Peter Lilienthal's film *David* (1979). Just how difficult it is for a German to face this topic without lapsing into peculiar rhetorical constructions to avoid extremes of cognitive dissonance, can be seen by the documentarist's well-intentioned, but embarrassing impulse to vindicate the victims. Apparently, Karalus felt that it was necessary to tell his viewers that the Jews were not "freeloaders and parasites," as they had been depicted by Nazi propaganda. Presenting archival footage of Jewish women at work sewing in a factory, he states that "these pictures give us the answer." However, the fact that the implied "question" can still be posed at all is disconcerting.

Most of Karalus's films are characterized by the attempt to present a subjectivized access to the period, to eliminate the safety margin provided by detached reportage. In *Mein Großvater—KZ-Aufseher Konrad Keller (My Grandfather—Concentration Camp Warden Konrad Keller*, ZDF, 1982), he chronicles the personal confrontation with one family's Nazi past as experienced by the journalist Kurt Kister, a member of the third postwar generation to be affected by the events during the Third Reich. This method brings home the double-bind situation in which young Germans were caught after the war. While they themselves were not responsible for the crimes, they faced the traumatic choice of either renouncing all ties to their parents or of somehow trying to preserve affection across the abyss of suspicion and, in some cases, the knowledge of the parents' complicity in the crimes. Kister's aunt remembers her father, the SS-man Konrad Keller, a prison guard in Dachau, as "a very good father." She stresses that he loved his children as much as they loved him, that he was "a man of the highest moral fiber," and that his "job" ruined his health.

Personal investigations like *Konrad Keller* bear a superficial structural resemblance to the "inquiries" of the 1960s, yet they differ from these in that a genuine historical interest in finding out what happened at the time has replaced the instrumentalization of the inquiries in some of the earlier programs. Rainer Hagen's 1981 *Warum haben 1933 so viele Protestanten Adolf Hitler gewählt? (Why Did So Many Protestants Vote for Hitler in 1933?*, ARD:NDR) destroys the denial strategies of the Protestant church by establishing historical links between the authoritarian mindset of the Nazi era and Luther's dialectical dichotomy of Christian freedom. He also documents the persistence of authoritarian behavior patterns among current church dignitaries.

From a different angle, Lea Rosh's passionate investigative reportage exposed the realities of *Vergangenheitsbewältigung* (coming to terms with the past) on the institutional level. *Holocaust: Die Tat und die Täter (Holocaust: The Crime and the Perpetrators*, ZDF, 1982) incriminates the abstruse dehumanized maneuvers with which sympathetic West German courts cleared particularly academics of any responsibilities for their acts. *Vernichtung durch Arbeit (Destruction by Work*, ARD:SFB [Sender Freies Berlin], 1984), another uncomfortable contribution relegated to a late-night slot, deals with a relatively neglected aspect of the Holocaust: the exploitation of Jewish (and other) slave labor by German industry—Krupp, Siemens, IG Farben.

The use of personalization and oral history in the documentaries of Fechner, Karalus, Demant, and others is probably rooted in the same rediscovery of regional, specifically antihegemonical traditions that also produced *Heimat*,[50] a renaissance that actually predated the broadcast of *Holocaust* but certainly was galvanized into action by the successful use of an identificatory diegesis in the American series. In a recent article on the background of the Historians' Debate, Mary Nolan describes these connections.

> In the last decade, Germany has experienced a perhaps unparalleled effervescence of interest . . . in its own most recent and troubled history. . . . Thousands of high school students enter the yearly history competitions, doing projects on such themes as "Everyday Life in the Third Reich." The extensive grass roots history workshop movement has encouraged all sorts of local and oral history endeavors. Like its counterparts in other countries, it has taken history out of the academy and taught nonhistorians how to investigate their own history. Local museums are thriving and historical books and television programs are enormously popular.[51]

Not infrequently, West German television has supported these endeavors. Wolf Lindner's *Jever: Schüler erforschen NS-Geschichte ihrer Stadt (Jever: High School Students Investigate Their City's Nazi Past*, ZDF, 1981) documents the efforts by the students of a Frisian (Northern German) high school to cut through the layers of oblivion that have accumulated over almost four decades. A particularly interesting aspect of this documentary is the fact that the voice-over narration was turned over to the students themselves, a Benjaminian gesture towards a more emancipatory use of the documentary's potential.

Without a doubt, the most moving, most distressing, most historically significant documentary film to emerge from this time period is Harald Lüders and Pavel Schnabel's *(Rhina) "Jetzt—nach soviel Jahren" ([Rhina] "Now after All These Years,"* ARD:HR, 1981).[52] Until 1923, Rhina, a small village in Hessia, had been the only Prussian town with a Jewish majority. Even at the time of the Nazi rise to power, Rhina still had a far higher percentage of Jewish inhabitants than other German communities. The filmmakers set out to explore what happens to the social infrastructure of a town that suddenly loses one-half of its citizens. The patterns of response during the first half of the film, which depicts the actual research in Rhina, are both eerily familiar and somewhat predictable. Nobody wants the filmmakers around to open up old wounds. The typical reaction is denial, displacement, and disinterested ignorance.

However, the most fascinating historical evidence surfaces in the film's second half, which chronicles the filmmakers' quest for Jewish survivors from Rhina. An advertisement in the New York German-language newspaper *Aufbau* put them in contact with a number of former inhabitants of Rhina, many of whom now live in Washington Heights, a German-Jewish neighborhood in New York City. Often called "The Fourth Reich," a bitterly ironical reference to the German Jews who came to this spot to escape the murderous policies of the Third Reich, this neighborhood, as depicted by the filmmakers, is not really a new home for the exiles but rather a constant reminder of the denial of Heimat. Few of them ever managed to integrate fully into American society. Their lives are on permanent hold; they do not really understand the society in which they live, and yet they certainly will not return to Germany.

With great hesitation, these German-American Jews accept the inquiring presence in their midst, passing them on to friends only as they begin to discover the filmmakers' genuine interest in learning about their fate. Some of the most moving scenes in the film are those in which Schnabel and Lüders bring out photographs they took at Rhina, pictures of the older people and of the Jewish cemetery there; in a small way, they return to the exiles part of the past from which they have been separated. A long shot, keeping the viewers at a respectful distance, shows us a small group of Jews gathering around one of the interviewees who shares his photographs with the others.

Perhaps more important still are the scenes in which the film-makers' presence becomes the catalyst for a dialogue between the exiles and their children, ending a conspiracy of silence that bears an uncanny similarity to its analog in Germany, with the significant difference that here it is the unbearable pain (and not the guilt) of the parent generation that enforced the long silence. One daughter tells the filmmakers that her parents had never before talked to her about their past but that it was her impression that the years in Germany, until 1933, had been the only happy years of their lives.

With a rare insistence on tying up loose ends, Lüders and Schnabel then take the New York footage back to West Germany and arrange a public screening in Rhina. Confronted with the statements of the exiles, the people of Rhina are provoked into breaking their silence.

A woman from East Prussia, herself a World War II refugee from the Eastern front, complains aloud that she only received 20,000 DM in compensation money while "the Jews got a lot more!" More shocking than these eruptions are the phony calls for reconciliation and forgiveness; the occasion reveals the self-serving hypocrisy of these "Christian" incantations.

Schnabel and Lüders employ an eclectic diegesis, using a cautiously subjectivized presentation to counterbalance the interview/compilation montage that forms the film's rhetorical base. Many of the New York sequences carry strong overtones of participatory cinema (bringing back the memory, catalyzing the intergenerational dialogue), with the self-referential narrative loops affecting the lives of the interview subjects as well as the later stages of the diegesis. In the final sequences, *Rhina* not only delivers the kind of feedback often omitted from documentaries, but it actually agitates against a "historicized," i.e., implicitly conciliatory reception of the evidence it presents by taking this material to the place where it is bound to have the most direct impact.

Reconstructed Memory

The other blind spot exposed by *Holocaust,* the inability to deal with the Nazi era through the discourse of everyday life in television's own, most medium-specific terms, turned out to be much more than a case of simple myopia. For if there is a real taboo broken by *Holocaust* in Germany, it is this: to portray the dialectics of mass murder and systematic political oppression on one hand and a frighteningly near-normal everyday life on the other, that was, in all probability, the key to the continued success of the fascist state.

There are some indications that a debate on the issue was about to break anyway, just about the time when *Holocaust* was broadcast. The rediscovery of regional traditions and the emergence of oral history towards the end of the 1970s would sooner or later have brought filmmakers up against the question of what everyday life was actually like in fascist Germany.[53] Hans Dieter Schaefer's essay "Das gespaltene Bewußtsein" (The Schizophrenic Consciousness)[54] dispelled the prevailing perception of the Third Reich as a monolithic unit of ubiquitous oppression by pointing to the relative economic security provided by the "German economic miracle" (as it was actually described), a miracle that was based on Hitler's arms build-up. Despite the official debunking of "negro music," American swing and even jazz continued to be popular (and commercially available) in Germany practically throughout the Nazi era. American films were shown, at least in major cities, right up to the American entry into the war. On the other hand, the *Kraft durch Freude* (Strength-Through-Joy) programs, the soup kitchens, the many community-oriented activities gave Germans a sense (however illusory) of self-worth, heightened even further by the Nazis' successes on the international stage and focused in the spectacle of the 1936 Olympic Games.[55]

In keeping with the tradition of the *Alltagsgeschichte* movement, but with a different inflection, Heinrich Breloer's documentary series *Mein Tagebuch (My Diary)*, broadcast in ten parts in 1984 (ARD:WDR), draws on a total of approximately one thousand private diaries from which the filmmaker selected twenty four for in-depth interviews and broadcasting. Although the focus of the series is not exclusively on National Socialism, the time before, during, and immediately after the Nazi years figures prominently in several of the broadcasts. Breloer complements a selection from the diaries with related interviews and archival footage. In his nonconfrontational but insistent interviewing style, he invites his subjects to comment or correct their historical impressions from the vantage point of 1984. There is some apologia, but on the whole, the interviewees speak freely about their early fascination with National Socialism (some were skeptical from the beginning) and the slow process of disenchantment, which, in most cases, had nothing to do with the Holocaust but usually was caused by the war, specifically by the realization that it could not be won.

Although *My Diary* is clearly not based on a revisionist agenda, it partakes of a larger movement—originating toward the end of the 1970s—to reframe the discourse on the Nazi era and the Holocaust, a movement of which the Historians' Debate may be merely the most conspicuous expression. This development has more to do with the need for personal memory-construction than with any national agenda, apologetic, or otherwise. The memory in question belongs to the generation born roughly between 1920 and 1935 (with slight deviations on either side), i.e., those Germans who were too young to be personally responsible for the crimes but whose formative and adolescent years were shaped by the experience of the Nazi era and World War II.[56]

It seems that as the members of this generation reach their late fifties and sixties, they feel a strong need to "script" a coherent personal biographical narrative. This process of individual memory-construction is threatened by the ruptures and discontinuities provided by the Nazi era and the memory of the Holocaust. It seems to me that such embarrassing scenarios as the 1985 spectacle at Bitburg (Helmut Kohl was born in 1930)[57] or the "apologetic tendencies" (Habermas) of the Historians' Debate[58] (Ernst Nolte, born 1923; Andreas Hillgruber, 1925–1989) may have more to do with these ruptures in personal memory than with any overt agenda of national revisionism. This is not to say that there are no revisionist agendas. I simply wonder whether they are not, in some cases, secondary phenomena of personal scripting. For instance, Andreas Hillgruber's problematic demand that German historians identify with the "heroic efforts" of the soldiers on the Eastern front to save Germans from the vengeful acts of the advancing Soviet army (problematic because of its renewed erasure from German memory of the thousands of German and European Jews who were killed in the death camps for each day the Eastern front held) is no less untenable but a little more comprehensible when projected against the backdrop of Hillgruber's own experiences in his youth (Hillgruber was born in the East Prussian town of Angerburg). Another example, on the opposite end of the political spectrum, is Alexander Kluge's (born 1932) obsession with depicting the sufferings of the German civilian population during the Allied bombing raids, which (as Anton Kaes has shown) also leads to the exclusion of the victims of the Holocaust from the field of vision.[59] In Kluge's case, the attempt to come to terms with the personal ruptures caused by the destruction of his parents' house in Halberstadt supersedes the necessity to deal with the issues surrounding the Holocaust.

Kluge's example shows that this kind of personal scripting is by no means restricted to the Right. Rainer Wolffhardt's 1977 production of Thomas Valentin's (born 1922) screenplay *Eine Jugendliebe* (*Young Love*, ARD:RB) thematizes the occlusion of political sensitivity by the adolescent protagonist's preoccupation with girls and issues related to high school and college problems. At any other time, these initiation problems would be expected to take precedence over political interests as a matter of course. However, the times, while often experienced as relatively normal by the protagonist, Wolfgang, are not normal at all, and his failure lies in the gap between this deviation and his acknowledgment of it. Twice his world is invaded by the Holocaust: the first time when a Jewish high-school classmate commits suicide to avert the fate he anticipates for himself and again when he is contacted by members of the French resistance while studying abroad in Luxembourg. The first time, upon finding the corpse, Wolfgang's girl friend expresses the irreconcilable contradictions between the world and the way they experience it when she exclaims in desperation, "But the *Führer* is not referring to Max when he says things against the Jews!" The second time, he mentions during a conversation with a young woman, Madeleine, that one of his former girlfriends moved away because her father "got some sort of position in Sachsenhausen, in the concert camp there." Both instances show the operations of the schizophrenic consciousness at work. While Wolfgang's girlfriend cannot accept the fact that the political and the private are intertwined in the most horrible way, Wolfgang himself has successfully screened out any knowledge about the existence of concentration camps by taking recourse to the Freudian construction of a "concert camp."

Young Love is part of a trilogy in which author Thomas Valentin traces the life of his protagonist Wolfgang in installments through the year 1965.[60] Although Valentin shows the emotional deformations caused by Wolfgang's early inability to face the reality of fascism, this connection comes across only for those viewers who have actually seen all three installments of the trilogy. In addition, each of the three self-contained parts focuses on a different variation of Valentin's underlying concern. Fascism and the Holocaust thus are only the first of three instances through which Valentin shows the damage inflicted on the personal sphere by political events, even (and especially) where this connection remains largely invisible to the individuals concerned. Yet, unlike Fassbinder's Maria Braun, the protagonist of Valentin's trilogy does not die in the end. Wolfgang survives the Third Reich, the repressive morality of the Adenauer era, and the formation of a prosperous yet self-satisfied and increasingly illiberal West German national identity in the early 1960s, with the same permanently disillusioned cynicism. Typically, while Valentin is quite critical toward his central character in the first episode, the critical stance weakens noticeably in the last two installments as Wolfgang is increasingly portrayed as the victim of societal repression.

In conjunction with the strangely conciliatory ending, (having survived both the suicide of his lover and the death of his mother, Wolfgang rides off into the sunset, accompanied by his latest love interest), the narrative falls prey to the temporality it attempts to master. As we get closer to the author's current time position, the initial critical impulse is superseded by the (unconscious?) need to construct a coherent biographical script, a script in which fascism and the Holocaust become necessarily relativized simply because time passes. Since Valentin, like Kluge and Reitz, can hardly be accused of revisionist intentions, this relativization process seems to be a consequence of the authors'/filmmakers' own needs for autobiographical scripting, which express themselves in their narratives.

A more recent and considerably more alarming document of large-scale personal rescripting is Wolfgang Menge and Horst Königstein's *Reichshauptstadt privat*, (*The Capital at Home*) broadcast in 1987 on the occasion of Berlin's 750th anniversary (ARD:SFB). The program consists of a two-part television play by Wolfgang Menge, complemented by four hours of oral history/documentary material by Horst Königstein (broadcast by the Third Programs only). Menge's play is a thinly fictionalized composite narrative based on material provided in Königstein's interviews. The interviews and the archival material assembled by Königstein, through a painstaking reconstruction of the relative normalcy of everyday life in Berlin up to the last war years, add up to an impressive oral/visual complement to Schaefer's essay on the "schizophrenic consciousness." Both programs draw on the recollections of a generation still in its early teens when Hitler came to power. For these youths, growing up under National Socialism seems to have been an experience not significantly different from the teenage years of any other generation. They dated, listened to their favorite music (including Ameri-

247

can swing), and went dancing or took advantage of the Strength-Through-Joy programs to go on a cruise down the Scandinavian fjords. In all these activities, the presence of Nazi-imposed restrictions were felt, but more as extensions of parental authoritarianism, annoying but not genuinely oppressive.

However, both Königstein and Menge are so bent on conveying the subjectively experienced normalcy of this life that the not-so-normal aspects, the persecution and the terror, are screened out once again. Most dangerously, both texts (Menge's television play more than the documentaries) at times flip over into an unabashedly nostalgic stance. "Es war auch schön" ("It was also beautiful"). This summary, by one of the witnesses, of her memories of the Third Reich indicates the whole ambiguity and the continuing trauma of the German discourse on the Third Reich. Presented within the context of a critical reframing of some of the basic questions, it could stand as a marker of the schizophrenic schemes invoked by Germans to screen out the horror. However, in the context in which it is embedded here, it signals instead the nostalgic redemption of a generation's "missing years."

By contrast, Egon Monk's *Die Bertinis* (*The Bertinis*, ZDF, 1988), adapted from Ralph Giordano's novel, depicts the same time period from the perspective of the victims. Tracing the lives of a half-Jewish German family, Monk shows an aspect of the terror also explored in Peter Lilienthal's *David:* the struggle to survive outside the concentration camps. Yet the format of the television miniseries, with its greater flexibility in the reconstruction of temporal dimensions, gives Monk a chance to convey a sense of the pervasiveness of terror, as experienced by the victims. As in *One Day,* the less significant, almost marginal events have the strongest impact. Lea Bertini's attempt to report to the police the anti-Semitic pamphlets written by her neighbor seems less naive when reinserted in the actual historical context: shortly after the Nazi takeover, Lea cannot yet comprehend the fact that basic human rights, which she has taken for granted throughout her life, should suddenly have ceased to exist for her.[61]

When the Bertinis's friends are deported by the Gestapo, Monk devotes one of the longest single sequences of the series to showing the complementarity of terror and the impeccably correct behavior of the arresting officers. Everything is taken care of, down to the key labels and the proper disposal of fresh food in the refrigerator. With a hint of real emotion, the Gestapo man makes sure that the family's pets will be provided for. In these scenes, which show the absurd lengths to which the Gestapo went in the effort to create the illusion of normalcy, Monk comes close to conveying a sense of immediacy, an understanding of the mechanisms that supported the schizophrenic consciousness. At the same time the series exposes the viewer to the relentless terror experienced by the Bertinis on an everyday basis.

Yet once again, extreme distantiation mitigates the series' effectiveness. The parallel montages of scenes showing the progressive deterioration of the family's predicament with archival footage and graphics that anchor the narrative historically are overly didactic. Furthermore, Monk's desire to show as many facets of the everyday terror as possible leads to a disjointed diegesis in which individual scenes or episodes often do not carry much narrative weight of their own but seem to be there mostly to illustrate a certain point.

The final sequence is a good example of the problems inherent in this kind of alienation technique. Having learned of the arrival of British troops in Hamburg, the family members slowly raise themselves from the floor of the dark basement hideout where they have survived the final months of the Third Reich. One by one, they stumble up a flight of stairs toward a light that indicates the door—and their liberation. Yet the camera does not accompany them, remaining instead in the dark basement, panning around their dismal quarters. Apparently, Monk wanted to avoid the danger of a false conciliation, but in doing so he deprives the Bertinis of some of their humanity: their only act of resistance, the only option open to them, lay in their survival. In denying to his audience the sight of the triumph that lies in this survival, he implicitly reduces them to their status as victims—as we have seen them throughout the film.

Private Rituals, Public Memory

The central paradox of Germany's attempts to construct a public memory of the Third Reich and the Holocaust has been inscribed into this discourse from the very beginning. The Mitscherlichs' project of the collective labor of mourning failed to suggest a way of bridging the mental gap between a quintessentially private endeavor, the process of mourning, and its public use in the construction of communal memory. Mourning is a deeply personal affair, not easily influenced by even the most well-intentioned educational efforts.

This study traces the rough outlines of the West German attempt to come to terms with Germany's fascist past as documented through the most sociocentral medium of communication currently available. While the broadcast in West Germany of the American television series *Holocaust* was by no means the first time the issue had been seriously addressed by the medium, the event marked by this broadcast did highlight the failure of the German texts to confront the genocide directly and on a personal level.

The broadcast opened the door for the productive reframings of the pertinent questions undertaken by documentarists like Fechner, Karalus, Breloer, and Schnabel and Lüders. On the other hand, it also may have prepared the ground for other attempts at rewriting the scenario. There is reason to suspect that the Historians' Debate may actually be part of the effective-historical aftermath of the broadcasting of *Holocaust*. Once the nationwide ritual mourning was over, there emerged from some very unexpected quarters the indignant complaint that the Americans, with *Holocaust*, had expropriated German history. The original title of Reitz's *Heimat*, "Made in Germany," is a reminder that some of the roots of this catalyst of West German identity formation are anchored in the filmmaker's feeling that Germans would have to tell their own stories about the recent past.[62] And Ernst Nolte's essay, "Die negative Lebendigkeit des Dritten Reiches," which anticipated some of the issues discussed in the Historians' Debate, was originally presented as a talk in 1980.[63]

There is certainly no dearth of programs about the fascist era on West German television. In fact, my summary of the most significant trends of West German electronic historiography has barely scratched the surface of the sheer quantity of texts available. More importantly, any attempt to identify dominant themes necessarily violates the individual voice of each text; also, different emphases are conceivable.

One of the alternative ways of organizing the material presented here is to move the discussion up yet another notch to consider the historicization of the Holocaust through the act of historiography itself. In his analysis of the issues underlying the Historians' Debate in *The Unmasterable Past*, Charles Maier writes about the Kohl administration's plan to build two museums of German history, the German Historical Museum in West Berlin, covering all of German history through 1945, and the House of History in Bonn, devoted to the history of the Federal Republic since 1945.

> Some nations are virtual museums; in Britain, for example, continuity and quaintness remain cultivated, often with an implicit political agenda. But West Germany has hardly been a museum. Its state had to be recreated, its cities rebuilt, its values transformed, its society opened up. . . . Hence perhaps the longing for a museum as sanctuary for continuity unavailable in public life.[64]

The controversy over the two museums has been an integral part of the Historians' Debate from the beginning. However, Maier's coupling of the issue with his reference to the material space of German history seems to me to be a felicitous notion since it reminds us that museums, among other functions, provide a site for the material objectification of collective memory/identity—or at least the dominant interpretation thereof. I would extend the analogy to the body of texts under discussion here. Together, they constitute another type of museum: the material traces of the West Germans' attempts at confronting the Holocaust discursively. When considered from this perspective, the term *museum* also conjures up connotations of ossification, distance, removal from personal experience through time, space, and, most importantly, the gap that separates the observer from the object under scrutiny. Together with films and literary texts, this discourse, as a corpus, historicizes—and thereby removes and to a certain extent relativizes—the memory of the Holocaust no matter what the specific ideological or aesthetic thrust of each individual text may be.

There may be a historical significance underlying the simultaneity of all these events: the spectacle of Bitburg, the controversy over the two museums, the increasing interest in oral historiography of the fascist era, the reception of *Holocaust* and *Heimat*, the Historians' Debate, and the concomitant emergence of biographical memory-construction as documented in the texts by Valentin, Menge and Königstein, Breloer, Fechner, and others. Perhaps the common denominator of these events is only tangentially related to the apologetic tendencies of Hillgruber, Nolte, et al. The controversy itself may be part of the passing rite in the transition of Holocaust historiography from contemporary history to general history (hence the current struggle over the control of this "history"). The question, then, would not be, Can the Holocaust be historicized? but rather, How can it pass into history without losing its sense of urgency and immediacy?

Despite the considerable risks involved in the method, the course taken by the practitioners of *Alltagsgeschichte*, i.e., the representation of history through personal testimony and in terms of the discourse of everyday life, is the most promising route. Commenting on his teleplay *One Day*, Egon Monk took issue with the contention that the Holocaust could not be represented in fiction because it exceeded our imaginative capabilities. "The horror was not incomprehensible, but physical, tangible, it was experienced in the most terrifying sense of the word. The suffering was not nameless, it had a million names. Nothing exceeded the imagination of our contemporaries, nor does it exceed our imagination. Only what human beings can imagine, will actually happen."[65]

Ironically, Monk's own television plays illustrate the trauma created by a confrontation with this subject. Yet his insight holds true. As the discourse on the Nazi period and the Holocaust constructs its own museum of the period, it becomes subject to the ways in which any museum is used. We can choose to build a traditional structure in which the memory of the Holocaust is safely enshrined in the solidified form of an official "history" of the Nazi past. The price to pay for this security would be a pervasive sense of distance and the complete lack of comprehension expressed in some of the interviews with the grandchildren of the perpetrators conducted by Peter Sichrovsky.[66]

By contrast, an approach to the Nazi era that relies on the methods of oral history and tries to reconstruct a multifaceted picture of everyday reality during the Third Reich has to face up to the risks involved in this method of inquiry, specifically those of falling for all sorts of rationalization and rescripting maneuvers. Yet when projected against the existing body of knowledge accumulated by traditional history, we may begin to gain at least a composite impression of what was actually going on at the time.

The labor of mourning, specifically mourning the Holocaust, is a private experience, a personal task. This private process can be facilitated by the public debate in which it is embedded, or it can be blocked. It can also be smothered by it. But it cannot be replaced by it. There is no public discourse that can assimilate the pain of the personal confrontation. The experience can be catalyzed by a confrontation with the victims, as in Claude Lanzmann's *Shoah,* or by facing the perpetrators, as we are forced to do if we watch the films by Fechner and Demant. It can be triggered by documentary and fictional text alike. But it seems to be most effective when conveyed through personal unmitigated encounters, even with all the risks involved.

Notes

1. The Bayerische Rundfunk, as it had often done before, threatened to sign off if the series were to go out via the (national) ARD network.
2. Cf. Uwe Magnus, "Die Einschaltquoten und Sehbeteiligungen," *Im Kreuzfeuer: Der Fernsehfilm "Holocaust,"* ed. Peter Märthesheimer and Ivo Frenzel (Frankfurt a.M.: Fischer, 1979) 221–24. Anton Kaes (*Deutschlandbilder. Die Wiederkehr der Geschichte als Film* [Munich: Edition Text und Kritik, 1987] 38, adapted and trans. as *From Hitler to Heimat: The Return of History as Film* [Cambridge: Harvard UP, 1989] 30) quotes the even higher figure of twenty million viewers, apparently going along with Magnus's arithmetic. Magnus simply adds the figures of all the viewers who saw one, two, three, or all four episodes, arriving at a total of twenty million. The problem is that this figure only represents those who have seen at least one of the episodes. However, according to Magnus's own figures, six million viewers only saw one episode, which reduces the total number to fourteen million if one wants to know how many people really watched the series. I would hold that only those who watched at least two episodes (approximately ten million) can be considered to have watched the series with the kind of concern suggested by the book's second subtitle: "Eine Nation ist betroffen." Moreover, it seems to me to be of crucial importance to know who turned off during or after the first episode—and why.
3. Marion Gräfin Dönhoff, "Eine deutsche Geschichtsstunde," *Die Zeit* 2 February 1979: 1.
4. Henri Nannen, "Ja, ich war zu feige," *Stern* 2 February 1979, reprinted in Märthesheimer and Frenzel, *Im Kreuzfeuer,* 277–80.
5. Cf. the two articles by Sabina Lietzmann, "Die Judenvernichtung als Seife-

Michael E. Geisler

noper" and "Kritische Fragen," both reprinted in Märthesheimer and Frenzel, *Im Kreuzfeuer* 35–39 and 40–42.
6. Anton Kaes, *From Hitler to Heimat* 38–40.
7. Siegfried Zielinski, "Uraufführung in den USA und erste Reaktionen bei uns," S. Zielinski and Friedrich Knilli, *Holocaust zur Unterhaltung* (Berlin: Elefanten, 1982) 115. This very useful compilation of personal reactions, reportage, project reports, and critical analysis is particularly interesting for the seismographic accuracy with which it reflects the complete consternation of the academic elite. Knilli and Zielinski, both well-established media analysts, vacillate throughout the book between a critical indictment of the series as a product of a manipulative, industrialized mass culture and a grudging admiration for the operative impact of the text. (Note: Unless indicated otherwise, all translations are my own.)
8. I refer to the studies by Zielinski and Dieter Prokop (*Medien-Wirkungen*, Frankfurt a.M.: Suhrkamp, 1981), to the various readers published by the WDR, and to the three issues of *New German Critique* published in 1980, which, taking the series' reception in West Germany as a cue, spiral out to a broad discussion of the historical relationship between Germans and Jews (*New German Critique* 19–21, Winter 1980, Spring/Summer 1980, and Fall 1980). Extremely useful are the materials compiled and edited by Wilhelm van Kampen, *Holocaust: Materialien zu dem amerikanischen Fernsehfilm über die Judenverfolgung im "Dritten Reich"* (Düsseldorf: Landeszentralen und Bundeszentrale für politische Bildung, 3d ed., 1982).
9. The manuscript for this article was completed in early 1990 and represents the status of the discussion up to that time.
10. Knilli and Zielinski, *Holocaust zur Unterhaltung* 130.
11. Kaes, *From Hitler to Heimat* 33–34.
12. On the way in which the reception of *Holocaust* tied into the political "narratives" of the United States and West Germany, respectively, see Bruce Murray, "NBC's Docudrama *Holocaust* and Concepts of National Socialism in the United States and the Federal Republic of Germany," *The Americanization of the Global Village: Studies in Comparative Popular Culture*, ed. Roger Rollin (Bowling Green, KY: Popular Press of Bowling Green State U, 1990) 86–105.
13. Cf. also the problems with questionnaires and viewer mail as described in Knilli and Zielinski, *Holocaust*, and in Prokop, *Medien-Wirkungen* esp. 92ff.
14. I gratefully acknowledge the assistance of the Deutsches Rundfunkarchiv in Frankfurt a.M.. The kind and knowledgeable support of the DRA and its staff was an invaluable asset in the preparation of this survey.
15. Since this article deals with the reception of the Holocaust on West German television, films are included only to the extent to which they are relevant in this context. For a broader discussion of cinematic texts that address the issue, see Annette Insdorf's *Indelible Shadows* (New York: Random House, 1983) and Ilan Avisar's more recent *Screening the Holocaust* (Bloomington: Indiana UP, 1988). To be sure, given the multiple entanglements of film and television in the Federal Republic, the distinction is a spurious one, made here for the purely heuristic purpose of looking at a body of texts produced within the general context of a medium more specifically defined by its affinity to mainstream discourse than is New German Cinema.

16. To this day, the most comprehensive general survey of West German television drama is Knut Hickethier's excellent compilation *Das Fernsehspiel der Bundesrepublik Deutschland: Themen, Form, Struktur, Theorie und Geschichte 1951–1977* (Stuttgart: Metzler, 1980). I would also like to acknowledge my debt and gratitude to Knut Hickethier for his expert advice and generous help with access to source materials.

17. Since few of these programs are in distribution in the United States, translations of television program titles are my own unless indicated otherwise. When citing books or films I have tried to give the accepted translation; in most of these cases I relied on the excellent compilation in Eric Rentschler's *West German Film in the Course of Time* (Bedford Hills, NY: Redgrave, 1984) 206–34.

18. To mention just a few: *Ein gefährlicher Mensch* (*A Dangerous Man*, again by Hubalek, NWRV 1958): a physicist refuses to hand over his plans for a nuclear bomb to the Nazi regime. Axel Eggebrecht, *Wer überlebt, ist schuldig* (*The Survivors Are Guilty*, HR [Hessischer Rundfunk] 1960): in her attempt to find out which member of a group of resistance fighters was a traitor and caused her father's death, a young woman discovers that she herself, through a careless act committed during her service in the BDM, is the culprit. Oliver Storz, *Der Schlaf der Gerechten*, (*The Sleep of the Righteous*, NDR [Norddeutscher Rundfunk] 1962, adapted from Albrecht Goes's story *Unruhige Nacht*): a non-Jewish woman, a butcher, is ordered by German authorities to hand out meager food rations to German Jews; in getting to know them, her initial reservations disappear to the point where she begins to identify with their plight and tries to help them; when she is caught by the Gestapo, she owns up to her actions. Peter Lotar, *Das Bild des Menschen* (*In the Image of Man*, SFB [Sender Freies Berlin] July 20 [!], 1964): during an air raid, a German count, awaiting the death penalty for his resistance activities, can move about freely in his prison, confronting fellow inmates, wardens, and even the judge who sentenced him; this is one of a number of programs that address the question of whether resistance against the German war effort was actually justifiable, a question still under discussion in parts of West German society, and not just on the neofascist fringes.

19. For a good, concise critique of the West German *Dokumentarspiel* see Manfred Delling, "Das Dokument als Illusion. Fakten und Fiktionen im Dokumentarspiel des Fernsehens," *Frankfurter Hefte* 4 (April 1974): 273–83.

20. Maria Matray and Answald Krüger, *Waldhausstr:20*, NWRV, 1960, about the underground rescue network of Swedish protestants in Berlin; and *Bernhard Lichtenberg*, ZDF (Zweites Deutsches Fernsehen), 1965, by the same authors.

21. Erich Kröhnke, *Paris muß brennen* (*Paris Must Burn*, ZDF, 1965); Helmut Andics, *Der Fall der Generale* (*The Fall of the Generals*, ZDF, 1966); cf. also Falk Harnack's (!) film *Der 20. Juli*, 1955, frequently broadcast on the anniversary of the assassination attempt.

22. E.g., Hans Hermann Hartwich, ed., *Politik im 20. Jahrhundert* (Braunschweig: Westermann, 3d ed., 1964). Of the 44 pages allocated to the discussion of the Nazi era in this reader only *two* (379–80) are reserved for a discussion of the Holocaust.

Also bracketed, at this time, is practically the entire socialist and communist resistance. On television the latter exclusion has been less pronounced since the rediscovery of the lost traditions of the workers' movement following the events of 1967 and 1968. In 1972, WDR aired a seven-part miniseries on the communist resistance organization *Die rote Kapelle* by Peter Adler; in 1978 the documentarist Paul Karalus, probably the West German filmmaker who has most thoroughly explored all the different aspects of fascism, came out with a four-part documentary programmatically entitled *Widerstand im Dritten Reich: Es gab nicht nur den 20. Juli (Resistance in the Third Reich: Beyond July 20th*, WDR III). The surge in oral-history research in the late 1970s and early 1980s brought experiments in counterhistoriography such as Gabriele Voss's and Christoph Hübner's interview series *Lebensgeschichte des Bergarbeiters Alphons S. (Biography of Alphons S., Miner*, WDR III, 1977ff) and Hans-Dieter Grabe's *Ludwig Gehm, ein deutscher Widerstandskämpfer (L. G.—A German Resistance Fighter*, ZDF 1983). Yet again it is significant that it was not until 1984 that the resistance years of West Germany's most prominent antifascist became the subject of a documentary. In the 1960s and at least the beginning of the 1970s, Heinrich Breloer's *Kampfname Willy Brandt (Alias: Willy Brandt*, ZDF, 1984) would either not have been broadcast, or if it had been aired, would probably have ruined Brandt's chances at the polls. At that time, the question whether a German had a moral right (not to mention an obligation) to fight against his/her own country, when that country had turned into a death camp, was a lively campaign issue.

23. Harald Focke and Uwe Reimer, *Alltag unterm Hakenkreuz* (Reinbek: Rowohlt, 1969).
24. Significantly, Jürgen Habermas, in the article that opened the Historians' Debate, insists on this very function of the Holocaust as a negative catalyst for the historical identity of the Federal Republic. "A commitment to universalistic constitutional principles which is anchored by conviction has unfortunately only been able to develop in the German *Kulturnation* since—and because of—Auschwitz." ("A Kind of Settlement of Damages [Apologetic Tendencies]") *New German Critique* 44 (Spring/Summer 1988): 25–39, trans. Jeremy Leaman. (Originally: "Eine Art Schadensabwicklung" *Die Zeit* 11 July 1986).
25. Alfred Grosser, *Geschichte Deutschlands seit 1945* (Munich: Deutscher Taschenbuch Verlag, 1974) 311.
26. Michael Schneider, "Väter und Söhne posthum. Das beschädigte Verhältnis zweier Generationen," *Den Kopf verkehrt aufgesetzt oder Die melancholische Linke* (Neuwied: Luchterhand, 1981) 18; trans. as "Fathers and Sons, Retrospectively: The Damaged Relationship Between Two Generations," by Jamie Owen Daniel, *New German Critique* 31 (Winter 1984): 3–51.
27. It is also worth reflecting on the fact that the only time in the text of the television play that a father and his son face each other directly is in the imaginary scene at the very beginning, apparently the only space where such an encounter was tolerable.
28. Among others: Gerd Oelschlegel, *Einer von Sieben (One of Seven*, NWRV 1960); Gunter R. Lys and Egon Monk, *Mauern (Walls*, ARD:NDR 1963); Jürgen Gütt, *Der Tod eines Mitbürgers (Death of a Fellow Citizen*, ZDF,

1967); Thomas Valentin, *Jugend einer Studienrätin (The Youth of a Teacher*, ARD:RB [Radio Bremen] 1972). Cf. also Lida Winiewicz, *Die Wohnung (The Apartment*, ARD:SWF [Südwestfunk] 1964) in which a young Jewish woman, whose mother was deported and killed in the gas chamber, returns twenty years later to her mother's former apartment. She finds out that the caretaker's wife reported her mother to the authorities to obtain use of the apartment. Hans Bachmüller and Jürgen Breest's slightly didactic *Die Gegenprobe (Cross-Check*, ARD:RB, 1965) confronts a young man (a student!), who accuses his father of being indirectly responsible for the death of prisoners in a concentration camp, with his own limitations. When he witnesses the brutal beating of an Italian "guest worker" by German factory workers he cannot gather up enough courage to interfere. It is interesting, and characteristic of the times, that the Antigone-theme is treated to two different updates, one by Claus Hubalek (*Die Stunde der Antigone* [*Antigone's Hour*], NWRV, 1960) and one by Leopold Ahlsen and Rolf Hochhuth (*Berliner Antigone*, ZDF 1968).

29. Cf. also the character of Ricardo in Rolf Hochhuth's *Der Stellvertreter* (*The Deputy*, 1963).

30. Cf. also the series *Das Dritte Reich* (ARD:NWRV/SDR [Süddeutscher Rundfunk], 1060/61), *Der SS-Staat*, (ARD:WDR/SDR, 1963), and others.

31. Dieter Boßmann, ed., *"Was ich über Adolf Hitler gehört habe . . ." Folgen eines Tabus: Auszüge aus Schüler-Aufsätzen von heute.* (Frankfurt a.M.: Fischer, 1977).

32. The taxi drivers were not alone in their demand for the reintroduction of the death penalty: Richard Jaeger, CSU, from 26 October to 30 November 1966 Minister of Justice in Ludwig Erhard's second Cabinet, was such an ardent proponent of the death penalty that he became widely known as "Heads-off-Jaeger."

33. In contrast to the war generation, the common ideological denominator of these texts is not "let's not talk about this, let's forget it, move on to other things." On the contrary, one must not forget that the generation of 1968 deserves a great deal of credit for putting the issue on the social agenda in the first place. The slip-up comes in the implicit referral to a projected consensus that says, "we all know what this led to, so let's concentrate on finding the people who are responsible and on fighting the perpetuation of the ideological holdovers in the current power structure." As it turned out, the implicit projection, apart from being the result of a displacement mechanism, was also false: apparently, "we" did not really know what this led to.

34. Kaes, *From Hitler to Heimat* 22.

35. Andreas Huyssen, "The Politics of Identification," *New German Critique* 19 (Winter 1980): 117–36.

36. Again, there are a few exceptions, mostly documentaries like Rolf Orthel's 1976 *Dr. W.—ein SS-Arzt in Auschwitz* (*Dr. W.—SS-Physician, Auschwitz*). It is significant, however, that this documentary depicted a man who, according to witnesses and victims, was a strange phenomenon. Eduard Wirth apparently had formed his own peculiar set of ethical values amidst organized terror: often volunteering for executions and death assignments, he tried to save as many of the victims as he could.

Michael E. Geisler

37. Umberto Eco, "Towards a Semiotic Inquiry into the TV Message," *Working Papers in Cultural Studies* 3 (1972): 103–26.
38. Stuart Hall, "Encoding/Decoding," *Culture, Media, Language,* ed. S. Hall, D. Hobson, A. Lowe, and P. Willis (London: Hutchinson, 1980) 128–38. See also John Fiske, *Television Culture* (London: Methuen, 1987) 62–83 and Ien Ang, *Watching Dallas* (London: Methuen, 1985).
39. Cf. Rick Altman, "Television/Sound," *Studies in Entertainment: Critical Approaches to Mass Culture,* ed. Tania Modleski (Bloomington and Indianapolis: Indiana UP, 1986) 39–54.
40. Peter L. Berger and Thomas Luckmann, *The Social Construction of Reality* (New York: Anchor, 1967) 25.
41. Even if, allowing for necessary narrative condensation, a single man may legitimately be cast as the agent responsible for every major phase of the Final Solution, from the *Reichskristallnacht* to the introduction of Cyclone B, such a personality would, in all likelihood, have a lot more in common with the *Freikorps* men analyzed by Klaus Theweleit in his *Male Fantasies* than with the soft-spoken, sensitive, androgynous Dorf; (Minneapolis: U of Minnesota P, 2 vols. 1987–89; trans. Stephen Conway et al.).
42. The intercultural problems raised by the fact that this was a fictional German everyday reality prepared in such a way as to intersect with American conceptions of everyday life, and finally, the German reception of this American image of the everyday reality of Germany's past, are outside the immediate purview of this paper.
43. It is no coincidence that the only program to rival the success of *Holocaust* in West Germany, Edgar Reitz and Peter Steinbach's 1984 *Heimat* (ARD:WDR/SFB) was also a miniseries with a sustained focus on patterns of everyday life.
    The problem with Reitz's attempt at showing twentieth-century German *Alltagsgeschichte* through its displaced reflection on the margins is that in appropriating the memory of the fascist years in terms of the discourse of everyday life, Reitz's text unwittingly continued the annihilation of the Jews by repeating the strategies of denial inscribed into the popular memory it sought to reclaim. However, this is part of the overarching problematic of oral history of which *Heimat* is an artistic expression. Its blind spots, as a historical document, reflect the shortcomings of the oral history method and need to be evaluated within those parameters. For a detailed discussion of *Heimat,* including the series' problematic depiction of the Holocaust, see my "'Heimat' and the German Left: The Anamnesis of a Trauma," *New German Critique* 36 (Fall 1985): 25–66. See also, in the same issue, Miriam Hansen, "Dossier on 'Heimat'" 3–24.
44. This does not mean that "the discourse of everyday life" cannot be escapist or removed from everyday life itself. To be sure, neither *The A-Team* nor *Dynasty* nor *Beauty and the Beast* directly reflect the everyday reality of many viewers. The emphasis here is on "patterns." Most, if not all, of the successful television series come with a number of structurally or personally encoded narrative hooks that link them to the viewer's paramount reality.
45. Sabina Lietzmann, one of the critics who changed her opinion on the series when she witnessed its impact, states this preference clearly, even in her follow-up review which indicates her change of heart. "We still hold that a

cool, well-made documentary is far superior as an instrument of enlightenment, but we know that the television series 'in terms of people,' . . . forces the masses to watch and to empathize" (*Im Kreuzfeuer* 41).

46. Ernst Bloch, *Erbschaft dieser Zeit* (Zurich: Oprecht und Helbling, 1935). One of the few texts that deals with this thorny issue is Eberhard Schubert's television drama *Flamme empor! (Fan the Flame!* ARD:SR [Saarländischer Rundfunk], 1979), which depicts the rise of National Socialism in an area where history easily might have taken a different course: the Saarland. This undercuts the sense of inevitability that renders so many excellent critical productions ineffective because the viewer comes away with the sense that nothing could have been done to change events. At the same time, Schubert shows the romantic attraction of the fascist solstice rituals and communal outings to the romantic "Wandervogel" mentality of large parts of the Weimar youth.

47. This project was complemented by Fechner's adaptation of Walter Kempowski's bourgeois family epic *Tadellöser & Wolff*, ZDF, 1975.

48. Cf. Karl-Heinz Janssen, "Über das Böse und das Tugendhafte," *Die Zeit* 47 (11 November 1984). The trial took five and one half years and another four years for the sentences to become final.

49. Press release *Neue Deutsche Filme*, Filmfest Berlin, 1980. Cited in Roth, *Der Dokumentarfilm seit 1960* (Munich: Bucher, 1982) 127.

50. On the regionalist matrix of *Heimat*, cf. Geisler, "'Heimat' and the German Left" 39ff.

51. Mary Nolan, "The *Historikerstreit* and Social History," *New German Critique* 44 (Spring/Summer 1988): 63.

52. Unlike too many other important television texts, *Rhina—"Now after All These Years"* is available in the United States (from Arthur Kantor Films, New York). I would like to express my gratitude to the Adolf-Grimme Institute, especially Ulrich Spiess, for making this and other films available to me and for many helpful suggestions concerning primary materials.

53. Cf. two book publications of 1979: Harald Focke and Uwe Reimer's collection *Alltag unterm Hakenkreuz* (Reinbek: Rowohlt) and Max von der Grün: *Wie war das eigentlich? Kindheit und Jugend im Dritten Reich* (Neuwied: Luchterhand).

54. Hans Dieter Schäfer, *Das gespaltene Bewußtsein. Über die Lebenswirklichkeit in Deutschland 1933–1945* (Munich: Hanser, 1981) 114–95 (*The Schizophrenic Consciousness: On Everyday Life in Germany 1933–1945*).

55. In his 1959 essay "Was bedeutet: Aufarbeitung der Vergangenheit," Theodor W. Adorno had already warned against omitting this aspect from an analysis of fascism: "Überdies ist es eine Illusion, daß das nationalsozialistische Regime nichts bedeutet hätte als Angst und Leiden, . . . Ungezählten ist es unterm Faschismus gar nicht schlecht gegangen. Die Terrorspitze hat sich nur gegen wenige und relativ genau definierte Gruppen gerichtet," reprinted in *Gesammelte Schriften*, ed. Rolf Tiedemann, vol. 10.2, *Kulturkritik und Gesellschaft II* (Frankfurt a.M.: Suhrkamp, 1977) 562.

56. Martin und Sylvia Greiffenhagen distinguish between three different postwar generations affected by the Nazi past: those who grew up during the years of the Weimar Republic and served the regime as adults (in some cases the perpetrators); those who grew up during the Third Reich and are now becoming the dominant generation in the Federal Republic; and those who

were born just after the war but confronted with the discourse about fascism—or its repression—from childhood on. See *Ein schwieriges Vaterland: Zur politischen Kultur Deutschlands* (Frankfurt a.M.: Fischer, 1981) 49.

57. On the historical continuities of the Bitburg scenario see Eric Rentschler, "New German Film and the Discourse of Bitburg," *New German Critique* 36 (Fall 1985): 67–90.

58. Most of the salient contributions to the Historians' Debate are reprinted in Rudolf Augstein et al., *Historikerstreit* (Munich: Piper, 1987). A useful summary of the major positions can be found in Charles Maier's excellent analysis, *The Unmasterable Past: History, Holocaust, and German National Identity* (Cambridge: Harvard UP, 1988).

59. Kaes, *From Hitler to Heimat* 132.

60. The second part, *Schulzeit (Back to School)*, covers the years 1952 to 1954; the third, *Stark wie der Tod (As Strong as Death)*, is set in 1964 to 1965, all broadcast by ARD:RB, 1977.

61. These events are, of course, reminiscent of Monk's famous adaptation of Feuchtwanger's *Die Geschwister Oppermann (The Oppermanns*, ZDF, 1983), which concentrates on the difficulties of a Jewish upper-class family in comprehending the changes in their everyday reality. I am not discussing this text here, simply because it is well known and readily available.

62. Cf. Reitz's essay "Unabhängiger Film nach Holocaust?" *Liebe zum Kino: Utopien und Gedanken zum Autorenfilm 1962–1983* (Cologne: KÖLN 78, 1984) 98–105.

63. See "Anmerkung des Verlags," at the end of Nolte's updated version, "Zwischen Geschichtslegende und Revisionismus?" *Historikerstreit* 35.

64. Maier, *The Unmasterable Past* 138.

65. Egon Monk, "Parteinahme im Fernsehspiel," *Theater Heute* 7.8 (1966): 49.

66. Peter Sichrovsky, "'Ich war's doch nicht, verdammt noch mal.'" *Der Spiegel* 6 (2 February 1987). See especially Stefanie's account of her history lesson.

9

On the Difficulty of Saying "We":
The Historians' Debate
and Edgar Reitz's *Heimat*

Eric L. Santner

I

As presented in 1967 by the Mitscherlichs in their groundbreaking study, *The Inability to Mourn*, the tasks of mourning in postwar German society are double edged and may, more radically, even represent a series of double binds.[1] In order to mourn for the victims of National Socialism, the Mitscherlichs claimed, the population of the new Federal Republic (and it is only for pragmatic reasons that I limit myself to this case) would first have to work through the more primitive narcissistic injury represented by the traumatic shattering of the specular, imaginary relations that had provided the sociopsychological foundations of German fascism. According to the Mitscherlichs, the political religion that was nazism had promised a "utopian" world in which what threatened the self with chastisements of its narcissism—including alterity in its multiple forms and dimensions—could be experienced as a dangerous Semitic supplement that one was free to push to the margins and finally to destroy. This was a utopia, of course, in which a mature self could never really develop. For that complex entity we call the human self constitutes itself precisely by relinquishing its narcissistic position and mournfully, and perhaps even playfully, assuming its place in an order—call it the symbolic—in which I and you, here and there, now and then, signifiers and signifieds, have boundaries, i.e., are discontinuous. It is this passage from a realm of continuity into one of contiguities that signals the advent of the *unheimlich* in human experience. According to the Mitscherlichs, there could be no real mourning for the victims of nazism, no genuine perception of the full magnitude of human suffering caused in the name of the *Volksgemeinschaft*, until this more primitive labor of mourning— the mastery of the capacity to say "we" nonnarcissistically, the integration of the *unheimlich* into the first person plural—had been achieved.

This complex interdependence of the way one says "we" in postwar German society on one hand and the way one positions oneself vis-à-vis the crimes of National Socialism on the other, seems in the last several years only to have become more vexing and complex. In the following I would like to explore two discursive events in which this interdependence has figured in a central way: the Historians' Debate and Edgar Reitz's film *Heimat*.

II

The beginning of this Historians' Debate might be dated with an essay by Jürgen Habermas entitled "A Settling of Damages: Apologetic Tendencies in German Historiography," published 11 July 1986 in the German weekly *Die Zeit*.[2] As the subtitle of that essay indicates, Habermas's concern here is a certain revisionist or "apologetic" tendency in recent German historiography of the fascist period. In the essay Habermas primarily addresses the work of three historians whom he sees as the main exponents of this new historiography: Ernst Nolte, Michael Stürmer, and Andreas Hillgruber.

In an essay published a month earlier in the *Frankfurter Allge-*

meine Zeitung, Ernst Nolte had argued for an empathic understanding of the anxieties that ostensibly led Hitler to the admittedly barbaric final solution of the Jewish question.[3] According to Nolte, Hitler had reason to fear that the Russians would subject the Germans to horrific tortures in the event of a westward expansion. Nolte evoked the so-called rat cage, an instrument of torture to which Winston Smith finally succumbs in George Orwell's *1984*, and which, according to anti-Bolshevist literature from the twenties, belonged to the Soviet arsenal, as the recurring nightmare that finally led Hitler to the prophylactic measures of Auschwitz.

> Is it not likely that the Nazis and Hitler committed this "Asiatic" deed because they saw themselves and others like them as potential or real victims of an "Asiatic" deed? Did not the "class genocide" of the Bolshevists logically and factually predate the "racial genocide" of the National Socialists? Doesn't the intelligibility of Hitler's most secret actions owe precisely to the fact that he could *not* forget the "rat cage"? May we not perhaps trace the origins of Auschwitz to a past that wouldn't go away?[4]

The missing link in this causal nexus is, of course, the equation Bolshevist = Jew, an anti-Semitic commonplace from the twenties and thirties.[5] Nolte had elsewhere offered further "evidence" also garnered from fundamentally anti-Semitic nightmare visions of the power of world Jewry, to support this empathic, not to say sympathetic, reading of Hitler's situation. He claims, for example, that Chaim Weizmann's declaration in 1939 that the Jews of the world should ally themselves with England, might justify the thesis "that Hitler was allowed to treat the German Jews as prisoners of war and by this means to intern them."[6]

Other aspects of Nolte's argument involve by now familiar comparisons between the National Socialist genocide and other modern examples of mass murder, from the Turkish slaughter of Armenians to Pol Pot's decimation of the Cambodian population. The thought here is, of course, that the Jewish Holocaust needs to be placed in the context of other cataclysmic events of twentieth-century history all of which may be seen under the general rubric *reactions to modernity.*[7] In defense of such comparisons, Nolte offers yet another familiar analogy, between Auschwitz and the Allied bombing of civilian populations. Nolte's example demonstrates rather clearly that the entire Historians' Debate is in many ways a continuation of the controversies surrounding Ronald Reagan's visit to the cemetery at Bitburg. Each event has, after all, served to challenge many people's understanding of the important differences between the Final Solution and other acts of war and mass murder, between SS-officers and soldiers in the field.

> To be sure, the American President's visit to the military cemetery at Bitburg provoked a very emotional discussion; but the fear of the charge of "settling accounts" ["Aufrechnung"] and a more general fear of making any comparisons at all prevented the consideration of what it would have meant if in 1953 the then chancellor had refused to visit the military cemetery at Arlington, justifying this refusal with the argument that men were buried there who had participated in terroristic attacks against the German civilian population.[8]

For Nolte, what finally distinguishes the Shoah from other cases of genocide in the twentieth century is the technical detail of the use of gas in the extermination of the Jews.[9]

In the end, however, Nolte's argument for a revisionist reading of the place of the Holocaust in modern European history is based on the notion that previous interpretations have been authored by the victors and are thus inherently biased and in need of rewriting from a German national perspective. He offers a curious thought experiment to dramatize his case.

> We need only imagine, for example, what would happen if the Palestine Liberation Organization, assisted by its allies, succeeded in annihilating the state of Israel. Then the historical accounts in the books, lecture halls and schoolrooms of Palestine would doubtless dwell only on the negative traits of Israel; the victory over the racist, oppressive and even fascist Zionism would become a state-supporting myth. For decades and possibly centuries nobody would dare to trace the moving origins of Zionism to the spirit of resistance against European anti-semitism, or to describe its extraordinary civilizing achievements before and after the founding of the state, to show its clear differences from Italian fascism.[10]

Although few professional historians have been guilty of the rhetorical excesses manifest in such prose, Nolte is by no means alone with regard to the general philosophical trajectory of his efforts. In recent writings by Michael Stürmer we find, for example, an explicit appeal to the historian as that figure in contemporary society who must carry on the work that can no longer be performed by religion, namely the unification and consolidation of the social group. By endowing meaning (*Sinnstiftung*) in the act of historical recollection and interpretation, the historian lays the foundation upon which a national identity may be constituted. Only after achieving such a firm national ego, as it were, may the Federal Republic come to occupy its rightful place as the "central unit in the European defensive arch of the Atlantic system."[11] The task of contemporary German historiography is to allow Germany to find its inner continuity with itself once more, to come home to itself, as it were, so that its Western neighbors may know they have a dependable ally anchored in a firm and unconflicted self-understanding. "For it is here a matter of the German Republic's inner continuity and its calculability in foreign affairs."[12] And like Nolte, Stürmer sees in the performance of this quasi-Homeric task of cultural *Sinnstiftung*—the historian becomes the new bard of the national epos, only now with scientific means—an antidote to the very disorientation that is seen as having given rise to fascism in the first place.

> It is doubtful that the uncertainty first began in 1945. Hitler's rise to power was a function of the crises and catastrophes of a secularized civilization tumbling from rupture to rupture; this was a civilization marked by the loss of orientation and futile searches for security. . . . From 1914 to 1945 the Germans were thrust into the cataracts of modernity to a degree that shattered all traditions, made the unthinkable thinkable, and institutionalized barbarity as political regime. It was for these reasons that Hitler was able to triumph, that he was able to exploit and pervert Prussia and patriotism, the state and the virtues of civil society ["die bürgerlichen Tugenden"].[13]

Finally, what scandalized so many readers of Andreas Hillgruber's study, *Zweierlei Untergang: Die Zerschlagung des Deutschen Reiches und das Ende des europäischen Judentums* (*Two Kinds of Demise: The Shattering of the German Reich and the End of European Jewry*),[14] was Hillgruber's declared identification with the perspective of the defenders of Germany's eastern territories during the period of their collapse, even though these "valiant" efforts to hold back the anticipated reprisals by the Red Army allowed for the machinery of the death camps to continue unabated. Hillgruber distinguishes this "ethics of responsibility" (*verantwortungsethische*) perspective from the "ethics of conviction" (*gesinnungsethische*) perspective of the conspirators of the 20th of July.[15] Perhaps even more distressing in Hillgruber's study is the assimilation of these two "national catastrophes" to a single, overarching narrative of the destruction of the "europäische Mitte" or "European center." As the rather asymmetrical treatment of these two catastrophes indicates—the "shattering of the German Reich" takes up a good two-thirds of the book—in this double plot it is the Germans of the eastern provinces who become the truly tragic protagonists of modern European history.[16]

The gist of Habermas's critique of these trends in the historiography of fascism and the Holocaust is that they attempt to recuperate notions of centrality and modes of national identity no longer feasible in the harrowed cultural matrix of postwar Europe; rather than exploring strategies of coming to terms with a historical experience that changed not just the geopolitical, but also the moral and psychological, landscapes of Europe and the West, these historians place historiography in the service of a "national-historical restoration of a conventional identity."[17]

A "conventional identity" signifies in this context a self-structure still rooted in a specular relation to the particular norms, roles, "contents" of a specific social formation such as family, *Volk*, or nation. A more distanced and critical dialogue with the intensely ambivalent cultural legacy of recent German history is thus for Habermas the sign of a cultural self-identity that has begun to work through the radically transformed conditions of identity formation of post-Holocaust and, I would add, postmodern German society. Habermas condenses these determinants of postwar political culture under the sign of what he calls "postconventional identity."

> If among the younger generations national symbols have lost their formative powers; if naive identifications with one's origins and lineage have given way to a more tentative relationship with history; if discontinuities are felt more strongly and continuities no longer celebrated at all costs . . .—to the extent that all this is the case, we are witnessing increasing indications of the advent of a postconventional identity.[18]

One can no doubt imagine a number of different explanations for the eruption of the Historians' Debate at this particular moment in the history of the Federal Republic. And indeed, as one observer has recently noted, efforts to explain the debate have since generated a minor cottage industry.[19] But there has been a hesitation on the part of commentators to depart from a narrowly drawn framework of political culture in the Federal Republic and attempt to link the Historians' Debate to larger questions concerning the discourses of national identity in postmodern politics and culture more generally.[20] As I have already suggested, Habermas's notion of a "postconventional identity" points us in precisely this direction. And indeed, once we begin to situate Habermas's concept of a postconventional identity within this more broadly drawn postmodern context, the texts of the Historians' Debate quite rapidly become legible as symptoms of a remarkable repetition compulsion; in good postmodern fashion, it is a repetition compulsion that reenacts history in the medium of representations, in this case, historiography.[21]

Where the Jews were once blamed for the traumas of modernity, it would now appear that the Holocaust figures as the irritating signifier of the traumas and disorientations of postmodernity. Now the conditions under which stable cultural identities may be consolidated have indeed *with* and *since* the Holocaust become radically different; the symbolic order to which a German is subjected, i.e., that social space in which he or she first learns to say "ich" and "wir," now contains the traces of a horrific violence.[22] But the conventional sites of identity formation have become destabilized, have become more and more *unheimlich* as it were, for a variety of other reasons that derive more directly from other, more global, social, economic, and political displacements. In the present historical moment, which, perhaps for lack of a better word, we call the postmodern, Orient and Occident, masculine and feminine, guest worker and indigenous host—to name just a few of the binary oppositions that figure in the process of cultural identity formation—would seem no longer to occupy stable positions. The postmodern self is called upon to integrate an awareness of multiple forms of otherness, to tolerate instabilities and complexities of new and rapidly shifting social arrangements, and to be open to more hybrid, more "creole," forms of personal, sexual, and political identity. Furthermore, in the postmodern, the availability of resources of legitimation and orientation in the narratives of European Enlightenment culture—all of which project some form of progressive synthesis of this heterogeneity under a teleological master term—has become highly problematical. The Jews, now no longer available as the signifier of ruptures and disturbances one would like to banish from the inside (of the self, the family, the city, the *Reich*), are being displaced by the event of their own destruction; the Holocaust now figures as the placeholder for the decenteredness and instability experienced as so painfully chronic in contemporary German society, and it is a national historiography to which the task is assigned to reconstitute the center—the "europäische Mitte"—once again, if only in the mode of nostalgic recollection or simulacrum. We are faced here with a refusal to mourn either the particular and deeply traumatic losses to the cultural resources of Germany, i.e., the real and ineluctable fragmentation of the cultural identity that results from Auschwitz or the more "structural" losses that result from a global remapping of political, economic, cultural, sexual, and moral power over the last forty years (I would include the division of Germany and the loss of the eastern provinces within this second series of losses).

In the texts of the neoconservative historians reviewed by Habermas, the subtext of the quest for a renewed and vigorous (virile?) national identity has not just a cold war/NATO component—Germany's unbroken self-identity with regard to the "struggle against Bolshevism"—but a postmodern one as well. A national historiography assumes the task of salvaging, or perhaps more accurately, simulating, sites of identity formation no longer available in a cultural space defined by the double "post-" of the post-Holocaust and the postmodern. If it has become difficult, under the burden of this double post-, to say "wir" in contemporary German society and to know at all times exactly what that little pronoun signifies, i.e., if a certain strangeness, a certain alien presence—call it, with Nolte, the "Asiatic"—has come to haunt the first person plural, splitting it from within, then a new national historiography has busied itself with working out strategies of narrating this *Unheimlichkeit* to the margins, of deporting it as it were. This new historiography thus performs double duty: all the difficulties that have come to complicate the enunciation of the first person plural in contemporary German society are assigned a delimited origin in the Holocaust, which in its turn may then be normalized and marginalized by various techniques of "historicization." Whereas once it was the Jews, it is now the Shoah itself that serves as a screen upon which is projected, as something that intervenes from the outside—from "Asia"—that which ultimately keeps Germans from feeling continuous with themselves.

In this respect we may think of the neoconservative moment in the Historians' Debate as symptomatic of a more general group psychological trajectory of desire toward a respecularization of the terms of German national identity. And in this context one wonders whether the efforts to construct two new museums of national history, the Haus der Geschichte in Bonn and the Deutsches Historisches Museum in Berlin, may not end up with a house of mirrors, an enclosed space in which Germans may go to see themselves reflected and thereby reinstated in an imaginary plenitude and wholeness.[23]

Habermas's interventions in these controversies are directed precisely against this tendency to return to narcissistic patterns of (group) identity formation, patterns that reinscribe, as we have seen, a refusal or inability to mourn. Habermas has of course himself been criticized by just about every postmodern theorist for his refusal to relinquish his commitment to an Enlightenment faith in rationality and the perfectibility of man, and to Western liberal notions of consensus, in short, to the project of modernity. This is not the place to rehearse these debates yet again. I would simply like to suggest that in the context of the Historians' Debate, Habermas's thoughts regarding the pressures placed upon German national identity at the present historical moment invite us to see a more radical potential in his notion of a postconventional identity, a potential that places him much closer to his postmodern critics than we might have imagined possible. For in the context of the Historians' Debate, Habermas has deployed the notion of a postconventional identity as a critique of current tendencies to respecularize the terms of national identity and as an insistence upon the necessity of a continued labor of mourning. Insofar as the "project of modernity" may itself be seen to reinscribe the specular pattern of self-identity, albeit at a very high level of mediation—i.e., if at the completion of this project we all end up looking into the mirror of a white, male, Europe-oriented *Weltbürger*—then the imperatives of a postconventional identity will demand that this project too be worked through—be deconstructed— according to the procedures of the labor of mourning. The following sketches out in a very preliminary fashion the ways in which the displacements and condensations we have seen to be at work in the Historians' Debate also figure in Edgar Reitz's hugely successful film *Heimat*.

III

Anyone who has seen *Heimat* is familiar with the absence of Jews in the film as well as the film's near total silence on the subject of the Holocaust. The composition of the one scene in which the Final Solution is mentioned is in itself quite revealing. In episode six, "The Home Front," we witness a party at Eduard and Lucie's villa in Rhaunen. In the course of the evening, which takes on a comic undertone through Lucie's exaggerated performance as cultivated hostess, we hear Wilfried whisper news of the extermination camps to two officers: "The Final Solution is being carried out radically and without mercy. I really shouldn't be telling you any of this—between you and me, we know what's what. Up the chimneys, every last one of them." A few seconds later the camera pans across the room and follows Lucie to Eduard who has been sitting alone the entire evening blinking his left eye. When Lucie inquires about this peculiar behavior, Eduard reveals the object of his preoccupation. "I . . . can't . . . stop thinking of little Hans, the basket weaver's boy. That he might still be alive today if only I hadn't taught him that."[24] Eduard, we recall, had tutored Hänschen in the art of sharpshooting, thus helping to begin the boy's short-lived military career. The effect of this sequence, whether consciously intended or not, is the creation of a symmetry: all victims of the war are equal, whether German soldiers killed in battle or Jews murdered in Auschwitz. The symmetry is further underscored by the fact that it was originally through young Hänschen's eyes that we first see a concentration camp earlier in the film. But to speak here of a symmetry may actually be too generous since the Jewish victims remain invisible and Hänschen is a figure we have come to know and for whom we feel quite a bit of affection (one thinks here of the asymmetrical symmetry of Hillgruber's book).[25]

Another quite interesting sequence, in which the fate of the Jews briefly intersects with the various narratives that constitute *Heimat*, comes in the first episode and prefigures, in a certain sense, the scene we have just described. It is 1923; Eduard and Pauline make an afternoon excursion to Simmern, the next largest town from Schabbach. Pauline wanders off alone and finds herself looking at the window display of the town watchmaker and jeweler. Suddenly a group of young men run up behind her—including Eduard, armed as usual with camera and tripod—and begin throwing rocks at the window of the apartment above the watchmaker's shop where, as we learn, a Jew—in this case also branded as a separatist—resides. They are chased off by police, but the shards of fallen glass have cut Pauline's hand. Robert Kröber, the watchmaker, signals her to come into the shop where he cleans her wound, thereby initiating the love story of Pauline and Robert. (Later on in the film—it is 1933—we hear that the now married Pauline and Robert are buying the Jew's apartment. As Robert remarks, "The house belongs to him and now he wants to sell it. . . . The Jews don't have it so easy anymore"[26]

The importance of this small "Kristallnacht" sequence is that it shows how the shards of the Jew's shattered existence—we never see him in the flesh—are immediately absorbed into a sentimental story of courtship and matrimony, i.e., into experience.[27] Now of course it is the filmmaker who is exposing this mechanism, who is showing us just how experience forms and constructs itself around such blindspots. One wonders, however, whether the filmmaker is not in the end complicitous with such mechanisms, that is, whether he too is not content to absorb the shards of suffering of the other into so many anecdotes of love and family in the provinces.

One way in which this complicity becomes manifest is the remarkable lack of curiosity on the part of just about every character in the film with regard to cases of historical suffering that become visible at various moments in the film. By *historical suffering* I mean precisely the suffering that disrupts, in a radical way, the normal rhythms of the kitchen and the blacksmith's workshop as well as the larger organic rhythms of birth and natural death that are so important to Reitz's vision of village life. The two most striking examples are Lotti's—and everyone else's—total lack of curiosity about her father, Fritz Schirmer, who, as we know, was a Communist and has been taken to a concentration camp. There is actually some confusion in the film regarding Fritz's fate, since there is a scene set in 1943 in which Ursel, Lotti's younger sister, born in 1936, refers to her father as a soldier on the Eastern front. Fritz, as the Schirmer's family tree reveals, died in 1937, in Dachau we may presume. That Lotti has not forgotten her father is suggested by the way she cuts off her sister when she begins to talk about him to Pieritz. And yet we never hear a word from Lotti herself who was, after all, already nine years old when her father was taken. The other, more striking example is the apparent lack of any curiosity concerning the fate of Otto Wohlleben's mother who was, as he himself reveals, a Jew. She is in fact mentioned only in the context of Otto's allusion to his own career difficulties. As a "Mischling" not professing the Jewish faith—Reitz refers to Otto as "the poor, propertyless half-Jew who could be kept at home and tamed"[28]—Otto was himself in no immediate danger. It is nonetheless quite uncanny—*unheimlich*, we might say—that no one in the film asks about Frau Wohlleben's fate before, during, or after the war. Implicated in this strange sin of omission is also, of course, Frau Wohlleben's (illegitimate) grandson, Hermann. The case of Hermann is especially significant since that figure is, after all, a rather thinly veiled autobiographical portrait of the filmmaker-artist as a young man.[29]

Much more could be said about the occurrences of direct references and allusions to Jews in the film. But in the present context I am more interested in other ways in which the Jews and the Holocaust figure in the narrative and characterological economy of the film (as well as in the conditions and history of its production).

Heimat is, one might say, less about the disappearance of a particular way of life than about the disappearance of a particular relationship to death. In Reitz's view, contemporary society marks the farthest remove from a way of life in which death figured in a central and organic way in individual and communal experience. The postmodern moment (to use a term with which Reitz would perhaps be uncomfortable) is for Reitz not so much the signpost of a heightened sensitivity to difference and marginality as of a world "in which one separates from everything. Where one can separate from parts of one's life and parts of one's soul, one's family, one's experience; wherever we look we find this pattern of seemingly painless separation."[30] What intrigues Reitz about peasant and so-called primitive cultures, is that they still appear to have a deep, existential relationship to death; these cultures still perform formal, ritualized responses not only to mortal loss but more generally to the passing of time as it comes to afflict objects of daily use. These are, as Reitz says in his essay on Chris Marker's film *Sans Soleil*, "ceremonies in which people formally take leave from objects no longer needed, with a dignity that is ever more foreign to us."[31] However, by losing this deep relationship to death and to time, by losing, in other words, the capacity to transform, with the aid of ritual, *chronos* into *kairos*, "consumer society [here Reitz uses the German *Wegwerfgesellschaft*] unconsciously surrounds itself with the ghosts of all these abandoned objects which will one day take revenge on us." The film *Heimat* basically tells the story of the emergence of the postindustrial, consumer society. And indeed, the first great, cataclysmic triumph of the *episteme* governing this society of consumption was, as Reitz has suggested, the Holocaust. Auschwitz is, Reitz has said, "the most extreme manifestation of this throwaway society the world has ever known, a monstrous radicalization of the throwaway society: human beings become waste products."[32]

The semantic field of this term *Wegwerfgesellschaft* includes another word that has proven to be of fundamental importance in Reitz's conception of modernization, that historical dynamic that destroys the idyllic matrix called Schabbach. The word is—and as far as I know it is a neologism of Reitz—*Weggeher* or "one who goes away, one who leaves home." The key *Weggeher* in *Heimat* is Paul Simon who, as Reitz has remarked, eventually becomes a "real American . . . a man without a home, without roots, a sentimental globetrotter."[33] And indeed, America represents for Reitz a land of *Weggeher*—Reitz himself has relatives in Texas who left the Hunsrück in the nineteenth century—a land where the metaphysic of capitalism determines every aspect of human existence.

> America is the foremost example of the development of this new, this second culture in our world, a culture of emigrants, of those who left home. Their basic principle is individualism, the value of the self. [This creates] a new society of human beings who have no commodity to offer except their selves and thus engage in a life-and-death competition. Whatever these many individuals bring forth in terms of abilities, inventions, products . . . becomes the exclusive object of commerce, a commerce which demands ever new, ever more spectacular offers and which relates everything with everything else through the common language of trade.

In the elegiac narrative that Reitz's film relates, it is ultimately the triumph of this language of capitalism—American English as it were—

that bears the greatest burden of responsibility for the destruction of the "Heimat."

But then Reitz adds this curious supplementary remark. "The Jews, since time immemorial 'people who go away' [*Weggeher*], fit well into this American culture, a culture that only seeks to expand and to compete in all areas, whose very own language is competition."[34] A remarkable twist is thus added to the story of Schabbach's demise. The Hebrews, whose name means "the ones from the other shore of the river" and who are cited here as the archaic embodiment of the ethic of the *Weggeher*, come to figure as a metonymy for the historical dynamic that rends the fabric of the idyll. As Gertrud Koch has quite aptly noted, this equation of the "plague of commercialization . . . with 'the Jews' [had] been a staple of antisemitic critiques of civilization already in pre-fascist Germany."[35] I have tried to indicate the ways in which the Historians' Debate repeats this ideological gesture in a postmodern, post-Holocaust setting. But the tropological slippages of Reitz's discourse would seem to suggest something more radical still: since Auschwitz is itself only an epiphenomenon of these deep historical processes governing the *Weggeher-/Wegwerfgesellschaft*, the Jews come to signify even further the very forces that lead to their own destruction. The Holocaust thereby becomes in some sense a Jewish dialectic of the Enlightenment.

These two phenomena, the Historians' Debate and *Heimat*, are in large part generated by a political unconscious attempting to undo, by way of various strategies of respecularization, the complexities that make use of the first person plural—that make saying "we"—in post-Holocaust, postmodern Germany such an ambivalent and ambiguous experience. Forgiving the Jews for these difficulties will, of course, not make the experience any easier.

Notes

1. Alexander and Margarete Mitscherlich, *The Inability to Mourn: Principles of Collective Behavior*, trans. Beverley R. Placzek (New York: Grove Press, 1975).
2. Jürgen Habermas, "Eine Art Schadensabwicklung. Die apologetischen Tendenzen in der deutschen Zeitgeschichtsschreibung," *Historiker-Streit: Die*

Dokumentation der Kontroverse um die Einzigartigkeit der nationalsozialistischen Judenvernichtung (Munich: Piper, 1987) 62–76. For an English translation, see "A Kind of Settlement of Damages (Apologetic Tendencies)" *New German Critique* 44 (Spring/Summer 1988): 22–39, trans. Jeremy Leaman. Unless otherwise indicated, translations are mine.

3. Ernst Nolte, "Vergangenheit, die nicht vergehen will," ("A past that will not pass away") *FAZ* 6 June 1986, reprinted in *Historiker-Streit* 39–47. The essay was originally intended as a contribution to the Frankfurt Römerberg-Colloquium. For a summary of the events surrounding the publication of Nolte's essay see his letter to *Die Zeit* 1 August 1986, republished in *Historiker-Streit* 93–94, as well as Hilmar Hoffmann's introduction to *Gegen den Versuch, Vergangenheit zu verbiegen: Eine Diskussion um politische Kultur in der Bundesrepublik aus Anlaß der Frankfurter Römerberggespräche 1986* (Frankfurt a.M.: Athenäum, 1987).

4. Ernst Nolte, *Historiker-Streit* 45.

5. Nolte, *Historiker-Streit* 46. A recent effort to historicize the Final Solution by an American historian, Arno Mayer, makes a powerful argument for the importance of the connections between anti-Bolshevism and anti-Semitism in Nazi ideology. Unlike Nolte, however, he does not use the former to displace or absorb the relative autonomy of the latter, nor does he posit the sorts of mechanical causalities that interest Nolte. In Mayer's reading, Nazi anti-Bolshevism is not defensive in the sense in which Nolte presents it but is rather part of an ultimately maniacal crusading ideology. See Arno J. Mayer, *Why Did the Heavens Not Darken? The "Final Solution" in History* (New York: Pantheon, 1988).

6. Ernst Nolte, "Between Myth and Revisionism? The Third Reich in the Perspective of the 1980s," *Aspects of the Third Reich*, ed. H. W. Koch (New York: St. Martin's, 1985) 28.

7. See Nolte, *Historiker-Streit* 33, 46.

8. Nolte, *Historiker-Streit* 42. One might also add to this summary of Nolte's remarkable capacity to equalize distinct historical phenomena the rather bizarre lesson he manages to learn from Claude Lanzmann's film *Shoah*, namely that the film "makes plausible that the SS-staff of the death camps were victims in their own right and that . . . a virulent anti-Semitism was not foreign to the Polish victims of National Socialism" 42.

9. Nolte, *Historiker-Streit* 45.

10. Nolte, "Between Myth and Revisionism" 21. For an insightful analysis of the "pseudo-interrogative mode" of such reflections, see Charles S. Maier's book on the Historians' Debate, *The Unmasterable Past: History, Holocaust, and German National Identity* (Cambridge: Harvard UP, 1988) 83. These sorts of comparisons and analogies are, of course, by no means new, nor are they necessarily clear markers of membership in a particular political or ideological camp. For, as Margarete Mitscherlich, Peter Schneider, and others have pointed out, the German left has deployed such rhetorical strategies quite as much as neoconservative historians and also, one might assume, out of interest in reducing the pressures of the historical burdens weighing upon the postwar generations in Germany. Commenting upon Helmut Kohl's comparisons of Mikhail Gorbachev's public relations skills with those of Goebbels and the work camps for political prisoners in the GDR with Nazi concentration camps, Peter Schneider points to similar

rhetorical moves on the part of the German left. "One has to concede that long before Kohl began formulating his hair-raising comparisons for Goebbels and the death camps, the children of the postwar period had de-historicized the concept of Nazism. After *fascism* had become a generalized term of opprobrium in Germany, it served hardly at all to refer to the twelve years that gave it its concrete meaning. The term was used mainly to denounce one's political opponents. The rebels of 1968 were as uninterested as today's revisionist historians in the uniqueness of the Nazi crimes. They were seeking comparisons, though for the students the term of the comparison was capitalist democracy, not Soviet communism. Only now has it become apparent that the leftist misuse of the accusation of fascism is an equally reflexive attempt at relief: for the reduction of the historical profile of nazism to general and transferable characteristics also had, apart from its instructive value, an unburdening function. If National Socialism was the 'conspiracy' of a couple of powerful industrialists, our parents, no matter what they had done, were the victims of the conspiracy." Peter Schneider, "Hitler's Shadow: On Being a Self-Conscious German," trans. Leigh Hafrey, *Harpers* September 1987: 52. Not surprisingly, one area that has become a key site for this process of political and psychological unburdening on the part of the German left has been Israel and its relations with the Palestinians. See, for example, Margarete Mitscherlich's remarks regarding the vehemence with which the German left has taken up the Palestinian cause, i.e., that of the "victim" against the Jewish, "fascist" oppressor (*Erinnerungsarbeit. Zur Psychoanalyse der Unfähigkeit zu trauern* [Frankfurt a.M.: Fischer, 1987] 102–3). Yet another circumstance in which the boundaries between left and right became somewhat blurred, was the controversy over the attempt to stage Fassbinder's play *Der Müll, die Stadt und der Tod (Garbage, the City, and Death)* at the Schauspielhaus in Frankfurt in the fall of 1985. There it was generally the Left that supported the staging of the play over the protests of the Jewish community which—for good reason—found the play to be full of undigested and unanalysed anti-Semitism, and it was generally from conservative circles, with the *Frankfurter Allgemeine Zeitung* at the forefront, that one heard the strongest public outcry against the staging of the play. These were the very circles that had more or less warned the Jewish community not to interfere with Reagan's visit to the cemetery at Bitburg. The controversy demonstrated, among other things, how the fundamental desire for normalcy in Germany is capable of instrumentalizing a great variety of ideological positions both from the Left and the Right. For an excellent summary of the debates surrounding the Fassbinder play see *New German Critique*'s special issue on the German-Jewish controversy, 38 (Spring/Summer 1986); see also Margarete Mitscherlich's remarks in *Erinnerungsarbeit* 28–30.

11. Stürmer, *Historiker-Streit* 38.
12. Stürmer, *Historiker-Streit* 38.
13. Stürmer, *Historiker-Streit* 36–37. See also Stürmer's *Dissonanzen des Fortschritts* (Munich: Piper, 1986). Martin Broszat, who has at times been associated with the revisionist camp of historians, has noted Stürmer's tendency to overburden historiography with quasi-theological social functions it can never fulfill. Broszat points to parallels with cruder, more explicitly political versions of the same vision of the task of the historian in the remarks

of Alfred Dregger, parliamentary leader of the Christian Democratic Union. "We are deeply disturbed by the lack of historical awareness and consideration vis-à-vis one's own nation. Without a fundamental patriotism, which is a given for other peoples, our own people will not be able to survive. Whoever misuses the process of 'coming to terms with the past,' as some have chosen to call it and which no doubt had its place, as a way of foreclosing the future of our people, must face our firm opposition." Quoted in Broszat, "Wo sich die Geister scheiden. Die Beschwörung der Geschichte taugt nicht als nationaler Religionsersatz," *Historiker-Streit* 194.

14. Berlin: Seidler, 1986.

15. "Looking back at the catastrophe of the winter of 1944/45, the historian is left with only one position, even if it is difficult to assume when it comes to the particulars of the case: he must identify with the concrete fate of the German population in the East and with the desperate efforts of the German forces on land and at sea, suffering casualty upon casualty. These efforts were dedicated to protecting the population of the eastern parts of Germany from the orgies of revenge of the Red Army, the mass rapes, the arbitrary murders and deportations, and to keeping escape routes to the West open in those last moments of the war" 24–25. In the narrative sections of the book this pathos of identification leads to some remarkable passages. "In these events, in which everyone was consumed by the single task of saving what could be saved, the destruction of entire armies stands side by side with the courage and selflessness of individuals; the loss of cities with the protection of river crossings upon which depended the fate of entire treks of refugees. In the catastrophe that was enveloping everyone and everything, many a nameless soldier and citizen found new strength and courage" 36. And further, "Among the National Socialist authorities, there were those who proved themselves in the hour of need . . . while others failed, at times pathetically" 37.

16. As Maier remarks about this asymmetry, "The sufferings of Jews are not evoked: no sealed freight cars, purposeful starvation, flogging, degradation, and final herding to 'the showers' parallels the accounts of the evacuation of East Prussia. If indeed these two experiences are two sorts of destruction, one is presented, so to speak, in technicolor, the other in black, gray, and white." Maier goes on to characterize Hillgruber's elegiac evocation of the lost center as the "geopolitics of nostalgia," *The Unmasterable Past* 23.

17. Habermas, *Historiker-Streit* 73.

18. Habermas, *Historiker-Streit* 75. The notion of a postconventional identity that Habermas has deployed in the Historians' Debate has been a key term in his thinking for some time. See especially his "Können komplexe Gesellschaften eine vernünftige Identität ausbilden?" in Jürgen Habermas, *Zur Rekonstruktion des historischen Materialismus* (Frankfurt a.M.: Suhrkamp, 1976), as well as in the same volume his attempt to use the psychological theories of Jean Piaget and Lawrence Kohlberg to theorize the formation of postconventional identities. See also, "Geschichtsbewußtsein und posttraditionale Identität. Die Westorientierung der Bundesrepublik," in Jürgen Habermas, *Eine Art Schadensabwicklung: Kleine Politische Schriften VI* (Frankfurt a.M.: Suhrkamp, 1987).

19. See Konrad H. Jarausch, "Removing the Nazi Stain? The Quarrel of the German Historians," *German Studies Review* 11 (1988): 293.

20. In the present context, *postmodern* shall signify a general remapping of political, technological, cultural, economic, and sexual power that has taken place since World War II. These shifts and developments include a redistribution of power and alliances within Europe as well as a general destabilization of European hegemony in the world; the ascendancy of the United States as a world power; the decolonization of the Third World (these three developments were the subject of a lecture by Cornel West entitled "Historicizing the Postmodernism Debate," at Princeton University, 4 December 1988); the women's movement and the emergence of gender issues more generally in the figuration and theorization of otherness; massive migrations of indigenous populations under political and economic pressures; a more international division of labor; the passage into a computer and information-based rather than industrial economy; the availability, with the computer, of vast memory banks allowing for the instant recall of unlimited "bits" of information; revisions within the sciences of the systems of logic considered to be natural; new forms of image consumption and spectacle; the availability, with nuclear weaponry, of technologies capable of eliminating life on the planet. These developments have put pressures on conventional, i.e., pre-modern and modern, notions of personal, sexual, and cultural identity that may be insupportable.

21. For a somewhat different reading of this repetition compulsion, see Dan Diner, "The Historians' Controversy—Limits to the Historization of National Socialism," *Tikkun* 2.1 (1987): 74–78.

22. See Habermas, *Historiker-Streit* 247. "Now as before we are faced with the simple fact that those born later also grew up in a form of life [*Lebensform*] in which *that* was possible. Our own life is not contingently but in its very essence, tied together with that life-context in which Auschwitz was possible. Our form of life is connected with the form of life of our parents and grandparents by way of a tightly woven fabric of familial, geographical, political, and also intellectual traditions that would be most difficult to untangle; we are part of a historical milieu that has made us into the people we are today. No one can escape from this milieu because our identity as individuals as well as Germans is indissolubly tied up with it. That reaches from the level of mimicry and bodily gesture to that of language and into the capillary divarications of one's intellectual habitus." The question that follows is the one we have been addressing all along. "But what are the consequences of this existential imbrication with traditions and forms of life which have become poisoned by unspeakable crimes?" This is, one might say, the central and ultimately suicidal core of Paul Celan's poetry.

23. For an excellent discussion of the debates surrounding the plans for these museums as well as the best evaluation to date of Habermas's interventions here and in the historians' controversy, see once more Maier, *The Unmasterable Past.*

24. Edgar Reitz and Peter Steinbach, *Heimat: Eine deutsche Chronik* (Nördlingen: Greno, 1985) 299.

25. I am very grateful to one of my students, Clare Rogan, for her sensitive discussion of this scene in her seminar paper.

26. Reitz and Steinbach, *Heimat* 148.

27. See Reitz's polemical essay on the American television film "Holocaust" for a discussion of this category so central to the aesthetic of *Heimat* in *Liebe*

zum Kino: Utopien und Gedanken zum Autorenfilm 1962–1983 (Cologne: KÖLN 78, 1984) 99.

28. Reitz, *Liebe zum Kino* 151.
29. Yet a third example that might be included in this series is the curious fact that Anton never seems to have any nightmares about the executions he witnessed on the Eastern front. See J. Hoberman, "Once Upon a Reich Time," *New German Critique* 36 (Fall 1985): 9.
30. Interview with author July 1987.
31. Reitz, *Liebe zum Kino* 128.
32. Interview with author July 1987.
33. Quoted in Michael Geisler, "*Heimat* and the German Left: The Anamnesis of a Trauma," *New German Critique* 36 (Fall 1985): 63.
34. Reitz, *Liebe zum Kino* 145–46, quoted in Gertrud Koch, "How Much Naivete Can We Afford? The New *Heimat* Feeling," *New German Critique* 36 (Fall 1985): 15. Perhaps one should add here that Gypsies (Appolonia) and refugees (Klärchen), i.e., those other people who since time immemorial "go away," would also fit well into this American culture.
35. Koch, "New *Heimat* Feeling" 15.

10

The New German
Cinema's Historical Imaginary

Thomas Elsaesser

The New German Cinema was no longer new when filmmakers
began to understand their protagonists' past also as history: many of the
films made in the late 1960s and early 1970s seemed studiously to avoid
reference to any precise temporality of events. Werner Herzog's work
rarely featured Germany even as geography. R. W. Fassbinder and Wim
Wenders in their early films preferred to explore the colonized state of
their heroes' consciousness. But asked why American music, comics, and
movies had been what he called his "lifesavers" in adolescence, Wenders
replied, "Twenty years of political amnesia had left a hole: we covered it
with chewing gum and Polaroids."[1] Yet barely half a decade later, after
the international success of Syberberg's *Hitler—Ein Film aus Deutschland* (*Our Hitler*, 1977), Fassbinder's *Die Ehe der Maria Braun* (*The
Marriage of Maria Braun*, 1978), Helma Sanders-Brahms's *Deutschland,
bleiche Mutter* (*Germany, Pale Mother*, 1979), and Kluge's *Die Patriotin*

(*The Patriot,* 1979), the New German Cinema appeared set to have its identity firmly located in a brooding obsession with Germany's recent past as a nation. This in itself is not unusual; other national cinemas have exploited their past in order to make it into a spectacle for the present. France, Italy, Britain, and Australia all had their *mode rétro* during the 1970s.[2]

The question that arises in the German context is nonetheless specific: What was it that prepared the ground for filmmakers to cut a passage through this amnesia to nazism and German history as a film subject, and what films, if any, thematize this amnesia itself to investigate the conditions of representing German history on film? One answer is that the New German Cinema discovered the past when filmmakers found history in the home and fascism around the family table. By taking up the more general debates and social conflicts of the late 1960s and early 1970s, such as the crisis of authority, the legitimation of power and the law, the actual and symbolic role of the father as head of the family, the West German cinema returned to history. The anti-authoritarian movement, the pressure of certain contemporary events (those depicted in *Deutschland im Herbst* [*Germany in Autumn,* 1978] for instance), but also the more conservative turn of academic historians (the *Historiker-streit*) gave history a new topicality.[3]

Another issue seems to be involved, one highlighted by Edgar Reitz's *Heimat.* Both the film and its reception are symptomatic not only of the New German Cinema's difficulty with German history but of our difficulty as film scholars with conceptualizing adequately the relation between film and history.[4] These difficulties have to do with two com-plexes that are at the same time the traces of historical traumas and conceptual impasses. One appears to be specific to Germany and German history, namely the question of continuity and discontinuity, of new beginnings and recurring cycles, of the return of the repressed, and the desire for radical breaks. The latter is usually referred to as "zero hour thinking," especially when serving politicians as the founding myth of the Federal Republic. Filmmakers have treated this cutoff point as prob-lematic, and many found in a novella by Heinrich von Kleist, *The Earth-quake in Chile,* an appropriate fictional precedent. Kleist took a natural disaster as the foil for criticizing the tabula rasa thinking of the French

Revolution. Conceptually, the "Chile complex" can be seen as a condensation of the question of historical agency and historical change (or lack of it).[5]

The other complex is the cinema/history debate generally. It centers on the question of how faithfully the audiovisual media and narrative films in particular can and ought to represent the events, sociopolitical forces, the heteronomies of historical processes. What claim does a given narrative make to authority and veracity (Ranke's "wie es eigentlich gewesen ist")? It is this guarantee of truth that is seen most threatened by the cinema getting hold of history. Giuliana Bruno makes the point well, "The historical obsession of contemporary cinema is not concerned so much with the representation of 'real' events in the form of a story, but rather with the representation of cinematic events in the form of other stories." Bruno concludes from this that the reference to the historicity of cinema in films like *Hammett* (film noir in color), to early comedy in *Broadway Danny Rose,* or the resumé of film history at the beginning of Fellini's *And the Ship Sails On* makes the obsession with history a formalist obsession because "it effaces the referent in order to replace it with a pure signifier."[6]

In West Germany the question of how film represents history not only affected (film) historians but stirred filmmakers too. One need only recall Wenders's polemical essay on Joachim Fest's *Hitler—Eine Karriere* (*Hitler—A Career,* 1977)[7] or Syberberg's and Reitz's interventions in the *Holocaust* debate.[8] Sensing that there was no easy way out of this problem, discussions in West Germany especially among filmmakers, tended to display a vivid concern with "authenticity": authentic "Filmbilder" (Wenders), authentic "Filmstoffe" (Kluge), or Reitz's demand that "films, literature, images [must] come into being that bring us to our senses and restore our reflexes."[9] So pervasive was the reaction to the "vanishing of the real"[10] brought on by the media that one can almost speak of the "authenticity complex" of the New German Cinema.

Reitz's *Heimat*

Heimat is a good example of how the two complexes often find themselves intertwined. Reitz had in earlier films explored the historical and personal aspects of the mythical search for a new beginning typical of postwar German culture. It is explicitly related to 1945 in *Stunde Null* (*Zero Hour*, 1976), which tells of the end of the war in a village near Leipzig, as American troops evacuate and cede part of their territorial gains to the Soviets. True to the topos as fixed by Kleist, the film details the villagers' depressingly swift accommodation to three different masters in as many months. In another of Reitz's films, *Die Reise nach Wien* (*The Trip to Vienna*, 1973), the ambiguity of a return to origins and the hope for a fresh start are translated into the dualism of home and abroad, rootedness in Central Europe and emigration to America, thus anticipating several motifs from *Heimat*.

Heimat, of course, is more ambitious than Reitz's previous films, also in its representation of history. There are Reitz's references within the film to the cinema but to the impact of the mass media, telecommunication, and transport as well. Not only are the first automobiles, the arrival of telephone wires, and the building of new roads major events for the village, the series as a whole thematizes its conflicts and characterizes its protagonists via the instruments of recording, diffusing, and consuming experiences in vicarious form. Paul's interest in radio, Anton's optics, Eduard's photography, Ernst's obsession with flying, and Hermann's electronic music become in the course of the film complexly handled symbols of (especially) the men's very displaced and mediated relation to their own selves-in-history. Reitz also includes an extract from a very popular 1938 Zarah Leander film, the movie star being a crucial reference point for several characters in *Heimat*. For the women who stay at home (and dream of Spain, Italy, the south) as well as for the men on the front (who dream of returning home) she becomes the convergence of several not quite symmetrically placed fantasies across the gender divide.

Against this we have to remember Reitz's by now well-known comments on Hollywood and *Holocaust*. To preserve a notion of authentic images, he makes a distinction between "opinion" and "experience," and condemns Hollywood for purveying opinions rather than experiences, which is tantamount, according to Reitz, to an act of theft.

> If we are to come to terms with the Third Reich and the crimes committed in our country, it has to be by the same means we use everyday to take stock of the world we live in. We suffer from a hopeless

283

lack of meaningfully communicated experience. As far as is possible,
we must work on our memories. This way, films, literature, images
come into being that bring us to our senses and restore our reflexes.
. . . Authors all over the world are trying to take possession of their
history, but they often find that it is torn out of their hands. The most
serious act of expropriation occurs when people are deprived of their
history. With *Holocaust*, the Americans have taken away our history.[11]

Reitz's plea for a cinema of individual and collective memory is one of
the most impassioned manifestations of the authenticity complex. Yet
Heimat also repudiates, in characters like Eduard and Lucie, the notion
of a zero hour and instead, across the Simon family, tries to document
continuity as politically and emotionally ambiguous. Part of the issue,
both of a false sense of and a necessary desire for continuity, comes from
the realization that, as Reitz is clearly aware, despite his attack on
Hollywood, to talk about memory and history in the twentieth century
is to talk about images and sounds electronically or optically produced,
an audiovisual representation of events, whether newsreel, family snap-
shots, big screen movies, or recorded music. Their fascination derives
from the instant presence they conjure up, their ability to annihiliate
time, distance, and death.

The dilemma of Reitz's project of "repossessing our history" is
therefore that the cinema, even where it is not a spectacular restaging
of the past but a "working through" in the sense of laying bare the different
intensities of moments in time, encounters the fact that photographic
memory is selective; what it preserves is often a conservative, nostalgic
sense of loss. From painful events, and even from historical disasters, it
draws the perverse but nonetheless powerful pleasures of regret. In
reviewing *Heimat* I was thus struck by a paradox. A return to history
through the subjective, the autobiographical, but even more, a return
to history through its images, cannot but be an elegy, a lament, a dwelling
on destruction. The trauma of burying and repressing the past—Wenders's collective amnesia—which is said to have characterized German
society for the first three decades after the war, seemed to have been
lifted only at the price of nostalgia, of a gratifying identification with
victims, and with oneself as victim, if not of history, then of time itself.
And since nostalgia is also the emotion typical for the cinema itself,
Heimat works with nostalgia for nostalgia: the memory and recognition

of images that have been seen many times before. History has become an old movie. And that—if the history happens to be that of Germany in this century—must give pause for thought.

Cinephilia: Rewriting German History as Film History

One needs to push this rhetorical flourish a little further and trace more closely how New German Cinema came to translate the question of history into questions of continuity/discontinuity/continuity (of fascism and postwar society) and the question of accuracy into a question of authenticity (autobiography, the personal, the domestic). Continuity and authenticity were made to bear a considerable conceptual burden. They tended to stand for such traditional categories as historical agency (which in the films became a negative and subjective category: a matter of guilt and responsibility), change (which emerged as the psychic "return of the repressed"), and truth (which became an almost religious need to bear witness). These transformations of history and appropriations of categories of the subjective, the psychic, and the spiritual are often summed up by the term *Trauerarbeit* (work of mourning) in which memory and commemoration want to establish a continuity across the very awareness of separation and loss, in a mode that converts the mirroring effects of nostalgia into the "sorrow and pity" of selfhood and otherness.[12]

Whatever its psychosocial implications, the widespread use of *Trauerarbeit* risks a certain telescoping of terms, with respect to historical analysis and the question of cinema. German history during the twentieth century has been particularly affected by the desire to posit radical breaks, figured as new beginnings, so that history may be given definite boundaries. In 1919 the Revolution was "betrayed" by the Social Democrats; in 1933 Germany "awoke" and banished as nightmare the so-called *Systemzeit*. Again, in 1945, the zero hour was supposed to have put an end to the "Nazi-Spuk." Similarly, if one cares to investigate the offical political discourses since 1945 in terms of Germany's role and identity as a nation, one finds that its fascist past has tended to be normalized or historicized in the rearticulation of binary oppositions and symmetries held together by the master-divide of Germany itself and its eventual reunification: East/West, Free World/Communism, exile and *innere Emigration*, and in the more recent *Historikerstreit*, "our" victims against "their" victims.[13] It might even be argued that some of the enthusiasm of German conservative politics for a United Europe stems from a similar wish to make Germany's past invisible as a concrete history, to better identify its future with another strong totality: at first the West and America, and now Europe. Just as the geographical borders were redrawn after 1945, so have the discursive boundaries with which to speak about Germany been reterritorialized.

Freudians like Alexander and Margarete Mitscherlich, recognizing the symptoms of such demarcations, interpreted this obsessive need to exclude and totalize, to disavow in order to reincorporate, as a sign of disturbed narcissism, the "inability to mourn."[14] From it, they exhorted West Germans to do *Trauerarbeit* with respect to their past. But one can also see it as a problem of representation, indeed *the* problem of representation in the age of the image: how to think the past without being seduced by polarization into a "politics of the Imaginary."[15]

In the forms that history was taken up by New German filmmakers one can in fact see a decisive attempt to get away from the binary lines and exclusionary formulations of the postwar period in politics and of Oberhausen in film politics. It will be recalled that the Oberhausen Manifesto was supported by the slogan "Papa's Kino ist tot": an oppositional gesture of confrontation typical of avant-garde aspirations but which was promptly denounced by a more radical avant-garde (Jean Marie Straub, Vlado Kristl, Hellmuth Costard) and also by women filmmakers such as Ula Stöckl not least because of its oedipal sentimentality and patriarchal presumptions. The New German Cinema that followed the Young German Film only partly endorsed either the commemorative return to the past (Kluge, Reitz, Syberberg, and *Trauerarbeit*) or the radical break with it (Kristl, Straub, and "Resistance"). Fassbinder, Herzog, Wenders, Schroeter, and Achternbusch by contrast all sought ways of figuring continuity and discontinuity not as an opposition but explicitly as a way of problematizing the imaginary, in terms of the relation between identity and otherness: the "politics of identification."[16]

Take the example of Werner Herzog and his celebrated claim

that his films affirmed West Germany's identity in that they represented "legitimate German culture" in the same way that Lotte Eisner, Murnau, and Lang had done. If what holds these names together is largely the projection into the past of an absence felt in the present, Herzog's dictum is only the most obvious case of a remarkable, self-consciously retrospective rewriting of a continuity across a break. What is interesting is that such identity as a national (film) culture appears only to have been formulated in dialogue with an "other," though not conceived as radical other, but as the other within the self, which is to say the other in the same. In the case of Fassbinder or Wenders, this other was American popular culture as the sign of authenticity for a German postwar child-hood. Such a gesture of recouping would have been impossible for Kluge, Reitz, Schlöndorff—all born a generation earlier, far less under the sway of popular culture, and indeed in the case of Reitz and Syberberg, openly anti-American.

But in what sense are the *Autoren* of the New German Cinema the sons of the Weimar cinema, or even the grandsons? Is there an Oedipus complex to be resolved between the filmmakers and the tradition to which they wish to belong? Are the films of Wenders, Herzog, and Fassbinder rewriting the Weimar cinema or Nazi cinema? Perhaps there is a splitting of the father image into good fathers (the Hollywood emigré directors: Fritz Lang, Douglas Sirk) and bad fathers (Veit Harlan, Wolfgang Liebeneiner). In a very public gesture, Fassbinder "adopted" Sirk as his father, Wenders Nicholas Ray, and Helma Sanders-Brahms DEFA-director Wolfgang Staudte.[17] Werner Herzog, in an act of calcu-lated homage, remade *Nosferatu*, and undertook a pilgrimage to the Paris home of Lotte Eisner. But Niklaus Schilling was happy to admit to his admiration for Harald Reinl, a representative, if ever there was one, of Papa's Kino.[18] And Syberberg paid tribute to equally ambiguous names: in *Karl May*, for instance, to Helmut Käutner and Kristina Söd-erbaum.

Faced with the discontinuity of German history at one level but the continuity of the German film industry at another, New German Cinema invented for itself a new kind of history—a genealogy of elective affinities—as a way not only of understanding the overwhelming pres-ence of the American cinema and American popular culture but also of

Thomas Elsasser

bridging the gap to reappropriate a good Germany: socialist or grand bourgeois, cinephile and professional, international and popular—in short everything that German filmmakers (and their films), at least in the 1950s, were not. The directors of the 1970s rewrote German history often enough as German film history.

Microhistory and Memory

Even more striking attempts to fashion continuity out of discontinuity often could be found in the work of women directors, who also focused on the experience of adolescence, though not in relation to popular culture. Neither Mickey Mouse nor chewing gum became the markers of a specifically historical subjectivity, but the mother's reaction to the heroine's first menstruation, or scenes of family strife, intensified by the recall of embarrassing moments—as if only pain and shame could furnish an affectivity adequate to the representation of history in its discontinuous, intermittent presence (*Germany, Pale Mother*, Helma Sanders-Brahms, 1979; *Hungerjahre* [*Hunger Years*, Jutta Brückner, 1979]; *Etwas tut weh* [*Something Hurts*, Recha Jungmann, 1980]). Here the autobiographical mode seemed to offer both a model of continuity and a notion of authenticity with respect to history. Dyadic bonds, such as mother-daughter relations (von Trotta, Helma Sanders-Brahms), mother-son relations (Fassbinder, Achternbusch) alongside father-son conflicts (Thomas Harlan's *Wundkanal* [1984] or Imhof/Vesper's *Die Reise* [*The Journey*, 1986]) became highly privileged metaphors not so much of the subjective in history but of specifically filmic ways of figuring continuity in discontinuity and the authentic as a property of the image.

The conjunction of painful memory and female masochism has in common with the search for continuity through elective paternity the paradigm of identification—identification with the self as other, the other as self (against the male "I want to be where/who my father once was" we get "I want to see myself from where my mother once saw/punished/embarrassed me"). Identification with parental figures in this mode often focused on figures who were themselves tied to the past by guilt, depression, and anxiety: ex-Nazis, cowards of conscience who survived by self-

288

deception and deceiving their children, or alcoholics and drug-dependents driving themselves to suicide. *The Marriage of Maria Braun, Die bleierne Zeit* (*The German Sisters*, United States title: *Marianne and Juliane*, Margarethe von Trotta, 1981), *Schwestern, oder die Balance des Glücks* (*Sisters or the Balance of Happiness*, Margarethe von Trotta, 1979), *Germany, Pale Mother, Malou* (Jeanine Meerapfel, 1981), and many other titles can be seen as attempts to enter into such a different relationship with history.

History and Paternity: Fathers and Fathers

Thus, the royal road in the 1970s of West German cinema to German history was family history, and one can speak of a veritable oedipalization of this history. The process can be studied in a relatively late attempt of the generation of Oberhausen both to oedipalize political history, as well as structure a story of generational social crisis around binarisms and oppositions: *Germany in Autumn*. It is a film developed for the most part around the drama of father and son, an attempt to explain via the nuclear family the relationship between economic affluence and political violence and also to find a model for the peculiar continuities within discontinuity and discontinuity within continuity. But as Fassbinder's contribution makes clear, neither the narrative closure provided by a double funeral symmetrically inverted nor the double father-son axis between Rommel and Schleyer could contain the truly paranoid power of the Imaginary that the events of Mogadishu and Stammheim projected, not only into the present but into history. The series of confrontations between Fassbinder and his mother, Fassbinder and his homosexual lover, Fassbinder and his former wife, Fassbinder and his obsession with Franz Biberkopf are designed to cast doubts on the notion that "Hitler is dead"—the narrative closure on which was built another founding myth of West German democracy. Fassbinder, however, goes further. He seems determined to deny history the symmetry of the heterosexual lineage cautiously and sentimentally imposed by Kluge and his collaborators in the framing events of *Germany in Autumn*. This refusal, also expressed in many of his other films as well as those of

Achternbusch and Schroeter, poses questions about history, its periodization and representation differently though still within the paradigm of identification: identification with the radical other. This, too, occurs in the name of authenticity, now based on perversion, deviance, marginality, and a play of inverted identification. Fassbinder's representation of the working class, of women, of ethnic minorities, of Jews, of homosexuality can most usefully be seen in this light, in films as different as *Der Händler der vier Jahreszeiten* (*The Merchant of Four Seasons*, 1971), *Die bitteren Tränen der Petra von Kant* (*The Bitter Tears of Petra von Kant*, 1972), *Angst essen Seele auf* (*Fear Eats the Soul*, 1973), and *In einem Jahr mit dreizehn Monden* (*In a Year of Thirteen Moons*, 1978). Schroeter's *Der Bomberpilot* (*The Bomber Pilot*, 1970), Achternbusch's *Das letzte Loch* (*The Last Hole*, 1981), and Sanders-Brahms's *Die Berührte* (*No Mercy No Future*, 1981) are similar and similarly anti-oedipal films about what another authenticity vis-à-vis German history might have been.

The Fear of (Mis)Representing History

Discussions of West German films about history tend to be marked by two fears. One is that a work would be seen as lacunary, that its representation especially of fascism might be selective or apologetic (Where are the Jews in Schabbach? Does Syberberg fall under the spell of "blood and soil" mysticism? Is Schroeter's flaunting of and flirting with 1930s kitsch irresponsible?). The second fear in the representation of German history is the fear of spectacle (Is Fassbinder not celebrating the *Reichskanzlei* in *Lili Marleen* rather than critiquing its architecture as indicative of a bombastic public life?). This anxiety culminated in the *Holocaust* reception and anti-Holocaust films like *Our Hitler* and *Heimat*. To counter this fear, filmmakers dealing with sensitive issues trimmed their spectacle ambitions to the point of making what Karsten Witte once called "Wunschkonzerte für Deutschlehrer" and Michael Rutschky complained of as "abgefilmte Schulfunkfeatures."[19]

It seems that the pervasive oedipalization of the New German Cinema in the late 1970s is in part a reaction to the strenuous attempt at an ideologically correct *Tendenz* during the late 1960s and early 1970s. Syberberg's *Hitler* and Reitz's *Heimat,* one at the beginning, the other at the end of the most intense phase of the New German Cinema's engagement with German history, are two films that mark extreme points in the spectrum of responses to both kinds of *Berührungsangst* (literally "fear of touching" [of a sensitive issue]) of the New German Cinema regarding history. Yet in both films, too, lies a suspicion of cinema as fundamentally inadequate for the representation of history, as well as its opposite, a suspicion of cinema's excessive seductiveness—if history is understood as the always contradictory manifestation of uneven forces, the constant battle between private, personal temporalities or intensities, and the chronology of public events.

A Shift in Paradigm; or, The End of *Trauerarbeit*

The concept of *Trauerarbeit,* useful as it may have been for West German filmmakers in articulating an ideologically and emotionally viable perspective on recent German history, leaves critics of the New German Cinema and theorists of the relation between cinema and history almost exactly where the issue was after Kracauer and *From Caligari to Hitler,* who (without using the term either analytically or prescriptively) had also highlighted the family, male subjectivity, patriarchy, and the authoritarian personality's identification with the other as constitutive for the films of the Weimar Republic. This "return" too is no accident. The Mitscherlichs, who introduced the term into cultural history, argue from within a configuration of generational conflict and the "fatherless societies" that come from the same critical tradition as Kracauer: Freud, Fromm, and the Frankfurt School. The continuity lies in the analysis at least as much as in the phenomena, but it gave the debate in the 1970s around the gesture of the commemorative, as opposed to the radical break in German culture, a particular political poignancy and even at this level illustrates the problem it was trying to probe in the first place.

Thus, film scholars, in order to understand the "representation of history in cinema" as a theoretical issue, must also be able to grasp the problem as one of "the history of cinematic representation" and, more specifically, address how the pervasiveness of visual representation has not only altered our perception of the past but concepts such as the private and the public, truth and evidence. If *Trauerarbeit* at a precise historical and ideological conjuncture served a very important function in raising the issue of the kinds of affectivity attached to events from the past, we also need to find different paradigms, in order to see the production and reproduction of this affectivity historically. For this we might also go back to Weimar film and cultural theory. When Kracauer argued that films reflected the deeper dispositions of the German psyche, he was obliged to claim that the films he singled out for analysis fostered attitudes that aided and abetted the rise of Hitler. The films thus played the role of determining agents. This has always been held against *From Caligari to Hitler:* how could something be both cause and effect, and equally puzzling, how could a writer like Kracauer proceed by such equivocal reasoning?

Kracauer, in fact, had recognized a problem that is still with us, even though he perhaps foreshortened its inherent dialectic, namely the historical agency not so much of the films but of the cinema, of which the films are both representations and products. Kracauer, in his essays from the 1920s,[20] was one of the first to articulate that as a mass medium and a creation of capitalism, the cinema is indeed a historically ambiguous phenomenon in that it is both effect and cause, effect without cause.[21] With Lukács one could even say that it is an ensemble of reality effects that annihilates causality and by that fact threatens the concepts at the heart of Western notions of reality and history.[22]

The Cinema as Historical Agent

To put it perhaps too hastily: The idea of cinema as expression and reflection, so prevalent in the cinema/history, cinema/society debate (and still often implicitly present in our discussions about the representation of historical referents in the cinema, such as class, gender, race, specific events, or social forces) seems to posit history as something that always happens elsewhere: in the domain of politics, of economics, of the struggles for national identity or cultural recognition. Cinema is either a transparent medium or an autonomous discourse on a par with other texts and discourses, other narratives of these events and forces, but rarely an event or force in itself.

On the other side, there is film history, or possibly the history of the cinema. Both are a reification and an abstraction, isolating by prising apart what only makes (historical) sense within a larger set of structures and phenomena. For cinema, as we know, is material and immaterial, an apparatus or *dispositif*, a power potential, and at the same time a mode of representation, a series of textual systems dedicated to the production of cognitive reality-effects and psychic subject-effects. Its function as part of public life and private culture in the twentieth century has therefore been as much an interventionist one as it has been one of representing phenomena discursively constituted elsewhere. Any theorization of the relations between cinema and history must begin by taking account of this, possibly along the lines of Lukács or Kracauer's thinking, who saw cinema as at one and the same time an aesthetic and a technological intervention into our notions of causality, agency, and change—what I have tried to identify as cinema's "irresponsibility towards the referent."[23] However, one might phrase the phenomenon more positively. We now recognize that television has created a historically distinct public sphere, which can no longer be opposed to a private sphere—a fact implicitly acknowledged in the dilemma on which Reitz and others in the debate about *Trauerarbeit*, spectacle, and retrofashion seem to be impaled: the dilemma that has made "history an old movie."

The Private and the Public Sphere

Thus, the New German Cinema, in a set of related moves, predominantly rearticulated the past as family melodrama, psychic trauma, and repetition compulsion, which can usefully be opposed to the retrofashion of Eurofascism and its sexualized, spectacularized, and demonized restaging of history. But in contrast to the idea of film/history as resistance,[24] most West German filmmakers consciously or not, renewed contact with the critical reception of Weimar cinema by attempting to forge a new (postwar) national identity out of the very traumatization and pathology of the public sphere for which the Nazi cinema and its demonstration of the power of the image had become notorious. Ambivalence in the representation of nazism derives not least from the fact that German fascism has left a more complete account, in sight and sound, in visual records and staged celebrations, of itself and its version of history than any previous regime or period.[25]

One could say that by "returning home to history" filmmakers had oedipalized German history to make it accessible to powerful intellectual scrutiny. But they had also sought to reclaim it by reinventing, as it were, a private sphere as (idealized) vantage point, whereas this private sphere (German *Innerlichkeit*) is itself at best a historical vantage point. The New German Cinema's oedipal version of the past was in the end a compromise that allowed for a credible figuration of continuity in discontinuity at two levels: at the level of film culture (rewriting German history as film history) and at the personal level (the dominance of primary bonds in the family—the same as different across the generations). It also—via the concern with identification—began to recognize the power of images in the relations between self and history, without however always fully confronting the taboo area of spectacle. The anecdotal and thematic, as opposed to structural or critical function that photography, newsreel, the cinema, and radio play in *Heimat* seems symptomatic in this respect.

For what is rare in the New German Cinema is the notion of the cinema playing the role of historical agent: through its technology, through its industrial and financial organization, through its inheritance of nineteenth-century narrative forms and thus the private realm of fantasy and desire, the colonization of memory. The perception of cinema's agency in the public sphere, through its mobilization of mass audiences and the social spaces created by movie palaces and entertainment architecture is also rare. These powerful presences of the cinema are acknowledged negatively in the phobia, the *Berührungsangst*, with regard not only to spectacle but to other social formations and figurations of power. In other words, the New German Cinema seems to have taken up only one side of the argument, conjuring up the memory of the Nazi regime's own self-dramatization, its narcissism of power and domination, and warning of the danger of film reproducing this fascination, without being able to displace it critically (the charge laid against Fest's *Hitler* film by, among others, Wim Wenders). Reducing identification, specular seduction, and other subject effects of cinema to memory and mourning work risks dehistoricizing them.

Cinema, Spectacle, and Warfare: The Other Paradigm

The media analyses of Weimar intellectuals (not all of them from the Left) are still instructive in several respects. First, in their remarks we find cinema, photography, and radio treated as interconnected and interdependent phenomena, bringing about profound changes in politics and aesthetics. Second, the media were inscribed in the crucial philosophical questions of German modernism.

In Ernst Jünger's metaphysical triangulation of modernity,[26] for instance, cinema, while intimately belonging to a cultural and existential complex he calls "pain,"[27] definitely does not belong on the side of memory but on the side of technology and the logos of domination. Acutely aware of the subject-effects produced by the new mass media and their power to summon, rally, gather, in short to mobilize (rather than motivate) the human subject struck Jünger as early as 1933 as the crucial feature. For him both radio and the cinema were integral parts of modern warfare, which he saw primarily as a revolution of the productive relations and the public sphere: war as the organized production of industrial waste and war as the mobilization of the civilian population for collective tasks. Because of the speed and instantaneity of communication they made possible, because of the density and complexity of organized information they provided, and above all because their presence and ubiquity addressed the masses as subjects, cinema and radio were indispensible logistical supports of any kind of modern societal power. Needless to say, the characteristics described by Jünger are wholly inimical to memory, mourning work, and anamnesis but all the more predictive of the historical uses the mass madia were to be put to.

Jünger may at first sight seem an odd source for an alternative paradigm for cinematic representations of history, and this is not the place fully to explore the Nietzschean tradition in thinking about the mass media.[28] But he can serve as a kind of introduction to those aspects of the New German Cinema that seem to me to have developed and rewritten Weimar film and cinema theory. Three directors come to mind: Syberberg, Kluge, Fassbinder. In some crucial respects, they have refused to re-oedipalize the cinema and history as their key to an understanding of Germany's recent past. Instead, they took up the challenge implicit in the cinema as itself a historical force, often by drawing on the complex of warfare, mobilization, and instant communication that so impressed Kracauer, Benjamin, and Jünger. These three directors, also spanning a wide ideological spectrum, have produced work amenable to a reading that poses the relationship of the cinema to history in terms not that dissimilar to Jünger's: Syberberg's *Our Hitler*, Kluge's *The Patriot*, and Fassbinder's *Lili Marleen*.

While these films' representations of the German past have often been discussed (among others, by me) within the dominant paradigms of mourning work, oedipalization, and subjective trauma, they also cohere around another paradigm, in which the cinema, spectacle, and radio do indeed figure as historical agencies. For instance, Reitz in *Heimat*, Syberberg in *Our Hitler*, and Fassbinder in *Lili Marleen* all allude to radio. Yet only in the last two do the narratives fundamentally depend on the transgressive function of radio, showing how, as a public and indeed global medium, it not only pervades and invades the private sphere but refashions the characters' subjectivity and the balance of power. In *Heimat*, when radio or newsreel traverse the lives of individual characters and make them participants (as in the case of the front broadcast of Anton's wedding) or invade their lives (as when the women go to the movies and do their hair like Zarah Leander) the media merely amplify a moment of personal glory or private consumption, not that different from "real people" today appearing on television game shows or beauty contests. Kluge's *The Patriot*—taking up a line of argument already present in his *Artisten in der Zirkuskuppel: ratlos (Artists at the Top of the Big Top: Disoriented*, 1968) and in most of his written fiction—explicitly poses the question of warfare, of images, and of memory—their startling similarities, incompatibilities, and antagonisms. Since I have discussed two of the films mentioned at length elsewhere,[29] I shall briefly summarize my argument here, to indicate the place of Kluge's film,[30] before concluding with some general remarks on how television might be seen to have imposed on us this new way of thinking about cinema and history.

Kluge

Because all of Kluge's films analyze processes of production, it is not surprising that history and cinema are also considered in this light. *The Patriot* can only be understood if its ostensible subject (German history teaching, a party-political congress) is understood as a parable of the way televisual discourse and media reality incessantly represent forms of socially approved productivity while inhibiting, destroying, or even criminalizing the more natural forms of productivity human beings invest in their lives. Such is the irony and dialectic of Kluge's world, however, that this natural productivity occurs, on a collective scale and in a socially useful form, only during wartime. This is why Kluge's other major subject is war.[31]

It would seem that the traumatic experience in recent German history is not nazism or the Holocaust but the final years of the war, the time of scattered armies, of migrating populations, of refugees, and of devastated cities. Emblematically, the complex in Kluge's work has the name Stalingrad, the midwinter battle that brought decisive defeat for the Reich's army and signalled the turning point in the war. Two major aspects of Kluge's view of the past come together in Stalingrad: the nonlinear, antagonistic nature of the historic process (as symbolized by war) and the utopian moment of radical change (the possibility of a zero hour and a new beginning resulting from the total breakdown of a social system). This second element refers again to New German Cinema's fascination with the "Earthquake in Chile" complex and the idea that only a cataclysmic event can break up social relations that have become frozen. Thus, Stalingrad is the retrospectively projected origin of the present, not only in that the Second World War becomes a rehearsal for the Third but in the way the historical energies of the twentieth century (fascism versus communism, the German working class vs. the Russian peasants, mass destruction of machines and people for the benefit of production) became frozen at Stalingrad, preserved like a mammoth in ice. In *The Patriot* the knee joint of a dead soldier—the part standing for the whole but at the same time a relation rather than an essence— literally voices this unreclaimed energy.

The nonlinear, antagonistic view of history is most clearly expressed in Kluge's distinction between a strategy from above (fascist, bureaucratic, globalizing) and a strategy from below (that of stubborn persistance, distrustful of strategy, disorganized, random but nearer to the ground). It, too, has its emblem derived from war: the blanket bombing of German cities, and more specifically, the bombing raids on Halberstadt, Kluge's native town. In the strategy from above, the U.S. Air Force and RAF bombers get confused with Hollywood movies in Berlin or Munich cinemas crowding out German independent films via block and blind-booking agreements. The strategy from below encompasses not only the emotional productivity of women, the ingenuity of ordinary people in conducting their lives, the dogged persistence of men and women planning one thing and achieving something else, but also the nation's nursery rhymes, fairy tales, and other scraps of popular wisdom—usually conservative and apolitical, irrational and fantastic, but preserving a kind of leverage in the play of uneven forces. These represent to Kluge what he calls the "friction-energy" of history, in contrast to illusionist spectacle, which to him is always the sign of a strategy from above. Events such as those chronicled in *Germany in Autumn* or the Bitburg episode in 1985 are fascinating to Kluge precisely because an official strategy from above is subverted and made incongruous by unexpected manifestations of a strategy from below.

What is interesting in the distinction between a logistical (molar) dimension and a molecular dimension (the energy of personal initiative, pluck, and unplanned productivity) is that Kluge here essentially transposes into the ideal of nonrepressive, utopian society the ideology of a class (the petit bourgeoisie), at a certain point in its history, when the ability to manage scarce resources, the tactics of survival in a war economy, and enterprise during the initial postwar reconstruction period were at a premium. Kluge's strategy from below belongs to the smallholder, the craftsman, and the artisan. However much he may make fun of them, it is from their values that his work draws its moral coherence. Apart from idealizing the dilemma of the New German film-maker facing the corporations and the multinationals in the marketplace, this risks misconstruing the historical relationship between cinema and war. For although Stalingrad and Halberstadt, the frozen armies and, air raid shelters in Kluge's films and books transcend their anecdotal or biographical origin (which is how similar events figure in Reitz), they nonetheless remain mere metaphors, picturesque or grotesque, humorous or touching.[32]

This has to do with the fact that Kluge overestimates and over-theorizes production. He does not seem to acknowledge that in the relation between the mass media and warfare—and thus in the significance of any historical parallel between them—the common element is consumption. Prior to the age of consumer society, war was the only way of managing the overproduction attendant on production for profit. In the struggle for new markets war has in common with cinema (or for that matter any service industry) the logistics of supply, manpower, transport, and distribution. In the fight with overproduction, the rapid obsolescence of weapon systems during peacetime and their rapid material destruction during war have their parallel in cinema's (or in the media of mass entertainment's) creation and rapid exploitation of blockbusters. Kluge has clearly recognized the productivity of war both for technology and for any strategy from above and for ordinary people and their strategy from below. Yet there is less evidence that he has developed an equally acute notion of the implied other of all production, namely the logistics of destruction or consumption.

Syberberg

Syberberg's *Our Hitler* is an unusual film in many respects but not least for attempting to offer a perspective on the cinema in the context of precisely this issue. Here too, the argument seems to be built on a relatively straightforward antithesis in which the film industry, fascism, and Hollywood are aligned on one side, from the vantage point of an art cinema that engages in a heroic struggle with the commercial cinema over the right to inherit nineteenth-century popular culture, with its romantic myths, its kitsch objects, its sentimentality, and peasant piety, but also its wit, sarcasm, and peasant slyness. But even if one recognizes the director's special pleading from the embattled position of the struggle with Hollywood over New German Cinema's own domestic audiences, the case for seeing Hitler as a failed Cecil B. DeMille, mistaking Europe for a movie set is not simply made polemically.

Just as Albert Speer conceived his buildings in view of their "ruin-value," and Hitler conducted World War II as the biggest film production ever undertaken, so—according to the film—Hollywood cinema's and TV's car chases, pileups, scenes of gratuitous destruction are indicative of a logic of production geared towards destruction, in order to organize consumption. Marketing, merchandizing, the campaigns for selling movies are to Syberberg the verso of war, itself the most spectacular production of industrial waste, production for waste as spectacle. The mass media in *Our Hitler* emerge as a power apparatus of specular seduction because they gave Nazi ideology its semblance of self-evidence. The appeal of *Lebensraum* and *Volksgemeinschaft* was finally not an appeal to history, tradition, or a promise of manifest destiny. Rather, its meaning was the experience of immediacy and presence itself, conjured up by nighttime radio broadcasts to the nation, creating the German Volk as the synthetic product of a media conglomerate that combined press, radio, and cinema. The logistic capacities of this new apparatus were such that, at the height of the war, live transmissions could join battlefronts with the homefront, in order for soldiers to intone "Silent Night" simultaneously in Murmansk and Tobruk, in Kiev and St. Malo. What satellite technology routinely achieves today, forty years ago still required the resources necessary for a world war. It is at this point that *Our Hitler* equates film production and cinema with the logic of militarization and warfare.

Fassbinder

If Syberberg explicitly refrains from restaging events, and in Kluge discursiveness always overwhelms the visual material, it was Fassbinder who with *Eine Reise ins Licht* (*Despair*, 1978) and *Lili Marleen*

(1980) broke the taboo against spectacle. But, as in his contribution to *Germany in Autumn*, Fassbinder was in fact in a countercurrent. It made his use of the dominant paradigms for representing history—strong female characters, biography, and oedipal crisis—highly ironic and an occasion for pastiche. At the same time, he was able to pursue more vigorously the connections between warfare and show business, femininity and the commodity, material and immaterial production, mass entertainment and mass destruction.[33]

It seems to me that *Lili Marleen* is the New German film that wanted to push furthest this deconstruction of cinema as a concentrated power potential, not unlike fascism, and fascism as the first self-consciously political organization of mass entertainment. By splicing together into one narrative a world war, an entertainment industry, a female star performer, and an oedipal melodrama, Fassbinder confronts directly the transformation of the power potential inherent in the film industry and cinema as a social practice and public sphere into textual effects of cinematic fascination. The film works out how "hard" military, organizational, economic, and political power gets commuted into spectacle power by way of three related topoi: that of mobilization, of productivity, and of consumption, figured as the effacement of the boundary between the material and the immaterial, of cause and effect.

In *Lili Marleen*, Fassbinder concentrates on something as ephemeral and banal as a popular song, albeit one that, like the cinema, commands its own imaginary and mythological space within history. This space can neither be metonymically collapsed with history (in the sense that one might be tempted to say that the song "Lili Marleen" stands for the use of the mass media under fascism) nor metaphorically separated from it (by treating the song as a symbolic representation of the cinema, for instance). What is at issue is precisely the complex status of the song as object—irreducible and recalcitrant to the uses it served—and at the the same time, product, expression, and signifier of a historical period. The narrative is charged with tying down, anchoring, and articulating these relations and effects in both their metaphorical and metonymic implications.

It is almost entirely from this perspective—which is obviously also the perspective of Fassbinder's construction of himself as a filmmaker, as a performer in the cultural contexts of sign and commodity production—that fascism becomes specific as well as historical in *Lili Marleen*. Although the well-known iconography of historical spectaculars invades the film, nazism maintains its metonymic ties with the war, or rather, with several kinds of warfare (the military fronts, the propaganda and media war, and the "secret war" between the Nazis and the Jewish resistance organization) mainly because of the rigorous and businesslike administration they both share. Fassbinder presents war from the point of view of production. It is seen as an acceleration and a unifying force that by speeding up the productive and reproductive cycles of the economy, intensifies consumption.

Consequently, the fascist war economy and its show-business operations appear as a kind of immense and universalized black market where those who have cornered the market—in this case the Nazi re-gime—impose their own rate of exchange, liable to the sudden and surreal reversals the film chronicles. Seen as eliminating surplus by simple destruction, while at the same time developing radio, and organiz-ing through it an elaborate system of transportation and communication, nazism becomes a particularly flamboyant figuration of capitalism in the sphere of representation—not merely because of its gigantic aspirations or the brutality of its public life but more because of its power to reorga-nize a society's ethical, material, and erotic relations in the direction of spectacle or rituals of communal consumption of sounds and images.

The identification in *Lili Marleen* of mass coercion (the Nazi regime and the army) with mass consumption (show business and the electronic "global village" of radio and television) is interesting in another respect. For one of the questions nazism raises for Fassbinder (as it did for Syberberg) apart from its relation to material production and capitalism and the monstrous scale and consequences of its demographic planning, was its ability to create a public sphere, a mass audience. The song of "Lili Marleen," endlessly repeated as a nightly ritual above and between the sights and sounds of war, is such a fascinating phenome-non—partly because of the discrepancy between the pure presence of the song, hermetically sealed by its technological immediacy from any contact and context, and the ceaselessly destructive and intensely busy machinery of war it serves. Media technology, in this case, binds together a whole array of social and communicative activities (performance, re-cording, broadcasting, listening, telephoning, and letter-writing) around something that, while still in need of some sort of material support (a phonograph record, a receiver, a broadcasting station), nonetheless has no determinants itself other than a kind of mirror surface for the projec-tion or reflection of desire.

Toward Television

The films of Fassbinder and Syberberg have an advantage in that they foreground those aspects of nazism that make of it a specific subject of filmmaking in Germany. The establishment of connections between fascism and show business, with a view to a historical and critical placement of their own practice, appears to be the implicit common perspective of *Our Hitler* and *Lili Marleen*. Both directors have, on the immoderate scale characteristic of the New German Cinema, found in the regime's use of radio as technology and as machine of social control a way of locating the present situation of the commercial film industry and state-sponsored German culture; and they have found in it a metaphor for the medium that would in time displace radio as well as the cinema, namely television. They agree that the cinema can deal with history only when and where history itself has acquired an imaginary dimension, where the disjunction between sign and referent is so radical that history turns on a problem of representation, and fascism emerges as a question of subjectivity within image and discourse (of power, of desire, of fetish objects and commodities) rather than one of causality and determinants for a period, a subject, a nation.

The inner logic of New German Cinema and central strategy during the 1970s and early 1980s was to set against the politics of spectacle as practiced by Hollywood the notion of personal experience as politically and cinematically authentic. With regard to the representation of history, this search for "authenticity" combined with an attempt to understand the relation between continuity and discontinuity in German history as a relation between the self and its other(s). It is to these two complexes that we owe some of the most impressive examples of cinematic *Trauer-*

arbeit. The more thoroughly, however, spectacle came to pervade not only television, but more crucially, personal experience and private fantasy itself, the more the paradigm of *Trauerarbeit* began to look esoteric, purely introspective, or merely morbid. Taking the total media environment as a political and cultural inevitability, Kluge, for instance, now talks of the "industrialization of consciousness,"[34] by which he means that the new media are only the vanguard of a more sinister move to turn public opinion itself into "corporate property." This may seem overly pessimistic, but there can be little doubt that in the current reorganization of delivery systems and their ownership in the film, television, newspaper, and publishing industries more is at stake than the profits to be made out of entertainment and culture. An industrialization of consumption is under way, of which television and the mass media are linchpins, allowing goods and services to circulate, from mailorder shopping to banking, from education to medicine. If the cinema and film culture become merely the muzak of the system, destined to enhance a consumer-friendly environment at the point of sale, then Fassbinder's *Lili Marleen* will appear no longer the Nazi soap opera faking history that some critics saw it as, but a film essay and a commentary on cinema, history, and spectacle that the names of Kracauer, Benjamin, but also Ernst Jünger tried to evoke in all its historical and finally typically German ambiguity.

What underlies their thought (and Fassbinder's film), is precisely the knowledge that the cinema as entertainment has played a crucial role in the wars of the twentieth century as well as in the development of military technology, and this in two ways. First, as in other branches of applied science and engineering, film technology became a testing ground and field laboratory for mobile camerawork and lighting techniques, for fast film stock and magnetic recording tape, for portable equipment and zoom lenses, for spying and surveillance work. More recently, the same is true of special effects and computer animation. The second major interface between cinema and warfare has to do with mobilization, where media reality acts as a kind of totalitarian invocation of presence. What the war was in terms of mobilizing the civilian population, the media reality of show business and news is in terms of mobilizing collectivities, as in monster events, media events, Olympic Games, or television series. Perhaps what television reformers ought to campaign about is not the wars on our screens, but the warlike mobilization of which the screens are capable.

The move of some independent filmmakers to undertake projects whose scale can generate television events to rival the nightly ones of the networks is symptomatic in this respect. It can be seen as an attempt to use film and cinema as release mechanisms for a discursive activity that crosses the boundaries of entertainment and even of the arts. This would be the contemporary and perhaps countercultural aspect of what I have called "mobilization," underlining television's powerful potential for creating something like an instant public sphere. In contrast to the packaging of experience as we find it in the movie megahit—which spawns everything from a novelization, or sound track album to a new line in fashion, toys, or tee-shirts—these television events exploit the various aggregate states not of the commodity cinema but of the discourse history/memory, as the interest and emotions aroused by programs like *Our Hitler, Heimat,* or *Shoah* cascade through television schedules, the press, and academic conferences or journals. By thinking of the cinema as spectacle in two senses (a *dispositif* of political power, mass mobilization, and the effacement of agency and a *dispositif* of subject effects, meaning effects and the metaphysics of presence), we might begin to understand the history of cinema as the cinema in history. Instead of history being just an old movie, the old movie needs once more to be seen for what it is. Its very inauthenticity might be its truth as history.

Notes

1. Quoted in Jan Dawson, *Wim Wenders* (New York: Zoetrope, 1976) 7.
2. See, for instance, "Michel Foucault: Interview," *Edinburgh Magazine* 2 (1977): 20–25; Jean Baudrillard, "Geschichte: ein Retro-Szenario," *Kool Killer, oder der Aufstand der Zeichen* (Berlin: Merve, 1981) 49–57; Fredric Jameson, "Nostalgia for the Present," *The South Atlantic Quarterly* 88 (1989): 518–37.
3. See, for instance, Dan Diner, ed., *Ist der Nationalsozialismus Geschichte?* (Frankfurt a.M.: Fischer, 1987).
4. See Miriam Hansen, "Dossier on *Heimat,*" *New German Critique* 36 (Fall 1985): 3–24.

5. See Thomas Elsaesser, *New German Cinema: A History* (New Brunswick: Rutgers UP, 1989) 87–92.
6. Giuliana Bruno, "Towards a Theorization of Film History," *Iris* 2.2 (1984): 53–54.
7. "That's Entertainment: Hitler," *Die Zeit* 5 August 1977.
8. See, for instance, Syberberg's interventions at the Aschaffenburg Streitgespräch in Karl-Heinz Janßen, "Wir—zwischen Jesus und Hitler," *Die Zeit* 14 July 1978.
9. Edgar Reitz, "Statt *Holocaust:* Erinnerungen aufarbeiten," *medium* May 1979: 21.
10. See the many book titles in Germany on this topic: e.g., Peter Hamm, *Die verschwindende Welt* (Munich: Hanser, 1985); Hartmut von Hentig, *Das allmähliche Verschwinden der Wirklichkeit* (Munich: Hanser, 1984); Hans Magnus Enzensberger, *Die Furie des Verschwindens* (Frankfurt a.M.: Suhrkamp, 1980).
11. Edgar Reitz, "Statt *Holocaust:* Erinnerungen aufarbeiten," *medium* May 1979: 24 (my translation). In the following, unless otherwise indicated, all translations are my own.
12. For a lengthier discussion of *Trauerarbeit*, see my *New German Cinema: A History* 255–58.
13. See especially the reactions to Andreas Hillgruber, *Zweierlei Untergang* (Cologne: Siedler, 1986) collected in *Streit ums Geschichtsbild,* ed. Reinhard Kühnl (Cologne: Pahl-Rugenstein, 1987).
14. Alexander and Margarete Mitscherlich, *The Inability to Mourn: Principles of Collective Behaviour,* trans. Beverley A. Placzek (New York: Grove Press, 1975).
15. See, for instance, Fredric Jameson, "Imaginary and Symbolic in Lacan," *Yale French Studies* 55/56 (1977): 338–95, here especially 380.
16. See Andreas Huyssen's essay on postwar drama, "The Politics of Identification," *New German Critique* 19 (Winter 1980): 117–36 and my discussion of identification in *New German Cinema: A History* 207–38.
17. See R. W. Fassbinder, "Seven Films by Douglas Sirk," *Douglas Sirk,* ed. Jon Halliday and Laura Mulvey (Edinburgh: Edinburgh Film Festival, 1971).
18. Quoted in Andreas Meyer, "Auf dem Weg zum Staatsfilm?" *medium* November 1977: 15.
19. Karsten Witte, "Wunschkonzert für Deutschlehrer: Syberbergs *Die Nacht,*" *Frankfurter Rundschau* 17 May 1985; Michael Rutschky, "Realität träumen," *Merkur* 363 (1978): 775.
20. Some of the most important are collected in *Das Ornament der Masse* (Frankfurt a.M.: Suhrkamp, 1962). For an English translation of the title essay, see "The Mass Ornament," trans. Barbara Correll and Jack Zipes, *New German Critique* 5 (Winter 1975): 67–76. Thomas Levin is preparing a translation of the entire collection (Cambridge: Harvard UP, forthcoming).
21. See my "Cinema, The Irresponsible Signifier," *New German Critique* 40 (Winter 1987): 65–90.
22. See Georg Lukács, "Gedanken zu einer Ästhetik des Kinos" (1913), *Kino-Debatte,* ed. Anton Kaes (Tübingen: Niemeyer, 1978) 114.
23. "Cinema, The Irresponsible Signifier" 88.
24. See my *New German Cinema: A History* 256–59.

25. See, for instance, Dieter Bartetzko, *Zwischen Zucht und Ekstase* (Berlin: Mann, 1985).

26. Jünger is typical of Weimar intellectuals directly under the sway of post-Nietzschean questions: Greek versus Judeo-Christian, techné versus memory/history, the individual versus the masses. The issue for Jünger was, among others, where the technological media (including the cinema) might belong in this metaphysical triangulation of modernity.

27. Ernst Jünger, "Über den Schmerz," *Blätter und Steine* (Hamburg: Hanseatische Verlagsanstalt, 1934). See also my "Fritz Lang and German Modernism," unpublished paper given at Yale University, February 1986.

28. Jean François Lyotard's contributions to the Heidegger debate could be a fruitful starting point.

29. See my "Myth and the Phantasmagoria of History" in *New German Critique* 24/25 (Fall/Winter 1981/1982): 108–54; and "'Lili Marleen,' Fascism and the Film Industry," *October* 21 (1982): 115–40.

30. *The Patriot* seems in this respect different from *Germany in Autumn*, where the framing story, as indicated, reinforces the oedipal paradigm. On the whole, Kluge seems to distrust Freudian psychoanalysis, tending more towards his own form of materialist cognitivism when analyzing the affectivity of cinema.

31. See, among others, his *Schlachtbeschreibung* (Frankfurt a.M.: Suhrkamp, 1968) and *Lernprozesse mit tödlichem Ausgang* (Frankfurt a.M.: Suhrkamp, 1973).

32. See, in this context, Thomas Pynchon, *Gravity's Rainbow* (New York: Bantam, 1974). Pynchon also sharply opposes the molar and the molecular, but for him, at the molecular level, all is disintegration, disarticulation, entropy. In Pynchon the link between the levels is copulation and sexual fantasy, whereas for Kluge it is productivity.

33. For a more detailed analysis, see my "'Lili Marleen,' Fascism and the Film Industry."

34. See Alexander Kluge, "Die Macht der Bewußtseinsindustrie und das Schicksal unserer Öffentlichkeit. Zum Unterschied von machbar und gewalttätig," *Die Industrialisierung des Bewußtseins*, ed. Klaus von Bismarck et al. (Munich: Piper, 1985) 51–129.

11

History and Film: Public Memory in the Age of Electronic Dissemination

Anton Kaes

A tormenting thought: as of a certain point, history was no longer *real*.
—Elias Canetti, *The Human Province* (1978)

In the middle of it all is Hitler, of course.
He was on again last night.
He's always on. We couldn't have television without him.
—Don DeLillo, *White Noise* (1984)

I

In February 1983, when its eighteen-hour miniseries *The Winds of War* came in within several points of the previous block-buster, *Roots*, an ABC newspaper advertisement boasted that "more people relived the war [on television] than fought in it."[1] One hundred forty million Americans "relived" World War II as it was restaged for television at a cost of $40 million (an additional $25 million was spent promoting the miniseries). "Before it is over," said ABC, "it will have reached virtually every American of twelve years of age and older." To capture viewers not familiar with the events of World War II, half a million copies of a twenty-four-page color magazine (with pictures from the series) were mailed to schools, libraries, and special-interest groups, introducing them to the period and, more importantly, to the upcoming television spectacle about this period. Identical images of this film version of World War II went out simultaneously to one hundred forty million people, many of whom obtained their first impression of German history and World War II from the television series. Although this adaptation of Herman Wouk's novel *The Winds of War* abounds with Hollywood clichés taken from adventure and epic war films and banks on the box-office appeal of recognizable film stars, it nevertheless maintains the illusion of providing images that claim to be a "true" depiction of German history under Hitler.

In a similar way, millions of Europeans have "experienced" the Vietnam War through the lens of Francis Ford Coppola's 1979 film *Apocalypse Now* or Michael Cimino's *The Deer Hunter* (1978). These historical films—I am using the term in analogy to the historical novel—do not show isolated pictures of accidental, contingent events but select, narrativize, and thereby give shape to the random material of history; they write history by "imposing meaning on what is meaningless," as Theodor Lessing once put it.[2] Various narrative patterns, often taken from literature or myth, structure the events and translate them into a story with a beginning, middle, and end. (*Apocalypse Now*, ostensibly a film about Vietnam, is based, for instance, on Joseph Conrad's 1899 novel *Heart of Darkness*.) Historical films interpret national history for the broad public and thus produce, organize, and, to a large degree, homogenize public memory. Surpassing schools and universities, film, and television have become the most effective (and paradoxically least acknowledged) institutional vehicles for shaping historical consciousness.[3] They are powerful because they can make history come alive more readily than commemorative addresses, lectures, exhibitions, or museums; they can resituate past events in the immediate experience of the viewer.

The Winds of War transmitted selected images of World War II to its millions of American viewers: images of heroic and likable American soldiers and their militaristic German counterparts, of intense battles, hard-won victories, and deserved defeats. Future representations of World War II will be based on, and compared to, the images from *The Winds of War*, just as this series used countless images from earlier representations of fascism and war. Thus images of images circulate in an eternal cycle, an endless loop, in a Möbius-strip of cliché images, validating and reconfirming each other, "swiftly spreading identical memories over the earth."[4]

Cinematic images have created a technological memory bank that is shared by everyone and offers little escape. It increasingly shapes and legitimizes our perception of the past. Memory in the age of electronic reproducibility and dissemination has become public; memory has become socialized by technology. History itself, so it seems, has been democratized by these easily accessible images, but the power over what is shared as popular memory has passed into the hands of those who produce these images. No wonder a struggle has erupted over the production, administration, and control of public memory.

President Reagan's highly symbolic visit to the military cemetery of Bitburg in May 1985, for example, was carefully staged as a public spectacle for television; setting, framing, camera, acting, and sound were planned in detail. The elaborate production triggered a major controversy, resulting in an embarrassment for all involved because the intentions behind this attempt to reshape public memory via television were a shade too obvious.[5] More recently, the equally acrimonious debates about government plans for museums of German history in Bonn and Berlin again centered around the self-representation, and thereby self-fashioning, of a nation's public memory. Since the late 1970s, numerous exhibitions, academic conferences, television documentaries, and countless books and articles have obsessively addressed the central problem of contemporary West Germany: what to do with the recent past that, no matter what, will not go away. No other country has more politicians, journalists, historians, writers, and artists preoccupied with the history and identity of their difficult fatherland.

Filmmakers play a special role in this mission. Their films—most of which have been shown, even repeatedly, on television—not only reach a much larger audience than, say, speeches, conference papers, or books; they also tend to move and manipulate spectators in a more direct emotional way. Moreover, films—as complex fictional constructs—offer ambivalent perspectives and contradictory attitudes that resist simple explanations and call for multiple readings. Films dealing with history represent a dynamic and complex balance between two referents: one appealing to the historical knowledge or memory of the viewer and to a certain extent verifiable, the other taking liberties with historical facts for the sake of inventive storytelling. Historical films thus toy with temporal ambivalences, associations, and identifications and have a tendency to expunge historical distance. Precisely because they present the past as pure presence (there is no past tense in film), historical films seem effective in engaging the viewer more than, for example, the historical novel. Moreover, historical films are as much about the present as about the past and often intervene in ongoing debates. For example, Hans Jürgen Syberberg's 1977 film about Hitler or Edgar Reitz's sixteen-hour film chronicle of 1984, *Heimat*, provoked debates that went far beyond the films that initiated them. The same holds true for the West German reception of the American television series *Holocaust* in 1979, which broke through thirty years of silence and left an indelible mark on German discussions of the Holocaust. A brief look at the response of the Federal Republic to this filmic representation of the most horrifying phenomenon of the German past may illustrate the intricate interplay between historical event and its fictional simulation, between authentic memory and its public appropriation.

II

Holocaust was the first major commercial film to deal with the persecution and systematic slaughter of millions of European Jews in a fictional form. As such, it was destined to evoke an especially strong response in the Federal Republic. The German discussion began in mid-April 1978, when NBC broadcast the four-part, eight-hour-long television series to an audience of approximately one hundred-twenty million viewers.[6] Initial reports from America castigated the commercial motives of the film, its consistently kitschy style, and the tasteless blend of concentration camp scenes and car commercials. When the series began on 16 April 1978, Elie Wiesel, himself a survivor of Auschwitz, described his revulsion at the series in a *New York Times* article called "The Trivialization of the Holocaust: Semi-Fact and Semi-Fiction":

> Untrue, offensive, cheap: as a TV production, the film is an insult to those who perished and to those who survived. In spite of its name,

this "docu-drama" is not about what some of us remember as the Holocaust. . . . Contrived situations, sentimental episodes, implausible coincidences: If they make you cry, you will cry for the wrong reasons. . . . *Holocaust,* a TV drama. *Holocaust,* a work of semi-fact and semi-fiction. Isn't this what so many morally deranged "scholars" have been claiming recently all over the world? That the Holocaust was nothing else but an "invention"?[7]

And Wiesel continues with the following statement: "I am appalled by the thought that one day the Holocaust will be measured and judged in part by the NBC TV production bearing its name. The Holocaust must be remembered. But not as a show." Wiesel expresses a fear that in the eyes of future generations—after all the survivors have died—the historical event of the Holocaust will be overshadowed and eventually obliterated and substituted by its filmic representation, by a simulation.

Presented as a made-for-television film, the historical Holocaust participates in television's medium-specific blurring of the lines between imagined and factual history, between invented and real spaces, between the documentary mode (operative, for instance, in news and entertainment shows) on one hand, and the fictional mode of TV films on the other. "Is fact watched as fiction? And fiction fact?" This question, posed by Gerald Green, author of the *Holocaust* screenplay, remains unanswered.[8]

In the case of *Holocaust,* an answer is not necessary, since it exploits this very indeterminacy. The realistic style, the carefully reconstructed historical *mise en scène,* and the occasional intercutting of documentary photographs and authentic film footage from the concentration camps imparts to the film a strong reality effect. This effect gains intensity in its appeal to the visual memory of the spectator. The pictures of concentration camps are well-known ones; no one would fail to recognize them. Seeing these images again as part of a television series produces a déjà vu effect that implicitly validates the historical correctness of the film.

Holocaust is a *mixtum compositum* both in its dramatic structure and visual style, offering something for everyone, much like a consumer commodity. The series contains such motifs as domestic happiness and its dissolution, love, war, humiliation, incarceration, survival, rebellion, and ultimate liberation—all universally valid narrative set-pieces whose combination guarantees the broadest possible public appeal. Not surprisingly, in the year of its first broadcast, *Holocaust* was sold to fifty countries—including the Federal Republic of Germany, where it was watched by twenty million West Germans (i.e., by every other adult) in the last week of January 1979.

The Holocaust that had been repressed for over thirty years, now came back in the form of *Holocaust,* a semi-documentary, semi-fictional film chronicle made in the United States. Germany, it seemed, had to import the images of its own past from Hollywood. German history—made in Hollywood: that was the real scandal someone like Edgar Reitz tried to counter with his film *Heimat,* which was originally polemically entitled "Made in Germany."[9]

The *Holocaust* film opened the floodgates. It was as if for the first time an entire nation dared to remember and to look at its own past. Yet the collective mourning in the Federal Republic itself became a public spectacle, played out, consciously or unconsciously, before the eyes of the world. There Germans knew the world would be waiting with bated breath for their reception of this film. Heinz Werner Hübner, director of WDR, admitted candidly, "The film is a political event, and if it is shown in the land of those who were affected by the Holocaust, in Israel, then we should expect the people in Germany who participated in those events and their successors to view it as well."[10] From this perspective, the *Holocaust* series seemed to be a challenge to the Germans to recognize themselves in the mirror held up by Hollywood. One advantage of the "right" reaction would be the chance to show the rest of the world that the Germans had learned from history, that they had changed.

No matter how hysterical or hypocritical the responses were,[11] it seemed in 1979 as if the Germans had finally become able to look their history in the eye. *Holocaust* allowed them to confront their own past precisely because it was vicariously presented and experienced in the innocuous form of a television show that could be switched off at any time. It appears that the horrors of the Final Solution could only be watched in a reflection. Just as Perseus was instructed to look at Medusa's mirror reflection in Athena's polished shield—to face Medusa's horrible sight directly would have petrified him—the German audience was given a chance to see representations of the Holocaust horrors on the polished shield of the television screen. In his *Theory of Film*, Siegfried Kracauer expressly links the Medusa myth to the filmic depiction of the unrepresentable.

> The mirror reflections of horror are an end in themselves. As such they beckon the spectator to take them in and thus incorporate into his memory the real face of things too dreadful to be beheld in reality. In experiencing . . . the litter of tortured human bodies in the films made of the Nazi concentration camps, we redeem horror from its invisibility behind the veils of panic and imagination. And this experience is liberating in as much as it removes a most powerful taboo. Perhaps Perseus' greatest achievement was not to cut off Medusa's head but to overcome his fears and look at its reflection in the shield. And was it not precisely this feat which permitted him to behead the monster?[12]

The question arises whether Kracauer's belief in the cathartic effect of the depiction of history's horror is still valid in today's specularized society in which a profusion of images pours forth from dozens of television channels twenty-four hours a day, trivializing the most horrific events (both real and fictional) into cliché images.

III

The past cannot be recovered and re-experienced, since it is not out there to be visited and photographed like a foreign country; the past always has to be reconstructed, reconstituted, represented based on representations that already exist. This of course is the aporia of historical representation in film: how to break out of the circular recycling of images that are mere replicas of previous images. Only if the spectator recognizes a film's images as historical ones, as images one has previously seen and knows, only then does the film qualify as a historical film. This is particularly obvious in the depiction of the Third Reich, which was obsessed with documenting itself on film. Both Hitler and Goebbels were cineastes: Hitler is reported to have watched newsreels of the war as a film director would examine the daily rushes (Syberberg claims that

Hitler staged the war as his home movie). And it is a known fact that Goebbels was actively involved in editing the weekly newsreels.

Nazi-produced images, precisely because they are recorded on celluloid, will remain with us forever; tens of thousands of meters of documentary footage testify to the collective madness: images of cheering crowds, of Hitler triumphantly towering over the masses, images of bookburning and of harassment against Jews, as well as images by Allied cameras of concentration camps and emaciated Holocaust survivors. All these images, which have been replayed again and again, do not age nor can they be erased or forgotten; they are part of public history; they have assumed a function that historical monuments erected in public places had in previous centuries. Unlike heroic monuments, however, these filmic images are everywhere, impossible to topple and destroy. It is as if the Germans had their eyelids cut off: they are forever condemned to stare at the images of their past.

Images of Hitler and the Holocaust have indeed so indelibly engraved themselves in the public consciousness that new images are hard to imagine. Historical films, in fact, predetermine and, to a large extent, prescribe our perception of the past and thus increasingly replace not only historical experience but also historical imagination. "How can the imagination survive if our capacity for free association is overpowered and occupied by these images?" Peter W. Jansen asks in his essay "Das Kino in seinem zweiten Barock" ("The Cinema in Its Second Baroque") in which he compares historical film epics like Bertolucci's *1900* or Coppola's *Apocalypse Now* with the encyclopedic political novel of the seventeenth century.[13] He is justifiably concerned that these "political novels of the cinema" overwhelm and colonize the audience's historical imagination instead of stimulating and liberating it.

It is true; we do not need to have experienced the Hitler era ourselves to be familiar with it. Soon after the war, an iconography of the Nazi era began to evolve that is now routinely reproduced time and again. Such internationally acclaimed films as Luchino Visconti's *The Damned*, Louis Malle's *Lacombe, Lucien,* and François Truffaut's *The Last Metro* have used opulent imagery to present fascism as a spectacle—imagery that has been used again and again in subsequent films on the Third Reich. Nazism as a semiotic phenomenon: colorful red swastika flags, tight-fitting SS uniforms, shaven necks, black leather belts and boots, intimidating corridors, and wide marble stairways. These stereo-typical signs do nothing more than provide a dramatic backdrop, de-signed to lend more historical weight and urgency to private events that dominate the foreground. Fascism in these films is reduced, more often than not, to a colorful setting for love stories; it is trivialized and coopted by the entertainment industry as mere *mise en scène*. The Hitler period as a referent for countless historical films has by now been so often recycled that it has become automatized. It can no longer provoke reac-tions, trigger memories, or yield an experience.

As early as 1946, Max Picard, in his book *Hitler in uns selbst* (*Hitler in Our Selves*) recognized how mass media increasingly expropri-ated independent personal experience. He was also one of the first to reflect how new technical media (the radio in his case) shape our percep-tions of historical reality.

> The radio not only reports history, it seems to make it. The world seems to originate from the radio. People still see things and events, but they become real only after the radio has reported the event and the newspaper has run a picture of it. The radio apperceives, registers, and judges for people. Our souls are immediately connected to the radio and no longer to our sensory organs. People no longer have an inner history, an inner continuity, the radio today is our history; it validates our existence.[14]

Anticipating subsequent reflections on mass media and the grad-ual disappearance of historical experience by Günther Anders, Marshall McLuhan, and Jean Baudrillard by more than a decade, Picard's misgiv-ings about radio apply even more radically to film and television.[15] The proliferating images that surround and control us everywhere constitute a second, artificial world that interposes itself between us and the world of our senses. For Baudrillard in particular, today's postindustrial, post-modern, consumer society is governed by signs and codes which consti-tute a new type of social order in which the "real" is the effect of signs that function only by reference to the internal logic of that semiotic system. "Abstraction today," writes Baudrillard in his essay, "Simulacra and Simulations," "is no longer that of the map, the double, the mirror or the concept. Simulation is no longer that of territory, a referential being or a substance. It is the generation by models of a real without origin or reality: a hyperreal."[16] Thus along with the simulation of meaning, identity, value, and even materiality in the exchange economy of signs typical of our commodity culture, history, too, is simulated in film and on television. Television, which developed worldwide in accord with the emergence of postindustrialized economies, is the medium that most clearly represents this logic of the simulation of the real. If distinctions between object and representation are breaking down and the contrast between the imaginary and the real (as still is the case in fiction) is no longer discernible, then the real itself is absorbed in the simulation: history dissolves into a self-referential sign system cut loose from experience and memory.

"I remember," says the French experimental filmmaker Chris Marker in his film *Sans Soleil*, "I remember a January in Tokyo, or rather I remember the images I filmed in January in Tokyo. They have replaced my memories, they are my memories. I wonder how people remember who don't film, who don't photograph, who don't use tape recorders."[17] As a technological memory bank, film saves and stores data so completely that human memory seems to become superfluous. As technical media, film and photography act as gigantic recording and storage systems, accumulating images from the past in constantly growing archives. Film constitutes a collective memory that, however much it splinters into innumerable individually remembered images, forgets nothing. While it is common to condense, to expand, and above all, to forget when experiences are related and passed on in an oral tradition, experiences recorded by the technical media are stored once and for all. They become documents, archivized and catalogued, reproduced and disseminated, used and appropriated. Since the development of photography, Roland Barthes says, "the past is as certain as the present, what we see on paper is as certain as what we touch."[18]

History preserved or re-created in filmed images does not fade or yellow, but the sheer mass of historical images transmitted by today's media weaken the link between public memory and personal experience. The past is in danger of becoming a rapidly expanding collection of images, easily retrievable but isolated from time and space, available in an eternal present by pushing a button on the remote control. History thus returns forever—as film. As the generation who lived during the

Third Reich is dying out, the Hitler era will slowly pass from the realm of experience and personal memory into the realm of images. Innumerable Westerns have made the Wild West a movie myth. Likewise, innumerable films about the Third Reich may make the Hitler period itself one day nothing but a movie myth.

IV

Is it impossible, then, to break out of this succession of endlessly recycled déjà vu images and to overcome the belief that we are all helplessly deluded by one gigantic simulation called history? There may be alternative ways of representing history in film, not however in the mainstream cinema of Hollywood or in West German television culture but on the margins and in full recognition of the theoretical aporias of historical representation in the age of electronic dissemination. Three examples must suffice.

Shoah, Claude Lanzmann's nine and one-half-hour semi-documentary film of 1986, for instance, consciously responds to the proliferation and cheapening of images from the Nazi period by *not* recycling those images once again; rather, the film is based on the power of personal memory and the immediacy of oral history. The terror of the concentration camps is here evoked not through a narrative and well-known images but by a search for vestiges of the past in the present and by the memory traces of the survivors. Conversations with witnesses and the images of faces and landscapes gain resonance because the film presents the past as an aspect of present experience. *Shoah*'s images evoke not so much the illusion of objective history as the individual memory of it. It is a memory that often fails; when confronted with the site of the concentration camp where he was a prisoner, one survivor falls silent; he cannot articulate the incomprehensible and unspeakable. Lanzmann implicitly makes a film about the impossibility of representing a past that is unrepresentable. He knows that terror loses its edge when cast into a narrative mold.

Alexander Kluge's film *Die Patriotin (The Patriot,* 1979) also sees the recovery of history as reconstructive work involving memory, archaeology, and an active interest in the present. His film features a fictional character, a female history teacher, who is involved in exploring and researching German history. As an amateur archaeologist, she searches for traces and vestiges of two thousand years of German history but digs up so many contradictory things that she can no longer make sense of them. History becomes a mere jumble to her. The film itself constantly intercuts her story with a motley array of documents, artifacts, and fragments, using photographs, illustrations, silent film clips, comic strips, and "found film," as well as poems and aphorisms that add to the disjointedness of the visual style. Kluge undermines any historical master narrative by emphasizing the wild dispersion of images that have survived over the centuries. History appears as a heap of mostly marginal remnants from various histories: political, artistic, filmic, etc.—impossible to systematize and narrativize in a logical and coherent manner. Like the teacher, the viewer is overwhelmed by the mass of material that history yields to those who look. Kluge uses the marginal to break up monolithic history into innumerable small stories. Both *Shoah* and *The Patriot* try to counter and subvert the dominant production of images, in order to reclaim a small area within the public memory that is not occupied by conventional images of the past. They can do this by either withholding worn-out images as in Lanzmann's case, or, in the case of Kluge, by self-consciously presenting unknown and far-fetched images that seem like lost parts of different puzzles. Kluge's Brechtian approach emphasizes that representation in film is always a construct.

Syberberg's *Hitler—Ein Film aus Deutschland (Our Hitler,* 1977) offers yet another possibility of escaping naïve historical representation.[19] According to Syberberg, no authentic or realistic depiction of the past is possible, only simulation and recreation in symbolic terms. He therefore does not even attempt to reconstruct the past: his film has virtually no visual documentary footage, no interviews, no location shots, no story set in the past. The entire film takes place in a studio on a sound stage, using the artificiality of the setting and the theatricality of the presentation as devices to counter any verisimilitude with the conventional Nazi imagery. The Hitler film tries to transcend the realm of simulation by openly acknowledging its own status as a simulation, as a theatrical event that has its own aesthetic laws independent of any outside referent. Syberberg offers, for instance, a proliferation of images of Hitler ranging from the image of the house painter to Charlie Chaplin's *Great Dictator*. His film does not represent Hitler but presents representations of Hitler. Most of the visual stereotypes about Hitler and the Nazi period still used in regular Hollywood movies are quoted in Syberberg's film only to be deflated by irony and exaggerated pathos.

History itself is expressed in this film as a bazaar in which popular myths are offered en masse; it is a carnivalesque closeout sale of new and old public myths in which, as in the preclassical age, the differences between high and popular culture no longer matter, and all styles mix promiscuously. Western cultural history of the last two thousand years provides the building blocks the author, as "bricoleur," constantly re-arranges and regroups. Syberberg's Hitler film uses and abuses, sets up and subverts, creates and deconstructs history and tradition; it self-consciously recycles tradition as a series of quotations and thus achieves an ambivalent effect, vacillation between irony and pathos. In radical opposition to conventional realistic narratives, his staging of history comes close to the static tableau style of Robert Wilson's postmodernist stagecraft, which displays, as one critic put it, "the paradox of highly reflective infantilism."[20] History for Syberberg means both puppet theater and horror show.

V

Films as radically different as Lanzmann's *Shoah*, Kluge's *The Patriot*, and Syberberg's Hitler film still have one thing in common: they defy the all-encompassing, homogenizing power of mass media and their control over public memory. They are not able to do more than puncture in some small fashion the grand narrative that is constantly being con-structed and endlessly elaborated and reconfirmed by the incessant flow of images. They are ultimately, of course, marginal phenomena in view of the mass audiences of one hundred-forty million viewers that watched *The Winds of War* or the hundreds of millions that saw the *Holocaust* television miniseries. Precisely because of their marginality, however, they deserve our attention. In today's media culture hope comes from the margins.

Notes

1. See "Wages of War: ABC Saga Storms the Ratings," *Time* 28 February 1983. See also the cover story, "The $40 Million Gamble," *Time* 7 February 1983. The sequel to *The Winds of War, War and Remembrance* was scheduled to run, with commercial breaks, for a total of thirty hours. The first twelve hours were shown on ABC in November 1988 at a staggering cost of more than $110 million; the miniseries about the events of World War II reportedly took more years to produce than World War II actually lasted. The ratings for the first parts of *War and Remembrance* were overall lower than those earned by ABC five years earlier with *The Winds of War*.
2. See Theodor Lessing, *Geschichte als Sinngebung des Sinnlosen oder Die Geburt der Geschichte aus dem Mythos* (1927; Munich: Matthes & Seitz, 1982). Unless otherwise noted, all translations are my own.
3. It is surprising how little research is done on the question of how the past is represented, how it is narrativized and visualized, shaped, and "rewritten" by film and television. On the value of film for the historian, see Pierre Sorlin, *The Film in History: Restaging the Past* (Oxford: Blackwell, 1980); John E. O'Conner, *Teaching History with Film and Television* (Washington, DC: American Historical Association, 1987); Marc Ferro, *Cinema and History*, trans. Naomi Greene (Detroit: Wayne State UP, 1988). See also Robert A. Rosenstone, "History in Images/History in Words: Reflections on the Possibility of Really Putting History onto Film," *The American Historical Review* 93 (December 1988): 1173–85; Keith Tribe, "History and the Production of Memories," *Screen* 18 (Winter 1977/78): 9–22; Mimi White et al., "The Conjuncture of History and Cinema: How Historians Do Things with Film," *Iris* 2 (1984): 137–44. The *Journal of Contemporary History* devoted two special issues (July 1983 and January 1984) to the interaction between history and film.
4. Botho Strauss, *Diese Erinnerung an einen, der nur einen Tag zu Gast war* (Munich: Hanser, 1985) 49.
5. The controversy erupted because the military cemetery at Bitburg also housed the graves of SS soldiers. Bitburg became the symbol, especially in the United States, of the attempt to declare the "culprits" as "victims" after the fact by means of the gesture of "reconciliation." All the major American newspapers and periodicals dealt in detail with the moral and political questions posed by Reagan's Bitburg visit. See the anthology of critical essays, Geoffrey Hartman, ed., *Bitburg in Moral and Political Perspective* (Bloomington: Indiana UP, 1986) and the exhaustive documentation, Ilya Levkov, ed., *Bitburg and Beyond: Encounters in American, German and Jewish History* (New York: Shapolsky, 1987). See also Eric Rentschler, "The Use and Abuse of Memory: New German Film and the Discourse of Bitburg," *New German Critique* 36 (Fall 1985) 67–90. And see "Reagan at Bitburg: Spectacle and Memory" (with statements from Hans Jürgen Syberberg and

Anton Kaes

Jean-Marie Straub, among others), *On Film* 14 (1985): 36–40; also Norbert Seitz, ed., *Die Unfähigkeit zu feiern; Der 8. Mai* (Frankfurt a.M.: Neue Kritik, 1985).

6. This means that every other American saw at least one episode of this television series. See Sabina Lietzmann, "Die Judenvernichtung als Seifenoper: *Holocaust*—eine Serie im amerikanischen Fernsehen," *Frankfurter Allgemeine Zeitung* 20 April 1978; Thomas Kielinger, "Wie das amerikanische Fernsehen deutsche Vergangenheit bewältigt," *Die Welt* 22 April 1978; Anon., "Fernsehen: Gaskammern à la Hollywood?" *Der Spiegel* 15 May 1978: 228–31; Rainer Paul and Hans Hoyng, "Massenmord gemischt mit Deo-Spray," *Stern* 27 April 1978: 202–7.

7. Elie Wiesel, "Trivializing the Holocaust: Semi-Fact and Semi-Fiction," *New York Times* 16 April 1978. To most German critics, his objections served as a substitute for an argument of their own. On the ambivalent fictional status of the televised "Holocaust," see Christian Zimmer, *Le retour de la fiction* (Paris: Les Éditions du Cerf, 1984) 75–76.

8. Quoted in Cecil Smith, "Docudrama: Fact or Forum," *Los Angeles Times* 17 April 1978. Although he is aware of the "inherent dangers" of the "docudrama," Gerald Green here legitimizes the process of mixing fact and fiction. "The technique, of course, is as old as literature itself. Tolstoy created all those Rostovs and Volkonskys and others—they didn't exist in history. Then he placed them among the Napoleons, the actual generals and the real events of *War and Peace*. . . . I think what's important is that even though in a dramatic structure you can't get every nuance 100% historically correct, you can get the thrust and the essence of history, probably more effectively than any other way. I think there's more truthful, documented history in *Holocaust* than in anything I have seen about the Nazi destruction of the Jews."

9. Cf. Edgar Reitz, "Unabhängiger Film nach Holocaust?" in *Liebe zum Kino: Utopien und Gedanken zum Autorenfilm 1962–1983* (Cologne: KÖLN 78, 1984) 98. Reitz was in fact so outraged by *Holocaust* that he accused the Americans of having stolen German history from the Germans.

10. Heinz Werner Hübner, "Kein Lehrstück, sondern Lernstück," *Süddeutsche Zeitung* 22 September 1978.

11. The literature on the German reception of *Holocaust* is immense. See Friedrich Knilli and Siegfried Zielinski, eds., *Holocaust zur Unterhaltung: Anatomie eines internationalen Bestsellers* (Berlin: Elefanten, 1982) and for further references Anton Kaes, *From Hitler to Heimat: The Return of History as Film* (Cambridge: Harvard UP, 1989) 221.

12. Siefgried Kracauer, *Theory of Film: The Redemption of Physical Reality* (New York: Oxford UP, 1960) 306.

13. Peter W. Jansen, "Das Kino in seinem zweiten Barock: Aspekte des internationalen Films," *Jahrbuch Film* (1979/80): 23. See also Wilhelm Roth, *Der Dokumentarfilm seit 1960* (Munich/Lucerne: Bucher, 1982) 194: "Do we have any memories left that are not shaped by film? Isn't everything mediated? How are our own memories and film images connected?"

14. Max Picard, *Hitler in uns selbst* (Erlenbach-Zurich: Eugen Rentsch, 1946) 46–47. For an English translation, see *Hitler in Our Selves*, trans. Heinrich Hauser (Chicago: Regnery, 1947). See also Eric Breitbart, "The Painted

Mirror: Historical Re-creation from the Panorama to the Docudrama," *Presenting the Past: Essays on History and the Public,* ed. Susan Porter Benson et al. (Philadelphia: Temple UP, 1986) 105–17.

15. Cf. Günther Anders, *Die Antiquiertheit des Menschen,* vol. 1: "Über die Seele im Zeitalter der zweiten industriellen Revolution" (1956; Munich: Beck, 1987), especially 97–211: "Die Welt als Phantom und Matrize: Philosophische Betrachtungen über Rundfunk und Fernsehen"; Marshall McLuhan, *The Gutenberg Galaxy* (1962; New York: Signet, 1969); Jean Baudrillard, *Selected Writings,* ed. Mark Poster (Stanford: Stanford UP, 1988).

16. Baudrillard, 166. See also Baudrillard, "L'histoire: un scenario rétro," *Ça cinema* (1976): 16–19. See furthermore the emergence of a similar debate about the problems and vicissitudes of representing the Vietnam war on television, in John Carlos Rowe, "From Documentary to Docudrama: Vietnam on Television in the 1980s," *Genre* 21 (1988): 451–77.

17. Chris Marker, as quoted in Edgar Reitz, "Das Unsichtbare und der Film," in Reitz, *Liebe zum Kino* 131. In his novel *The Moviegoer* (1960; New York: Noonday, 1967), Walker Percy refers to the phenomenon of moviegoing as "certification": "Nowadays when a person lives somewhere, in a neighborhood, the place is not certified for him. More than likely he will live there sadly, and the emptiness which is inside him will expand until it evacuates the entire neighborhood. But if he sees a movie which shows his very neighborhood, it becomes possible for him to live, for a time at least, as a person who is Somewhere and not Anywhere"(63). Similarly, a Hunsrück farmer is reported to have said about Reitz's *Heimat* television chronicle (quoted in Press Materials on *Heimat*): "I've been living here in the Hunsrück for fifty years, I was born here, it's my home. But I see how beautiful it is only now, after the television show."

18. Roland Barthes, *Camera Lucida,* trans. Richard Howard (New York: Hill and Wang, 1982) 88.

19. Syberberg's nearly seven-hour-long Hitler film had its premiere in 1978. The controversial, politically revisionist project of this film cannot be discussed in this context. My analysis is here directed (as in the discussion of Kluge and Lanzmann) at the way history is encoded in the film. On Syberberg's politics, see Saul Friedländer, *Reflectons of Nazism: An Essay on Kitsch and Death* (New York: Harper and Row, 1984) and the chapter on Syberberg in my *From Hitler to Heimat: The Return of History as Film* 37–72.

20. Hans-Thies Lehmann, "Robert Wilson, Szenograph," *Merkur* 437 (July 1985): 554.

Notes on Contributors
Index

Notes on Contributors

BARTON BYG is assistant professor in the Department of Germanic Languages and Literatures at the University of Massachusetts at Amherst. He has published numerous articles on European and American film, DEFA, and Konrad Wolf. He also is working on a book on the films of Danièle Huillet and Jean-Marie Straub for the University of California Press.

THOMAS ELSAESSER is chair of the Department of Film and Television Studies at the University of Amsterdam. His essays on film theory, film genre, national cinema, and film history have appeared in many collections and anthologies. He is the author of *New German Cinema: A History* and editor of *Early Cinema: Space Frame Narrative*.

MICHAEL E. GEISLER is associate professor of German at Middlebury College. He has published a variety of essays on German cinema and television. Geisler also is the author of *Die literarische Reportage in Deutschland: Möglichkeiten und Grenzen eines operativen Genres*.

SABINE HAKE is assistant professor in the Department of Germanic Languages and Literatures at the University of Pittsburgh. Her book on the early films of Ernst Lubitsch is forthcoming from Princeton University Press. She also has published widely on early German cinema and Weimar culture.

JAN-CHRISTOPHER HORAK is senior curator at the International Museum of Photography at the George Eastman House and associate professor at the University of Rochester. He is the author of numerous books, including *Anti-Nazi Filme der deutschsprachigen Emigration von Hollywood* and *The Dream Merchants: Making and Selling Films in Hollywood's Golden Age.* He also has published widely on the history of cinema in Germany and the United States.

ANTON KAES is professor in the Department of German at the University of California, Berkeley. He is the author of *Expressionismus in Amerika* and *From Hitler to Heimat: The Return of History as Film,* and editor of *Kino-Debatte: Literatur und Film 1909–1929* and *Die Weimarer Republik.* His essays on Weimar culture and film studies have appeared in many journals and anthologies.

BRUCE A. MURRAY is assistant professor in the Department of German Languages and Literatures at the University of Illinois at Urbana-Champaign. He is the author of *Film and the German Left in the Weimar Republic* and coauthor of *Film and Politics in the Weimar Republic.* His book *The Dialectic of Antifascism; National Socialism in Postwar German Cinema* is forthcoming from de Gruyter. Murray also has published a variety of articles on German cinema and culture.

ERIC L. SANTNER is associate professor in the Department of Germanic Languages and Literatures at Princeton University. He is the author of *Friedrich Hölderlin: Narrative Vigilance and the Poetic Imagination* and *Stranded Objects: Mourning, Memory, and Film in Postwar Germany.* He is the editor of *Friedrich Hölderlin: "Hyperion" and Selected Poems.* He also has published articles on postwar German cinema and culture as well as modern Austrian literature.

THOMAS J. SAUNDERS is assistant professor in the Department of History at the University of Victoria, Canada. His publications include articles on American slapstick in Germany after World War I, war films in the late 1920s, and social change in the Third Reich. He is currently engaged in a study of cinema, state, and the press in Weimar Germany.

LINDA SCHULTE-SASSE is assistant professor in the Department of German and Russian at Macalaster College in St. Paul, Minnesota. She has published articles on Weimar and Nazi cinema, is coauthor of *Film and Politics in the Weimar Republic,* and has completed a book manuscript on Nazi cinema's appropriation of history.

Notes on Contributors

MARC SILBERMAN is associate professor in the Department of German at the University of Wisconin at Madison. He is the author of *Literature of the Working World: A Study of the Industrial Novel in East Germany* and *Heiner Müller*. He is the editor of *Interpretationen zum Roman in der DDR* and the author of numerous articles on German cinema, postwar literature and theater in East and West Germany, and Bertolt Brecht.

WILLIAM URICCHIO is associate professor in the School of Mass Communications at the Pennsylvania State University. He is the editor of *Die Anfänge des deutschen Fernsehens: Kritische Annäherungen an die Entwicklung bis 1945*, coeditor of *The Many Lives of the Batman: Critical Approaches to a Superhero and His Media*, and coauthor of *Reframing Culture: Intertextuality and the Conditions of Production/Reception in the Vitagraph "High Art" Moving Pictures*, which is forthcoming from Princeton University Press.

CHRISTOPHER J. WICKHAM is assistant professor in the Division of Foreign Languages at the University of Texas, San Antonio. He has published articles on German film, literature, and pedagogy, and a monograph on the dialect of Diendorf (Oberpfalz). He also is the editor, with Karl-Heinz Schoeps, of *"Was in den alten Büchern steht . . .": Neue Interpretationen von der Aufkläring zur Moderne*.

Index

331